the small details of LIFE
twenty diaries by women in Canada, 1830–1996

This rich anthology presents twenty diary excerpts written between 1830 and 1996, reflecting the upper-class travails of nineteenth-century travellers and settlers as well as the workaday struggles and triumphs of twentieth-century students, teachers, housewives, and writers. The diarists are single, married, with children and without, and range in age from fourteen to ninety years old.

The excerpts – each preceded by a biographical sketch of the diarist – make compelling reading. Elsie Rogstad Jones endures the sudden death of her baby in 1943; Constance Kerr Sissons, writing in 1900, discovers that her husband already has a Metis wife 'à la façon du pays'; and Dorothy Duncan MacLennan ruminates on her married life with Hugh MacLennan in 1950s Montreal. Writers Marian Engel, Edna Staebler, and Dorothy Choate Herriman contemplate the creative process. Two diarists, Phoebe McInnes and Sophie Alice Puckette, writing in the first decade of the twentieth century, reveal the contradictions and difficulties of their lives as unmarried schoolteachers. In an excerpt from a diary written in 1843, Sarah Welch Hill, a newly arrived settler, describes her violent marriage in what must be one of the few nineteenth-century documents describing domestic abuse in the first person.

With an introduction that examines diary writing by women in Canada from a historical and theoretical perspective, The Small Details of Life represents a significant contribution to the fields of Canadian women's history and life-writing. It enriches our understanding of women's literature in Canada, especially the strong tradition of personal non-fiction writing, and provides compelling glimpses into the lives of a range of Canadian women.

KATHRYN CARTER teaches Canadian literature at Wilfrid Laurier University (Brantford).

the small details of LIFE

twenty diaries by women in Canada, 1830–1996

edited by kathryn carter

UNIVERSITY OF TORONTO PRESS
Toronto Buffalo London

© University of Toronto Press Incorporated 2002
Toronto Buffalo London

Printed in Canada

ISBN 0-8020-4339-9 (cloth)
ISBN 0-8020-8159-2 (paper)

∞

Printed on acid-free paper

National Library of Canada Cataloguing in Publication Data

Main entry under title:

The small details of life : twenty diaries by women in Canada, 1830–1996
   Includes bibliographical references.
   ISBN 0-8020-4339-9 (bound)   ISBN 0-8020-8159-2 (pbk.)

   1. Women – Canada – Diaries.   2. Canadian diaries (English)
   3. Women – Canada – History – Sources.   4. Canada – History –
   Sources.   I. Carter, Kathryn, 1966–

   FC26.W6S59 2002   305.4′0971   C2001-904089-X
   F1005.S59 2002

COMMITTED TO THE DEVELOPMENT OF CULTURE AND THE ARTS

'Not the Music' by Lorna Crozier, reprinted by permission of the author.
From Lorna Crozier, *A Saving Grace: The Collected Poems of Mrs. Bentley*
(Toronto: McClelland and Stewart, 1996).

University of Toronto Press acknowledges the financial assistance to its
publishing program of the Canada Council for the Arts and the Ontario
Arts Council.

University of Toronto Press acknowledges the financial support for its
publishing activities of the Government of Canada through the Book
Publishing Industry Development Program (BPIDP).

Contents

PART FOUR: EXPLORATION

PART FIVE: LOVE, LOSS, AND WORK

PART SIX: REFLECTIVE ENDINGS

Acknowledgments

The need for a Canadian collection of women's diaries became obvious to me when I was studying the topic at the University of Alberta. I found published collections of diary excerpts by British women, American women, and Maritime women, but no book featured a geographically wide range of Canadian women. Yet literary scholars and historians alike agree that personal writings by men and women are one of the identifying features of a Canadian literary tradition. Compiling the bibliography that was eventually published as *Diaries in English by Women in Canada*, I found evidence of over 500 archived diaries, many with fascinating stories to tell. I knew that there was material enough for a book of this kind, and put out a call for papers to solicit contributions. That call brought to my attention some diaries that I did not know about. Although finalizing the selection was difficult, I am very pleased with the quality of the excerpts that appear here.

My first and largest debt of gratitude goes to those contributors who devoted their time and energies to this project and who have been remarkably patient in answering my persistent and probably repetitive questions over the past years. This book has had a long journey, and I truly appreciate their endurance. By extension, I wish to thank the diarists, living and dead, whose words appear here. To those diarists who are still alive – Edna Staebler and Elsie

Rogstad Jones – I thank you for your bravery in sharing your writing with a wider audience than you had likely anticipated.

Like many diary manuscripts, this manuscript went on a circuitous journey involving life changes and physical relocations. Just after putting out a call for contributions, I discovered that I was pregnant with my first child; she and the contributions all arrived in the middle of January 1998. Barely beginning motherhood and the book, we uprooted and moved to the United States. I packed up the manuscript and moved it from dry Edmonton to humid Durham, North Carolina. Then, eighteen months later, the growing file of papers and notes were transplanted again, to Ontario, where the book finally reached maturity. I was always keenly, though theoretically, aware that material conditions affect the creation of any written work, but that awareness translated into acute personal experience as I packed and unpacked the piles of papers in each new location, and as I learned to accommodate my writing schedule to an infant's sleeping and eating habits. A new respect grew for those women who enjoyed large families, managed busy households, suffered dislocations, and still made time to write in their diaries. The small details of life do indeed interrupt and shape all of our writing activities.

I am indebted to Bill Harnum and Gerry Hallowell at the University of Toronto Press, who first agreed that a book like this was needed. Jill McConkey, Siobhan McMenemy, Frances Mundy, and Barbara Tessman were gentle guides as this book went through its process of becoming. Three anonymous readers offered incisive comments for which I am very grateful. George Elliott Clarke and Uma Parameswaran graciously shared research and ideas. In North Carolina, this project benefited from the support of Jean O'Barr in women's studies and John Herd Thompson in the North America Program at Duke University. At Duke, I found supportive readers in Roxane Head Dinkin and Monica Russel y Rodriguez, who broadened my horizons by introducing perspectives from psychology and anthropology. I am also grateful to Suzanne Bunkers, Isobel

Grundy, and Craig Rintoul for offering valuable comments on various versions of the introduction. This project was sustained by a very timely writing grant from the Alberta Foundation for the Arts for which I am immensely grateful.

Finally, I dedicate this collection of women's words to my daughter, Rachel Bishop (who slept well). This book is one small act of saving the past for the future that she will inherit.

the small details of LIFE
twenty diaries by women in Canada, 1830–1996

Introduction

Not the music.
It is this other thing
I keep from all of them
that matters, inviolable.

I scratch in my journals,
a mouse rummaging through cupboards,
nibbling on a crust of bread, apple skins,
chewing the edges of photographs, the small
details of a life. I hoard and save,
place one thing inside another
inside the next.

Start with the prairie, then Horizon
and inside it our house,
the kitchen, the table where I sit
with my journal, and inside it
everything I write – dust, moths,
wind speaking in whispers
across the page, the absence of rain
forgiveness –

everything shrinking
to the smallest
thinnest letter,
I.

Lorna Crozier, 'Not the Music'

In Sinclair Ross's 1941 novel *As for Me and My House*, Mrs Philip Bentley keeps a diary as she navigates the rocky shoals of married life during the Depression in a fictional small prairie town called Horizon. Lorna Crozier's poem imagines the importance of such writing for Mrs Bentley: how it moves her ambiguously towards forgiveness (which might be as absent as the rain); how it functions as a sacred place, a saving place; how it sustains a diminishing self. Crozier calls it a journal. I call it a diary. Whatever it is called, it comprises the act of writing down the details of a life – for a few days, a few weeks, or a few years – and it often has tremendous value for the writer and her readers.

This is a collection of excerpts from diaries written between 1830 and 1996 by twenty women who are Canadian or who wrote in what is currently called Canada. A few of the names will be familiar from the worlds of history, art, or literature, but most are not. The choice to present writing by women who are not necessarily 'names' is deliberate. This is a book for anyone who has stood in a cemetery reading the brief epitaph of an unknown woman, wondering at the details: What pleasures did her body know? What losses did she survive? What was the rhythm of her day? This collection presents the extraordinary daily achievements of allegedly ordinary women. It seeks to enrich the history of Canada with the voices of 'unknown' women who lived from coast to coast, and urges readers to become acquainted with the rhythm of women's days and women's work. The writings range from the upper-class travails of nineteenth-century travellers and settlers to the workaday struggles and triumphs of twentieth-century students, teachers, housewives, and writers. In words and in silences, these excerpts

tell stories of successful and unsuccessful courtships; bigamous, violent, and loving marriages; the death of children; travels; all kinds
of work.

The diaries served a number of purposes for their authors. Poet
Dorothy Choate Herriman used her 1933 diary to 'write things out
of [her] system.' In 1976, writer Marian Engel used hers to knead
creativity. Travellers sometimes used their diaries as an *aide de
memoire*. Observing with the eye of a journalist, Miriam Green
Ellis, for example, made careful notes about her northern journey.
The diarists are single, married, with children, and without children, and one is squelching a 'case' – a crush – for another woman.
They are Mennonite, Catholic, and Protestant. Frances Simpson's
narrative of arriving in Rupert's Land with her husband, Hudson's
Bay Company Governor George Simpson, is the earliest, written in
1830. The most recent, written in 1996, is writer Edna Staebler's
sometimes comical account of receiving the Order of Canada.
Writing of a prestigious ceremony to mark the occasion, during
which she is engaged in conversation by a fellow recipient, she
remarks unselfconsciously, 'I couldn't hear what he said because I'd
taken out my hearing aid.' The portrait of Staebler that emerges
from her diary is that of a woman who does not take herself too
seriously: earlier in the entry, she grudgingly and laughingly accepts
that her wild mane of hair will not be tamed for the 'Grand Event.'
At ninety, Staebler is the oldest diarist; fourteen-year-old Amelia
Holder is the youngest, documenting life at sea with her father in
the late 1860s.

The decision to refer to 'diaries' in the title of this book is deliberate. Although the *Oxford English Dictionary* declares that 'journal'
connotes 'something more elaborate than a diary,' it is misleading
to believe that there are two types of daily writing. 'Diary' and
'journal' share etymological roots. Diary evolved from the Latin
dies for day, and journal from the French *jour*. Any distinctions
between the two are spurious, arbitrarily introduced as a way to
separate lesser 'diaries' from more introspective and coherent 'journals' usually produced by those who have had access to various

degrees of literary training. In practice, both terms are applied to such a variety of texts and styles that attempts at categorization prove fruitless. Over twenty years ago a commentator noticed that the term 'diary' was, in practice, applied to spiritual account books, desk memoranda, business journals, and farmers' logs.[1] Sometimes a diary doesn't amount to much more than a list enumerating phone calls, friends visited, medicine taken, or groceries bought; at other times it initiates an evocative exploration of self. The protean form of the diary has persisted since at least the 'pillow books' of tenth-century Japan,[2] and its current popularity – evidenced by the proliferation, for example, of diaries posted on the internet – ushers in new formal possibilities.

The diary is perennial and plastic, spanning a register of writing styles from reportage to confession, polemic to introspection. This collection includes writers' notebooks and brief daily memoranda, and ranges from writing that is introspective and eloquent to writing that is factual and sparse. As one might expect in a collection that spans over 160 years, the styles and functions of diary writing change over time. Some things, on the other hand, stay remarkably the same. The basic format of the diary does not change, so this collection defines diaries as texts that are not retrospective but written at intervals – daily or weekly – in the midst of a lived experience, whether that experience is a whole life, a journey, an illness, a courtship, or a season on the farm.

The premise underlying this work is that the best history is biography and that reading the details from lives of individual women can do much to broaden and challenge our understanding of Canadian history. Although Canadian history has benefited from primary sources written by women, it would be wrong to think that primary sources written by women present anything approaching a progressive, linear narrative of that history. Used to interpret the history of women in Canada, women's personal writing creates instead a palimpsest, a fact that becomes more obvious as new voices are introduced. Writings contest and contradict each other. They illuminate the unevenness of historical developments. This collection seeks to add new voices to the corpus of personal writing by women in Canada to enable a critical search for continuities between past and present, and to lead current readers to reflect on how the self is constructed at specific historical moments in particular geographic spaces.

Some of the excerpts found here came from archives, but others, such as the diaries of Constance Kerr Sissons, Mary Eidse Friesen, Mary Dulhanty, Edna Staebler, Mina Wylie, and Elsie Rogstad Jones, remain in private collections. I am pleased to bring them to public attention because this kind of writing by women has a way of disappearing. With its story of serendipitous survival, one of the diaries in this collection illustrates this point. Mary Dulhanty's 1927 diary, written in Halifax, was discovered in 1987 between the walls of a house being renovated. Other diaries are lost in basements and attics. In decades past, women's diaries chosen for archival preservation were those thought to be of historical value, as determined by an androcentric model of historiography: women's records were saved for what they revealed about the lives of important men or about historical moments made significant by men's involvement. Women's lives (especially their domestic activities) have not always been considered historically important. In 1978 historian Veronica Strong-Boag urged Canadian archives to reassess their collection policies in an effort to make accessible historical materials about women from diverse economic and social strata. She argued that the 'real neglect' of archives stemmed 'in large part from time-worn classification systems which emphasise the activities of political, military, diplomatic, and economic elites.'[3] Historiography has changed significantly in recent years but, although many archivists now express an eagerness to preserve as much as possible, resources are limited.[4] Strong-Boag's call to rescue the records of 'women both prominent and obscure' is worth respecting and one of the reasons why I wanted to collect a diverse selection of the fascinating unpublished diaries, archived and unarchived, written by women, prominent and obscure, in Canada.

The following transcriptions have been carefully prepared and rechecked many times to ensure that they faithfully reproduce the originals; the mistakes and struck-out words that appear in these selections are mistakes that occur in the originals. With these excerpts, square brackets signify that a contributor has interpreted a word, expanded cryptic initials, or indicated where a word is missing. Square brackets are also used to correct the first instance of a spelling mistake that would hinder comprehension, but repetitions of that same mistake are left uncorrected. Creative spelling is left untouched. For example, Marian Engel coins the word `wonderf' for 'wonder if,' and uses it several times. She and Ellis both used typewriters, which introduced a new set of problems: their machines sometimes jammed and skipped letters. With these excerpts, I have removed the mistakes introduced by the typewriter in terms of spacing errors, but I have retained the spelling mistakes, on the theory that it would be impossible to tell which mistakes were created by the author and which by the typewriter. And, in the case of Engel's diary, making such corrections would have meant losing word-play like 'wonderf.' Many of the diarists used punctuation sparingly, so extra word-spaces have been inserted to indicate syntactical breaks that are sometimes more obvious in the manuscript versions.

I encouraged contributors to be judicious in their use of end-notes, to get away from the notion that the diary is of service mainly to social history, and to direct attention to the ways in which and the conditions under which these texts are written. Although diary writing is but one step removed from oral communication, it is, in the end, an act of writing, and I want to emphasize that these are written texts. Therefore, the transcriptions stay true to the diarists' idiosyncratic grammatical styles, their spelling habits, and their method of dating entries. The excerpts reproduce as closely as possible the manuscript versions of the original diaries.

What follows are chunks of diaries complete with meandering plots, dead ends, and repetitions. Contributors were asked not to edit excerpts for the purpose of following a narrative thread. In all cases a terminal point was chosen by the contributor or by me, and in each case the decision was fairly arbitrary. This is also the case for diarists who sometimes end simply because they have run out of paper. Closure in diaries is almost always artificially imposed, whether by authors or editors, except in diaries covering a discrete event (like a journey or a love affair) whose end signals a sensible stopping point. Some of the excerpts here cover crucial life decisions while others document a span of average days. The selections are not meant to be equivalent to one another in any sense; they represent some of the widely varying functions of diary writing and constitute an eclectic group designed to stimulate discussion. When faced with the difficult decision of what to exclude, I eliminated those that duplicated each other – I tried to limit, for example, diaries written by school teachers on the prairies in the early 1900s, of which there are many. I aimed for diversity.

The excerpts were not adjusted to or judged by literary standards. Imposing narrative by removing 'boring' passages would have meant losing details that bring texture to a wide range of women's lived experiences. Choosing excerpts only because they are successful in terms of literary style would have meant, paradoxically, ruling out some very moving diary writing.[5] After reading a great quantity of women's diaries, I discovered that they are remarkably engaging even when not – sometimes especially when not – aiming for literary effects. Diaries can inadvertently meet literary expectations when they elicit the emotional affect that readers associate with good fiction or when the plots engage readers deeply. Diaries frequently arouse empathy. Diaries that do not conform to literary expectations can be even more interesting. Indeed, neatly packaged stories seem rather predictable after one has become accustomed to reading between the lines of a woman's diary; then, even the terse notations in a reticent account-book diary begin to speak of abundant experience folded into inadequate space.[6] The excerpt by Elsie Rogstad Jones is an example of a sparse diary entry that packs an emotional punch; the excerpt by Constance Kerr Sissons provides an example of diary writing that hides more than it discloses. At the other end of the spectrum lies diary writing by Dorothy Choate Herriman and Marian Engel, who are more comfortable with and more conversant in literary techniques; both authors strive to achieve what they see as appropriate levels of self-critique and emotional expressiveness. Herriman is even self-conscious about her self-consciousness, apologetic about 'straining for "individuality".' But diaries are not always fluent in literary style, and after the reading the following selections, you may agree that diary writing is more energetic and direct when it lacks such fluency.

I have resorted to two fictions to structure this collection, borrowing from thematic and chronological schemes. The first fiction is a narrative appropriated from the *künstlerroman* (the story of an artist's growth to maturity), a shape deliberately and provocatively chosen to suggest that a woman diarist is the artist/creator of her life story. The excerpts proceed through an imagined series of stages that imply a process of growth, discovery, creation, and reflection. Putting pen to paper, this imaginary female diarist might proceed through turbulent beginnings and periods of conflict and confusion until, after a time of hesitation and pause, she gathers herself before setting out on a mental or physical adventure where she encounters love, loss, or vocation – maybe all three. She ends by reflecting, with comic or tragic undertones, on her life. The diary excerpts that appear under each heading are written, roughly, at these particular life stages. The *künstlerroman* offers a useful fiction to shape this collection while maintaining respect for the idiosyncrasies and differences of the individual diarists and their power to create and fashion their own stories; in effect it names each diarist an artist. But it is a fictional shape, for every life has a unique pattern that cannot necessarily be mapped by any prototypical psychological journey.

The second fiction underpinning this collection is a timeline. The excerpts are arranged in a chronological order proceeding from the earliest to the most recent because diaries are in dialogue with history. What I mean by this is that the expectations and norms of a culture or community at a given historical moment will inflect diary content. The content of a diary is predicated upon the historical moment of its creation. However, the chronological format should not be interpreted to mean that I think diary writing has a *literary* history in any commonly understood sense of the term.

Diaries tend to defy commonly accepted notions of what constitutes a literary history because they are rarely distributed through the usual channels of published works. If a diarist seeks immediate publication for a recently penned diary, it is quickly dubbed a fiction, its sincerity and authenticity doubted. With this tacit injunction against publication in place, diary circulation is more diffuse and therefore more appealing to those who wish their writing to remain at a distance from the public for whatever reasons.[7] Readers of private writing are not found through commercial transactions (such as buying a published book) but informally in networks of friends and family, if at all. In fact, private writing is supposedly defined by the way it withholds itself from the 'public,' usually represented by commercial exchange in the marketplace. The censure of women, in particular, for mingling in the marketplace and going public with any kind of writing has been more acute, but the theory applies to diary writers of both sexes. British literary history offers the instructive example of Samuel Pepys, whose seventeenth-century diary, often cited as a classic of the genre, remained unpublished until 1825. He wrote in code to hide sexual content from prying eyes, and the text remained undeciphered for years. Like Pepys, diarists usually restrict their audience; consequently, any potential 'literary' influence on other would-be diarists is also restricted. Pepys's influence on other seventeenth- or eighteenth-century diarists, for example, was non-existent. In another scenario, a diary might tentatively enter the public domain by being donated to an archive, but sometimes it is not made available to the public until a specified time has elapsed. The circuitous routes to readership confirm that diary writing does not have a straightforward literary history. Diaries that are significant and innovative from a literary point of view may remain submerged for many years after their creation, so literary advancements in the genre erupt unevenly and asynchronously. The matters of circulation and publication complicate the connection between 'literary history' and diaries.

Although readership is restricted, it is not non-existent. Diaries find readers. The alleged frisson that results from reading an unpublished diary is based on the idea that the diarist does not want her words read by other eyes, but the idea of complete privacy is peculiar to the late nineteenth and twentieth centuries. Diary writing engages in dialogue with an audience – a real or imagined community of one or many – who already understands a great deal of the narrative. That audience may be a future self, a trusted friend, a sister, a husband, a family, or an entire village. Fifteenth-century commonplace books, one of the early forerunners to diaries, were 'promiscuous in ownership' and content and set out in public places to receive scribblings from any number of community members. The books might include recipes, prayers, and fragments of copied verse, along with the odd notation about current events.[8]

Nineteenth-century families sometimes kept collaborative diaries. In 1833, for example, sisters Ellen and Millie Steele co-wrote a travel diary, which is housed in the Provincial Archives of Ontario. More common, however, was a shared culture of diary writing within a family context that valued such an exercise as a spiritual and mental discipline.[9] In two cases, this collection contains extracts from nineteenth-century diaries written by members of the same family, although each is individually authored: those by the Nagle sisters and by Sarah Crease and her daughter Susan. Another Crease daughter, thirteen-year-old Josephine, kept a school diary that is not in this collection. Some of the Crease men were also diarists. Sarah and Susan Crease were clearly aware that other family members engaged in this activity. In addition, they probably knew that other women in their community wrote diaries: Jessie Nagle, whose diary is reprinted here, lived with the Crease family for a time and continued to visit them afterwards (see Jessie Nagle's entry for 29 April 1870). That the Crease family and the

Nagle sisters were writing and interacting in the same community hints at the popularity of diary writing among this particular class of Victoria women during the 1870s.

Earlier in the century, settlers and travellers kept journal letters addressed to friends and family, which then circulated among the domestic circle and beyond; such journals were sometimes published by newspapers as information for prospective immigrants.[10] For example, Frances Simpson's contribution to this collection is a journal letter she wrote in 1830. The familial, social, and sometimes public circulation of diaries throughout the nineteenth century calls into question what we mean when we label diary writing of that period 'private.' Diaries were, in fact, semi-public documents. They did (and do) circulate. The relationship between diaries and their deliberate or accidental audiences sets diaries apart from other forms of published writing. Diaries have a tradition, but it is not fitting to say that this is a literary history.

Despite having argued against literary history in a general sense, I do think that Canadian diarists are inheritors – consciously or unconsciously – of a legacy of life writing essential to understanding Canadian literary history. Anglo-Canadian literary history has been very receptive to autobiographical works by women and men. Francess Halpenny, former editor of the *Dictionary of Canadian Biography*, notes that 'it has been customary in Canadian studies to bring within the purview of literary history, at least, if not always literature as such, a good deal of material that originally had a private purpose (such as the records of explorers).'[11] Scholar Susan Jackel comments that 'autobiography in its many variant forms and proto-forms has been prominent in Canadian writing since the seventeenth century,'[12] and critic Helen Buss bluntly asserts that 'to be a Canadian is to be an autobiographer.'[13] Although we may not be able to establish a literary history of the diary genre, the cultural importance of life writing for women in a Canadian setting cannot be doubted.

Looming large in this aspect of Canadian literary history are the non-fiction personal writings of Anna Jameson, Susanna Moodie, and her sister Catharine Parr Traill, which enjoy canonical status.[14] Susanna Moodie settled with her husband northeast of present-day Toronto and endured the trying circumstances described in *Roughing It in the Bush* (1852) before her writing and her husband's appointments altered, to some degree, their financial prospects. Her prose is remarkable for its emotion, while her sister's tone, in *The Backwoods of Canada* (1836) or *The Female Emigrant's Guide* (1854), tends to be factual, scientific, and optimistic. Margaret Atwood and Margaret Laurence, among others, have reworked their legacy in contemporary Canadian literature. Anna Jameson, who enjoyed friendships with literati in England, France, and Germany, forges a feminist perspective in *Winter Studies and Summer Rambles in Canada* (1838). In the process of separating from her husband, who worked for the British government at Toronto, Jameson spends a miserable winter there before embarking on a tour around present-day Ontario, befriending Ojibwe and Ottawa peoples, shooting white-water rapids, and eventually earning the name 'The Woman of the Bright Foam.' Jameson is an example of a woman travelling through Canada who left a mark on the cultural landscape, her literary initials carved into a metaphorical tree. She is the precedent that justifies, in this collection, writing by women who were not Canadian by birth but who documented their time here, such as Sophie Puckette, an American emigrant writing about settler days in Alberta and about teaching in Washington State.

As engrossing as are the texts by Jameson, Moodie, and Traill, and as vital as they are to the larger project of Canadian history and literature, they were written by women who had both the literacy skills and the time to write, and then the great good fortune to have their words preserved for posterity. Others would not have had the literacy or the time. Finding a moment alone, a diary or some paper, a pen, and enough light are all prerequisites for writing and are not always readily available. The women who gave birth to the large families of the nineteenth century found their lives knit up in the endless demands of pregnancy, nursing, and childcare (assuming that they survived childbirth), and this would have directly affected the amount of time they had for writing (as it did with Moodie and Traill, who were also busy mothers).[15] At the same time, other factors conspired to make diary writing a more accessible activity for men and women during the nineteenth century than it had been previously.

Evidence of diary writing in Britain, specifically, multiplies during the 1820s. This may be proof that more diaries from that period have survived to the present day, but the increased numbers arrive in tandem with the invention of cheaper paper and more convenient pens, which would have made diary writing accessible to a wider range of people.[16] Diaries proliferate again after the 1850s in Britain and Canada, signifying a growing population in Canada, increased literacy in general, and more leisure time for women, in particular, which was concurrent with the growth of the middle class. The rising number of servants employed in middle-class homes meant that daughters in those homes had more leisure time. Historians assert that household labour was well entrenched by the 1880s in Canada; by 1891, domestic servants accounted for 41 per cent of the female work force.[17] While one segment of the population, the daughters of middle- and upper-class families, had little to do at home, the women doing the housework had a lot to do and little time for diary writing. Diary writing thus became a way to indicate class standing. It marked women of leisure and was regarded as a conventional habit among people of culture, associated with a genteel life and an ideology of refinement. Coincidentally, public education was becoming more widespread – Nova Scotia introduced the Free School Act in 1864, for example, and Ontario mandated compulsory schooling for children in 1871 – which meant that more people could read and write.[18] Moreover, universities began opening their doors to women in the 1860s: Mount Allison University in New Brunswick was one of the first to do so, in 1862. Thus, social-historical factors determined which women would have the time and skills to keep diaries.

Women of the twentieth century enjoyed lower birth rates and higher literacy rates, but they too encountered impediments to writing. One of these – a lack of time – was nothing new. Although gaps in diaries occur when a woman is both overwhelmed and underwhelmed by life events, more common are the variations on this typical entry from Elsie Rogstad Jones's record of vigorous housewifery during the Second World War: 'Up early again   we were busy all day   canned peas and beans.' If the entry offers little in the way of narrative, it shows that Jones's days were full and productive, and the accumulation of such entries is dense with information about what it meant to live as a woman in Canada at a particular historical moment and about the continuities that link women's lives across generations. Jones scrubs and waxes floors, tends to her children's illnesses, bakes, irons, shops, harvests, cans, launders, and churns – sometimes, it seems, all on the same day. Not only is she frequently 'up early,' but she often works until midnight. Once, with some enthusiasm, she writes, 'Finally got work done up!' Jones's daily grind does not differ significantly from that described by Sarah Welch Hill exactly one hundred years earlier. Hill irons, washes, makes Knickerbocker pickles, boils jam, and tends to her child's seizures.

Marian Engel's 1976 diary shows her to be a woman of her generation, newly separated and struggling with her dual role as an income-earning author and a single mother of twins. She tries to imagine how she can reconcile the demands on her time: 'Much, much more silence. Good babysitter. Better rules. You can't do all the things you used to do without domestic help any more ... Therefore: good help.' As the Royal Commission on the Status of Women discovered during its interviews between 1968 and 1970, the status of women in Canada was not easily summarized – differences in living conditions from province to province to territory make that impossible today as well – but there are threads of similarities stitching together women's lives across the years. Is Engel's need to manage her domestic space really so far removed from the household management put into effect by Sarah Crease one hundred years earlier? Perhaps more noteworthy is the fact that women made time to write in their diaries, despite a sometimes endless round of chores or a hectic schedule.

Of the records in archives and museums, the majority are written by upper- and middle-class women of European descent, women who were native English-speakers. This collection reflects that disproportion. No diaries included here are written in languages other than English.[19] Although examples of such diaries are extant, usually in other European languages (for example, the diary by German writer and Canadian immigrant Else Lubcke Seel at the University of Victoria Archives), no archived diaries are identified as being by women of colour. Still, there is some evidence of personal writings left by pioneer African-Canadian women. George Elliott Clarke reproduces an example in *Fire on the Water*: part of a letter written by Susannah (Susana) Smith, a Black Loyalist who had moved to Nova Scotia after the American Revolution and then left with a group for Sierra Leone after they faced intolerable prejudice. Smith's letter, written on 12 May 1792, asks her colonial authorities at Sierra Leone for soap: 'I have bin Sick and I want to git some Sope verry much to wash my family Clos for we ar not fit to be Sean for dirt.'[20] Benjamin Drew's *The Narratives of Fugitive Slaves* includes memoirs dictated by nineteenth-century Black women.[21] Poet Dionne Brand more recently solicited oral histories. With the assistance of Lois De Shield, Brand compiled *No Burden to Carry: Narratives of Black Women in Ontario, 1920s–1950s*.[22] Clarke, Drew, and Brand offer oral histories, memoirs, and letters. I have not, however, been able to discover evidence of diaries existing in archives; and of the unarchived diaries known to researchers in the field, none are in the public domain.

Similarly, there is no archival or reported evidence of diaries by South Asian, Japanese, or Chinese women. Chinese men appear in the 1878 diaries of Sarah and Susan Crease, whose taken-for-granted assumptions about other classes and other races are uncomfortable to read. The leisure time enjoyed by the Crease women – which leaves them free for diary writing – is made possible by the servitude of these men, who look after the nonglamorous work of running a household. Their service receives consideration in the diaries only during their strike in 1878; at most other times it is an invisible precondition that makes life run smoothly in that house.

Although collections of oral stories told by First Nations women exist, such as *Our Grandmother's Lives as Told in Their Own Words* (in Cree and English),[23] I have been able to find only one archived diary identified as being written by a Native woman. It is by Jennie Healy Gladstone, from the Blood nation in Alberta, written between 1937 and 1945 and housed at the Glenbow Museum and Archives in Calgary. It seems likely that there are other diaries written by Native or Metis women but not identified as such.

There are a few possible explanations for these archival absences: that women of European descent have been more liter-ate, historically, than women of colour; that archives, faced with budget constraints, are restricted to working with documents writ-ten in the two official languages; or that the diary format is unat-tractive or dangerous to women in non-white cultures. Writing may not be alluring to those who have seen the written word used to perpetuate a system of domination. And fear of reprisal from one's own community might be a factor for those who name the internal tensions or sacred knowledges of those communities.

Sadly, examples of explicit and implicit racism are evident in some of the excerpts that constitute this book. Frances Simpson, writing in 1830, and Constance Kerr Sissons, writing in 1900, mar-ried men who had previously established significant relationships with Metis women; their silence about the issue demonstrates how they deny and occlude the truth (even to themselves) and begins to unravel the ways in which women, often acting out of shame or insecurity, manage to oppress each other. Evidence of racism in women's diary writing powerfully affirms that cultural conventions cannot be escaped even in allegedly private writing. In other words, prevailing attitudes mandate and elicit these racist views, and indeed many other opinions expressed. Any conclusions we might be tempted to draw from these records regarding women's history in

Canada is limited, compelling readers to read attentively against the grain. What this collection can do is bring into inquiry prevailing myths about Canada as a 'raceless' society, and some of the romantic stereotypes peopling women's history, such as the blameless English gentlewoman scribbling in 'newly discovered' territory. The selections here complicate such stereotypes and the sometimes optimistic assumptions made about race relations in Canada. In particular, the excerpts by Frances Simpson, Amelia Holder, Sarah Crease, Susan Crease, Constance Kerr Sissons, Mina Wylie, and Miriam Green Ellis are written in what literary critic Mary Louise Pratt calls the 'contact zone' where disparate cultures meet.[24]

The women writing on these pages are not stereotypes. The details and idiosyncrasies in their diary writing make manifest their individuality. They have flaws; they have strengths. If they do not always crusade tirelessly for social improvement, neither are they the unwitting dupes of historical determinism. Their diaries provide evidence that they capitalized on opportunities and materials available to them in order to leave a record of self, an activity of value for them.

'It is this other thing / I keep from all of them / that matters,' says Crozier's Mrs Bentley, who is an emblematic diary writer, hoarding and saving, tucking away the small details of her life in furtive notes scribbled when she has a moment. Diary writing matters because it has the potential to trace threads of meaning in the fragmentation that characterizes human life. The dailiness of diary writing speaks to a desire to give meaning to the chaos of everyday events, and in this way redeem life from the chaos of unmeaning. In short, it promises (even if it doesn't always deliver) narrative, a function that it shares with fiction. The unspoken syllogism of diary writing is this: if all of the seemingly unconnected details of life are written down – waiting in traffic, filling out tax forms, battling ice storms, making mincemeat tarts – then maybe the sense of it all will emerge. The act is one of preservation or putting up stores; the diary is a Mason jar packed with a rich harvest of details. Women's work and women's diary writing are intentionally collapsed in my metaphor – as they are in Crozier's poem, where Mrs Bentley writes on the kitchen table, the figurative ground zero of women's work. Tasks traditionally associated with women (like the preservation and preparation of food) are repetitive daily tasks whose sum total is not always evident.

Women's diaries, like women's work, are frequently accused of being too partial, too jagged, too boring, and too detailed to amount to much. But the dense rich fruit of the diary is the seemingly minor details nestled among 'big' events such as births, deaths, illnesses, and marriages. In this collection, for example, Susan Crease records the price of an umbrella in Victoria, British Columbia, in 1878. (It was an exorbitant $4.50.) More poignant details are found in Mary Eidse Friesen's 1990 chronicle of her husband's death. Friesen's attention to detail (the nurses putting in his dentures after his death) drives home the reality of her loss. Even in excerpts that chronicle the creative processes of writers and artists (such as those by Marian Engel, Dorothy Choate Herriman, or Dorothy Duncan MacLennan), daily life interrupts. MacLennan, for example, enjoys artistic energy during the winter of 1953 but still needs to eat: 'Marian came in again – this time with a casserole she had made for our dinner.' The profusion of details, 'the mundane, repetitive realities, domestic rituals, [and] patterns,' creates a cumulative effect described by Canadian diary scholar Donna Smyth: 'If we think of the tiny trickles of snow which signal an avalanche, what accumulation can do is overwhelm us with a sense of beingness.'[25]

Diaries are usually, but not always, a daily practice. Dailiness figures more importantly as a theme or motif, found first in descriptions of the material conditions for writing upon which diarists comment at length. The quality of the day at hand – its weather, its limits – and the scene of writing are the seemingly banal details that form the backbone of a diary. To a degree that far exceeds other forms, diary writing foregrounds the material conditions of its making; these are the details of the writing scene. Pen and paper are frequently the subject of diary entries, especially when it is a problem to find something to write on or with. Some diarists attribute gaps in their diary writing to a lack of paper or other similar difficulties: 'We did not get our things unpacked for a long time ... only now found my diary,' writes Caroline Porter to explain an extended interruption. Mary Dulhanty summarizes a visit from her mother this way: 'Ma didn't bring me anything much. This pen I'm writing with.' Another time she notes 'This is Bea's pen. It certainly is nice to write with.' Marian Engel puzzles over her typewriter: 'How does the ribbon turner work?' she types. 'Mebbe with this thing? Close it up and hoe [*sic*] for the best. Hope. Hope. Yep, it worked.' The main purpose of these few sentences is to test her writing technology. Only by typing can she tell whether or not her ribbon turner is working. The writing that results in each case comments self-reflexively on the physical act of writing.

The physical location or scene of writing also figures importantly. As diary scholar Andrew Hassam notes, diary writing is intimately fastened to the 'then and there' of its composition.[26] You know you are reading a diary and not something else when the writing announces its daily time and place: 'Monday July 9. Weather fine. We arrive in Portage la Prairie.' Nowhere is this more obvious than in travellers' diaries (such as those by Frances Simpson, Mina Wylie, Miriam Green Ellis, and Amelia Holder), where the point of the narrative is to record the coordinates of a person moving through time and space, but it is evident even in diaries apparently less concerned with such details. Caroline Porter writes on Christmas Eve 1907, 'Pa [her husband] is reading. he does not even notice that I am writing beside him.' Porter explicitly locates her writing self in a particularized setting. Mrs Bentley is placed at a kitchen table, and her writing, too, is situated within the telescoping boundaries of the page, the journal, the kitchen table, the house, the town, and the prairie. Because diary writing is attentive to place and space, it offers an ideal vehicle for uncovering the material conditions of women's daily lives. Of course, historians have for many years harvested evidence from diaries as a way to comment or elaborate upon public events, but the diary itself has been generally understood as somehow exterior to public discourses. Now, however, scholars use evidence of place and space to situate diaries as texts produced under specific material, social, and institutional conditions. This critical practice heeds an argument put forward by critic Jerome McGann, that 'every text, including those that may appear to be purely private, is a social text.'[27] When we read women's diaries, we are not at a remove from more public discourses. The writing is materially and socially situated, bringing the words into the purview of cultural analysis.

The materiality of diaries is a theme expressed in content, and a fact expressed in its physical existence. The actual diary manuscript is a vulnerable thing: Did the diarist use cheap paper that crumbled quickly? Did she store the diary in a place where it was chewed by mice or destroyed by water? Did she burn her work? Who found the diary, and why was it not thrown out? Each is an artefact with a provenance. I asked contributors to remark on the physical appearance of the diary manuscript because it matters what kind of container a diarist chooses for her words. Readers can infer something about a woman's self-perception and about her living conditions if she selects an expensive leather-bound book; a different portrait emerges if she left scraps of loose-leaf papers carelessly arranged, especially if these papers are torn from other books. Fourteen-year-old Amelia Holder used one of her father's discarded ship's logbooks, and the remaining pages became a scrapbook. Dorothy Duncan MacLennan, like many other diarists in Canada, used daybooks provided by her insurance company – a practical choice: these were promotional giveaways. Eight decades earlier, in the 1870s, Sarah Crease wrote in a tiny black Colonial Almanac of the Standard Life Assurance Company. Her daughter, Susan, stitched together larger unlined sheets that offered more room for recording the emotional events of young adulthood. Some diarists grow attached to a particular format. Edna Staebler's journals began in a science looseleaf notebook with punched loose pages seven by ten inches in size. Because a standard sheet of paper is eight and half by eleven, she went to some lengths to find paper just her size. As

Suzanne Bunkers summarizes in the introduction to her recent sampler of diary excerpts by women in the American midwest, 'Diaries are artifacts of material culture as well as texts ... When considered from this dual perspective – as text and as artifact – a thorough exploration requires not only analyzing individual diary entries but also analyzing the size and shape of the diary in an effort to determine how its physical format might have influenced what was or was not written as well as how it was or was not written.'[28]

The physical format of a text controls, to some extent, the volume of writing in its pages and the depth of exposition. Often a sort of narrative flattening occurs, as events tumble onto pages, compressed by the physical limits of the paper. Diarists and readers are forced to leap from one event to the next without benefit of connecting statements. Yet, time and again, diarists inventively overcome the arbitrary boundaries of the text by ignoring the allotted space for a daily entry, adding extensive marginalia in cramped spaces, or simply using unlined, unmarked books. Others do not restrict themselves to writing. When words are not adequate, diarists paste in invitations, menu plans, receipts, recipes, letters, theatre programs, dance cards, cruise-ship passenger lists, *cartes-de-visites*, obituaries, birth notices, and even cookies.[29] Diaries often serve double duty as scrapbooks, like fifteenth-century commonplace books, and interpreting a manuscript diary seems incomplete without reference to these extra-textual mementos that are subject to the same principles of selection and editing as the written entries. Diary scholar Cynthia Huff agrees that 'a picture, postcard, a newspaper account, a pressed flower, a lace handkerchief, a lock of hair ... are as much a part of the diarist's life as is her writing.'[30] Contributor Barbara Powell notes that other archival texts influence the reading of the diary proper. For instance, the Crease family archive includes photographs, letters, and scrapbooks, so that the diaries written by the Crease women are only a portion of any given year's written account.

A printed anthology such as this cannot solve the problem of how to incorporate extra-textual material, but its existence needs to be stated. To make sense of women's lives we need to look at their diaries along with their recipe books, their letters, and other material legacies left to us in quilts, baskets, and stitching samplers. This point is made elsewhere by historians Margaret Conrad and Gwen Davies and by diary scholar Suzanne Bunkers, among others, but it bears repeating. For the community of readers bequeathed such documents, the fact of a diary manuscript and its extra-textual mementos is a relic of human life, evidence of a deliberate act of creation: editing, choosing, pasting, writing. Readers too must find inventive ways to overcome the arbitrary boundaries of the text.

Andrew Hassam cites an evocative entry from an emigrant's mid-nineteenth-century diary that describes shipboard diarists lobbing their journal letters, attached to lumps of coal, onto a passing ship said to be heading for Cork, Ireland, hoping that these manuscripts would make it back to loved ones, or perhaps anyone.[31] The journal letters are thrown despite significant threats from uncontrollable material factors. These texts might very well drop into the ocean, be discarded by unsympathetic travellers, or fail to reach the intended audience. Still they are thrown like a message in a bottle. The anecdote is a fitting analogy for the diary flung into the future – it also faces unknowable and uncontrollable material factors. Not knowing the outcome of the narrative, the fate of its material existence, or who (if anyone) might see the work, each of the following diarists – carefully or rashly – set down one word and then another. The accidents of survival and publication that befall diaries demand a certain gentleness from us, the accidental readers. We need to respect the idiosyncrasies of history as they play out in the diarist's diction or her self-conception. We need to approach the diaries that have washed up on these pages with generous hearts ready to listen for the poetry of the mundane.

A final caveat. Even if we proceed as the proverbial gentle reader, we can not be ideal readers. In some cases, we will not even be accurate readers. The messiness of human life complicates interpretive acts because the records of that life resist narrative closure and rebuke our attempts to self-identify. Although the brief epitaphs in cemeteries may pique our interest, we are thwarted in our desire to speak with the dead. We will know some but not all of the details. Ultimately the diarists remain other – separated from us. So we let them go, not to their original obscurity, but to a field of Canadian history newly enriched with their voices, arguing, cajoling, laughing, wondering, reflecting, and grieving.

I prefer to envision for these diarists a return to an obscurity thick with traces of human life, such as that described by Virginia Woolf in 'Lives of the Obscure': 'Gently, beautifully, like clouds on a balmy evening, obscurity once more traverses the sky, an obscurity which is not empty but thick with the stardust of innumerable lives.'[32]

NOTES

1 John Stuart Batts, 'Seeking the Canadian Pepys: The Canadian Manuscript Diaries Project,' *Archivaria* 9 (winter 1979–80): 130.

2 The earliest known women's diaries are those written by Japanese women in the tenth century, a time not only when arts and literature had begun to flourish, but, significantly, when women were well educated, were allowed a share of inheritance, and often owned homes. Of three Japanese 'pillow books' anthologized in *Diaries of Court Ladies of Old Japan*, the one most like contemporary western diaries is the anonymous pillow book of a woman born in Saroshina in 1009, chronicling her travels, the books she has read, her pilgrimages, dreams, and philosophies. See Annie Shepley Omori and Kochi Doi, eds, *Diaries of Court Ladies of Old Japan* (New York: AMS, 1970).

3 Veronica Strong-Boag, 'Raising Clio's Consciousness: Women's History and Literature,' *Archivaria* 6 (summer 1978): 73.

4 In some communities, volunteer organizations like the Alberta Women's Archive Association (based in Edmonton) have emerged to take up the slack. AWAA's mandate is to ensure that the widest possible variety of women's records are preserved for the future. This means that they actually retrieve women's records and do some of the prelim-

inary cataloguing work before the collection is delivered into the care of trained archivists.

5 Other diary scholars advocate a similar approach. In Canada, an anthology edited by Margaret Conrad, Toni Laidlaw, and Donna Smyth presents everyday writing by Nova Scotia women (*No Place like Home: Diaries and Letters of Nova Scotia Women, 1771–1938* [Halifax: Formac, 1988]). American and British diary collections with a similar methodology include Margo Culley's *A Day at a Time: The Diary Literature of American Women from 1764 to the Present* (New York: Feminist Press; New York University Press, 1985) and Harriet Blodgett's '*Capacious Hold-All*': *An Anthology of Englishwomen's Diary Writings* (Charlottesville: University of Virginia Press, 1991).

6 Readings of account-book diaries and the kind of information they can yield are offered by Marilyn Ferris Motz in 'Folk Expression of Time and Place: 19th-Century Midwestern Rural Diaries,' *Journal of American Folklore* (April–June 1987): 131–47, and Kathryn Carter in 'An Economy of Words: Emma Chadwick Stretch's Account Book Diary, 1859–1860,' *Acadiensis* 29, no. 1 (1999): 43–56.

7 This is true even for those who 'publish' their diaries on the Internet. Such a method of self-publication withholds the work from the vagaries of the marketplace while maintaining artistic control for the author/diarist. My discussion of the ways in which unpublished diaries work to fortify concepts of 'authenticity' and 'sincerity' in contrast to published works is elaborated in 'The Cultural Work of Diaries in Mid-Victorian Britain,' *Victorian Review* 23, no. 2 (1997): 251–67.

8 Thomas Mallon, *A Book of One's Own: People and Their Diaries* (St Paul, MN: Hungry Minds, 1995), 120.

9 At the beginning of their collection of Ontario women's diaries from the nineteenth century, Frances Hoffman and Ryan Taylor cite a provocative editorial from the *Millbrook Reporter* of 12 January 1893, which enumerated four worthwhile reasons for diary keeping: '1. A temporary expedient for training one's memory; 2. To record a special purpose; 3. To remember a special event, such as a trip; 4. Jotting down in its proper place any remarkable occurrence whose exact date and

description may be a matter of interest at a subsequent time.' See *Much to Be Done: Private Life in Ontario from Victorian Diaries* (Toronto: Natural Heritage/History, 1996), 1. I would argue that the practice of diary writing at this time was seen as a useful habit because it invited its writer to monitor personal failure and success and thereby assess the way in which she did or didn't live up to society's ideals.

10 Andrew Hassam, *Sailing to Australia: Shipboard Diaries of Nineteenth-Century British Emigrants* (Manchester: Manchester University Press, 1994), 1.

11 Francess Halpenny, 'Problems and Solutions in the *Dictionary of Canadian Biography,* 1800–1900,' in *Re(Dis)Covering Our Foremothers: Nineteenth-Century Canadian Women Writers,* ed. Lorraine McMullen (Ottawa: University of Ottawa Press, 1990), 39.

12 Susan Jackel, *A Flannel Shirt and Liberty: British Emigrant Gentlewomen in the Canadian West, 1880–1914* (Vancouver: University of British Columbia Press, 1982), 98.

13 Helen Buss, *Memoirs from Away: A New Found Land Girlhood* (Waterloo, ON: Wilfrid Laurier University Press, 1999), 2.

14 The high regard in which the accounts by Moodie, Traill, and Jameson are held has been used to justify studies of other non-fiction personal writing written by settlers and travellers. Among the better-known writers are Elizabeth Posthuma Gwillim Simcoe, who wrote a circumspect diary (1791–6) detailing her move to Upper Canada, her husband's work, and her growing appreciation of a new landscape. Frances Barkley kept a diary while she explored the West Coast with her husband between 1786 and 1787. Settler Frances Stewart described her situation in journals and letters home (some written to author Maria Edgeworth) after emigrating in 1823. Mary Gapper O'Brien and Anne Langton also wrote personal accounts of pioneering in the 1830s. Jane Ellice detailed events leading to the 1838 rebellions with a spirited sense of humour, and Letitia Mactavish Hargrave wrote engaging letters about life at a fur-trading fort between 1840 and 1847.

15 'For all of British North America, the average number of children born

to families in 1851 – slightly more than seven – was still remarkably high,' Alison Prentice et al., *Canadian Women: A History*, 2nd ed. (Toronto: Harcourt Brace, 1996), 66.

16 For a discussion of the history of writing implements and paper, see Joyce Whalley's *Writing Implements and Accessories: From the Roman Stylus to the Typewriter* (London: David and Charles, 1975).

17 Geneviene Leslie, 'Domestic Service in Canada, 1880–1920,' in *Women at Work; Ontario, 1850–1930*, ed. Janice Acton, Penny Goldsmith, and Bonnie Shepard (Toronto: Women's Press, 1974), 71.

18 Marilyn Färdig Whitely, *The Life and Letters of Annie Leake Tuttle: Working for the Best* (Waterloo, ON: Wilfrid Laurier University Press, 1999), 49; Marta Danylewycz and Alison Prentice, 'Teachers' Work: Changing Patterns and Perceptions in the Emerging School Systems of Nineteenth- and Early Twentieth-Century Central Canada,' in *Women Who Taught: Perspectives on the History of Women and Teaching*, ed. Alison Prentice and Marjorie Theobald (Toronto: University of Toronto Press, 1991), 140.

19 There has been no attempt to include French-Canadian diaries in this collection; they have a distinctive tradition that is receiving attention in several critical studies. For more information about the tradition of French-Canadian diary writing and its uses in Québécois fiction, see two books by Valerie Raoul: *Distinctly Narcissistic: Diary Fiction in Quebec* (Toronto: University of Toronto Press, 1993) and *The French Fictional Journal: Fictional Narcissism; Narcissistic Fiction* (Toronto: University of Toronto Press, 1980); see also Pierre Hébert's *Le Journal intime au Québec* (Montreal: Fides, 1988), as well as Daphni Baudouin's article 'Le journal intime féminin québécois au XIX siècle,' in *Littérature québécoise: la recherche en émergence* (Saint-Laurent, QC: Nuit Blanche, 1991).

20 George Elliott Clarke, ed., *Fire on the Water: An Anthology of Black Nova Scotian Writing*, vol. 1, *Early and Modern Writers, 1785–1935* (Lawrencetown, NS: Pottersfield Press, 1991), xiv. See also Clarke's 'Africana Canadiana: A Primary Bibliography,' *Canadian Ethnic Studies* 28, no. 3 (1996): 107–209.

21 Benjamin Drew, *The Narratives of Fugitive Slaves* (Boston: John P. Jewett, 1856; reprint, Toronto: Prospero Books, 2000).

22 Dionne Brand, with the assistance of Lois De Shield and the Immigrant Women's Placement Centre, *No Burden to Carry: Narratives of Black Working Women in Ontario, 1920s–1950s* (Toronto: Women's Press, 1991).

23 *Our Grandmothers' Lives as Told in Their Own Words*, ed. and trans. Freda Ahenakew and H.C. Wolfort (Saskatoon: Fifth House, 1992).

24 Mary Louise Pratt, *Imperial Eyes: Travel Writing and Transculturation* (London: Routledge, 1992), 4.

25 Clara Thomas, Carol Shields, and Donna E. Smyth, '"Thinking Back Through Our Mothers": Tradition in Canadian Women's Writing,' in *Re(Dis)Covering Our Foremothers: Nineteenth-Century Canadian Women Writers*, ed. Lorraine McMullen (Ottawa: University of Ottawa Press, 1990), 5–21.

26 Hassam, *Sailing to Australia*, 1.

27 Jerome McGann, *The Textual Condition* (Princeton, NJ: Princeton University Press, 1991), 21.

28 Suzanne Bunkers, *Diaries of Girls and Women: A Midwestern American Sampler* (Madison: University of Wisconsin Press, 2001), 21–3.

29 For example, Marjorie Saunders's 1908 diary, written while she attended the private girls' school Glen Mawr in Toronto, has a greasy spot and a caption indicating where a cookie had once been. The diary is housed in the Provincial Archives of Alberta in Edmonton.

30 Cynthia Huff, '"The Profoundly Female, and Feminist Genre": The Diary as Feminist Practice,' *Women's Studies Quarterly* 3–4 (winter 1989): 11.

31 Andrew Hassam, *No Privacy for Writing: Shipboard Diaries, 1852–1879* (Carlton South: Melbourne University Press, 1995), 27.

32 Virginia Woolf, 'Lives of the Obscure,' in *Collected Essays* (London: Hogarth Press, 1967), 4:122.

PART ONE:
TURBULENT BEGINNINGS

Frances Ramsay Simpson
(1812–1853)

S. LEIGH MATTHEWS

On 4 March 1830, Frances Ramsay Simpson, daughter of Geddes Mackenzie Simpson, a 'successful London merchant,' and Frances Hume Hawkins,[1] embarked on a journey that would take her from her home in London, England, to the Hudson's Bay Company (HBC) outpost of York Factory in the interior of Canada, a journey that lasted four months and required arduous physical exertion over hundreds of miles. At the age of eighteen, Simpson had left England on 24 February 1830 as a new bride, married to George Simpson, governor of the Hudson's Bay Company in North America and then in his mid-forties. Simpson was both her maiden name and her married name, as she had married her cousin.

George Simpson and his friend HBC chief factor John George McTavish had travelled to England in 1829 in 'search for a suitable wife,' one 'who would live up to their middle-class ideal of womanhood – a lady pure and devout, of beauty, genteel accomplishment, and dutiful obedience,'[2] a prescription admirably filled by young Frances Simpson. Like many men who served in trading posts in the British North American colonies, George Simpson had previously engaged in liaisons with a number of Native women, although he eschewed the traditional custom of marriages between fur trade officials and Native women *à la façon du pays*, or 'after the custom of the country,' a ceremony that provided for solemnized unions according to 'traditional native marriage rites,' consolidated economic relations between the two cultures, and resulted in 'distinct family units.'[3] In setting out to England in search of a white wife, George Simpson sought to change the customs of the British North American interior and introduce the 'civilizing' moral influence of the British lady into the far reaches of the empire.

Whether or not Frances Simpson knew the magnitude of her journey in terms of her husband's 'civilizing' project before she left the shores of England, she certainly very quickly became aware that her presence on the journey to York Factory was a matter of great public interest; this was true, too, for her companion, the newly married Catherine Turner McTavish, who travelled with her husband, John George McTavish, only as far as the 'Establishment' – that is a trading post or depot – at Michipicoten. In the excerpts that follow, Simpson begins her journal account of this journey with a narrative that brings the reader up to date on her voyage across the Atlantic and her initial inland journey from New York to Lachine, Lower Canada. At the end of this narrative, Simpson writes that the voyage 'seem[s] to excite a general interest – being the first ever undertaken by Ladies' (2 May). Equally important to her position as a representative of British cultural values was Simpson's position as a woman in the British North American interior. Late in the seventeenth century, a 'resolution was passed forbidding any female a passage to Hudson Bay,' a resolution barely abrogated in the century and more prior to Simpson's arrival.[4] Immediately after her acknowledgment of a public interest in her journey, Simpson indicates her intention to keep a record of her experiences 'in order to amuse [her]self, and likewise to refresh [her] memory' (10).[5] On first consideration, it would appear that Simpson's journal was meant to be 'a record of events or matters of personal interest kept by any one for h[er] own use, in which entries are made day by day, or as the events occur.'[6] Nevertheless, at the end of her journal Simpson makes explicit reference to an intended audience when she states that she trusts 'that such of my friends as may take the trouble of perusing the foregoing unconnected Memoranda, will examine them with an indulgent eye' (55). As Kathryn Carter suggests, Simpson's journal represents more accurately a 'journal letter,' a sort of 'diary written in installments and explicitly addressed to a particular person or set of persons. Generally, it features periodic diary entries addressed to distant loved ones in the form of an extended letter.'[7] Simpson was evidently an avid letter-writer – indeed, at the precise moment that her ship left the Liverpool docks, she 'went below for the purpose of writing a few lines to [her] Father' (2) – and her journal represents a clever (and popular) generic adaptation of the letter to New World circumstances. Travellers in British North America soon found that mail service was periodic at best; keeping a daily log of experiences and observations was the only way to ensure remembrance of events over the long periods of time that passed between mailings.

As modern-day readers of Simpson's private/public journal letter, we must remain aware of our cultural and temporal distance from Simpson's intended audience; we must keep in mind the material and social conditions that brought Frances Simpson to the New World, as well as her individual imperative for choosing to write down her experiences. Indeed, in our attempts to read the woman represented in her writing, we must remain sensitive to the paradoxical nature of Simpson's position in the colony. On the one hand, as the wife of the highest-ranking man of a major British corporation, she writes from a position of extreme economic and social privilege, as seen from her description of the 'Ladies' Cabin' inhabited by herself, Mrs McTavish, and their servants while onboard ship crossing the Atlantic. When in New York City, Simpson mentions the fashions and shops of the town, going to the theatre, and visiting with the 'first people in the City' (4). As a British traveller with an interested audience back home, Simpson displays the social privilege of education when she describes the landscapes through which she passes as being 'highly picturesque' and as 'wild & romantic' as some of those appearing in 'Sir Walter Scott's beautiful tales' (6, 20). Simpson thus carries with her to the

New World the 'aesthetic baggage' of the old;[8] she translates the feast of colonial scenery to the tastes of the British palate, thereby complying with the project of making the New World an economic and social product of British imperialism. Simpson also shows herself complicit in her husband's desire to 'civilize' the furthest reaches of the empire, as seen when she figuratively draws a map of the colony along the following racialized lines: speaking of the HBC establishment at the 'Chats,' Simpson writes, 'The Establishment at which we encamped last night, may be considered the boundary between the Civilized and Savage Worlds, as beyond this point, the country is uninhabited by Whites, except where a Trading Post of the Honble. Hudson's Bay Compy. occasionally presents itself' (16).

On the other hand, as a woman entering into a world dominated by masculine adventurers and the romanticized image of the Canadian voyageur, Simpson writes from a relatively weakened position within the fiercely gendered social economy of the colonial outposts. As the following excerpt from Simpson's journal illustrates, the writer uses a traditionally sentimental portrayal of her departure from the family home in order to establish her emotional ties to her familial community and to emphasize the personal loss that she sustains by making the decision to travel abroad. No sooner does the ship leave the docks of Liverpool than Simpson succumbs to seasickness and shows herself to be less than strong enough to undertake her journey. Her husband's immediate reaction is to use his economic privilege to secure her retreat to the Irish coast and to continue on his journey, which Frances Simpson describes as 'indispensable,' alone; however, the ship is unable to go into port, and Simpson recovers sufficiently to endure the voyage. It is tempting to view the passage and the illness as representative of the symbolic death of the old Frances Simpson – indeed, she says she feels 'at times perfectly indifferent as to whether I lived, or died' (3) – and the writing of the journal/journey as the construction of a new and stronger self inhabiting a vastly different community in the New World conditions. Simpson tends to paint herself as a stranger in a strange land, but rather than being daunted by her relatively isolated position as one of the first white women to travel into the Canadian interior, she instead maintains a sense of humour about her social privilege by laughing about having to ride on the backs of 'sturdy Canadians' across rapids and by commenting ironically on getting up one morning at the 'unfashionable hour' of 5 A.M. due to bad weather (11, 33). Usually the entourage got up much earlier.

As a woman in a man's world, Simpson displays an amazing ability to adapt to her new environs. By engaging wholeheartedly in the privations and risks of her situation, she subtly draws a distinction between herself and some young voyageurs who, 'finding the labor greater than they expected,' desert the travelling party (16). While writing to maintain her ties to the old world, Simpson increasingly defines herself in terms of her position as a member of the community of voyageurs. Indeed, she eventually begins to relinquish the part of a stranger and aligns herself, by her considerable use of the pronouns 'our,' 'us,' and 'we,' with her travelling companions; she is no longer apart from, but a part of a larger communal identity. In fact, her new 'strong fellow-feeling' for the other voyageurs even results in her making not so subtle comments against her husband's policy of travelling at an almost inhuman speed, thereby underscoring his almost tyrannical personality, as when she states of his meagre allowance of one hour of sleep on one night that she 'could not help thinking it the height of cruelty, to awake them at such an hour' (34).

The excerpts from Simpson's diary illustrate the change in a woman who, at the outset of her journey, finds 'the exertion of talking quite painful' aboard a noisy ship, but who, by the end of that journey, can write rather routinely that she 'ran several Rapids in fine style' (2, 35). What is particularly engaging about Simpson's diary is the author's ability to negotiate between her two subject positions – her ability when placed beyond the margins of English social customs to travel within herself and create her own unique subjectivity, expressed in her diary in her own unique voice.

Although excerpts from the manuscript have appeared in texts devoted to the representation of early exploration and travel writing, both in the *Beaver* magazine in the 1950s and in Germaine Warkentin's 1993 anthology, *Canadian Exploration Literature in English*,[9] this is the first time that portions of Simpson's diary will be read within the context of the tradition of Canadian women's diary writing. That Simpson probably expected her journal to attain a wider audience than just family and friends is evident from the condition of the extant manuscript, apparently rewritten some years after her initial journey, likely when she had returned to England.[10] The neat handwriting and careful construction of the manuscript – appropriate dates, pagination, and catchwords at the bottom of each page – suggest that the surviving journal is a fair copy and not the notes hastily composed during the journey.

While one might suggest that George Simpson sought to use his young wife to inscribe certain middle-class cultural values of civility and morality on to what he deemed a 'primitive' world ripe for imperial influence, we must be aware that Frances Simpson's decision to keep a journal letter represents an attempt at self-inscription, at preservation of a psychological journey for selfhood, for herself, for her family, and for readers, like us, of 'a future period' (10).

Photograph of a miniature portrait of Frances Ramsay Simpson,
ca. 1828.

DIARY, BRITISH NORTH AMERICA, MAY–JUNE 1830

Journal of a Voyage from Montreal, thro' the Interior of Canada, to York Factory on the Shores of Hudson's Bay commencing May 2nd – ending June 26th, 1830.

1830

On the 4th of March, I arose from my Bed at 5 A.M. (for the first time in my life) with an aching heart, and a mind agitated by the various emotions of Grief, Fear & Hope. Grief, at parting from my beloved Parents, and a large & united family of Brothers & Sisters, from whom I had never been separated: Fear, for the changes which might take place among them during my absence: and Hope, which in the midst of my distress, diffused its soothing influence, and acting as a panacea, seemed to point to the home of my infancy, as the goal at which, at some future period, (however distant) I should at length arrive.

After taking leave of my dearest Mother & Sisters, (my feelings at which time, I cannot attempt to describe) Mr. Simpson & Myself, were accompanied into Town by my Father & eldest Brother, who conducted us to the 'Swan & Two Necks,' to wait the arrival of our fellow-travellers Mr. & Mrs. McTavish, & Mr. McMillan, who, (with our respective Servants) formed the party who were shortly to leave the shores of their native Country, for those of the New World.

I can scarcely trust myself, to think of the pang which shot thro' my heart, on taking the last 'Farewell' of my beloved Father, who was equally overcome at the first parting from any of his Children – suffice it to say, that this was to me a moment of bitter sorrow, and one over which in pity to my own feelings I must throw a veil.

We started from London at 7 A.M. and the day being fine, we had a delightful ride; tho' a great part of its beauty was lost upon me, as my thoughts were constantly wandering back to that spot, and to those scenes, where I had hitherto passed a life of as much comfort & happiness, as I believe it possible to enjoy.

We arrived at Birmingham between 9 & 10 O'clock, and put up at the 'Swan' Inn.

At 8 O'clock the following morning, we were on our road to Liverpool, which place we reached at 11 P.M. – we took up our quarters at the 'Waterloo' Hotel, & remained there two days during which time, we occupied ourselves in writing to London, walking about the Town & its environs, and visiting the Ship which was to convey us across the Great Atlantic.

She was a beautiful vessel named the 'William Byrns,' well manned, and handsomely fitted up, with every accommodation: the Ladies' Cabin was entirely at our disposal (Mrs. McTavish Myself & our Servants, being the only female passengers) and a very pretty appearance it had; the Wainscot being formed of the Curly Maple, highly polished, and bearing a strong similarity to the finest Satinwood, this ornamental work however, was more for show than comfort, as the carved partitions were constructed so as to slide backwards & forwards, with every motion of the vessel, accompanied by the most tiresome & distressing noise, sometimes so loud, as to render the exertion of talking quite painful.

The 8th of March, at 9 A.M. we left the Hotel, and about 10 embarked, (altho' blowing a gale) and bade 'Adieu' for some time to Old England. Immediately upon clearing the Dock-gates, I went below for the purpose of writing a few lines to my Father (to be sent ashore by the Pilot) but had scarcely put pen to paper when I felt the Cabin reel, and saw every color of the Rainbow dancing before my eyes: in less than half an hour, I was safely deposited in my Berth, where I remained for three weeks, during which time I was so extremely ill, that Mr. Simpson at length thought that from want of nourishment, and such constant & violent sickness, I should be too much exhausted to recover: and he therefore struck a bargain with the Captain for 5000 dollars, to land me on the coast of Ireland, and give him one hour ashore, in order to place me under the care of a Doctor, or a Clergyman, until my Father or Brother should arrive for me from London, while he should proceed on his journey, which was indispensable. Our Captain could not resist the bribe, altho' going into Port except when the safety of the Ship is concerned, was contrary to his instructions. The attempt however was made, but the darkness of the night, and the stormy state of the Weather, rendered it dangerous to approach the land: this attempt had nearly proved fatal to us all, as the wind shifted in the course of the night, and the utmost exertion was necessary to prevent the Ship from drifting ashore. – from that time I began gradually to recover, after having experienced the distressing effects of Sea Sickness to such a degree, that I felt at times perfectly indifferent as to whether I lived, or died.

I must pass over in silence the rest of the voyage, remarking only the tempestuous weather, and head winds, which kept us beating about the coast of Ireland, for 20 days: after which the wind came round, and continued favorable, till we got within sight of Sandy Hook, at the entrance of New York harbour, where we were provokingly detained 5 days by thick weather, each morning preparing and expecting the pleasure of again setting foot on Terra Firma: at length a breeze sprang up, the Sailors sung merrily to their work, the Pilot came on board, and I believe no one ever felt more perfectly delighted than I did on entering the harbour: the day was fine, clear & warm – but how to describe the appearance of New York and the surrounding villages, and country, I am at a loss, as any representation will fall far short of the reality.

The beautiful Basin was crowded with Shipping, the banks on either side clothed with verdure, Houses, Garrisons, & Buildings of every description scattered along the shore, and in front was seen the City (which is built on an Island) with its seven beautiful Spires, shewing themselves at a great distance, the most conspicuous objects, and glittering in the Sun, as if proud to be exhibited in full splendour to welcome the approaching Strangers. The Town is flanked on the left side by a strong battery, which, with the fine gravel walks, and tastefully arranged gardens surrounding it, forms one of the principal places of fashionable rendezvous, in the Summer Season.

The main Street is called 'Broad-Way,' and is the Bond Street of New York, as the Ladies & Gentlemen here promenade dressed in the gayest manner, rows of Trees are planted on either side of the

Street forming a cool & pleasant shade from the heat of the Sun, which at times is quite overpowering.

We took up our residence at Mrs. Mann's Boarding-house where we had a suite of private apartments, and were here called upon by many of the first people in the City, who were very polite & pressing in their invitations, especially Mr. Wilkes President of the Bank, and Mr. Aster (founder of the Settlement of 'Astoria' since rendered famous in story by Washington Irving) he pressed us to spend a few days at his seat at Hockham, situated at some distance from the Town, but the limited time at our disposal, was received as an ample excuse for declining visits. During our stay we were fully employed in walking, riding &c. we also went to the Theatre, which is a very pretty house, but did not at that time shine in performers.

The principal Edifice is the Senate House, built of White Marble, in a very chaste and handsome style.

There are several fine churches, at one of which we were all delighted with the chanting which was very Superior.

The Shops are excellent, and the fashions the same as those of England.

On the 19th of April, at 9 A.M. we embarked from New York in the 'Commerce' Steam-vessel, and proceeded up the beautiful river Hudson, the banks of which exhibit all the variety of Rock, Wood, Hill & Dale, and are thickly studded with Villages, Farm-houses, & Gentlemen's seats: it is also rendered interesting from the different spots being visible where so many battles have been fought and where so many brave fellows have perished.

The following morning about 5 A.M. we arrived at Albany, a considerable town, with an excellent Hotel, where we had Breakfast (which is a meal of no ordinary magnitude, & variety in America, the table being loaded with Beef Steaks, Fish, Potatoes, Eggs, Cider, Tea, Coffee &c.) after which, having provided a Stage Coach which was to be entirely under our controul, and which our party (nine in number) filled, we set off, in order to reach 'Sandy Hill' that evening where it was intended we should sleep.

I must now describe an American Stage – it is much higher from the ground than an English Coach – instead of Springs, it is loosely hung on thick leathern straps: it has three seats inside, and carries no outside passengers. The sides are open, but provided with leathers to button on in case of rain: – the heavy baggage is placed in the fore & hinder boots, and the lighter portion on the roof, which is surrounded by a railing: – the whole has a clumsy effect, but is found to be the safest vehicle for the rugged roads over which it has to travel and it is always furnished with excellent horses.

Travelling in this part of the Country is not only disagreeable, but at some seasons dangerous. The roads are seldom or never repaired; the ruts are so deep as to bury half the Wheel, immense stones are scattered in all directions, and to crown the whole, at every five, or six yards, logs of wood are placed across the path, (usually known by the name of 'Stripes of Corduroy') over which, the unfortunate traveller is jolted & shaken, till he can with difficulty retain his seat.

The Bridges are formed of planks, laid loosely upon a wooden foundation, and roofed like a Barn, with a door at each end, fastened by a staple & chain.

At some parts of a river which frequently intersected our road, there are Boats stationed, which are wrought by horses, and machinery, (as a horse Mill) and known by the name of 'Team Boats,' in which carriage, horses, and passengers are conveyed just as they stand.

The Country thro' which we travelled is highly picturesque, fertile, and abounding with large & fine Orchards: the Inns clean, & well furnished, and the people obliging & attentive: these however must be late improvements, as they were noted for want of cleanliness and incivility a few years ago.

We left Sandy Hill the following morning at 6 O'clock and reached Whitehall, which was the last stage, between 12 & 1 – where we remained till about the same time the following day, when we embarked on board the 'Franklin' Steam-boat, to cross Lake Champlain, the banks & Islands of which, form perfect Fairy Land: – Stupendous rocks, some covered with verdure, others barren; the Apple & Almond trees in full blossom, and here & there, a few houses forming little Villages, at which we stopped to take up, and set down passengers.

In the evening we witnessed what was supposed to be the approach of a heavy storm – the Heavens from being clear, and serene, suddenly became disturbed by clouds, which appeared charged with mighty volumes of dense smoke in some parts, and in others bore the appearance of an awful conflagration having taken place: – the water was agitated, & assumed a darker hue than it had previously worn; the wind howled mournfully, and the whole face of Nature seemed to have changed: it however passed over, and the Sun after gratifying us once again with his generous beams, set beautifully, leaving the prospect of fine weather the following day

At 5 A.M. we took leave of this beautiful Lake, 160 miles in length, and landed at 'St. Johns,' which appeared to be a small dirty village, tho' the time I remained in it was too short to entitle me to pass any remark as to its actual extent or appearance – at this place we breakfasted, and three Stages being ready to start we took possession of one, while the others were occupied by our Steam-boat companions, with many of whom Mr. Simpson was well acquainted. – This Stage was 19 miles, to a Village called La Prai-rie, and the roads in this district were even worse than those we had previously passed. – On our arrival here, I was introduced to Mrs. Moffatt a genteel, pleasant woman resident in Montreal, who had that morning crossed over for an airing, (a frequent custom among the Ladies who reside in the City) and was waiting the return of the Steam Boat. She received me very kindly, and expressed a wish that we would make her house our home during the time we remained in Montreal – this kind invitation we how-ever declined, it being Mr. Simpson's intention to proceed immedi-ately to his house at La Chine situated nine miles from the City.

The Boat having returned we were conveyed down the noble river St. Lawrence at the breadth of which I was perfectly amazed, and which added to the view of the Town, and the beauty of the surrounding Country, would have made a fine subject for an Artist.

The first appearance of Montreal from the Water is striking in the extreme: all the buildings are roofed with Tin, which causes it to glitter in the Sun, like a City of Silver – the most conspicuous object is the Roman Catholic Church (the largest place of Public Worship some Cathedrals excepted I have ever seen) situated nearly in the centre of the Town, and which rises with an air of grandeur, to a height which appears almost gigantic. – The 'Mountain' (which is one of the chief 'Lions') is also an attraction on account of the relief its verdure affords the eye.

On approaching the Quay the vessel was soon crowded with friends who came to welcome us to Montreal, among them were Messrs. Gale, Moffatt, McGill, Le Rocque &c. &c. Mr. Moffatt then conducted us to his house where a large party was assembled at Luncheon – I was here introduced to Dr. & Mrs. Robertson, Dr. & Mrs. Pardy &c. &c. We were invited by our host, to accompany his family in the evening to a grand Military Ball, given by the Officers of the Regiment then stationed in the Town – we were however too much fatigued by travelling to avail ourselves of this invitation – Before taking leave of our kind entertainers, we were surprised by the entrance of Mr. Keith, (the Gentleman in charge of the Hudson's Bay Compys Establishment at La Chine) who learning by accident, that the Boat was that day expected at St. Johns, had driven into Town to meet us – We then took our departure, and arrived at La Chine to dinner at 5 O'clock.

The Country is beautiful, being varigated with Farms, Orchards, & Meadows as far as the Village in which the house is delightfully situated, having the St. Laurence running in front: – it was almost too early in the Season to judge of the productions, and vegetation, but it must be a charming Summer residence.

We remained here 8 days, during which time we were visited by all the principal families, far & near, but declined accepting their numerous invitations, and dined only at Mr. Moffatt's, and Mr. Richardson's, the latter of whom, is the oldest inhabitant of the City, known for his upright and honorable character, and a general favorite – We were very handsomely, and kindly entertained at both houses, where large parties were invited to meet us.

Mr. Simpson's time & attention were devoted to business while here; and I found full occupation in writing to my dear friends in England, and viewing the 'Lions' of the City viz. the New Church, the Nunnery, the Mountain, and other attractive objects.

The interior of the Church is not however equal to the exterior, at least according to my taste, as it appeared to me too gaudy and light, to suit the sacred purpose to which it is dedicated.

At the Nunnery we were ushered into a large room with one very high window, white-washed walls and every article of furniture of the plainest description – this is occupied by the principal Nuns, seven of whom we saw: they were very lively, & agreeable, and seemed much gratified by our visit, but regretted they could not show us over the house, as it was being cleaned and prepared for the reception of the sick whom they attend. Their dress consists of a black stuff gown, a broad white linen Tucker fastened round the throat, & reaching to the waist, a bandage of linen covers the forehead, and is surmounted by a long black veil, which descends to the feet, very thick high-heeled shoes, a string of Beads with a Crucifix, and a Girdle which contains a pair of Scissars & a Key.

Mrs. McTavish and myself were escorted round the 'Mountain' by Mr. Gale (the Barrister) who resides in the City, and is well acquainted with all the beauties of the surrounding neighbourhood –

This is a spot worthy the attention of all Strangers – There are two roads, one winding up each side, till it reaches the summit, from whence the eye is feasted with a magnificent, and extended prospect. The sides exhibit patches of large Timber, clumps of young Trees, Underwood, & ornamental Shrubberies; rich Orchards, & gardens belonging to several fine houses which overlook the Town, River, & opposite shores.

After occupying the morning with this delightful ride, we returned home, accompanied by Mr. Gale, who was to favor us with his company, the first two days of our voyage to the Interior.

Speaking of this voyage, I must observe that it was regarded as a wonder, was the constant subject of conversation, and seemed to excite a general interest – being the first ever undertaken by Ladies, and one which has always been considered as fraught with danger.

In order to amuse myself, and likewise to refresh my memory on subjects connected with this voyage, at a future period, I determined on keeping a Journal, which I now commence.

[The travelling party left Lachine on 2 May 1830, to continue their journey to Fort Garry and on to York Factory. The following excerpt picks up as the party leaves Fort William.]

[May] 26th   Left 'Fort William' between 2 & 3 A.M. Breakfasted at the Parepeux Rapids: the Weather fine & warm.

Made the 'Mountain' Portage, about 3/4 of a mile in length, from which, is seen one of the finest Falls in the Country – it is upwards of 100 feet in height, dashing over stupendous rocks; boiling, foaming, and roaring with the noise of Thunder – the Spray flying in all directions appears studded with precious stones, and surrounded by thousands of Rainbows.

Soon after, made a Rocky Portage, which was closely followed by one rather wet & dirty.

Encamped at 8 P.M. on the Couteau Portage.

27th   Started at 3 A.M. – got to the Dog Portage, (Portage de Chien) at 11.

This Portage is about 2 miles in length; the road good, with a steep hill upon each side, about 300 yards in height, from the Water's edge. The view from the upper end is beautifully picturesque, overlooking a Lake which is formed at the lower end of the Dog-fall, and a portion of the river farther down. The banks surrounding this Lake, elevating themselves about 200 yards, are clothed with a variety of the richest verdure.

Crossed the 'Lac de Chien,' and ascended the river of the same name, about 25 miles – & encamped at 8 O'clock, on the best spot we could find, after much examination: but bad enough, as it was covered with burnt wood, & fallen timber, and accessible only, by clambering over the men's shoulders, which formed a bridge across the deep, slimy mire of which the bank is formed.

This abominable spot was surrounded by stagnant pools, from which our ears were assailed by the croaking & whistling of thousands of Bull-frogs: and here the Musquito first introduced himself to our notice, exerting his sting vigorously, and giving full employment to our fingers in allaying the irritation occasioned thereby.

28th   Off at 2 A.M. This I may say was the most fatiguing day I ever experienced having walked between Breakfast & Dinner (under a scorching Sun) upwards of 7 miles, over the 'Prairie,' 'Middle' & 'Savanne' Portages, the last of which, deriving its name from its character, is formed of a bridge of Logs in a very crazy, & decayed state: so slippery, unsteady & uneven, as to occasion the greatest difficulty in crossing it.

This walk (if, so it may be called, as it was an operation of 6 hours, of hopping, slipping & climbing) completely overpowered me with fatigue, and on arriving at the end I threw myself upon the grass, unable to move for some time.

The Afternoon exceedingly wet, and uncomfortable, but it was cheering to know that we were now within the Territory of 'Rupert's Land,' as the Middle Portage is the height of land, separating the Waters which run into Hudson's Bay, from those which fall into the Gulf of St. Lawrence.

Descended the river Embarras about 2 miles, which takes its name from the frequent obstructions of wind fallen timber, which is carried down by the Spring floods: requiring the constant use of the axe, to cut a passage through it.

Encamped on the edge of a filthy Swamp at ½ past 7.

29th   Torrents of rain during last night, and a snow storm this morning, which prevented our starting till after breakfast, rather an unfashionable hour 5 A.M.

Off at 6, and occupied until 11, cutting our way thro' this tiresome little river, which was completely choked up with Drift-wood:
when as ill-fate would have it, our Consort Canoe in following us
round one of the points, formed by the winding course of the
Stream, ran against a stump, which did not show itself above
Water, tore up about 9 feet of its bark, and in a few minutes (altho'
all the people were occupied in baling with every vessel they could
get hold of from Hats downwards) was up to the Gunwales in
water: but Providentially, the river was so shoal when she sunk
that no lives were lost, and we got to her assistance in sufficient
time to save what was not perishable of the baggage: so that no evil
was sustained by the accident, except the loss of half this day,
(occupied in repairing the Canoe) and of a great portion of our
Tea, Sugar, & Biscuit –

Employed from 11 till 3 O'clock putting our wreck in a 'Sea worthy state,' which was a very simple process; by introducing a piece
of new bark, inside the damaged part, sewing it with the thin fibre
of the root of a tree, and covering the Seam with melted Pine
Pitch, or 'Gum,' which rendered it perfectly water-tight.

We then entered Mille Lac; deriving its name from the thousand
Islands it comprehends, and continued our route until ½ past 8
P.M. when we encamped, but without our Consort, which thro'
some accident had taken the opposite side of the Island, to that on
which we put up, so that her passengers were supperless, the rem-
nant of provisions, happening to be in our Canoe.

30th   The rain & snow of yesterday had so completely soaked into
our Clothes, that it was necessary to sit up till 11 P.M. drying them
before the fire, when we laid ourselves down, but I had scarcely
closed my eyes when I was roused by the well known, and (to me)
unwelcome signal of 'Léve Léve Léve,' and found on enquiry the
time to be a few minutes after 12 –

Embarked, and had just fallen asleep again, when we were
obliged to start up for the purpose of crossing a very bad Portage;
the dry parts slippery, from the frost of the former night, and

covered with fallen Timber, and the miry portions (which were not a few) almost impassable.

Over this rough & disagreeable road we groped our way in the dark, and found Mr. Christie & his party fast asleep at the farther end – I could not help thinking it the height of cruelty, to awake them at such an hour, having a strong fellow-feeling for them, as it was with the greatest difficulty I managed to keep my eyes open, and more than once fell on the slippery & uneven ground – not much ceremony was however observed, and in a very short time we were all again afloat –

Got to another Portage at day-break; where, out of charity to me, a fire was lighted, and Breakfast prepared; the most seasonable and welcome meal, I ever sat down to. In starting from this Portage, we had a similar mishap to that which befel our Consort yesterday, as a Stump caught the bottom of our Canoe, ripped up several feet of the bark and it required the utmost exertion to get ashore before sinking. I was fortunate in escaping a ducking, by being caught up in the arms of one of the men, and carried to a dry spot.

The repairs occupied about an hour & a half, when we continued our voyage, and encamped at 8 P.M. on the Deux Rivieres Portage.

31st   Started at 1 A.M. Entered the river Maligne at 6, ran several Rapids in fine style, and got into Lac le Croix at 12 O'clock – crossed one of its Bays about 10 miles wide, and descended the river Michan, which is not the usual route, but much shorter; yet seldom or never passed by Whites, being considered dangerous – The other route is understood to be within the American territory, and this, to be the line of demarkation: being the great outlet of the Waters running from the height of land thro' Lac and Riviere la Pluie, into Lac des Bois. Mr. Simpson therefore in order to ascertain its state, mounted its current last Fall, in low water, and descended it this Season in high water, and considers it not only a practicable, but a safe route in any state, either for Boats or Canoes.

We made 3 Portages, and ran several Rapids, which before entering had rather an alarming appearance; but once over the brink, the rapidity with which they were passed, left no time for apprehension; on the contrary, I could but admire the address of the Bowsman in leading our beautiful & airy bark, thro' the Breakers, Whirlpools, & Eddies occasioned by this great body of water pent up between immense walls of Rock, and hurled over huge masses of the same material.

The river we had been descending, empties itself into a beautiful Lake of the same name; where we fell in with a large Camp of Indians attending a Sturgeon Fishery. They received us with a salute of fire-arms, and we replied to them by a present of Tobacco, which seemed to afford great satisfaction.

Crossed a Bay of Lake Michan, and got into Lac la Pluie, where we encamped at 7 O'clock, drenched to the skin, by the spray of river Michan, and a down-pour of rain which had continued since 12 O'clock.

June 1st   The rain fell in torrents all night, and until 9 A.M. today: we however were afloat again at 12 P.M.

Breakfasted at 8 O'clock on an Island in Lac la Pluie, and almost immediately after we re-embarked, our Canoe struck on a rock, and sustained so much damage, as to occasion considerable alarm; and it required the utmost exertion of the people to keep her above water, till she reached the Shore.

We could receive no assistance from our Consort, as she had started a few minutes before us, and was out of sight; having doubled the point of an Island when the accident took place: & to complete our misfortunes we found on gaining the shore, that we had neither Bark, nor Pitch on board, to repair the damage, the whole of our stock having been consumed in making good the injury we sustained two days ago – Necessity, however, is the Mother of Invention: a piece of Oil-cloth answered as a substitute for bark; a piece of Twine for 'Wattap,' (or sewing roots) and the whole smeared over with Butter inside & out, (instead of Pine Pitch) which stopped the leak sufficiently to enable us to proceed, till we reached the Establishment of Lac la Pluie, at 12 O'clock, just as a Canoe was being manned to go in search of us: it being apprehended that some accident had occurred from our non-arrival.

At the Establishment we found Mr. Cameron, and Mr. McMurray, who received us with a degree of kindness, which satisfied me that our welcome was cordial, and unaffected.

The Establishment is delightfully situated, on the East bank of the river, overlooking a beautiful Waterfall to the South, also the American Post, on the opposite side, and a long reach of this noble Stream to the North.

While Mr. Simpson & Mr. Cameron were transacting business, Mr. McMurray beaued me round the Fort, and Garden; and old & weather beaten as he was, he surpassed all the Gentlemen I had met with in these Wilds, as a Lady's Man; but altho' our walk did not occupy an hour, it quite exhausted all his fine speeches, and the poor man seemed as much relieved when we returned to the house, and were joined by Mr. Christie, as if he had just been freed from an attack of the Night-Mare.

Dined on fresh Sturgeon, and dried Beaver Meat; and continued our route at 5 O'clock, having exchanged our damaged Canoe, for one, new off the Stocks. proceeded down the river, passed several bands of Indians, and encamped at 8.

2nd   Yesterday having been a broken day, Mr. Simpson determined on making up for it, and he accordingly gave the call at 12 P.M. [midnight]

I was exceedingly sleepy, and being well wrapped up in Cloaks, soon settled myself into a comfortable nap, when in running a Rapid, a wave broke in upon the side of the Canoe on which I was, and gave me a benefit in the shape of a Cold Bath – We however put ashore soon afterwards to an early Breakfast, when my clothes were dried, and we then proceeded down this truly beautiful stream, the banks of which, are clothed with a variety of fine Timber, and laid out as regularly as if planted by the hands of man.

Got to the Lake of the Woods at 2 O'clock, continued our route

thro' it about 30 miles; when we put up for the night in an excellent encampment.

3rd   Raised Camp this morning at 1 A.M. Made a small Portage
in the Lake, at 6 O'clock, and another into river Winnipeg at 10.

Descended that noble Stream, the scenery of which is finely
diversified: comprehending all the varieties of Hill, Dale, Mountain & Rock: rich Meadows, Timber of all sizes, heavy Waterfalls,
strong Rapids &c. and every few miles as we proceeded, the river
expanding into Lakes, with their Islands, Inlets & Bays: in short,
nothing can be more beautifully picturesque than the route of
today.

About noon an Indian met us, with a packet of letters for Mr.
Simpson, which brought favorable accounts from the Northern
Establishments.

In the evening, we had a great deal of very heavy rain, and put
up at dark, in a very uncomfortable swampy Encampment; it being
too late to look out for a better.

4th   Embarked at ½ past 1 A.M. We had not proceeded far,
when the heavy rapid of Portage de L'Isle, made itself known to
us, by breaking over the sides of the Canoe and giving us a
moistening –

Made several Portages over smooth rocks of Granite, some of
which, were troublesome, and dangerous to pass, owing to the rain
of the former night, having made them very slippery. The principal
were, 'Chute de Jacob' (the torrent of which foams, & boils, with
a thundering sound for a considerable distance) 'Point de Bois,'
the 'Barriere,' 'Chute des Esclaves,' and 'Grand Galet' – the last a
beautiful Rock, of about one hundred & fifty yards in length; the
breadth between the Water and the Woods by which it is flanked,
varying from 20 to 30 yards, with a perfectly smooth & level surface. We encamped here, and I found it by far the most pleasant
foundation for a bed, I had yet tried.

The scene around this spot was very fine – the dashing Waters
sparkling beneath the clear light of the Moon, together with the

Tents, Fires &c. of the Encampment, forming a picture at once striking & romantic.

5th   Off at ½ past 1 A.M. Drizzling rain, during the morning, and heavy after breakfast, until 12 O'clock, when the Weather became fine – Made several Portages and ran 4 heavy rapids.

At the last Portage in this river (Winnipeg) the crews of both Canoes shaved, and dressed in their gayest attire, previous to landing at Fort Alexander, where we arrived at 1 A.M. and were welcomed with no ordinary degree of kindness by Chief Factor John Stuart, the Gentleman in charge of the Establishment.

Dined here, and took our departure at Sun Set, encamping about a mile below the Establishment.

6th   Mr. Simpson being anxious to get to Fort Garry (about 100 miles distant) today, gave his usual 'Léve Léve Léve ['] at 12 P.M. [midnight] and although it blew very hard, occasioning a heavy swell on Lake Winnipeg when we embarked, we got to the mouth of Red River at 11 A.M. The beauty of this Stream surpasses that of every other I have yet seen in the Interior. – The banks are richly clothed with Timber of larger size and greater variety than is generally met with, and the soil when properly cultivated as fertile as that of a manured garden.

This rich Country forms an immense sea of level plains, which extends upwards of 500 miles back, on the West side to the foot of the Rocky Mountains, on the South to the Missourie, and on the North to the Saskatchawin.

On advancing in the Settlement, signs of civilization began to appear in the form of houses built of Logs, and surrounded by patches of ground which bore the marks of the Plough & the Spade: – from this point, cultivation is continued along the banks with very little intermission, as far as nine miles beyond the Fort, which is situated 50 miles from the mouth of the River.

As the houses and farms increased in magnitude, & improved in quality, the pleasing & domestic sight of Cattle appeared, which added much to the beauty and interest of the Scene.

About 2 O'clock we came to an Indian Camp, the Chief of which was recognized as 'Peguish' or the 'Cut nosed Chief,' who embarked in his Canoe, attended by six or seven of his followers, to congratulate Mr. Simpson on his return, he being very popular among the Indians, on account of treating them with uniform kindness: which in my humble opinion (except perhaps in extreme cases) is the surest way towards attaining the desired end of improving their condition, as it is far more likely to succeed in weaning them from their Savage life & roving habits, than authority harshly exercised could be – and they are thus frequently induced to give up the fatigue & uncertainty of the Chase, for the more peaceable and certain occupation of husbandry. – The Chief welcomed me very cordially in his Native Tongue, to his 'Native Land' – shook me by the hand several times, and promised to come to the Fort next day to pay me a visit.

On stopping to prepare for Dinner, Mr. Simpson gave all the Wine & Liquor that remained to the men, who made it into Punch in their large cooking Kettle, and regaled thereon, till some of them were 'powerfully refreshed.' – This debauch (the first I had seen on the voyage) infused into our Crew a degree of artificial strength & spirits, otherwise we should not have reached the Fort, as they were quite overpowered with sleep and fatigue; but after it began to operate, they paddled and sung, with much gaiety, bringing us to the Establishment at 12 P.M. after a hard day's work of 24 hours.

The first respectable looking house to be seen, belongs to Mr. Cocrane, one of the Clergymen of the Settlement, and is situated about 16 miles from the Fort: near it, is his Church, the sight of which, had the most cheering effect, after passing so many Wilds without the smallest trace of a Sacred Edifice, or even of a Civilized habitation, and seemed to raise the Soul to its Creator, who is to be found in the remotest corner of the Globe, and whose Fatherly care, and protection are equally divided, between the poor untutored Savage, and the Monarch who reigns over an enlightened people.

This was the first place of Worship I had seen, since leaving

Montreal, and I hailed it as a favorable sign of the moral state of the Colony.

Mr. Cocran was from home, but his Wife on seeing us approach, came from the house, and pressed us very kindly to land, which invitation we were obliged to decline, as it was then late in the Evening.

A Courier was sent on horseback from the foot of the Rapids, to make known our arrival, and at midnight we landed at 'Fort Garry.'

The reception I here met with, convinced me that if the Inhabitants of this remote Region were plain & homely in their manners, they did not want for kindness of heart, and the desire of making every thing appear favorable, and pleasing, to the eye & mind of a Stranger.

NOTES

Frances Ramsay Simpson, Journal: May 2nd–June 26 1830. D.6/4 (copy and microfilm of original), Hudson's Bay Company Archives, Provincial Archives of Manitoba, Winnipeg.

1 Sylvia Van Kirk, 'Frances Ramsay Simpson,' *Dictionary of Canadian Biography*, vol. 8, *1851–1860* (Toronto: University of Toronto Press, 1985), 811–12.
2 Sylvia Van Kirk, *'Many Tender Ties': Women in Fur-Trade Society in Western Canada, 1670–1870* (Winnipeg: Watson and Dwyer, 1980), 183.
3 Ibid., 28.
4 Ibid., 173. For a discussion of those white women who did penetrate to the interior of the colony before Simpson's arrival, see ibid., ch. 8.
5 The numbers refer to Simpson's own paging in the original diary.
6 *Oxford English Dictionary*, 1989 ed., s.v. 'journal.'
7 Kathryn Carter, 'A Contingency of Words: Diaries in English by Women in Canada 1830–1915' (PhD diss., University of Alberta, 1997), 51.

8 I.S. MacLaren, 'Touring at High Speed: Fur-Trade Landscapes in the Writings of Frances and George Simpson,' *Musk-Ox* 34 (1986): 78.
9 'Journey for Frances,' *The Beaver*, nos. 284 and 285 (Dec. 1953): 50–5; (March 1954): 12–17; (summer 1954): 12–18. Germaine Warkentin, ed., *Canadian Exploration Literature: An Anthology* (Toronto: Oxford University Press, 1993), 384–96.
10 A clue to when the manuscript may have been rewritten is found in Simpson's musings on the people and places in New York State. She specifically mentions having met 'Mr. Aster (founder of the Settlement of 'Astoria' since rendered famous in story by Washington Irving).' Irving's *Astoria* was published in 1836, six years after the events of her journal.

Sarah Welch Hill
(1803–1887)

ROBYNNE ROGERS HEALEY

'A fine day & mild but the roads must be *very bad* – Do not feel so
cold as I did yesterday – It seems almost nonsense writing down
these trifles, but I have had a habit of writing down daily what
occurs & no events of more consequence have transpired,' wrote
Sarah Hill on 26 March 1863, closing another entry in her diary.
Sarah Hill did indeed have a long-established habit of daily diary
writing.[1] Her diary – located, along with other family papers, at the
Archives of Ontario[2] – encompasses sixty years of her daily activities and thoughts. The diary comprises thirty-three bound, covered
books, and six bound, uncovered books, the latter consisting of
some odd-sized bits of paper sewn together and filled with the
small, even script that details the events in the life of Sarah Welch
Hill from her first entries at eighteen years of age until her final
entries at the age of seventy-eight. An advantage of having access
to a diary that covers such an extended period of time is that the
changing circumstances and situations in Sarah Hill's life course
reflected in the diary serve as a reminder that single diary excerpts
should not be taken out of context and assumptions made about an
entire life based on one or two entries.

Sarah Welch was born on 16 March 1803 into a gentle family in
Birmingham, County of Warwick, in the midlands of England. She
was the eldest child of Joseph Welch and his wife Sarah Langley.

The young Sarah's diary writing reflects her family's status and circumstances: much of it is occupied by discussion of visitation, family health and illness, attendance at church, and benevolent activities such as her involvement with the Committee of the School of Industry. Following the death of her mother on 11 December 1832, Sarah Welch became the mistress of her father's home. Her only sister, Elizabeth, had died on 1 January 1825, and her brother John Langley Welch had died on 30 July 1827. Her only surviving sibling, Joseph, appears to have been rather irresponsible.[3] Although her brother's behaviour caused Sarah's relationship with her father to be strained at times, as she tried to play the role of peacemaker, it also placed her in an uncommon situation for a Victorian woman in that she became executrix and sole beneficiary of her father's will.[4]

It was through her brother that Sarah was formally introduced to Edwin Hill, born 15 January 1799, of Birmingham. Edwin Hill also came from a gentle family and was owner of a brass foundry. Mr. Hill, as Sarah would forever call him, began to figure prominently in her diary in 1839. From Sarah's descriptions of her feelings and his actions, Edwin Hill was obviously both charming and persistent. Judging from her comments on Christmas Day 1839, Sarah was infatuated: 'Mr E Hill dined with us, he was very kind and attentive to me & I think I could like him better than any one I have ever seen, he is so well informed & sensible & there is a refinement about him that pleases me.' However, whether it was her age, temperament, or her situation, she was also cautious and unwilling to leave her father alone. Early in January 1840 Edwin Hill had requested the consent of Joseph Welch Sr for the hand of his daughter in marriage. Welch thought it might be prudent to wait, and Sarah, confident in being guided by her father's advice, consented to being married after Lent. Hill's response to having to wait was one of the first indications of his volatile temper. He left Welch's home early one Sunday after dinner '& we did not part pleasantly, he having said I was capricious, because I will not marry him till after Lent[.] I think he likes to have his own way,

he seemed very vexed, & was anything but pleasant.' The pre-
wedding situation, as described in entries of 1 and 2 May 1840, was
not made easier by 'the *innumerable* reports [Sarah heard] to his dis-
advantage,' or his continued resistance to signing a marriage settlement due to a particular clause that he thought was 'only put in to
vex him.' That Sarah had to endure this situation after the shock of
finding her father dead in his bed on the morning of 24 February
1840 gives a certain edge to her comment on the eve of her wedding: 'I have however the most perfect confidence in Mr Hill &
hope to be happy.' Their wedding on 5 May 1840 began a long
period of physical and emotional insecurity for Sarah, marked by
frequent nervous headaches, heart palpitations, and generally
being, in her words, 'very poorly.' Before the birth of their first
child – a son, Edwyn Welch Hill – on 10 December 1841, Edwin
Hill began to make inquiries about selling his brass foundry and
emigrating to Canada. A second and last child, Sarah Margaret
Hill,[5] was born on 26 March 1843 and within weeks began to have
convulsions. The baby was so ill and convulsed so frequently that
she was quickly baptised at one o'clock one morning to prepare for
what appeared imminent death.[6] Against all odds, the baby survived. In the midst of this turmoil Edwin Hill sold his brass foundry
and the family prepared to leave for Canada in the summer of
1843.

It is here that the diary excerpt begins; it covers the period just
preceding the family's immigration to Canada until the following
year, when they settled on a farm they purchased in Hope Township, Canada West.[7] Sarah's domestic circumstances changed suddenly with their arrival at the farm. She had to bake her own
bread. She began to collect recipes for making yeast, candles, and
medicinal remedies, and for preserving meat in hot weather;
instructions on washing various fabrics; and advice on how to deal
with the over-zealous Canadian mosquito. Following the family's
settlement, the diary reflects Sarah's metamorphosis into a farm
woman. Even though she regularly had tea with her social equals
and remained involved in the intensive ritual of visitation,[8] Sarah's

day-to-day labours producing and exchanging food for her family and sewing clothing for her children began to figure more prominently in her life. At the same time, the family was never entirely free from Edwin Hill's volatile temper.[9] How much of this anger was related to the family's financial situation is unclear, but Hill did insist that his wife begin to draw on her marriage settlement and on her deceased father's estate.[10] With no family on whom to depend, Sarah was without recourse to change her situation.

A most abrupt change in the family's circumstances occurred with Edwin Hill's sudden death on 14 December 1854, leaving Sarah Hill a widow with two young children and a servant to care for. Ironically, for all the ill treatment Sarah received at the hands of her husband, every reference to him following his death is to her 'dear husband.' Sarah decided to remain on the farm with her children, where, with drastically reduced finances, she valiantly attempted to maintain a lifestyle consistent with her station. As her daughter, Margaret, got older, Sarah agonized over her difficulty in providing adequate clothing and accoutrements such as singing and piano lessons. Worse than her concerns over her daughter, however, was her feeling of helplessness in assisting her son to find an adequate 'situation.' Starting in the autumn of 1864, Edwyn taught at a school in Port Hope, a less prestigious position than Sarah would have hoped for. After two years of teaching, he left for Toronto, where he enrolled first in the Military School and then in BA Commercial College. From there he went to Missouri, where he began to practise law. After Edwyn became a successful lawyer in St Louis, Missouri, and as it became obvious that Margaret would not marry, Sarah set herself to providing for her daughter's care following her death.

On 26 September 1887 at eighty-four years of age,[11] Sarah Welch Hill died on her farm after a six-week illness. Margaret continued to live on the farm until she died in 1896; Edwyn, a successful barrister, died in St Louis in 1901. There were no further heirs.

All that remains of the life of Sarah Hill is her diary and a few other family papers. In the diary's meanderings over sixty years, certain themes emerge. Sarah Welch Hill was not a passive participant in the circumstances of her life; she actively responded to her often changing circumstances, drawing heavily on her faith for both spiritual support and explanation. She changed what could feasibly be changed and lived as best she could with the rest. The richness of this diary comes from both its repetitiveness and its transitions. Sarah Welch Hill, like most women, faced a round of daily tasks that were largely repetitive in nature and focused on family. The transitions that occurred over Sarah's adult life are reflected in her diary writing and followed a pattern similar to that of most women, regardless of their status. It could be said that Sarah Welch Hill lived a rather ordinary life. Unlike her more prominent peers, Susanna Moodie and Catharine Parr Traill, her scribblings were entirely private. Sarah Hill's diary is her monument, her daily entries a reminder of the circumstances and achievements of many immigrant women in Victorian Canada.

Excerpt from the diary of Sarah Welch Hill.

DIARY, CANADA WEST,
JULY 1843–JANUARY 1845

Tues [July 25th 1843]: Jane Ann[12] & both children went to town   Mrs Horton came to tea.   Wed: 26th   went to town – Had a Letter from Mrs Joseph – very sorry Joseph is much worse: His body and legs sadly swell'd. J Piercy called in the afternoon – Wrote to Joseph & Mrs James   very low and anxious about him –   Thurs 27th   Mrs Chambers came to tea brought the little shirts. Walked as far as the warehouse with her. Mr Hill & I called of Mr James – he has written to Joseph – Went shopping – Had a note from Miss Hawksley –   Fri 28th   called of Mrs Cairns, to ask me to introduce me to a lady who had been with her children to N. York & back again – am to call of Mrs Cairns on Tuesday   People tell me I look thin. The afternoon rainy – The [illegible] did not go –   Sat: Master Chambers came, gave him 5/ for 8 skirts & 6 Flannel petticoats. Went to town in the afternoon with Mr Hill   bought Edwyn two pr. Shoes. Edwyn & baby both colds – Yesterday Mr Hill had a letter from Mr G Ryley.[13] Sun: Ducks for dinner, Mr Hill very cross – we went to Edgbaston[14]   in the evening   Mon: Mrs Hill[15] & Miss Budd came to dinner –   Tues: washing day, at dinner Mr Hill gave me a letter from Joseph which he received yesterday but being so low he did not give it to me – He seems to think his *hours* are number'd & it is a very affectionate Letter; *felt very low* & fretted about him. Wrote to Mr James & my dear brother – Mrs Thos Hill[16] called – went to town and called of Mrs Cairns & she called with me of Mrs Newstead a Lady who has been at New York.   Wed: August 2   Up by 5. Mr Hill gone to Liverpool – Ironing day – boiled some black currant jam   sent Mrs Hudson her money, she is very poorly. Very rainy. Wonder how poor Joseph is, think very much of him   Drank tea in Digbeth.[17] Thurs: Dined in Digbeth & went shopping with Mrs T. Hill   came home after tea & surprised to meet Mr Hill on the road. Mr Gittens sent the things,   Fri: Mrs Jas Welch called – went with her to Miss Broomhead, no letter from Wales. Rainy – Had a kind Letter from Mrs N Langeley. Sat [August] 5th: Wrote to Miss Hawksley   Had a Letter from Joseph, he writes very affectionately, he asked the surgeon plainly

his opinion – he told him no earthly power could save him
He says his legs & thighs are not so swelld but that his body is more
so. He does not write to excite any feelings which at this time I
think very kind of him.   Very busy   Mrs Chambers sent home
the skirts –   Sun: Mrs J Welch, Alfred & Louisa Green called,
Mr Hill & I drank tea with Mr Thos Hill   Mon: Very busy
Tues: Mrs Hill & Mrs Horton called, the Latter surprised to find
our sale would be so soon & asked us to stay in Calthorpe St[18] –
Wed: The first days sale – Jane the two children & I went to break-
fast & spend the day with Mrs James Welch. In the evening Mr
Hill called for us & went in a car to call of Mrs T Hill & Mrs
Fitter   Miss Budd went with us – Mr Hill & I went to call of
Mr James who was from home. Slept at Mrs Hortons,   Thurs:
Mr Hill left immediately after breakfast having a great deal to do –
Jane & I with the baby went to the 'Old Church' (walked *very fast*)
where Mrs Tom & Mrs Charles soon after joined us – Mr Starrall
christened the baby he was very kind & civil – Gave him half a
sovereign. Edwyn was registerd wrong – had it made right & certificates of both children written out to take with us. Coming out
met Miss Burbridge & went with her shopping   Called of Mr
James – Thinks he should have known sooner of our going & so do
I[19] – Had a letter from Mrs Jos   Joseph still living but speech-
less, wrote to her. Very tired & hurried when I got to Mrs Horton's,
when Mr Hill told me he had ordered a car to come at 4 o'clock to
take us to the station. Mr James had said if he *possibly could* get the
writings[20] he would call at Mrs Hortons so agreed to go by the six
o'clock train instead of the one at 4 – He did not come. Mrs Hill
came while we were at dinner and gave me *two* sovereigns for the
children. At 6 the car came & Mrs Horton & Mrs Charles went in
another car with us to the station & little Ann. The Children very
good – Got to Liverpool a half past 10 – Slept at the 'Star &
Garter'   Fri: 25th After breakfast Mr Hill & I went to see the
ship & look a little at Liverpool   dined at the Inn – In the afternoon took Jane & the children to see the Ship – Thought perhaps
we could have slept on board – Could not. Went early to bed as the

ship was to sail next morning at 9 – Wrote to Mrs Joseph Mrs Lang-
gley & Mrs Robinson. Sat 26th: Up early – went in a car to the
River where we found the 'Steam Tug,' waiting to convey us on
board. When we went on board, it was very calm & I wrote a letter
to Mrs Hill. Found we had no Brandy, & that Mrs Cook had sent
Sherry & Port. Dined at table, began to feel giddy, our first dinner
not well cooked, all after were very well done – Sunday night *very*
rough. I slept in Jane's room with the baby – *Very* sick the first fortnight & Mr Hill very poorly his bowels is confined. A whale was
seen – Began to feel better at rather more the [entry stops or there
is a small blank space][21] Dined at Table & much better the last
week, two days becalmed. Very glad to see land, a fine harbour,
went in a steamer to land – The Custom House officers did not
examine any of the Ladies trunks & only slightly the gentlemen's.
Drove to the Post Office no Letter from Mr J. Hawksley[22] & so
went to the Inn. Next morning found out where Mr J Hawksley
lived called on him & saw his wife, he told us he had written a letter & left it for us at the Post Office, which we found to be true &
that he had looked out for apartments for us, which were very genteel & comfortable at a Miss Parkinson's. The society very pleasant
& well informed. Dined on Sunday at Mr Hawksley's – Saw a good
deal of N Y   walked in the Broad way, & Mr Hill took us about
in a cab, Jane children & Mr H – Went to church on Sunday 'St.
Georges' & on the Wednesday to a 'Convention,' never saw so
many clergymen – Think NY a very gay place, sorry to leave it, but
Jane & the children sadly bitten by the moschetos particularly poor
Edwyn – The Thermometer 90 and 92 – went in a Steamer the
'Troy,' up the River Hudson   very fine scenery – The steamer
such a one for size as I had never seen – Landed in time for tea at
Albany a (poor town)   Up by 4 o clock & set off by the railroad
carriage for Syracuse   A very fine Inn   had tea & took
a walk after to look at the town, with which we were much
pleased   Up early the next morning & set off again by the railroad carriages for 'Rochester.' The first Inn we went too, we could
not be taken in but staid there while Mr Hill went to look after our

luggage which I rather fear'd was gone, when Mr Hill came back, we went to, 'Blossoms,' next morning went to St Lukes to hear Dr Whitehouse preach. In the afternoon went to see the 'Genesee Falls,' & after tea called of Dr Whitehouse where we saw his wife Father & Sister: very friendly, The Dr took Mr Hill to see the different manufactories next morning & called with his sister in a Cab to take Mr Hill & I to see the Cemetery at 'Mount Hope' in the afternoon. About 8 at night the 'Gore' was to sail for 'Cobourg' & 'Port Hope,' on Lake 'Ontario.' They thought it would be too rough, but set off & went about 15 miles when they were obliged to turn back – very sick, the Ladies cabin very close, three nights on the water. Met at 'Port Hope' by Mr George & Mr Robert Ryley who took us to lodgings at Mr Barnetts. Staid there a week – Drank tea the first day we spent at 'Port Hope' at Mrs R. Ryley's, Jane & the children we all went in the lumber waggon & met Mr & Mrs G Ryley there   Sun: Dined at Mrs G Ryley's, children & Jane at the weekend went to the 'Queens Arms,' very comfortable there, Mr & Mrs Short, Mrs Whitehead, Mrs Kirckhoffer, 'Smith, 'Innis,' Hickman,[23] &c &c called upon us. 26th Oct   Went to our new house[24]   Mr Hill slept there the night before alone   very much against me as I thought both the house & beds must be damp. Snow on the ground. Did not take cold; while at Mr Hastings the baby had an attack of Dysentry. Dr Evett, Mr Jacobs & Mr Waller called of us – Returned some of the calls – Jane not very well – consulted Dr. Hickman – said it was cold. 10th November, 'Florinda Brake'[25] came to us; a month upon trial   Mr Hill's temper very trying. Mr G Ryley & Mr Hill went to Cobourg   Mrs Ryley dined here. Baked bread for the first time, Snowy.   16th   Mr Hill hurt his leg. Mr Hill bought a sleigh £4 currency. Very mild & damp, think it must be the Indian Summer. Have not yet had any Letters from England. Jane poorly –   Sun: Mr Hill very cross. Mon: 20th [November] Delightful weather   Mr Hill's leg better. Our goods came – Medicine, my Cloak, Fur Tippets   Dr & Mrs Hickman dined here & Mr & Mrs Ward[26] called here in the afternoon. It was a very lovely day – Have no doubt it is what is called the Indian Summer – Jane better. Tues: Mr Hill very poorly – Rainy   Thurs: Jane in bed all day. Mrs Chambers came to see her & Dr Hickman called, did not think her very bad. Mr Hill bought a pig, I did not feel very well, I want a little more rest & fresh air. Sun: Advent; Went to Church[27] with Mr Hill, heard a very good sermon from Mr Short   [December] 5th:[28] Mr Hill very much out of temper, which made me feel very low & poorly – The English Mail came, *no letters*. Wrote to Mrs Horton and Mrs Langley last week   Mr and Mrs G Ryley came to tea.   Tues 6th   Very cold   Mr Hill spent the evening at Mr Whiteheads, a party and dancing, singing & music, Mr Hill said he enjoyed himself very much. Wed: Got a bad cold. Jane better.   Sun 10th December Edwyn's birthday two years old. I lay in bed all day being *very unwell* with a cold & Catarrh. No one went to Church. 11th Mon: 11 years today since my dear Mother died. I was very poorly and lay in bed most of the day. Mr Hill cut Edwyns hair & put the Grange curtains to our bed. I do not feel strong or well, my chest feels weak. Tues: Dr Hickman called said I got the Influenza   Wed: Lay in bed, took medicine   very poorly. Thurs: Poorly –   Sat 16   Dr Hickman called to see me in a Cutter, brought his little girl. Had an invitation to an evening party on Thurs: last at Mr [Kirckstry ?] but too ill to leave my bed, and Mr Hill too had a cold, so both declined   Jane had a letter from her sister. The Doctor still says she has no complaint but that her teeth are bad & advised her to go out as much as she can, she looks thin & out of spirits. My face sadly broken out & I am very weak. Sun 17th: Feel better. Jane went with the Chamber's in a sleigh   none of us went to Church but Mr Hill took Edwyn a walk. Mon 18th: Mr & Mrs Short called in their sleigh – Mr Hill went in our sleigh (or Berlin) for the first time, broke it. I am better but my face still broken out. Tues 19th: A large meeting at Cobourg. Mr Hill went. A great number of sleighs passed by here.   Wed 20th   Mr Hill went twice to 'Port Hope,' had his hair cut. My face continues to be broken out, but I am better.   21st   The

shortest day. Mr Hill went a long ride on horseback, & brought
3 bushels of Apples – He went to P Hope after tea. Fri: Mr Hill
went a ride on horseback, in the afternoon   Dr Hickman &
3 children called, recommended me to take some medicine
Mr Hill went to Mr Hughes for it after tea. Sat: Very poorly –
Sun   Xmas eve, lay in bed most of the day – Mr Hill did not
go to Church –   Mon Xmas day, no one went to Church,
Florinda's Mother came for her & she went home for
the day at breakfast time and is to stay all night. Upon the
whole I feel better though very weak & poorly and the glands
of my neck continue swelled. The weather very mild and open,
a little snow this morning. Jane has been better the last two or
three days –   26th   Florinda came back. Mrs & Miss Innis
& Mrs R & Miss Ryley called. Mr Hill takes medicine. Surprised
Dr Hickman has not called to see me, or sent the flour.   Wed
27th   Two bags of flour came. Thurs: Mr Hill called of Mr Ward
Mrs King & Dr Evett. Mr & Mrs G Ryley called. Fri: Mr Hill
gone to Mr G Ryley's   *never heard* any one swear so dreadfully
as he does.   Sat 30   Mr Hill, Florinda & Edwyn went to Port
Hope   brought me a very kind affectionate letter from Mrs
Horton   It's the first letter I have had since I came to Canada &
contained what I expected to hear, that my dear brother had died
about a fortnight after I left, it was what I expected & thought I
was prepared for, never the less it was a *great shock*, I hope & trust
through the merit of our Saviour that he is happy he has had a long
illness & time to prepare   He has suffer'd much in mind on
account of his circumstances. I feel much for his wife & family &
my very *dear* sister. Mr Hill wrote to Mr Charles   has taken our
house in the Park, a lease for 7 years –   Sun: The last day in the
Old Year   Mr Hill & Jane went to Church, A fine but cold day
felt very poorly   1844   Mon: New Year's day   Fine &
bright but cold, walked a little in the yard – have not been out for
more than a month   my face still broken out though getting
better. Feel very low about poor Joseph whose death I heard of on
Saturday by Mrs Horton's letter – Sent Florinda with a note to

Mrs G Ward's accepting for Mr Hill an invitation for this evening.
I of course declined it. Mr Hill went & had a pleasant rubber at
Whist   Florinda went to Mr Chamber's at night and had a
dance. Tues 2nd. At times feel a *very sickly* feeling & low & dull,
want something to chear my spirits, Mr Hill so very irritable that
I am constantly in a flutter at the breast. Mrs Fanny[29] here wash-
ing. Wed 3rd – Mr Hill more out of temper than ever – very
poorly   think I am a good deal abused in appearance, feel
Joseph's Death very much. Thurs. Mr Hill's temper rather better,   bought 3 bus[hels] of Apples – Snow –   Fri: Dr.
Hickman called & in the evening   Mr Whitehead & Mr G
Ward & the Doctor came to tea & play a rubber. Sat: Walked to
Port Hope. Sun: Snow   Florinda went home & stayed all night.
Mon: Mr Hill & Fanny thrown out of the sleigh, Mr Hill & I
walked out. In the afternoon Mr Hill rode to Mr G Ryley's – Mrs
Smith called. Wrote to Mr James by the post & Mr Hill to his
brother Charles. Thurs: Mr Hill, Florinda & Edwyn went a ride in
the Sleigh, it was the first time I had been in one. Called of Mrs
Hickman, the Doctor gone to 'Toronto.' Fri: 12th   Rainy. 13th:
Drew a gallon of Whiskey. Mr Hill went to P.H. posted a letter to
his brother & Mrs James, also 9 newspapers.   Sun: 14th   went
with Mr Hill to Church, the young Wards took us up in their sleigh
& brought us back. Called after Church of Mrs Hickman & Mr
Hill invited the Doctor & Mrs Hickman to dine with us tomorrow it being Mr Hill's birthday, also the young Wards to come
& play a rubber. Fell down the steps going into the kitchen.
Mon: 15th   Mr Hill's birthday, he and I went to Cobourg in the
Sleigh, Old Dolly drew us. Dr Hickman dined with us & Mr G
Ward came to tea, I played at Whist & Mr Hill was my partner,
we have spent a pleasant day –   16th   All went a drive in the
sleigh .   17th   About 5 in the morning Jane woke us to say the
baby was ill, she was in a fit, but very slight, Took an emetic & Castor Oil,   Very well all the day   Dr & Mrs Hickman called –
Snowed all day   18th   Mr Hill, Edwyn & I went to 'Port
Hope'   called of Mrs Kirckhoffer invited them to tea on Mon-

day. Called of Mrs Hughes in the afternoon   Mr Hill & Jane
went to Cobourg. Mr Walter called. The baby pretty well. Lost a
good deal of blood in the evening. Fri: Poorly – Mr Mrs & Miss
Whitehead called & Dr Hickman & Mr Hill going to play a rubber
at Mr Whiteheads tomorrow, think them pleasant people. Sun:
Lay in bed most of the day. Mon: Mr & Mrs Kirckhoffer Mrs Read
spent the evening with us – Expected the Doctor & Mrs Hickman –   Tues 23rd   Paid Mrs Breaky two months wages for
Florinda up to the tenth of January. Very mild – I am better.
Wed: A note from Mrs K. inviting us there tomorrow: Thurs
25th   Very Cold, Mr Hill & I went to Mrs Kirckhoffers, they
had invited a large party but had had many disappointments.
Fri: 26th   Very Cold. Sat: *Very Cold*, went to PH with Mr Hill, a
sleigh overturned close by me –   Sun 28th   a *wretched day*, Mr
Hills *temper unbearable*   cannot live in the way we do, think we
had better part. Tues: Called at Mrs Fortune's   29th Bought a
loaf of sugar   Mr Hill's temper better   Wed: Did not go
out   Fri: Mr Hill had a letter from his brother Charles, called at
Mr Aldrich's – Felt very poorly in the morning   Mr Hill, Jane &
baby went to Port Hope[30]   A lovely day Jane got quite well –
Florinda going to leave us, had rather she had staid another month.
Sat: Out twice in the cutter, called at Mrs R Ryley's   Sun: Feb
7   Mr Hill and I went to Church, a very good sermon from Mr
Short, 'On the Duty of keeping Holy the Sabbath day.' Walked
in the afternoon – Florinda went home took Edwyn with her. I
feel much better, baby I think is about more teeth, she looks
paler   Tues: Mr & Mrs G Ryley dined here. Wed: Spent the day
with Mrs G Ryley – lovely weather –   Thurs: very fine   Sat:
Edwyn poorly, Dr Hickman saw him, *did not* think he was going to
have the scarlet fever which is very prevalent at this time. Sun:
Got ready to go to Church but did not go – Mr Hill more provok-
ing than ever. A *very bad* headache. In the afternoon Florinda & I
set out to go to Church, but found there was no service. Edwyns
eyes badly bloodshot.   Mon 19th   Wrote part of a letter to Mrs
Joseph   Mrs Alldrett & daughter called, & brought us a present

of a couple of fowls. In the afternoon Mr Hill and I went to
Cobourg to buy some tea   went with Mr Soden's Mare –
like her very much   My head very bad. Florinda Breaky
left us, and seem'd highly delighted to do so. My dear sisters
birthday.   13th   Went a drive with the new Mare, called at
Mrs Robt Ryley's   Finished my letter to Mrs Joseph.   Wed:
14th   Mr Hill exchanged our Mare for one with Mr Soden – gave
£2 for the exchange   A lovely day – none of us very well.
Thurs: Mr Hill had been *very angry* that the flour was gone, I felt
very ill   violent Palpitation of the Heart. Mr G. Ryley dined
here but I was too poorly to get up. Mr Hill going to PH met the
Doctor & asked him to call – Baby's eyes very bad – The Dr lanced
her gums –   Sat: 17th Maria Ashby came [9] dollar a month.
Sun: Went a drive with Mr Hill, he was very poorly at night Mon:
19th Better. The babys upper teeth quite through, she has now
4. Went to PH with Mr Hill & called at Mrs Fortunes, they were
come here but did not meet them. The Doctor called in the morning. His daughter ill with Rheumatic fever.   Tues: 20th   A lovely
day, drove as far as Dr. Hickman's at the Farm. I am getting better.
Mr Hill looks poorly. Wed: Drove as far as Mr G Ryley's. Thurs:
Called of Mrs R Ryley   Fri: Snowing greatest part of the day. Mr
Hill went for some flour to the Mill.   Sat 24th   Four years this
morning since I found my dear Father a corpse, thought much of
him before I got up. A lovely day, Dr. Hickman called – We are
better than we were. Drove as far as the Doctors & staid tea took
Edwyn with us. Sun 25th: First Sunday in Lent, Mr Hill and I went
to church, came home in Mr Ward's sleigh   Mon 26th – Mrs
Fanney here, a very large wash –   Tues 27th   Ironing day – did
not near finish the wash.   Wed: 28th   Mr Aldrett called at the
Post Office   brought Mr Hill two letters, one from Mr [illegible
due to ink spill] & the other from his brother Charles. A good
account of all their healths [except?] Mr Hills who *is* not very
well   Fri: [March] 1st   Mr Hill, Edwyn & I went in the buggy
to Cobourg   Mrs R Ryley to dine with us. Mrs & Miss [ink spill]
came to tea.   Sat: 3rd   The snow going fast. In the afternoon Mr

Hill & I went in the Buggy to Mr Aldrett's.   Sun 4th   About 5 in the morning Jane called to us to say the Baby was convulsed, Mr Hill & I got up – It was a slight attack, but do not like the recurrence of them, Hope please God that it be the last. Snowing slightly during the day. Mon: Mr Hill all day at Mr Aldretts Tues: About 5 in the morning the baby was again convulsed – After breakfast Mr Hill went for Dr Hickman gave her a powder, does not think she will be subject to these attacks. Said her her [*sic*] head was not so much closed as most some children of her age but did not think it of consequence – In the afternoon Mr Hill drove Edwyn & I in the buggy to P Hope for ingredients for the Knicker-bocker pickle.[31] Wed: A lovely day – Baby much better, took another powder. Baby better   Dr Hickman called, Mr Hill offended with [him] for not being more attentive –   8th March   wrote to Mrs Horton & wrote to Mrs Robinson, by the same mail   the letters went the 8th of March, Mr Hills temper *very bad indeed*, I think no wifes can be more tried in that respect   The baby is better, but Edwyn has a bad cold. Think it was croup the baby had a few days afterwards, she had 3 convulsions in the night and I think it was a fit she had in the morning, Mr Hill went for Dr Hickman   he ordered when is a fit immedeately to put her in a warm bath. She is now very much better. Said we must not over feed her and observe the state of her bowels – Occasionally if they were not as they should be give her a grain of Calomel or a dose of Castor Oil. Called during the week of Mrs Short, Mrs Mileard & Mrs Innis – Went in the sleigh, suppose for the last time. Mr Hill has been irritable in temper, but has been better the last day or two. He was much offended with the Doctor about the baby – but they are getting friendly again.   25th Mrs Fenny here washing –   26th   Little Margaret one year old to day – Ironing – All had a glass of wine – walked with Mr Hill & Edwyn into the 'Bush'   saw Mr Chambers boiling Maple Sugar – The baby pretty well –   Sun: 31   Went to Church – Mr Short *very severe* to some persons in his sermon who did not behave themselves well at Church & to those who came late.

Frosty.   April 1st   A lovely day over head but cold – gradually
weaning the baby, she is got quite well. Mr Hill bettered tempered
– went to look at some farms – Mrs Hallon called   wish the
roads were better – want to walk out, and begin to be tired of the
winter. At night called up about 2 as the baby was convulsed. Had
another attack about an hour after, in all 6 – Dr Hickman saw her 3
times during the day. Mrs Chambers & I sat up till half past 2 then
called Jane   next day Miss Ward called, the baby had a fit while
she was here – Mrs Short called – The baby better – Mr Hill's temper *very bad* –   April 13th   Had '[Stovis?] Gazette' sent by Mrs
Horton   saw my Aunt Lovelace's death in it   The paper
dated 12th of February   Sun: Went to Church   sat down
stairs   Mon: Tues: & Wed: Mr Hill's temper *awful*. Thurs [May
2nd]: Mr Hill at work with Mr Fenny in his garden, his temper better now he is employed – Fine but a keen air – I do not feel strong.
Mr Hattons's Mill burned May 2nd   had letters from Mrs
Charles, Mrs James & Mrs Davis, my dear Brother's widow. Mrs
Charles & Mrs James mentioned she was married, never was so
much astonished. In her letter she spoke of the last days & death of
my dear brother & the end spoke of her having been married to Mr
Davis 5 weeks. My dear Brother died Sept 9th 1843   Her letter
was dated March 16th 1844. Drank tea the day the letters came to
hand at Mrs Wards for the first time.   May 5th   Anniversary of
our wedding day – Went to Church in the morning & Jane in the
afternoon – Did not keep it all.   May 10th   Mr Hill has agreed to
buy a Farm as the title is now made good – I am sorry as I should
have liked to have lived here.   9th   Mr & Mrs Ward Miss Ward
& Mr & Mrs Short drank tea here –   10th May   Drank tea at
Mrs G Ryley's   11th   Poorly[32] the first time since Baby was
born – she is very well. 11th May, Thundering & lightning all
night – We have had a good deal of thunder & lightning lately –
but every one says they never knew *so early or so fine a spring* –
Sun 12th   The little Lamb died – A Good deal of wind. Little
Margaret has had no titty the last 3 days so may call her wean'd –
she is very well. Not very well myself – Mr Hills temper *very bad* &

his language very abusive. Wish I was not going to so lonely a place
his temper at times is so awful. Mon [May 13th]: Mr Berriman here
tailoring for Mr Hill. Tues: Mr Hill Edwyn & I went to the Farm –
very fine weather, saw some pretty wild flowers & pretty birds,
Woodpeckers &c *Do not* like so retired a situation –   Wed [May
15th]: A lovely day – Mr Hill swore dreadfully said he would *kick
me & my servants* out of *doors* that he would not live with me if it
were not for the children & do not know what he would have – We
all do our utmost to please him   I *am poorly,* and my breast hard
& painful I often *feel* as if I had *no inside,*   Thurs: 16th Heard
Mrs Charles Hughes was dead of the Scarlet Fever, Dr Hickman
dined here & he & Mr Hill went to the Farm   very low and
poorly – wrote a letter.   Sat: 18th   Mrs Hughes *Eldest* child dead
– went to Port Hope after tea, saw the Funeral   Put a letter in
the Post Office for Mrs Davis & one for Mrs Hill and Mrs Horton
the two last inclosed in one envellope, understand the mail does
not go till Friday –   Sun: May 19th   Went to Church alone, a
Funeral sermon for poor Mrs Hughes the text there is but a 'Step
between me and death.' And a funeral anthem 'I mount I fly,' [']O
death where is thy sting O grave where is thy victory.' In the afternoon Jane Maria & children went a walk – Mrs Waller came to
tea   Mon: 20th   Our wash, a rainy morning, Maria had to go
to 'Port Hope' for Soap. The *Fever* bad at 'Port Hope.' The baby
has had no milk for a week, she is quite weaned & bore it better by
far than I expected – she is looking remarkably well. Tues: Ironing
day – busy in the morning & in the afternoon went with Mr Hill to
the Farm. Mr Hill measured the height of a tree that was lying on
the ground, found it 142 feet and the top was sawed off which we
supposed would be 10 or 12 feet more. Wed. Fine but very cold – A
barrel of flour Mr Chambers brought – Rode as far as Mrs Robert
Ryley's –   Thursday 23rd   Mr Hill went to the Court house
Cobourg. Sent 2 newspapers to Mrs Davis 1 to Mrs Green 1 to Mrs
Langley and 1 to Mrs Robinson   Friday May 24th   Had an
uncomfortable night   Mr Hill had been so out of temper all the
day – He brought me from P Hope a Letter from Mrs James and one

from Mrs Horton who I am pleased to hear is better in health. Mr Hill had a letter from his brother Charles and some English newspapers – Mr Gibbs dead & Mr Ingram – Jane gone to put the newspapers in the Post Office. Sun: Went to Church with Mr Hill   Mon: Mr Hill gone to Port Hope   took an invitation for the Kirckhoffers   In the evening went a drive with Mr Hill who caught a Jay – Gave Mrs Fanney a [Mop?] – Maria poorly   think there is thunder in the air –   Tues: Mr Hill all day at the Farm with Mr Maryfield sewing Clover seed   Miss Ward called & brought some flowers. Wed: Mr Hill took the sheep to Mr [Slade's?] to be washed   Thurs: went with Mr Mrs & Miss Ryley to our Farm – drank tea at Mrs Ryleys –   Thurs: 30th A very rainy day – Expected company but no one came   Mrs Kirckhoffer sent a note – Mrs Aldrett called   Think the weather trying as it always is in the Spring.   Sun: 2nd June Trinity Sunday   Mr Hill & I went to Church[33] – In the afternoon Mr Maryfield & Mr Sanders helped Mr Hill to catch the Mare & came in & had some Grog. Mrs Waller had tea here – Mon 3rd   *before* half past 6 some one knocked at the door   Mr Hill called the girls, who got up, he swore at them *dreadfully* & then at me *ordering* me to get up with the most abusive language in which blasted b...h &c was repeatedly used   not getting us with this insolent treatment he *kicked* me several times. Very poorly all day – After dinner Jane gone to Charlotte's wedding. She came out with Mr George Ryley as his servant.   Tues 4th   Yesterday and today A man & his son here at work making pig stys & working in the garden, they came from Yorkshire but have been living 5 years at Montreal. Mr & Mrs George Ryley called on their way to Cobourg   The weather very fine. I have not yet taken a meal with Mr Hill since he kicked me. Wed: Very poorly & out of spirits. The men at work in the garden. After dinner Mr Hill, Mr Clark, Maria Edwyn & baby went to the Farm – Showery – heard our goods were arrived at Montreal.   Fri: 5th   Mr & Mrs Ryley dined here & after dinner Mr & Mrs G Ryley Mr Hill myself Jane Edwyn & baby went to the Farm. Had a letter from Mrs Robinson

& Mr Hill had the Times newspaper from his Brother. Sat: After dinner Mr Hill Maria & I & children went as far as Cobourg but did not go into the town. Mr & Mrs & Miss Ryley called on their return from Cobourg. Sun 9th   Very rainy – Maria went to see her sister. Mon: Very blowing.   Tues 11th   Wrote a few lines in Mr Hills letter to Mrs Horton and asked her to purchase a black dress for me & get Miss Dowler to make it. A fine day, the Mail goes at four this evening. Mr Hill Jane & children went to put the letters in the post office & call at Dr Hickmans for him to look at the childrens gums, Edwyn had his lanced.   Wed 12th   Mr Hill got up early & went with Mr Whitehead to his farm. A lovely day, Swarms of flies.   Tues: [June 11th]   Drove as far as Mrs G Ryley's & called at the Dr   Wed: Mr & Mrs Millard came to tea and our cases arrived here from England containing crockery, one feather bed, carpets & writing from Mr James, on account of which Mr Hill and I shall have to go to Toronto. Thurs: Busy Friday   Miss Aldrett spent the day here and her Father and Mr G Ward came to tea. The roads by here being mended. Sat: Busy, think of going to 'Toronto' on Tuesday. Sun: Mr Hill & I went to Church   two clergymen officiated. Fine & warm, had an early tea & Mr Hill rode over to Mr G Ryley's. Our parlour looks nice with the looking glasses pictures & carpet. Mrs Horton sent little Margaret a parasol. Had a note from her   no letters from any-one else.   Tues: June 18th   Up soon after 4 o clock – Rainy – clear'd up soon after 6 & before 7 set off in our own buggy – Got to 'Pugh's Tavern' & had a lunch   set off again & met a waggon loaded with flour, the wheels of which & ours got entangled & broke one of our wheels the shaft & c   Mr Hill set off with the Mare for Bowmanville & I remained to take care of the Buggy & follow Mr Hill in the Stage – After waiting a long time in the Hot sun & no stage appearing I was very glad to see Mr Hill return Went to Mr Tiffanys cottage while Mr Tiffany got a waggon with which we proceeded to Bowmanville. The buggy being tied behind it. Dined at the 'Cottage Inn' next door to Dr Lowe's Exceedingly hot – the thermometer 100 in the sun – After tea

took a short walk & called at Mr Suttons, very civil people – Came
to the Inn to a *very small* room & *bed*.   Wed: 19 June   poor
Joseph's birthday – Had breakfast with Dr Knower & set off soon
after on our journey, had not proceeded far before we were over-
taken by a thunder storm. Got to 'Posts' just before one of the
heaviest showers I almost ever saw, dined & had our clothes dried.
In some parts the roads very good & in others very bad   Got to
Stones in the evening – had tea & to bed – Comfortable room –
Breakfasted & then went to call upon Mr Smith, he had no personal knowledge of us but did not doubt our identity – Called two
or three times of him & signed the writings in the presence of Mr
Day & Mr Moore   He is to convey them to Mr Simcox
Saw the Market Hall. Came to the Inn to Lunch – Dined at 5 &
walked out again – bought Edwyn a top and both he & his sister a
cup with their names upon it, Came home and to bed – Up by 5
next morning & set off on our return home – breakfasted at the
'Scarboro' Arms, a very nice breakfast strawberries & cream
&c   Set off after it for 'Posts,' where we again dined,   Drank
tea at Mrs Pughs & got home soon after 11 at night the latter part
of the way dark, as the moon only in its first quarter was gone down
– A distance of 67 miles in one day & with one horse – Went [sic]
we got home Mr Hill found the girls gone to bed, Jane got up while
I waited at the gate in the buggy the roads being repaired we could
not drive through our gate, The baby had been sick & Dr Hickman
was sent for and staid all night – Sadly agitated, feared it had been
worse than I found it was. Sat [June 22nd]: Edwyn did not seem to
care about us, baby delighted   looked thin –   Sun: Were set
off for Church, Mr Hill said *some very unkind things* to me about the
uncomfortableness it was to him when I was in the family way, that
if I ever was so again he would not sleep with me & c. Felt so hys-
terical that although we were at the Church gates I turned back &
Mr Hill followed, Lay in the bed in the afternoon. Mr Waller came
to tea & staid supper – During the week went several drives – very
far from well[34]   Mr & Mrs Hughes drank tea with us, Mr Hill &
I went a party at Mr James Smiths – wrote to Mrs James,   Sat:

Mr Hill called of Dr Hickman as his foot pained him – the Dr said
it was rheumatic gout – Sun: did not go to Church –   Mon
called at Hoopers Mill & at the Doctors Mrs Millards son *very ill*,
he was thrown from his horse & kicked.   Tues 2nd July   Went
shopping to 'Port Hope.' Called at Mrs Aldrett's. Had an early tea
& Mr Hill drove Maria and baby to the 'Farm' – Sultry, think we
shall have thunder – Edwyn very sick yesterday, Mr Hills foot painful – Got our hay in. Mr Maryfield, Mr Sanders & Mr Fanny Jane
helped to rake. Paid Mrs Sanders for milk & butter.   Wed 3rd   A
fine day Mr Hill drove to Port Hope took Edwyn with him. Mr
Waller & Mr Hill drove over to the Farm – Mr Mrs & Miss Ryley
& Mr G Ryley & his wife dined here – had the centre leaf in the
table for the first time. Roasted beef and Fish – Agreed to dine
at Mr G Ryley's next Tuesday – Dr Hickman called – At night
wished to be friends with Mr Hill as we had appear'd to be before
our company – 'said he wished to have nothing to do with me' –
Thurs 4th   Sold our wool to Mr Quinlan 13 1/2 lbs a shilling a
pound – received 13/6 –Thought the wool weighed very light. Had
an early cup of tea & Mr Hill went a drive swore *dreadfully* before
setting out –   Sat: Mr Hill went intending to bring home the
cow but did not.   Sun 7th   Mr Hill did not go to Church, but
Jane and I did   Mr Harness from Cavan[35] preached – In the
afternoon Mr Hughes and Mr Waller came; staid tea   said Mr
Newman was married last night. Mr Hill still continues out of temper but I content myself with thinking I have tried *all in my power*
to please & live peaceably with him but find it impossible   I
hope I shall not find I wear myself to a skeleton as I have done –
His foot is better he does not walk at all lame –   Mon 8th
July   drove Mr Fanny nearly to Joplins, where he was going for a
cow Mr Hill bought a few days ago   Mr Hill gave [blank] dollars
for it – It is a very nice looking cow called 'Brandy' – went & called
for Miss Aldrett & took her to see our farm – very low and
depressed in spirits. At night Mr Hill thought he had heard some
one about, got up –   Tues 9th   Maria came to say Jane was
sick, got up – she took some Castor Oil – poorly all day – Mr Hill

gone to dine at Mr George Ryley's – I was neither in health nor
spirits to go, & Jane poorly – I almost think it will be impossible for
us to live together,   'he said this morning that he had married
me for *spite*' & my health & spirits both giving way – In the afternoon Miss Smart called – had an early tea, & surprised to see Dr
Hickman & Mr Reynard & Mr Palsgreave   The Doctor gave
Jane a dose of Calomel – Said I looked *very* thin & my pulse was
exceedingly weak and feeble. They would not stay tea as Mr Hill was
from home, but thought they might meet him as they returned
10th Wednesday – Mr Hill breakfasted at Mr Hastings with Mr
Reynard & his friend – Sent [word?] expecting they would dine
with us – They did not,   Mr Reynard has been married again
about two months since   Had an envellope with simply two
cards, Mr & Mrs Hill – Does not say when they were married –
Miss Ryley called, lent her some drawings – Engaged to dine at Mrs
R Ryley's Friday next   Jane got pretty well.   Thurs 11th   Mr
Hill's foot bad – think he has taken cold – Went to the Post Office
after tea – no letters or English newspapers – Called at Mrs
Millard's   their son better – said they had the Scarlet fever at
Mr Williams. Very Sultry.   Fri: 12th   Mr Hill complained sadly of
his foot – Dined at Mrs R Ryley's –   Sun: Jane and [illegible]
went to Church   Mr Kennedy preached   Tues 16th   Dr
Hickman a son – [blank] Mr Jacobs called –   Sun 21st [July]
Expected Mr Jacobs to dinner – Went to Church alone – Mrs
Ward drove me home   Mr Murloch preached   Mrs Eli
Ward dined with us –   Mon: up in good time – Mr Hill and Mr
Maryfield gone to the Farm   Saw a humming bird – Mr Hills got
quite well – I have felt better the last few days. A dreadful thunder
storm. After tea went to PH   Maria bought a bonnet. Tues [July
23rd]: Miss Knowles here. Went to Port Hope in the morning –
found a letter from Mrs Horton & two newspapers – After dinner
went with Mr Hill to the farm, thought it looked pleasanter than
I have before done. Thurs: Expected Miss Knowles, she did not
come. Maria & baby gone a drive with Mr Hill   Friday   Miss
Knowles   Sat Maria went to Mr Barretts for some currants – I

had to go afterwards to Mr Whiteheads to sign a paper about Mr
Hills giving up his right to Mr Short house – Mr Hill could not find
the paper · they were at Mr Whitehead's office   Picked
& boiled the currant jelly – At night very tired and poorly –
Sunday [July 28th] – went in Colour to Church – Mr Hill went.
Took a walk after tea. Mon & Tues: The Wash – Called at
Wode's –   Wed 31st   Very poorly all night, & in the morning
had a sever attack of cholera – Mr Hill went for the Doctor – bowels
relaxed sick cold [one word illegible] pinched & cramp – Doc-
tor came twice   Thurs: Very poorly & weak   Friday &
Saturday   ill & weak came down stairs –   A newspaper from
Mrs Horton.   Sun August 4   Very poorly – The Doctor says I must
keep quiet   Mr Hill gone a drive with Dr Hickman   Mrs
Hughes & Mrs Waller called   Edwin passed *one* worm some days
ago   been taking the [illegible] but none have come from him.
Very sultry – Oppressed with the heat – Very weak –   Mon:
August 5th   Very *poorly* indeed   Tues 6th   Mr Hill gone to Mr
G Ryley's The Doctors & Mr R Ryley   He dined at the Doctors – wrote a long letter to Mrs Horton – better   Thurs: Up
early   Mr Hill gone to Mr Pengellys   do not know wheth
er he will return to night or go on to Peterborough – Continued
my letter to Mrs Horton – Mending   Jane busy washing –
Thurs 8th   Mr Hill gone to Mr Pengelly's –   Fri 9th August
Had a long letter from Mrs Davis – Sent Jane to the Post Office
with a *long letter* to Mrs Horton. Getting better. Sat: In the morning Mr & Mrs Whitehead called – Mr Jacobs Mrs Ward & Mrs
G Ward   in the afternoon went to Port Hope   Mr Jacobs
came to tea.   Sun 11th   Mrs Ward kindly called to take me to
church   Dr Bethune[36] preached. James Aldrett drove us home
& Miss Aldrett dined here – Feel far from strong   Mon:
12th   Mr Hill gone to Port Hope   Tues   Drank tea at Mrs
Fortune's & called of Mrs Wallace –   Wed: Went with Mr Hill
to the Farm   Thurs: Mr Hill sadly out of temper – Nothing
yet fixed about the house – talked of going for the winter to
Mr Charles farm   called at Mr G Ryley's – The Doctors &

Mr Robert Ryley's – In the evening Mr Hill rode to Mr Nelson's –
People are busy with the harvest   sent Mr Maryfield a bottle of
wine   he is very poorly –   Fri 18th   Both Mr Hill & I have
diareah & Edwin   I called to see Miss Ward, who is poorly – Mr
Hill went after tea to Port Hope –   Sun 18th   A man came
about being hired as a farm servant, Mr Hill drove him in the buggy
to see the farm & I thought it a good opportunity to be driven
to Church   a missionary preached –Mrs Ward brought me
home – After dinner Mr Hill Edwyn & I went to Mr R Ryley's
& staid tea.   Mon: 19th Jane washing. very sultry – rain & lightning in the night   Mr Maryfield ill   Mr Hill gone to see
him –   Wed: Went to the Farm drank tea at Mr Aldretts –
Thurs: A great deal of rain – Mr Hill dreadfully irritable, gave Maria
a cut with his whip –   Fri: Mrs Ashby came   Sat: Mr Hill
went to P Hope – after dinner I went with Mr Hill to Perry's Mill –
He went in the evening to the Aldrett's   Sun 25th   I went
alone to Church – Rainy – Maria went with baby to Mrs Fanny's
Mon 26th   Killed a pig – Maria & the children gone a walk – Feel
better, the weather cooler   Went a drive with Mr Hill & Edwyn
in the afternoon. A Letter from Mrs Horton to Mr Hill & me –
Tues: Washing day – Rainy the early part of the morning   Wed:
Ironing day – Mr & Mrs Hughes called to ask us to tea there next
day – Mr Hill & I went in the Buggy to Mr Hughes met there
Mr Mrs & Miss [illegible] – Cake & wine but no supper   Mr Hill
very ill tempered –   Thurs: Mr Hill gone out on horseback
went to Cobourg   Sun: Sept   A man came, who Mr Hill has
hired   Mr Hill took him to see the Farm & drove me part of the
way to Church   Mr Short did the duty   came home with Mr
Ward's family   Mon: Neither Mr Hill or I went out – The children taking brimstone & treacle –   Tues: Mr Hill gone to the
Farm . Sun 8th   Went to Church alone   came as far as Mr
Wards with Mr & Mrs W in their Buggy – Drove with Mr Hill to
the Farm in the afternoon   Mon: Mr Short called. Three English newspapers – Jane sent a Letter to her sister –   Tues: very
hot   boiling preserves – In the afternoon Mr Hill & I drank tea

at Mr G Ryley's   He is better tempered lately – Expected
James Sherwood the man Mr Hill hired as farm servant, Mr
Hill disappointed he did not come as he wished to begin to
plough –   Thurs 12   Mr Mrs Two Miss Fortunes & Miss Aldrett
came here to tea   Fri 13th   Mr Hill, Maria & Edwyn went to
Perrytown – Had an early cup of tea & Mr Hill & I went
to the Farm   Lovely weather – Fine climate –   Sat 14th
Sun Mr Hill & I went to Church –   Mon: Mr Pengelly dined
here, Ellen came to tea, Jane Maria & children went to Port
Hope   came home *late*   Tues: Mr Pengelly breakfasted
here   Wed: Mr & Mrs Kirckhoffer called & Mr & Mrs Ryley &
Mr Pengelly drank tea here –   Thurs Sept 19th   Mr Hill
Edwyn & I went for the Side saddle to [illegible]   called of
Mr Johnson   had Nelson & plums went to the Farm, overtook Brines his wife & children on the road in our waggon – They
are gone for the present while they get there [*sic*] house ready to
live in the one we intend to occupy –   Sun 22   Fine & Cold
no one went to Church –   Mon 23rd   Mr Hill Jane & baby
went to the Farm in the morning –   Sun: None of us went to
Church,   Mon: Very Cold. Mr Hill & I drove over to Johnsons &
had tea with them   Tues & Wed: our wash & Called at Mrs
Wards   Thurs: Drank tea at Mrs Wards & in the morning
called at Mrs Shorts & Mrs Whitehead's   Fri: Dined at Mr G
Ryleys   met Mrs Griffiths there –   Sat: Very Cold   Sun:
29th   Went to Church Mrs Waller called   Mon 30th   Mr &
Mrs G Ryley & Mrs Griffith called on their road to Cobourg with Mr
Hill   Mrs Kirckhoffer came to tea   lent her some drawings –
Staid late waiting for Mr K to come for her   Tues Oct 7th   Fine
& Cold   Mr Hill gone with Mr Kirckhoffer to the Farm   Fri
4th   The Agricultural Show   Mr & Mrs Ward, Mrs Smith, Miss
Ward & Mr & Mrs Pengelly & little boy came to tea   Mr Buck
killed a pig for us –   Sat 5th   Mr Hill at the Farm   Brines had
23 lbs of pork –   Sun 6th   Went to Church alone – Jane Maria
& children went to Church in the afternoon, called at Mrs Fanny's –
Jane had some Whisky   Mon 7th   Mr Hill in one of his ill tem-

pered fits – *impossible* to please him – try as much as we can –
Maria & I went in the Buggy to P Hope   met Mr Whitehead
invited us to tea there tomorrow. The foliage very beautiful – the
weather clear & cold. Tues: Mr Hill again swearing & cursing –
Got the headache owing to his constant abuse, or should be very
well – Drank tea at Mr Whitehead's – Felt low & out of Spirits –
Frightened by some men coming home – They did it for fun – Mr
Hill & I more friendly –   Wed: 9th   Drove to the Farm.   Thurs
10th   Begun the Farm work of the house on the premises, 4 men at
work – Slept there   Called to see Mrs Aldrett   Mr Hill Maria
& children went to the Farm in the afternoon   Fri: Mr Hill gone
to a sale   Jane Edwin & I went in the Buggy to call & invite Mrs
Smith Mrs G Ward & Mrs Kirckhoffer to take tea with us on Tuesday
next. The English mail went yesterday, Mr Hill intended writing.
Sat 12th   Mr Hill, Edwyn & I went in the Buggy for the poney –
it is a pretty grey poney – I drove home   Sun: 13th   Went
to Church alone   Mrs Hughes & George came in the afternoon
Mon: 14th   Tues: 15th   A note from Mrs Smith declining our
invitation   Mr & Mrs Whitehead, daughter, a young lady visitor
of theirs, Mr & Mrs G Ward, & Mr & Mrs Kirckhoffer spent the
evening with us   Wed 16th   Rode the Mare & Mr Hill the
poney to the Farm   Thurs: 17th October   Mr Hill gone to Mr
Charles sale – Maria gone to Port Hope for bread   Very rainy all
the day, sent Mr Fanny with one of the pigs to the Farm. Mr Hill
bought 30 sheep, sleigh, pigs   Friday 18th   Mr Hill gone to the
farm   Fanny went to drive two of our pigs over   Bad travelling. Sat Mr Clark called   Mr Hill came to a late dinner   In
the night the most violent storm of winds ever remembered ·   Sun
20th   Went to Church *very early*   Mr Hughes dined here he &
Mr Hill drove to the Farm in the afternoon   Lost the poney –
Mon 21st   Our wash – killed a sheep – Miss Smarts called.   Tues
22nd   Ironing day   Mr Hill Maria & children gone to Port Hope
& the Farm   Mrs Wallace sent Maria to invite me to tea – went –
Mrs [Kennedy?] & Mrs Kirckhoffer Mrs Hughes walked home with
me – The Election – The poney threw Mr Hill   Sun 27th   Did

not go to Church, a charity sermon   not very well   Mr Hill
lame, but better   He had a providential escape of being
killed   Mon: 28th Brines came, when we got up in the morning
found the ground covered with snow, snowing all day   A letter
from Mrs Horton – Poor [Parmena?] Langley dead –   Tues:
Snowing again   Mr Hill gone out in the *Sleigh* – very cold – Mr
Hill feels very little of his lameness –   Wed: [Oct 30]   Mr Hill
Maria & children went in the Sleigh to the farm – Expected Mr &
Mrs G Ryley to dinner   Alfred came to tell us they would not
come   Sat Nov 2nd   Went in the afternoon to the Farm with
Mr Hill   They have got the staircase up & hope by this day
week to have the plastering done   Sun 3rd   Damp – Went to
Church alone – Mr Hill's temper more trying than ever – Indeed I
think *no one* has more need of patience than I have   Mon
4th   A dinner at Mr Hastings – Do not know whether Mr Hill
will go. Mr Williams was returned [to his seat in government] &
the dinner is on his account   Mr Hill went to the dinner &
came home before I   Tues   Mr Pengelley came here to breakfast – Mr Geo Ryley dined here – Called & returned the 'Mysteries
of Paris' to Mrs Waller   Thurs: Drove to P Hope with
Maria   went to the Bank. Mr R & G Ryley came & Mr Hill
went with them to Mr Fortunes & to our Farm: Fri: Mr Hill
Edwyn & I went & dined at Mr G Ryley's   Called at Mr
Aldretts. Very cold – Snowed all the way home   Mr Hill pleasanter. Sat Mr Hill & Mr G Ryley gone to Cobourg.   Sun
10th   Went to Church alone, Brines drove me there – Mr Hill
and Mr Maryfield went to the Farm – turned out very rainy,
Mon: 11th Mr Hill went to the Farm   Tues: 12th Mr & Mrs
Aldrett dined here for the first time very rainy – A Fox has taken
one of our geese –   Wed   Fine & Cold – Mr Hill has bought
a chest of tea   The house being plastered   Mr Hill had a
Letter from his brother Charles on the 11th   Mr Hill has had
congestion of the brain –   Thurs: went with Mr Hill to the
Farm – The house nearly finished Edwyn has a bad cold. Lawrence
Short came with an invitation there to tea this afternoon   Mr

& Mrs Ward Miss Ward Mrs Smith & Mrs Hughes there to[o]
Mr Hill came to bring me home   a dark walk – Had a pleasant
visit   Fri: Mr Hill went to the Farm with Fanny after dinner I
went with Maria & the children to P Hope – Mr Hill had his dinner the instant he came in & I think never stirred from his chair
till he went to bed –   Sat: the children *bad colds* & hoarse &
both the girls sore throats. Mr Hill called them up & they did not
immediately rise as the children had disturbed them   He
became *outrageous* threw the clothes off *me & became extremely
violent*   I kept up my spirits, but the agitation caused me to loose
a good deal of blood. I sometimes think we must part, he is so very
insulting – he is the most insolent & self indulgent man I ever saw.
Sun: Did not go to Church. Maria went. A deep fall of snow. Mon:
Mrs Fanny & I packing   very cold   Tues: Went in the Sleigh
with the china & glasses. The sleighing not very good but nothing
broken. Wed: A [illegible] bason 2 tea cups & some other trifles
broken –   Sat 30 Believe Mr Wetheral has finished his job.
Jane's hand has been bad the last fortnight   Brine's also has a
bad hand.   Sun Dec 1st   Did not go to Church although the day
was fine   felt afraid of it being slippery – Dined early & Mr Hill
Jane & children gone to the Farm, expect it will be the last Sunday
we shall spend here   Mr Hill wrote a letter to his brother
Charles & enclosed mine to Mrs Davis – not any thing like so cold
– Had a letter from Mrs Horton   Thurs: Dec 5th   Up early –
Maria the two children & I came to the Farm soon after breakfast,
followed by the waggon with kitchen stove, Brines & young
Fowke   Mr Hill & Jane came to tea which we had got very
comfortably for them in the kitchen   Fri: Mr Hill & Jane went
to our old house. Sat: Very rainy   Mr Hills fingers festering
Sun: no one went to Church   Mon: 9th Mr Hill & Jane gone
to the house & P Hope   Mr [illegible] came – busy in the afternoon getting carrots & c into the cellar   Mrs Brines very poorly
– In the evening Mr Hill and I went to see her. Tues: 10th Mr Hill
Cross   The man came to do the well. Feel not very well – hurried Edwyn's birthday   Mr Clements & Thos dined with

us   Mrs & Miss Fortune called, told us Mrs Howe's baby was dead, went to see Mrs Brines who I found better   Wed: 11th Brines & Maria gone to Port Hope   Mr Hill gone in the Buggy   Killed two pigs & made some pies   Sun: [Dec 15th] None of us went to Church, a bad headache   Mon: Set off with Mr Hill & Edwyn intending going to Port Hope but found it such bad sleighing that Edwyn & I staid at Mrs Aldretts till Mr Hill returned   Feel all the better for having been out   Thursday 19th   Mr [Aldred?] called & bought the white sow for 4 dollars – Brines brought us the 'Advertiser' yesterday, but no English letters. Have made Edwin two comfortable frocks out of my old dress – Mrs Brines cut out the body   helped me to make it   The House warm and comfortable   Tues: 24th Mr Hill posted a letter to his brother Charles with one enclosed to Mr Langley. I wrote a short postscript to Mrs Langley – Mr & Miss Ryley dined here. Xmas day very fine & mild, had the house decorated with Hemlock & a Turkey & plum pudding for dinner – A comfortable day   no one went to church.   26th   Mr Hill gone to Cobourg in the waggon with 'Bessy & Buddy'   Mr Clemments sinking the well   very mild   Sun [Dec 29th]: Mr Hill & I went to Church   Mon: Mr Hill Edwyn & I dined at Mr R Ryley's –   Tues: Mr Hill & I spent a pleasant evening at Mr Fortunes   met Mr Adred's family there   The last day in the Old Year Walked home it was 2 o clock when we got home.

NOTES

The diary is in the Sarah Welch Hill Papers, Provincial Archives of Ontario (PAO), F 634, MU 113–114.

1 Sarah made every effort to make daily entries. After the birth of her children she even had her husband make entries for her. However, readers will notice that there are portions in this excerpt where she has not made her entries on a daily basis. This occurs on the ship coming across

to North America and at times when the family is moving or one of the children is very ill. Sometimes, to counter missed events, Sarah back-tracked.

2 Because Sarah Hill's children died with no issue, her papers became the property of Thomas Benson, the executor of Hill's will. The Benson family donated the papers to the Archives of Ontario, so the boxes carry the title Benson Family Papers.

3 Joseph Welch was obviously somewhat of a spendthrift and a gadabout, which caused considerable tension between him and his father, Joseph Welch Sr. At one point in 1828 Sarah expressed her feelings thus: '15th of March the anniversary of Joseph's wedding day, just twelve months since. Lately he has been very steady, hope it will turn out for the best – spent a most wretched day this time last year, heard he was married and did not know who to.' Joseph did not, however, become more responsible in his financial pursuits or in his relationship with his wife.

4 In addition to Sarah Welch's appointment as executrix, William James and James Shipton were named as co-executors and administrators of the will. See 'Power of Attorney to Misters William James and James Shipton,' 1861, MU 114, PAO.

5 In the diary Sarah Margaret is first referred to by her entire name, then as Margaret, and finally as Maggie.

6 The 'fits,' as Sarah called them, were at times as numerous as twenty-eight in a day; one entry indicates 'constantly fits.' Sarah Margaret did recover from this particular session of convulsions but, as is seen in the diary excerpt, she suffered another session after the family settled in Canada. There is no indication that Margaret suffered with seizures throughout her life.

7 Edwin Hill purchased eighty-seven acres on the south half of Lot 5 in the 4th Concession of Hope Township, just north of the town of Port Hope. Smith's Creek, sufficiently large to support a mill, ran through the farm. 'Brooklands,' as the farm was called, in 1852 was reduced when six acres were taken by the Midland Railroad, which, according to the *Illustrated Historical Atlas of Counties of Northumberland and Durham*,

ran directly through the middle of the property. Edwin Hill received three hundred pounds compensation for the loss of land.

8 For an excellent examination of the lengths to which the ritual of visitation could go, see Katherine M.J. McKenna, 'The Role of Women in the Establishment of Social Status in Early Upper Canada,' *Ontario History* 83, no. 3 (1990): 179–206.

9 For instance, Edwin Hill seemed to get some perverse pleasure out of frightening his wife and children by driving the cutter in a reckless manner. On 19 February 1851 Sarah recorded: 'Mr Hill I & the children went in the cutter to Port Hope – All thrown out & sprawling on the ground   Poor Margaret's nose bled & her eyes & nose sadly swelled & discoloured   I am very stiff and sore ... Mr Hill will drive on high ridges of snow   expect several times to be thrown   It makes me quite nervous.' Hill's explosive anger continues to surface occasionally throughout the diary but is definitely less frequent than it had been in the early years of their marriage and settlement in Hope Township.

10 For instance, in March 1847, Sarah noted that her husband 'took a solemn oath never to do a days work after my settlement was made that bread & water was quite sufficient for me & as for clothing he did not care what I wore or how shabby I looked &c & c   The things affect my health & cause me to be in a constant flutter.' By 1 November 1851, Sarah had signed away her dower, commenting 'Hope it is for the best.'

11 Death Certificate 23074, MS 935, Reel 49, PAO.

12 Jane and Ann were servants. Jane immigrated to Port Hope with the Hill family and remained with them until her death.

13 The George Ryley family lived in Port Hope, as did the Robert Ryley family. Both were acquaintances of the Hills. According to Harold Reeve, *The History of Hope Township* (Cobourg: Cobourg-Sentinel-Star, 1967), there was a private school for girls run by Mr and Mrs George Riley in 1844–5 on Lot 1, Concession 1.

14 This is the parish in which the church was located that the Hills attended.

15 Her mother-in-law.

16 Her sister-in-law.

17 Digbeth is the home of Edwin Hill's family.

18 This is the home of the Horton family.

19 William James was one of the executors of the will of Sarah's father. It appears that Sarah had understood that her husband would notify her accountant and solicitor of their travel plans.

20 These are agreements about her inheritance and her marriage settlement.

21 The next short portion of the diary that covers the actual passage to North America appears to have been written all at once, after the Hills' arrival in Port Hope.

22 Family acquaintances who had moved to New York from Birmingham, UK.

23 These families and individuals represent some of the well-established citizens of Port Hope. The Reverend Dr Jonathan Shortt was the First Rector of Port Hope, 1836–7; Mrs Whitehead's husband, M.F. Whitehead, was the registrar of the Surrogate Court of Port Hope, the collector of customs, and notary; Nesbitt Kirchhoffer was a barrister and attorney in Port Hope and was also a solicitor in the Chancery. Dr Hickman was a local physician, and Mr Smith became a judge in Port Hope. The Innis family is not listed in the *Directory* for Port Hope: they lived outside the town and he had no particular position listed. However, Innis, along with Hughes, Benson, and Fortune – other families mentioned in the diary – is a prominent name among the officers in the corps that was enlisted to ward off the Fenian raids in 1866. Many of these families would have been known to the Hills, as can be seen in their contact with the Ryleys prior to the Hills' arrival in Upper Canada. In the 1830s Port Hope had experienced large-scale immigration and was incorporated as a town in 1834.

24 This was the home in which the Hills lived for approximately one year before moving to the farm mentioned earlier. No information is given as to its exact location, although it was not in town.

25 Florinda Brake (pronounced Bray-kee) is the hired girl. She was related to James Breakey, a shoemaker in Port Hope. He was also

deputy master of Lodge 44 of the Loyal Orange Association; George Ward was the county master.

26 There is only one Hickman family, and that is the family of the doctor. There are at least two Ward families. The *Port Hope Directory for 1856–1857* lists George Ward as registrar for Port Hope and deputy clerk of the peace; Thomas Ward is listed as clerk of the peace. The 1839 muster roll for the militia lists George Ward as lieutenant in the cavalry; James Ward is listed as an ensign in the Durham 1st Regiment.

27 The Hills attended St John's, the Anglican church in Port Hope. As the town grew and the building aged, it was eventually replaced by a new church building in 1869. Some members, especially those who lived close to the old building, such as the Wards and the Whiteheads, were unhappy about its closure and were instrumental in its reopening as St Marks. Peter C. Moffatt, *Time Was: The Story of St. Mark's Anglican Church, Port Hope* (Cobourg: Haynes Printing, 1972).

28 Hill seems to have the wrong date here. No explanation is given. It happens again on 1 March and in June.

29 This appears to be Mrs Fanning. The Fannings had a farm on Lot 16, Concession 2. There are further references to this family, who, it seems, lived rather close to the Hills. This distance would account for the references to walking to Port Hope or to taking two trips a day into the town.

30 In between the lines is added, 'at night after being out baby convulsed.'

31 Sarah had the following recipe for Knickerbocker Pickles in her recipe book: 'Take six gallons of water 10 lbs of Salt 3 lbs of coarse brown sugar 1 quart of Molasses 3 oz salt petre 1 oz Pear[l] ash. Boil and skim. When quite cold pour over pork or beef previously placed in a barrel. 16th January made this pickle but only put 6 pounds of rock salt, & used Sallerata instead of pearl Ash.'

32 Sarah's references to being 'poorly' in this way are to her menstrual cycle, which she diligently kept track of in the back of her diary.

33 Written in between the lines is 'Jane went to Church.'

34 In between the lines: 'Our wash.'

35 The township north of Port Hope.

36 The Reverend Alexander Neil Bethune was first put in charge of the

Hamilton District. When the district was divided into smaller areas and Dr Shortt became the minister at St John's in Port Hope, Bethune was named the first rector of St Peter's Anglican Church in Cobourg. He later succeeded John Strachan as the second lord bishop of Toronto. Moffatt, *Time Was*, 10.

Amelia Holder
(1855–1936)

JOANNE RITCHIE

In March 1867, eleven-year-old Amelia Holder set sail from Saint John, New Brunswick, with her sea-captain father and her dying mother in a 112-foot, square-rigged, wooden brigantine, the *Mina*. That voyage, which kept Amelia at sea or in ports around the world for fifteen months, was followed by five more long, adventurous voyages over the next six years. One of Amelia's regular shipboard activities was keeping a diary, and her delightful adolescent journals have been carefully preserved by her family.

Over the dozen or so years Amelia kept a journal, she used a number and variety of books. The original journals of her six sea voyages were kept in several hard-covered, lined notebooks, and some of Amelia's later journal entries were made in what might have been her father's discarded log book. Most of the notebooks include scraps of verse, songs, stories, lists, newspaper clippings, and the like, as well as diary entries. There are occasional passages written by one or two of Amelia's siblings, and some of the books also contain scraps of writing and childish drawings made years later by Amelia's daughter as a young child. Some of Amelia's original notebooks have been misplaced, but, luckily, not before they were microfilmed and placed in the New Brunswick Provincial Archives. Also, a typescript was made of the journals before some went missing, and this was placed in the archives of the New

Brunswick Museum. And finally, when Amelia was in her seventies, she laboriously copied her original journals by hand into a black, hard-covered book, nine by eleven inches, with 'Sea Voyages' lettered in gold on the front cover, as a gift to one of her sons. This 'edition' includes postcards, sketches, poetry (both her own and sea-related poems of others), and some explanatory notes added at the time she made the copy. On the whole, her handwriting is quite legible, although it changes considerably from her first childish, sometimes messy, entries (at age ten) to the neat, careful hand in which she copied her journals when she was over seventy.

Amelia, born on Christmas Day in 1855, was the third of eight children born to Edwin Jacob Holder and his wife, Hannah Parrett, of Holderville, near Saint John. Holderville itself was named after the family, going back well before Amelia's time. Like many New Brunswickers of the day, the Holders were a seafaring family, and counted ship-builders and -owners, sailmakers and master mariners among their number.

Shortly before Amelia's first voyage, her father wrote to his wife encouraging her to come with him on his next trip: 'I do not know where we will go yet but think we shall go to the Mediterranean. I do not know whether I can stand it to go again without some of you with me. I shall feel so lonesome.'[1] Hannah had sailed with her husband on previous occasions, and although she had seven children at home, including a seven-month-old infant, she made arrangements to have her sister look after the house and the children, and, taking young Amelia with her, joined her husband. On that occasion, Hannah was motivated by more than just providing companionship to Edwin; she was suffering from consumption, and a family 'council' had concluded that a sea voyage, which was to include time in the warmer climate of the Mediterranean, would be good for her health. That was not to be, and two days after the shipboard family returned to Saint John in June 1868, Hannah Holder died.

Two months later, Edwin was again at sea, aboard the barque *Hannah H.* bound for Ireland, accompanied this time by Amelia and her younger sister Aggie. They sailed from Ireland to Spain, then back across the Atlantic to South America before returning to New Brunswick. The journal excerpt reprinted here chronicles part of the voyage, which began in August 1868 and ended in March 1869.

The *Hannah H.* was a square-rigged, wooden vessel used primarily for carrying cargo, although occasionally a passenger might hitch a ride for some portion of the journey. She was a barque, just over 120 feet long, with three masts and twenty to twenty-five sails, most of them 'sqaure' (actually rectangular) in shape, which suggests the label 'sqaure rigged.'

Amelia's journals give a lively and articulate account of family life aboard a sailing vessel. The long days at sea were full and happy ones, and she was only rarely bored or lonely. Even at sea the usual domestic routine – cleaning, washing and ironing, knitting and sewing – was observed. She also shared the task of supplementing the shipboard menu by fishing – for shark, porpoise, dolphin, and flying fish – and tending to the chickens, which provided fresh eggs and meat. Young Amelia was a voracious reader, and devoured anything she could get her hands on – Gibbon, Shakespeare, Byron, novels borrowed from the British Consul in Barcelona, her father's navigation books, and the newspapers they were able to get whenever they were in port. She was also an avid writer, and her journals and notebooks contain poems, stories, and sketches in addition to her daily diary entries.

Amelia had a keen interest in navigation and learned early on to use the chronometer and to help her father 'take the sun' and work up the longitude and latitude. On occasion, he also let her take the wheel and 'skip' the ship. Not surprisingly, her diary entries reflect the constant and careful attention those aboard a small sailing vessel must pay to the elements, with regular references to the weather, the wind, the condition of the waves and the sky, the barometer, as well as the position of the ship, its speed, and its rigging.

Shipboard routine extended beyond domestic and sailing concerns. In addition to time set aside for lessons, there were games and music to be enjoyed, and almost every day the natural world brought forth something to delight the lively and curious Amelia: the changing geography when they were on or near land, the variety of seascapes and atmospheric phenomena as they moved around the oceans of the world, and the abundant marine life. Indeed, about the only time Amelia was bored or anxious was when they were in port, waiting for cargo, waiting for 'Pa' to take care of business, or waiting for the right wind to take them out again on the 'old Atlantic.' Life was not completely idyllic, though, and she also recounts tales of mutiny and terrifying storms at sea.

Amelia's final sea voyage took place when she was seventeen. In her last seafaring journal, we meet a more sophisticated young woman, well read and well travelled, more interested in visiting and parties in port, and also more introspective. Like many girls their age, she and Aggie also fussed occasionally about their hair and clothes, bantered good naturedly with the young men they met, and teased each other about snaring rich planter husbands in Barbados. Amelia didn't rush into marriage, though, and worked as a dressmaker after she returned home. She married Benjamin Henderson (who had gone to sea himself as a young man) when she was thirty, and she and her husband settled in New Brunswick to farm and raise three children. Amelia died in 1936, in her eighty-first year.

Amelia's seagoing adventures coincide with what is often called the 'golden age of sail' in Canada's Maritime provinces. The region's primeval forests were the source of a highly marketable cargo, and also provided the raw material to build the ships that could carry the cargo. New Brunswick and the other Maritime provinces were well positioned to take advantage of opportunities created by a number of world events. In the 1840s, trade between England and the rest of the world was thrown open to competition for ships of all nations; gold was discovered in California in 1848 and three years later in Australia, creating demand for fast ships to carry cargo and emigrants; war in the Crimea and the Civil War in the United States created demand for fighting ships. The elegant Maritime square-riggers, such as those built and sailed by Amelia's family, enjoyed a prominent place in the world shipping community during the heady years of New Brunswick's great timber trade and the boom years in shipbuilding.

Amelia Holder's journals represent an interesting subset of diaries, those of seafaring women. The long-standing and widely held superstitions about the undesirability of having women on board ships has led to an assumption that women rarely went to sea. Although it cannot be said that women shipping out on their own was commonplace, current interest in women and the sea is producing research that suggests seafaring women are not the aberration they were thought to be.[2] Women did go to sea: as common deck-hands, as pirates and warriors, aboard whalers and traders as crew, and as companions to sea-captain husbands and fathers. Some women occasionally disguised themselves as men or boys, sometimes just to get aboard but also for entire seafaring careers. While their motivation was often to be with a husband or lover who was himself a common sailor, this was by no means the only reason women went to sea. The irresistible call of the sea that drew men to the seafaring life was also heard by women, and many of them found ways to answer it.

The experience of Hannah and Amelia Holder and the other women from maritime communities was probably the most common – going to sea as the wives and daughters of merchant marine captains. Indeed, it was the rule, rather than the exception, for sea captains to take their wives or some of their family with them. The fear of loneliness expressed in Edwin's letter to Hannah is a poignant reminder that the prospect of a long voyage alone was a daunting one for most sea captains, who didn't generally socialize or have much contact with the crew 'before the mast.'

With the captain's family along, shipboard life took on much of the appearance of life on shore. When the ship was in port, the captain's cabin was often transformed into a floating Victorian parlour, complete with carpet, fancy tablecloths, knick-knacks, and likely an organ; families visited back and forth for tea and other entertainments. At sea, domestic routines were established, lessons were taught, and leisure hours were filled with reading, writing, and needlework.

Yet these women faced remarkable challenges on their voyages. In addition to the inconveniences of seasickness, cramped living quarters, and quarantine in foreign ports, they were constantly tested by the elements – violent storms, sweltering heat, and bone-numbing cold – from which there was no escape. Giving birth and raising children on board ship was a demanding undertaking, but leaving young ones at home, as Hannah Holder did, was also difficult. Often, the captain's wife or daughter was the only female on board the ship, and many longed for the support and companionship of other women. Shipwreck, disease, and childbirth also took their toll – many of the women didn't come home.

What has survived, though, is a wealth of journals, diaries, letters, and memoirs. Like Amelia Holder, many of the women kept diaries to record their journeys, and wrote countless letters to loved ones to take the edge off their homesickness and to fill the hours when time hung heavy on their hands. Luckily, hundreds of these records are emerging from collections of family papers as well as from official records. The remarkable stories of these women and their families are being told largely through these documents, and Amelia Holder's delightful journals are part of that legacy. They chronicle a slice of a unique period of maritime history, and make a contribution, along with those of other seafaring women, to our understanding of the fascinating subject of women and the sea.

Amelia Holder, aged thirteen, in Montevideo between April and November 1869, shortly after the period from which the journal excerpt was taken.

DIARY, NEW BRUNSWICK,
SEPTEMBER 1868–MARCH 1869

Aboard the barque *Hannah H.* bound for Ireland

September 6, 1868
Left Saint John August 17th with a fair wind. Uncle Abram and
Aunt Elmina and three aunts and three cousins came out past Partridge Island and went back in the steam-tug that took us out. We
had not gone far after they left when one of the men stabbed the
first mate. We turned back, the steamboat came out to us again and
we anchored and left one man and the second mate and brother
A[bram] on board and took three men in irons and the mate on
shore, and Pa, Agnes and I all went on shore again.[3] We laid at
Partridge Island four days and sailed on the 21st. We had fine
weather. We passed a vessel bottom upwards, her bows were under
water and the sea was breaking over all of her except the after part.
We have had very fine weather so far except once when the wind
blew pretty hard. This is the third Sunday at sea and the 6th of
September. It is a fine day with not much wind. She is going one
mile an hour. There is a brigantine not very far from us.

January 27, 1869
In Tarragona, Spain. Raining very hard, it has been raining this
two or three days, it is very dull, I wish we were out to sea. Aggie is
playing with her doll this morning.[4] Pa has gone up to town, he
brought us down some *Illustrated London News* last night, they are
only lent to us. We have got a carpet for the cabin floor since we
have been here and a fancy tablecloth and the cabin looks quite
comfortable. There is only one American vessel here, she is a large
ship and the captain has been on board several times. We are
acquainted with the captain of a Danish schooner that is lying
alongside of us, he has been on board once to tea and speaks very
good English. There was a young Mr. Gibbon here to dinner with
Pa, he came from Barcelona. I have been reading some today in
Gibbon's *Decline and Fall of the Roman Empire* and sewing some on
my patchwork. It is raining this evening.

January 28, 1869

It is pretty fine today and we washed. My bird has been singing a good deal today, I had it up on deck this afternoon, we have been on deck a good deal today. Pa has been up to town, he brought down a newspaper. The Danish captain gave us a crock of butter this afternoon, we have not got much. We have been knitting some today and reading. This is a very fine evening, the sky is clear and the stars are shining bright.

January 29, 1869

It is raining this morning again. Pa has gone up to the town. Aggie and I are sewing on our patchwork this morning. It is pretty fine this afternoon. I have been on deck some. Pa got a letter from Mr. Jones asking him to charter back to England. We have been sewing and knitting some this afternoon. The bird has been singing, it is shedding its feathers. Pa telegraphed this afternoon that he would take the charter so now we will have to go back to England again when we get to Buenos Aires. It will be a long time before we get home, we will have to go up the River Plata too. This is a fine evening. Pa got a newspaper today.

January 30, 1869

This is a very fine morning. Pa has gone up to town. I took the mats up on deck and shook them. Aggie is reading and I am writing, it is dull this morning. We ironed this afternoon. It is pretty fine this evening.

January 31, 1869

This is a fine day. We took a walk down the Mole[5] this morning and up to town, we got to the vessel by dinner time. We have been reading old letters this afternoon. There is no church to go to here and it is pretty dull. I hope we will soon get out of here but we do not expect to till the last of the week. I am tired of being in port.

February 1, 1869
This is a fine day. Pa was up to town this forenoon. I was cutting
out some things for Aggie and me, we were making them this afternoon. My bird is on deck and is singing nicely. We have had no letters from home yet, I would like to get one very much, we have
written two since we came here. I am going up on deck now. This is
a very fine evening.

February 2, 1869
It is blowing very hard today, the wind roars almost like thunder.
Pa did not come to dinner but he came this afternoon and brought
Aggie some little dishes, he got his dinner ashore. We have been
sewing and knitting. It is not blowing quite so hard now.

February 3, 1869
This is a very fine day. We went on shore today and had our dinners. We had it in the Spanish style, it was very nice. We came
right on board again. The American captain started to go out but
there is not enough wind and he is anchored. This is a very fine
evening.

February 4, 1869
This is a beautiful day and we went out this afternoon to see the
Devil's Bridge. It is about three quarters of an hour's ride. The
country looks green in the valleys. The Devil's Bridge is a very old
bridge, it is very high and narrow. The coachman said it is more
than a thousand years old. There is no water under it but there
once was a river there. We were down underneath it. It looked
dreadfully high and it has a great many arches, we got a piece off of
it. It was four o'clock when we came back, we came right on board
again.

February 5, 1869
It is very fine today. We washed a little and scrubbed out our rooms
this forenoon.

February 6, 1869
Pa went up to Barcelona this morning at six o'clock, he expects to
be down this evening. We ironed this forenoon. This is a very fine
day. We expected to get some cargo today but none has come yet,
we have been waiting for some these two days, they are very slow
here. My bird is singing beautifully now, I take it up on deck every
fine morning. It is pretty lonesome on board now. Pa came home
about nine o'clock this evening.

February 7, 1869
It was pretty cold this morning but this afternoon it is very fine. We
went ashore this afternoon and went away up the town. We went
in an old Cathedral that they say was built in the time of Pontius
Pilate. It is very large. This is carnival day and there are a great
many people with masks and queer dresses on, there is a great stir.
This is a fine evening.

February 8, 1869
This is a fine day. I have been reading almost all day. Pa got some
novels in Barcelona from the British Consul. We got some hens
today.

February 9, 1869
This is a fine day. We got some cargo today. We have not been
doing anything much. I have been reading most all day. Pa has
been on shore.

February 10, 1869
We went on shore this forenoon and bought some things. It is fine
today. We came on board at dinner time. I have been reading a
good deal this afternoon.

February 11, 1869
This is a very fine day. We have all our cargo in and expect to go
out tomorrow. Pa did not come home to dinner today. I have been

reading and knitting all this forenoon, this is a very fine afternoon.

February 12, 1869
We have hauled out from the wharf this forenoon. We went on
shore and bought a few things. Wrote a letter home this afternoon.
We expect to go out tonight. This is a very fine day. We did not go
out because Pa could not get ready, one of our men swam ashore
tonight to get the boat to take the rest ashore but the steward told
Pa and he would not let him come near the vessel.

February 13, 1869
It is blowing hard today and there is quite a sea. Pa has gone on
shore, it is blowing too hard to go to sea.

February 14, 1869
This is a fine day, there was no chance to go out this morning but
about twelve o'clock there came a fair wind, there is a pretty big sea
out. Aggie is a little sick, it is a good wind.

February 15, 1869
This is a fine day. The wind was fair this forenoon and ahead this
afternoon. I bound one of Pa's charts today. Aggie is almost well.
The land is in sight yet. The vessel has been rolling pretty hard.
This is a fine evening.

February 16, 1869
This is a fine day, the wind is ahead. There is more than there was
yesterday. We have been up on deck a little. We have been knitting
and sewing most all day.

February 17, 1869
The wind is still ahead this morning, there is a little more than
there was yesterday. We are down to Cape St. Antonio this afternoon. We have not been on deck much, we went up a little this

evening. Aggie and I were playing dominoes this evening. The vessel is close to the land now.

February 18, 1869
This is a fine morning, wind ahead, we have not gone much today. We have not been on deck today. The wind is blowing harder tonight and there is a heavy head sea. The wine smells very badly.

February 19, 1869
This is a fine day, the wind is ahead yet. We have not been on deck today. The bird is singing beautifully. We have been crocheting most all day, Aggie is a little sick yet. There is hardly any sea this evening and the vessel is not rolling any.

February 20, 1869
It has been raining hard this morning but it is fine now, the wind is fair. We caught some rainwater this morning. The wind is blowing pretty hard this evening.

February 21, 1869
It was very fine this morning but it is blowing pretty hard this afternoon. The wind is ahead. We are down to Cape Gata. There is a very heavy sea. I feel a little sick this evening.

February 22, 1869
The wind is ahead this morning. We have not been on deck much today. There was a little fair wind this evening but it did not last long, we have gone hardly any. It is raining a little this evening.

February 23, 1869
It was calm this morning but this afternoon we are going pretty fast. We have not done much today. We had one of the chickens for dinner, one of them flew overboard.

February 24, 1869
Fine day with a good breeze. We were almost down to Vélez-
Málaga this morning. Aggie and I have been on deck a good lot
today. We are abreast of Málaga this evening. We were up on deck
this evening when the moon was up, it is a beautiful evening.

February 25, 1869
Passed Gibraltar this morning with a good breeze, we went right
through the Straits, the land looks much greener than it did last
year, but everything else looks the same. We have a fair wind this
evening and are fifty miles from Gibraltar. We are in sight of land
yet.

February 26, 1869
Fine day and fair wind. We have gone a good lot. We are out of
sight of land on the old Atlantic again. We have not been on deck
much but have been sewing most all day. Pa was playing on the
accordion this evening. We were 75 miles from Cape Spartel at
noon.

February 27, 1869
This is a fine day. I have been on deck some today. Aggie is a little
sick. It is a fair wind and we have gone 168 miles today. We caught
a porpoise this afternoon with the harpoon, it was a very large one.
We had the liver and heart for tea, it tasted like any other. There is
a heavy sea on, Pa thinks we are in the Trades. Lat. 34°16′.

February 28, 1869
Fine day, fair wind. I have been on deck a good lot today. There is
not so much sea as there was yesterday. We have gone 120 miles
today, there is a little more wind this evening and it is pretty cold.
Lat. 33°13′.

March 1, 1869
Fine day, fair wind. We have not been on deck much today, we

have been sewing and knitting most all day. We were forward to feed the hens with Pa.

March 2, 1869
Fair wind, it is pretty fine today. We have been on deck a good deal. We expect to see one of the Canary Islands sometime tonight. There is a pretty heavy sea.

March 3, 1869
It is almost calm today, there is a very heavy sea. Passed the Canarys before we were up.

March 4, 1869
It has been calm this forenoon but this afternoon there is a good breeze. We have not been on deck much today.

March 5, 1869
There is good breeze today. We have been on deck a good deal. One of the hens laid an egg today. We have sewed and knit a good lot.

March 6, 1869
Fine day and fair wind. We have been on deck a good deal today. We got another egg today and we have been forward to feed the hens. I was up on deck this evening.

March 7, 1869
It is raining some today in showers. We have not been on deck much today. It is lonesome on board with no church to go to. I have been reading. There is not much wind.

March 8, 1869
Very fine day, there is not much wind. We got two eggs today. We have been on deck a good deal. Caught two porpoises this evening.

March 9, 1869
It is nearly calm today. I have not been on deck much. We had our
room cleaned out today. Pa had the stove and carpet taken out, we
are getting into warm weather, it has been warm today.

March 10, 1869
It is calm today and very warm. We have been up on deck a good
deal. We have not done much only knit a little.

March 11, 1869
There is a little breeze today. It is pretty warm. Pa is going to make
a little tent out of some cotton for us to sit under. We sighted one
of the Cape Verde Islands this afternoon very far off. Saw a steamer
this evening. We have not been on deck much. We got two eggs
today.

March 12, 1869
There is a good breeze today, we are going seven miles an hour. We
are in sight of the land this morning. It is very high land (Peak of
Teneriffe). We are out of sight of it this afternoon. There is a heavy
sea on today.

March 13, 1869
Fair wind and a good breeze. We have not been on deck much
today. There is a pretty heavy sea on, we are going seven miles. We
saw two vessels, they go faster than we do. A flying fish flew on
board this morning. The hens did not lay today.

March 14, 1869
There is a good breeze today. A vessel passed us just before dinner
and spoke us, she was the *Paragere*, Spanish, from Liverpool bound
to Hong Kong 18 days out.[6] This is a fine evening.

March 15, 1869
Fair wind, we are going seven miles an hour. There is a heavy sea.

We got our cotton awning up, it is very cool under it. This is very sultry weather, we are now in the calm belt, there is not much calm this month. We see a great many flying fish.

March 16, 1869
This is a fine day and a good wind. It is very warm. We had a flying fish for breakfast this morning, it tasted very good, much like a trout. We have been on deck a good deal today. We have knitted and sewed some.

March 17, 1869
Fine day and a fair wind. It is very warm. We have been on deck most all day under our little awning where it is nice and cool, we sit up there and knit. We got five eggs today, we have thirteen now beside what we eat. This is a fine evening.

March 18, 1869
It has been raining very hard this forenoon, we caught plenty of water. It is pretty fine this afternoon.

March 19, 1869
This is a fine day. We washed some today. There is a good wind, it is fair. It is very hot weather.

March 20, 1869
Very fine day, there has not been much wind today and it is very hot. We finished washing. There are some fish around but we have not caught any.

March 21, 1869
It is calm today with occasional showers. We crossed the Line[7] about four o'clock this morning and at noon today are 17 miles south of it. There was a very heavy shower this evening.

March 22, 1869
Calm with frequent showers. We have been on deck a pretty good

lot. Caught a young shark and had some for tea, it tasted very good.

March 23, 1869
It is calm today again, there are a good many vessels in sight and one is pretty close to us. It is showery today and we have not been on deck much.

March 24, 1869
There is a breeze this morning, it has the appearance of the South East Trade Wind. We had our clothes up on deck today and the steward scrubbed the walls of the room. There is more wind tonight.

March 25, 1869
The wind is blowing pretty strong today and we are going along nicely. We have not been on deck much today.

March 26, 1869
The wind is blowing some today but we have all sail set.[8] Aggie and I have been in bed all day she is rolling so. We have run another vessel out of sight which is the only one I guess we have passed since we left Tarragona. She shipped some water[9] in the cabin this afternoon.

March 27, 1869
There is not so much wind and sea today as there was yesterday but we are going along as fast, we have made two degrees a day since we entered the Trades. I have been on deck a little. I have sewed a good deal today.

March 28, 1869
This is a very fine day. We had eggs for breakfast and a chicken for dinner. I have not been on deck but have been reading most of the time.

**Account of hurricane we experienced in the gulf stream
on our way from Buenos Aires to New York**

We were bringing as passengers Mr. and Mrs. Mahar from the
Argentine where they had been farming but finding the country
unsettled they had decided to come back to the U.S.A. They were
of Irish extraction. The hurricane began in the morning with a
very low glass and squalls increasing in force all the time. All the
sail was taken off or what was left was soon torn to pieces, while
one of the sailors had his clothes blown off coming from aloft. The
squalls continued to increase in force sounding like thunder coming from the sky. Two men stood at the wheel while my father
stood by calling to them, 'keep her up, keep her up,' meaning 'keep
her before the wind.'

We could hear them saying, 'there go the boats,' but fortunately
although washed adrift they did not got overboard, and the hen
coop was washed overboard too. After a while as the wind
increased they could keep her up no longer and she broached to
and lay on her side. We thought the last moment had come then
but after going a certain distance she stopped and did not go any
farther. After awhile the squalls began to abate a little, each one
not quite as hard as the last. We could hear the mate and my father
shouting to each other, for it was only by shouting that one could
make themselves heard, that they had better set a staysail. My sister, aged ten, who had been nearly crazy with fright, when she
heard that, called the steward, a mulatto, and told him to go on
deck and tell my father she wanted to see him, he went and told
him but he said he could not come, again she sent the steward up
and again my father sent word he could not come, to send up and
tell him what she wanted, so she told him and we could hear the
steward shouting her message, 'She says not to set the staysail.' Of
course they took no notice of this but set the staysail which was no
sooner set than it was torn into ribbands.

Mr. Kerr, the mate, comes and talks to us for a few minutes, he
has an axe strapped to his waist ready to cut away the masts if he

has to, he was in a hurricane before and they cut away the masts.

As we huddled in our room Mrs. Mahar, who was a devout Catholic, kept repeating her prayers and saying to us, 'Say your prayers girls, say your prayers.' At last she whispered something to her husband. He started for their room, reaching it with great difficulty as it was on the lee side, and got what he wanted, a bottle of holy water, which he threw up against the side the wind was blowing. It was soon after this the storm began to abate and I suppose they always believed it was the holy water that saved them. She was a dear woman of middle age and Mr. Mahar was a nice quiet man too. The hurricane lasted six hours.

NOTES

A microfilmed version of Holder's diary is at the New Brunswick Provincial Archives, MC665. A typescript is held by the New Brunswick Museum, CBDoc. The originals remain with the Holder family. The typescript held by the NB Museum was the primary source for this excerpt.

1 The letter, dated 8 February 1867, is held by the Holder family.
2 Studies of seafaring women include Daniel Cohen, *The Female Marine and Related Works: Narratives of Cross-Dressing and Urban Vice in America's Early Republic* (Amherst: University of Massachusetts Press, 1997); Annette Brock Davis, ed., *My Year before the Mast* (Toronto: Hounslow Press, 1999); Linda Grant DePauw, *Seafaring Women* (Boston: Houghton Mifflin, 1982); Joan Druett, *Hen Frigates: Wives of Merchant Captains under Sail* (New York: Simon and Schuster, 1998); Joan Druett and Mary Anne Wallace, eds, *The Sailing Circle: Nineteenth-Century Seafaring Women from New York* (Long Island, NY: Three Villages Historical Society and Cold Spring Harbor Whaling Museum, 1995); Ulrike Klausmann, Marion Meinzerin, and Gabriel Kuhn, *Women Pirates and the Politics of the Jolly Roger* (Montreal: Black Rose Books, 1997).
3 Amelia related this tale of mutiny to her children in later years. She was put in a cabin and given a gun, with instructions to shoot if anyone

came into the cabin. Their voyage was delayed several days while her father went back to Saint John to get a new crew.

4 Agnes [Aggie], Amelia's ten-year-old sister, who had come to say good-bye to her family, decided at the last moment that she wanted to make the trip. Her father writes to his sister-in-law Mary Ann Parrett, who was looking after the children ashore: 'Agy [sic] wanted to come so bad that Uncle Abraham let her come and we will have to fit her up with clothes and what she may want.' This letter is among the Holder family letters that the family has kindly given me access to. They include letters written by many family members (including Amelia and her father) while they were on long voyages, to other family members who remained at home. Whenever their father was at sea, Mary Ann Parrett (the sister of Amelia's mother) looked after Amelia's siblings after the death of their mother.

5 A mole is a massive work formed of masonry and large stones or earth as a pier or breakwater.

6 'Speaking a ship' was a sometimes tricky procedure whereby two vessels manoeuvred in a set sequence that brought them close enough together so that the captains could speak to each other without the aid of a speaking trumpet.

7 The equator.

8 That is, the ship was flying all its sails.

9 Because of wind and high waves, the water washed over the boat's side into the cabin.

PART TWO:
CONFLICT AND CONFUSION

Jessie Nagle and *Susan Nagle*
(1844–1873)   (1840–1921)

ANITA BONSON

Sisters Susan and Jessie Nagle arrived in Victoria soon after the creation of the colony of Vancouver Island in 1858. The second and third daughters of Captain Jeremiah and Catherine Nagle,[1] they had wandered far with their family by this time: Susan was born on board ship ten days out of Sydney, Australia, in 1840; Jessie was born in New Zealand in 1844; and they had lived in San Francisco for several years before their final major move. Over the years, their father took on various government posts, including Victoria harbourmaster, as well as engaging in several business ventures. Although he was, at one time, one of the major landowners in Victoria, Jeremiah's business sense (or luck) was apparently not of the highest calibre, and the family eventually lost its land holdings and was frequently in a tenuous financial condition. This was certainly the case in 1870, the year in which most of these excerpts were written.

The ambiguities of the Nagles' social and economic status (as part of a social but not economic elite) had profound effects on the courses of the sisters' lives. While they were fairly well acquainted with most of the prominent members of Victoria society, and would often be invited to functions at Government House, they were also required to contribute substantially to the household economy through extensive housework and earning what money they could outside the home. Like many educated young women of their background, both turned to teaching in one capacity or another. Since, as Susan remarked in her diary, there were in Victoria 'already ... almost more [schools] than scholars' (7 April 1869), this usually meant that they had to move away from home, a difficult decision for women with such close ties to their family. At the beginning of 1870, Susan had been teaching for half a year in Yale, then head of navigation on the Fraser River. Jessie had recently returned home from work with a family in the area near Victoria.

The need and desire to help their family out, and particularly to provide more comfort for their frequently ailing mother, were also major considerations when the sisters contemplated marriage. Their choices in this area were complicated by their status: as they were relatively high in social status, their suitors would have had to be equally 'respectable,' but the Nagles' generally poor economic circumstances did not necessarily recommend them to the limited pool of 'suitable' young men. They themselves wished to be able to benefit their family through their marriages, as had their younger sister Isabel, whose husband, Philip Hankin, had embarked upon a successful diplomatic career. Unlike Isabel, Susan and Jessie, at thirty-one and twenty-seven, respectively, both married considerably later than was the norm for women in British Columbia at the time.[2] Both also had been engaged more than once before they finally married, the broken engagements arising from both practical and personal factors.

At the time of her arrival in Yale, Susan was engaged to Algernon (Algy) Hill, a young man she had not seen in some time: he was attempting to build a career in the Colonial Services and, by this time, had received a minor posting in British Honduras. The diary excerpts reproduced here encompass the breaking of this engagement. Those from Jessie's diary cover both her engagement to Christopher Berkeley (whom Jessie called Willie) and its subsequent breaking. This was apparently Jessie's third engagement. Although both sisters were dealing with similar romantic circumstances at around the same time, the extent to which they differ in their articulations of these events and their feelings about them is quite remarkable. Susan dwells very little on her personal feelings as such, whereas Jessie's long passages clearly convey the emotional turmoil she was undergoing at this time. Every development in the story and her emotional reactions are described in detail, sometimes verging on the melodramatic. In contrast to her sister, Susan wrote sparingly and calmly about her own foundering engagement. The extent to which her mind was occupied with this situation is impossible to tell from Susan's journal entries alone, which succinctly record each event, such as letters sent and received and their essential content, but seldom mention either Algy or her feelings about him at any point in between.

Diary writing fulfilled different functions for these two sisters. For Jessie, it was a vehicle for expressing her feelings or 'individual consciousness'; for Susan, it was more a means of recording what was happening in her family and community.[3] Susan had other outlets for expressing her feelings: throughout her life she wrote extensively, even publishing some poetry, children's stories, and articles. Some of the conflict she felt with regards to Algy came to light in dreams that she described elsewhere.

Jessie's diary, begun in 1867, ends shortly after the final entry given here, with her engagement still broken. However, she and Willie eventually were able to marry, apparently with the family's blessing, in December 1871. Their marriage was not to last long, as Jessie did not survive the birth of their only child (a daughter, who also died shortly after the birth) in 1873. Susan's diaries continue on, with some gaps, from 1865 to 1911. Soon after her remarks in this excerpt about David Holmes (the Anglican clergyman at Yale), she 'promised to try for the next two months to like him' (5 January 1871). They became engaged in February and married in June 1871, moving to the Cowichan Valley on Vancouver Island in 1873. Between the ages of thirty-two and forty-four, Susan had six children, all surviving to adulthood. When they were older, she was able to devote more of her time both to her community activities (on both individual and organizational levels) and to the writing she had long desired to do seriously.

Susan's earlier diaries were generally written in relatively small or medium-sized (four-by-six or five-by-seven-inch) softcover notebooks, most of them lined. Her later diaries tended to be larger in size, and most were hardcovered, although some have lost their covers and bindings. Jessie's diary writings were all contained in one maroon leather-bound 'records' book; indeed, she did not completely fill this book. After her death, her journal was in Susan's possession, and Susan at some point filled the empty pages at the back of the book with her own poetry. On the front page of the book, she wrote: 'The writer of this Journal (my dear sister Jessie Melville Berkeley) died on the 13th of April 1873 in Victoria B. C. Her baby was three weeks old at the time and only survived her mother three weeks, she was buried in the same grave in the Ross Bay cemetery. S. A. Holmes.'

Jessie Nagle, ca. 1870.

JESSIE MELVILLE NAGLE DIARY, BRITISH COLUMBIA, DECEMBER 1869–JULY 1870

17th December 1869 – Mr. Berkeley proposed to me & I accepted him.

March 16th 1870 – The Active left V[ictoria] this morning with Isabel Capt Stamp, the Needham's & many others on board   Isabel has gone to San Francisco for change of air   she has not been well for a long time   Capt Stamp has gone to England, the Needham's have gone to Trinidad

April 10th – The Active arrived this morning & Philip received a letter from his sister in-law Emily Hankin telling him of the death of poor Graham[4]   he died on the 23rd of February   I feel very very sorry for him but at the same time I'm very thankful to know that he became very much changed before his death & that we may feel that he has gone to heaven. He wrote to me on the 19th of January & it was his last letter that he ever wrote. He is the first friend that I have ever lost by death, 'not lost but gone before.' May God grant that my end may be as peacable as his & may this sad news which I have heard this day, soften my heart and make me love my Saviour while on earth and lead others to do so too so that we may all meet in heaven at last. O Heavenly Father hear my prayer for Christ's sake. Amen. May my darling Willie become a true & sincere Christian.

Easter Sunday April 17 – Went to Sunday School this morning & to Pandora St. Church. Willie & I stayed to Sacrament   we went for a walk in the afternoon, & to St John's in the evening after coming home he told me that he was afraid that our marriage wd have to be put off as he would not be in a position for some time   I was not at all pleased to hear [it] for I do not like long engagements

Monday April 18th – Miss Cridge died of consumption last Friday morning & was buried to-day, Ella & I went to church, after which we called on Mrs. Aikman & Mrs. Guild from whence I got some

Ivy & Periwinkle but I don't think it will grow. Willie has been very good putting the garden in order   I planted some seeds on Saturday, & Ella & I have been working in the garden for two hours this morning.

Tuesday April 19th – Woke up this morning with a bad sore throat & cold   I became overheated & chilled yesterday so this is the consequence   Willy came to see me today.

W[ednesday]. – Did not get up until late on account of my cold   Willie came in the afternoon & brought me some oranges. There was no Dorcas to-day.

Thursday 21st – My cold a little better   Mrs. Beaden & Mrs. Elliott called to-day, Willie was working in the garden when they came

Friday April 22nd – Did not go to the Practice on account of my cold   Willie came in the evening & told me that he had lost $400 from the Treasury & that that was his reason for putting off our marriage, he also told Papa & Mama about it   they are both very angry with him for not having told us how his affairs stood [when?] we were first engaged for he is very much in debt

Saturday April 23rd – Did not get up till half past nine had no breakfast   felt very wretched, Willie came about 12 to see if I could go up the Arm with the Bushby's[5] but I had told Mr. Bushby yesterday that my cold would not let me so he went away, not being quite certain whether he would go or not   about three he [Willie] came back not having gone with them   we went for a walk to-gether and strolled about in Mrs. Young's field gathering flowers & talking about our troubles   he put such a bright face on them that they almost vanished   when we came home Mrs. Clark was there with her baby   Mama w'd not ask him to dinner as she feels so vexed with him.

Sunday April 24th – Went to Sunday School & church in the afternoon   Mama had a long talk with Willie about his affairs & conduct & the substance was that he had behaved very dishonorably and that she thought our engagement should come to an end   I feel very wretched & I do not know how it will end, I went for a short walk with Willie and I told him that I wd wait until November & not break the engagement   Ella & I went to St. John's with Willie then he poor fellow had a long talk with Papa   I did not see him again. The 'Newtons' arrived on Saturday from S[an] F[rancisco].

Monday April 25th – My week in the kitchen. up at half past six   after the kitchen work was finished I ironed until about half past two, Philip came to see me in the morning & talked of Willie's difficulties, I promised to go for a walk with him [Philip] at 4 o'clock, strange to say I was ready before the time   we went to the beach & sat on some rocks   he advised me to wait for six months that is if he could promise to be ready to get married by that time, if not to break off the engagement and to promise to keep myself free for a year and at the end of that time if we both cared for each other still, then to be married, I did not like the idea of it very much but I would not decide as I wanted time to think it over. We went back to Philip's to-gether & there I met Willie who walked home with me   I had not time to say half I wanted. Since all this trouble has come upon us we have not been to-gether nearly as much, he will not come into the house, he is so angry with Mama but he ought not to be as it is her duty to question him   I'm so sorry, putting aside the fact of having to wait so much longer than I intended, he will not be so welcome here   Papa & Mama liked him so much and now they both feel that he has not behaved honorably in not telling us many things that he ought to have done.

Tuesday April 26th – Up at 1/4–7. Breakfast was ready before eight, I finished my ironing this morning   Philip came over to ask me

if I had made up my mind what to do & gave me different advice to
what he did yesterday   he wants me to keep on the engagement
but to tell him that if at the end of six months he had not been
paying off his debts & was no nearer being in a position to marry
then most certainly to break it off   I listened to all he had to say
& then said I would not decide yet, it is better to wait & not to
decide hastily to regret it afterwards   I went over to Philip's at
four to see Willie as I promised & as he was not there I practised till
he came, we had intended going for a walk to-gether but it was too
late so we stopped talking there, he said that he would love no one
but me but that I was to do as I liked   he would not hear of it
from any one but myself   I said that I would wait before I would
give an answer   poor darling he must feel very wretched also. he
walked home with me but would not come in. I had then to get the
dinner ready in a great hurry as it was almost six and in consequence it was so late that it made Papa very angry as he dislikes to
eat his dinner when it is too light for lamps & almost too dark to
see without, I'm sorry to say, I was very cross too and spoke disre-
spectfully to him   I must not do it again.

Wednesday April 27th – Up at 20 minutes to 7. Baked bread for
breakfast from Yeast which I set last night   Went to bed last
night at eleven, after the breakfast things were washed I cleaned
the inside of the kitchen windows & black leaded the stove, it was
then past one   I was a long time dressing & then thought of
what sewing I should do & concluded to finish a white petticoat
that I began when I was at the Wood's, I had no sooner begun it
when Philip came over to ask me to go to see Willie at four but I
had told Papa I would have dinner at half past five so could not
go   I walked up and down the garden talking to Philip, I feel
much more cheerful to-day   Willie explained many things to
me satisfactorily to me yesterday and I begin to think that after all
it will turn out better than we expect though I know we won't be
married for a long time, I would not have accepted him if I had
known he was so much in debt   I should have said wait till

your debts are paid & then come   Mr. Crease does not like
our engagement, Willie thinks he dislikes him but does not
know why he should   Ella went to the Dorcas to-day &
then did some shopping   she bought me some cards, &
some broad nibbed pens   I must not forget to send some to
Sue   after dinner Papa Ella & I went to Mrs. Ogilvy's for some
plants   we got daisies, sweet williams, & two or three other
things. we want to be up at half past five to plant them   I must
again write down more faults   I got very angry with Papa this
morning talking of Willie   I know I was wrong but he does say
such things in such a way. Mama has just been telling me that she
thinks I ought not to go & see Willie but that he ought to come if
we see each other at all so I am going to write to him and ask him
to come over to-morrow afternoon if he wishes to see me he must
come, Mama has promised to cook the dinner for me so that I can
have time to see him. it is now eleven.

Thursday April 28th – I wrote a note to Willie asking him to come
over this afternoon which he did   I had a long talk with him
but came to no decision

Friday April 29th – I wrote a letter to Sue last night and told her of
our troubles but I do not think I spoke of Willie's debts only of the
money which he has lost. I feel very wretched and I do not know
how to decide   both Papa & Mama advise me to break it off.
but I do not want to do so   I did not go to the practice tonight.

Saturday April 29th[?] – C   Up not very early   Willy
went out to the Richmond for Philip, Ella & I called at the
Crease's[6]   after seeing Mrs. & Miss Crease I asked to see Mr.
Crease   I wished to ask him about something I had heard he
had said about Willie, he assured me that he did not believe that
at all for it was told him by a person in whom he had no confi-

dence   I felt a very great weight of[f] my mind. but he is
strongly opposed to our engagement and thinks I ought to take
Mama's advice   he does not like his having lost so much
money & being so very much in debt. I felt better this afternoon
than I did in the morning   I was scarcely able to walk to the
Crease's & w'd not have gone but I was so anxious to see Mr.
Crease.

Sunday May 1st – I very stupidly went into hysterics last evening
what with feeling so worried all the week & then being unwell I
gave way altogether   Mama helped to undress me and bathed
my head with cold water until I became quieter & then Ella read
aloud to me   I went to Sunday School but was rather late, just
before I started Philip brought me a letter from Willie but I did not
stop to read it then, he walked as far as the Govt buildings & then
went to meet Mr. Good who was going to Esquimalt with him.

May 26th – Went to San Juan[7] with Capt & Mrs. Delacombe to
spend a few days   We went over in Pritchards boat & were 4
hours & 20 minutes going over

June 8th – Willie's Birthday   I returned from San Juan in the
Boscer[?] with Papa who went over for me

June 18th Saturday – Rained all day. Up at 20, to 7. When I woke
I was holding my watch in my right hand. Willie was here this
afternoon & I was not ready to see him and was rather saucy I
think & said if he wished to see me he must go into the Drawing-
room   he was standing at the bottom of the stairs & I having on
a short dress did not want to go down   We nearly had a quarrel
or should have had I think if I had not kept quiet   he had asked
me if Philip had said anything to me about our engagement and
so after some hesitation I told him that he had said 'if the engagement should be broken off that he ought to do it & not I.' he was

annoyed and then he asked if I wished him to do so and when I said nothing he jumped up and said if I wished it broken off I had only to say the word and then walked up & down the room abusing Philip for giving me such advice. I said nothing until he was a little cooler and then said, You fiery creature come to me, he came saying that he was not so at all. After some more conversation he told me that he would do anything I wished if I thought it better or that it would make me happier in any [way?] he would break it off though he did not wish to   I do not know how it will end. I do not want a long engagement like poor Sue's she has been engaged nearly three years & is as far off being married than at first   she is talking of breaking it off. I've very nearly come to the conclusion that it will be broken off (mine). Rained all day

Sunday June 19th – Went to Sunday School & church   Mr. Cridge preached a sermon about spiritualism. the text 4 Chapter of the 1st epistle of John 1 verse. he spoke very strongly against believing in spirits appearing to people   Willie went to Esquimalt to the Pooley's   I got a letter from him a short time ago & I've just written to him.

Monday June 20th – There was a Regatta up the Arm to-day I rode with Philip and saw one or two of the races   we went to the Beach to look for the steamer but she was not visible   I dined with him & returned home about eleven

Tuesday June 21st – The Pelican arrived early this morning Isabel & Harry were on board   they both look very well in spite of the shipwreck.

Wednesday. 22 – Philip Isabel Lady Franklin Miss Musgrave & several others went to Gold-stream & returned about seven to a Meat Tea, I went over in the afternoon & helped Wing to set the Table etc. And then went over to Tea   Miss Zoe was also there. Willie promised to be there in the evening but could not get back from Esquimalt in time. Mr. Musgrave walked home with me.

Thursday June 23rd – Ella & I went into town this afternoon & did some shopping. I bought a white straw hat for 1.37 1/2 & some braid. Handkerchiefs 1/2 dozen for 1.62 1/2 [added on line above]   we also called on Mrs. Anderson, Mrs. Philippo & Mrs. Powell

Saturday 25 – Philip & Isabel went to San Juan to-day & intend spending a few days there.

Sunday June 26 – Went to Sunday School & church in the morning   Willie was at church & walked home with us. In the afternoon Ella, Harry Willie & I went to the Beach   it was too warm to walk far. I told him I would go to church in the evening but when he came for me I felt too tired to go out so Ella went with him

Wednesday June 29th – Harry Willie & I went for a short pull across the harbour & enjoyed it very much   on our return we went into town   Harry to see the Doctor & to ask him to see Papa.

Thursday June 30th – Isabel Philip & Capt D returned from San Juan   Ella & I went into town   I bought a hat & some other little things. We called on Mrs. Philippo Mrs. Anderson & Mrs. Powell

Friday July 1st – I went over to Isabel's this morning & took my sewing   I was helping Ella in her preparations for meeting Mrs. Musgrave. The Admiral Mr. Bickman, Mr. & Mrs. Philippo, Mrs. Pierce & Miss Pemberton, Mrs. Anderson and Mrs. Davie called while I was there. Harry & I went to the practise this evening   Willie walked home with us.

Saturday July 2nd 1870 – About ten o'clock this morning we were startled by hearing a gun which was a signal to get ready to meet the Governor & Mrs. Musgrave. Ella had to get ready in a great hurry, all the young ladies who were to throw flowers were at Government House in time, after welcoming the happy pair, they partook of cake & champagne and then returned home   Susan arrived from 'Yale' this afternoon for a months holydays   she has been away a year, all but a week   we were all very glad to see her   she is look[ing] much the same as ever. Our family party is larger now than it has been for a long time with the addition of Harry & Sue. We played Whist this evening.

Sunday July 3rd 1870 – Sue & I must have talked till 2 or 3 this morning   I felt very tired and sleepy when I woke, I did not go to Sunday School, but cooked the breakfast   Mama went to church for the first time since Easter   She Ella & I drove to church & Harry & Ella walked, we stayed to the Sacrament and then drove home. Sue did not go   it was very warm   The Governor & Mrs. Musgrave were in church. Willie came to see me in the afternoon   we did not go for a walk it was too hot. Harry, Ella & I went to church in the evening   it was very hot in the church   I could scarcely attend to the sermon.

Monday July 4th – This has been kept as a general holyday & everyone seemed to be at picnics   Papa Mama & Sue drove to town this morning   Sue wanted to do some shopping   Ella & I were at home all day. Philip asked me to go out in a boat with them & Willie, but I declined as Harry had said he would go with us, but it was so very hot that we did not go.

Tuesday July 5th – Another very hot day, the thermometer was 93 in the kitchen without the fire   Willie came to see me after having been for a bathe with Harry   I apologized to him about the going in a boat last evening. I did not get the dinner till 7. he

did not leave till nearly six. This is the warmest day we have had
for several years   there was a hot wind which was stifling
almost.

Wednesday July 6th – Harry said good-bye to us this morning
he has gone to Olympia on his way to S[an] F[rancisco].
he is travelling agent for a life Insurance Company   Susan
insured her life yesterday. Another very warm day but not
as hot as yesterday. Sue drove into town [with?] Isabel & did
some shopping and then began to make a grenadine dress for
the dance on board the 'Zealous'   I cut out a cape like
my gauze dress. Ella & I went for a walk to the beach after dinner
it was so mild and delightful. Sue & I went over to Philip's for a
short time in the evening   Judge Begbie[8] was there & we sang
some duetts and Trios   Philip walked home with me and we
stood at the gate for a long time talking, he was advising me to
keep on our engagement and that he would help him to pay his
debts, but he makes so many promises that he does not fulfil that I
cannot trust to what he says.

Thursday July 7th – Another hot day. this is my cooking week and
I find it very hard work during the heat   I do not feel at all well
and I am so worried about my engagement not being able to decide
whether to keep it on or not   Willie came to see me to-day but
Papa went to him and had a long talk   the principal thing was
that he ought to release me from my engagement and that, when
he is in a position to marry & we are both of the same mind, to
come and ask me again and then Willie said he would not do
that   Papa forbid him the house   he went away at once
with out waiting to see me. I did not know what to think when
Papa told me what he had done but thought that our engagement
ought to be ended. I had promised to go out boating in the evening
with Philip, Isabel, and & several others & Willie too. I went over
and walked with Philip Isabel & Mr. Colwell to the bank near the

Philippo's, Willie & Mr. Good were there and the Philippo's came two or three minutes afterwards   we had only started a few minutes when we saw the Steam Launch coming in from San Juan with the Delacombe's Mrs. Bird & Miss Bowman, the two latter were going to Philip's until after the dance on board the 'Zealous.' So our boat was turned and went to the landing again   Philip and Isabel got out to escort their visitors to the house & then we went for a short pull and then returned to have some tea at Philip's   I had no chance of talking to Willie coming from the boat as Mr. Colwell was with us nor could I during the evening but I fully expected him to walk home with me, but I was disappointed for he did not come out of the drawing-room when I came down stairs and after waiting some time I went home alone not feeling at all pleased   I thought he might have thought of me in time to see me home

Friday July 8th – Just a month to-day since I arrived from San Juan   The Admiral gave a dance on board the Zealous, Susan went with Isabel, & Ella with Mrs. Trutch,[9] I did not care about going & spent the afternoon partly in sewing & partly in shelling peas & cooking the dinner, I was very tired and low-spirited & went to bed early. Began to read Her Majesty's Tower.

Saturday July 9th – It was nearly seven when I got up this morning & I was hard at work all day in the kitchen cleaning, baking, & I was feeling very unhappy for I had made up my mind to see Willie and tell that the engagement must come to an end. I had had a letter from him on Friday telling me what Papa had said to him on Thursday & also said that if I wished him to he would break it off but only because I wished him to and for no other reason and that just so soon as he was in a position to marry he would come & if necessary ask me again   My dear darling could not say more. I would not tell any one that I had made up my mind until I could see him. I went for a short drive with Philip and he kept telling me to keep it on but I left him without saying much in return. After dinner, Isabel came over with Mr. Diegle[?] to ask Sue & me to

go over in the evening   I declined at first for I was tired &
unhappy and did not care to go over there to talk and sing when I
felt so far from being cheerful, but when in the course of conversation Isabel said Willie was over there I said I would go as I wanted
to see him. he met me on the Veranda and then we went into the
drawing room where I told him I had come on purpose to tell him
my answer   I could not say any more just then but he guessed
what it was. I cannot write down my feelings only that we were
both very wretched but he said all he could to cheer me, but at last
poor fellow he gave way and then I had to console him   My
darling has promised that he will still care for me as much as ever
and that he will work as hard as he can & be steady and good and I
have promised not to believe what I hear against him but to trust
him.

Susan Nagle, ca. 1865.

SUSAN ABERCROMBIE NAGLE DIARY, BRITISH COLUMBIA, JANUARY–DECEMBER 1870

Jan 28th [1870] – Recd letter from Algy, also from Mama & Papa, my watch arrived all right at last, I was afraid I should never see it again, heard of Jessie's engagement to Mr. Berkeley. The cold snap seems over for the present, the Th[ermomete]r which last Sunday but one was 8 below Zero, is now up to 48. The snow too is fast disappearing, it began to go in the river this morning   we watched it gradually floating off, I think we are in for some rain tho!

Jan 31st – Wrote to Algy, Mama Papa Jessie Eddie & Capt Stamp, weather rainy but mild, snow nearly all gone.

Feb 4th – Received letters from Papa & Mama enclosing others from Harry & Fred & the latters likeness, Jessie's wedding is settled for the 9th of July, if all goes well I hope to be down to it. She will be married after all before me, rather hard lines after being engaged so long, & with every prospect of its being as long, or longer before the happy event can take place, unless something fortunate occurs differe[n]t to what is at present. The weather continues very mild, nothing like the dreadful winter I was led to expect. We received invitations yesterday to attend a dance in the town. I dont know whether Nellie[10] will accept, as for myself I should much prefer stopping at home, these kind of entertainments are very well occasionally but having been to two, with[in] a short time do not feel anxious for another at present

Sunday Feb. 6th – Received letters from Algy, Jessie, Mr. & Mrs. Green & Dick Berkeley, no news of importance from any one   Mrs. Green is in charge at the Ladies College pro.tem.

Sunday 13th – Recd letter from Papa. There was a very small mail, Nellie was very disappointed at not getting a line from her husband. A great deal of snow fell last night, and this morning we had the pleasure of driving to church in a sleigh, the first time in my life. We went to the dance after all last Wednesday evening and enjoy'd it very well, that is as could be expected. I was called upon to sing & gave them 'Home they brought her Warrior dead' which being loudly encorred, sang 'My Lover is over the seas'!

Feb. 14th – Wrote to Papa Algy Mrs. Young Mr. Berkeley. The snow has changed to rain which comes down steadily and our anticipated sleigh drive of today did not come off. The express leaves early in the morning   Mr. McKay has not yet returned, Nellie did not hear from him by this Mail, for which she was not pleased.

March 2nd Ash Wednesday – This usually blustering month has began with beautiful weather, bright, but a little colder than we have been having it. I gave the children a half holiday that we might go to church   the congregation was not very large, only ourselves, the Baileys, Minnie Burr, & some few of the other children. We had the morning service & then Mr. Holmes read a homily on the subject of fasting, I was very glad of it, for at breakfast this morning we had an argument about it, Nellie thinks it is all folly and maintained that our Saviour when on earth did not teach that people should fast – Which is certainly a mistake, for he would not have given a rule to go by in the performance of anything he thought unnecessary, and when he tells his disciples not to be as the hypocrites 'Moreover when ye fast be not as the hypocrites of a sad countenance, for they disfigure their faces that they may appear unto men to fast, verily I say unto you they have their reward, but thou, when thou fastest anoint thy head & wash thy face that thou appear not unto men to fast but unto thy Father which is in secret and thy Father which seeth in secret shall reward the[e] openly ·   St Matthew VI ch. 16.17.18vs.

I feel sure did we follow the teachings of the church and our Bibles in this matter we should feel great benefit from the conscientious performance of this duty, people may say what they like, we are not so fit, or inclined to either pray or reading the Bible after eating or drinking heartily as we are when we abstain in some measure, and another thing is the taking part in idle amusements during Lent. Forty days out of three hundred and sixty are not many in which to give up some few pleasures and occupy the time in a better preperation, for another life. How often do I regret the little improvement I see in myself as year after year goes on instead of which I fear I often go backwards   it seems so strange that knowing the uncertainty of our life here, any moment liable to death or injury, that we think so little about it and strive so little if at all for the crown we hope to wear. How much better we should all be did each individually strive to do his or her duty after the example set us by Christ. The example of even one consistent Christian is not without good, if we could always remember this, and feel what an amount of influence either for good or ill, we are constantly exerting on those around us, and try and to use this influence for their good, we should be much happier ourselves, and help to make others so. May this be my desire and effort for the future.

March 11th – Much to our astonishment this morning the ground was covered with snow, and extremely cold the wind blowing & altogether a very wintry day.

12th – Continues cold & windy   went up to the school for a book and in that short distance got nearly frozen.

13th – Sunday colder than ever, the Th[ermomete]r down to 7 below zero, none of us went to Church   it was all we could do to keep warm in the house. Mr. Vernon dined with us, he intends going down to V[ictoria] by the Express tomorrow. I have written to Mama. I have several other letters to answer but my hand is too painful yet to allow of much in that line.

April 3rd – The Steamer[11] came up today the first time this year. Mr. McKay returned & Mr. Work on route for Cariboo. I received the parcel that has been missing for some weeks the Copy books I sent for, & letters from Papa Mama Jessie & Ella, enclosing others from Kate & Harry, Isabel had arrived safely in San Fran after a pleasant voyage of four days. Wrote to Mama, Ella, Eddie Mrs. Green, Harry. My watch also turned up again, I have been very bothered for the want of it.

Harrys address Messrs Cubery & Co

April 10th[12] – Recd letters from Mama Ella & Eddie, they were all well at home but Philip had had a bad attack of Lumbago.

April 9th – Began this morning to take Cod Liver oil.

April 10th – Wrote to Mama Papa & Mrs. Edwards. Mr. Vernon came up from V[ictoria] also Mr. Somerville   the latter spent the evening here   he appears a well informed man, and very communicative. The boat is expected up again on Thursday, no letters from Algy yet. I suppose there must be some for me on the way.

April 13th – I have often heard it said that there was electricity in peoples hair and this evening I have had full proof of its being true. I had been lying down, and when the tea bell rang rose and took the comb to put my hair a little in order when much to my surprise every time I put the comb in bright sparks eminated from it. I found too after trying several times that the comb retained the Electricity and that after putting the comb into the hair and tuching any other substance with it that the electric light showed plainly on this substance. I have always been so interested in Electricity and should like much to know more about it, there is so much to learn in this world and we know so very little. How I should like to make some discovery in this wonderful Science.

Recd letters from Philip and Algy the former containing the news of poor Graham's death & the latter that of Algy's brother Herbert. Algy talks of going to England in hopes of getting a better app[ointmen]t. I do hope something may be done soon.

May 1st – Recd letter from Jessie telling of her engagement having been put off.

May 9th – Recd letters from Jessie Philip & Dick, Philip has received his promotion as Commander on half pay. Mr. Cornwall came up, he spent the day with us.

13th – Wrote to Papa, Jessie Philip & Mr. Berkeley. There seems every chance of Jessies engagement with him being broken off, he is much more deeply in debt than we at first supposed, and it may be years before he can marry therefore the wisest plan appears to bring it to an end, poor Jessie she has been very unfortunate in her love affairs; I am beginning rather to despair about mine   I am afraid its rather hopeless.

26th – Recd a letter from Mama with account of the Ball at Gov. House, she went to it also Papa Jessie & Ella the latters first ball, it was a very gay affair and they all seem to have enjoy'd themselves.

1st June – Nellie & the Children went down to Hope to spend a week. I expect to join them on Friday afternoon.

15th – Recd letters from Philip Papa Jessie & Ella. They brought news of the loss of the Active, thank God tho' no lives were lost. They were wrecked on the 5th and did not get off until the 12th in the Pacific   we have heard very few particulars yet. Amongst the list of passengers I see Harrys name but cant imagine why he should be coming up.

July 1st – left Yale for Victoria

July 5th – Recd a letter from Algernon

July 8th – Went to a dance & luncheon on Board the Zealous

given by the Admiral. Went with Isabel   Mrs. Bird & Miss Bowman from the American camp accompanied us. We spent a
very pleasant day returning about 7 P. M. Ella went with Mrs.
Trutch.

10th – Went to Christ Church with Ella, afterwards called on Mrs.
Ash & Mrs. Charles & Mrs. Crease

11th – Went into town with Ella   did some shopping.

12th – Went into town with Jessie   called on Mrs. McMick-
ing   sent the carriage for Mama, met Harry who went with us,
called on Mrs. Evans Mrs. Jenns & Mrs. Trutch & the Harveys.
Wrote to Algernon telling him I think our engagement had better
be broken off as there seems no prospect of our meeting, it was hard
work when it came to the point, still I believe it will be best

13th – Harry has just wished us good bye   he goes back to
S[an] F[rancisco] today in the Pelican, I hope he will get there
safely.

August 2nd – Left Victoria on board the Otter for New West-
mins[ter]   Mrs. Trutch, Messrs. Gribbell Robertson, McCreight
Alic Davy Capt Raymeur Capt Cooper ret. were also to make the
Journey   Got to New Westminster about 7 'OC   went with
Mrs. Trutch to the Hotel, after having tea walked to the Camp
with Alic Davy   saw the Woods   left Mrs. Hancocks
cap with them to be given to her. Left the following morning for
Yale   Mrs Trutch very nearly left behind. The first part of the
Trip delightful then the mosquitoes began to be troublesome. Mr.
Gribbell was the only gentleman of the day before who was going
any further but we had some Ladies Mrs. Henry Work, Mrs Oglevie
& daughter, Mrs. McKenzie & Baby   all but the first named came
on to Yale when we arrived next morning about 1/2 7 O'C

Monday 8th – Began school today with 20 Scholars   I am afraid
I dont take to it very kindly   I shall soon get broken in
tho'   Mr. Gribbell came in for a little while & asked the children some questions; we all went for a walk in the evening.

Thursday 11th – Mr. Finlayson came down unexpectedly this
evening and leaves in the morning   we are all sorry as he will
take Mary with him. Recd a letter from Mama & a short one from
Jessie   Isabel Philip Ella & Mr. Berkeley had started on their
camping out party to Cowichan.

Friday 12th – Mr. Finlayson Mary and Mr. Gribbell left this
morning   the house seems so quiet now that they are all gone,
we had Mrs. McKenzie and Baby for a week, she has now gone to
Kamloops to join her husband. Mr. Alston came up by the Thursday boat also Mr. Holmes   the weather is extremely
hot   Tho. varies from 95 to 100 in the shade.

Saturday 13th – Dont feel very well today   went for a walk with
Mr. Alston after breakfast up the creek and felt better afterwards.

Sunday 14th – Very hot day, had great difficulty in playing on the
Harmonium, what with my being hot & the Instrument out of tune
I dont think the music was very edifying   Steamer came up but
no letters for me

Sunday 21st – Not so warm as the last   A good congregation   Harmonium a little better   went for a walk in
the afternoon, our family & the O'Reillys & Mr. Harvey & Mr.
Dewdney.[13]

Thursday 25th – Steamer came up. I got a letter from Papa &
enclosing one from Harry   He wants to get the place here in
Mr. O'Reillys office but I fear it is too late. I should have liked his

being here very much but dont know whether it wd. be a very good thing for him   however I dont think there is much chance of his getting the place. I have written to Papa, Philip Mrs. Woods & Mrs. Handcock   Papa tells me that Mr. Mrs. Heathfield & two children have gone to board with them for the summer months The camping out party, have returned and did not enjoy themselves as much as they expected owing to the fires & smoke

Sunday 28th – Pleasant day went to church. Kenny has chicken-pox   was not well in the night, Nellie & the other children did not go out until evening when we took a walk to the Bluff   The only letter recd today was from Jessie.

Monday 29th – Wrote to Mama, Mr. Pope will remain in Mr. O'Reillys office so there is no chance for Harry   I hope he may do better where he is   Went up the Creek this Ev'n'g with Aunt Willie & Agnes the latter tumbled into the water and made herself uncomfortably wet. Kenneth getting better.

Thursday Sep 1st – Wrote to Harry Hibben & Co. Weather warm again   Thor. & 7. 92 yesterday   Every body grumbling except self, like it.

Thursday Sep 7th – Steamer came up but no letters for me Much to our astonishment Charley Hankin made his appearance this evening, he is on his way to Victoria. Wrote to Mama Jessie Philip Isabel & Dr. Bellamy & sent him a box of ferns. Sent Mama $50. & returned P. the $25. he lent me. Willie & Agnes both ill with the chicken pox, nearly all the children in the school have had it. Mrs. Dewdney came up to stop with Mrs. Trutch during the absence of the O'Reillys. Heard today that the Gov. Mrs. & the Misses Musgrave wd. be up in the Sundays boat. Heard or rather saw in the Victoria paper that Harry had arrived. I wish he could have got this place   it would have been so nice for me in the winter, but its not to be.

Sep. 21st – Wrote to Kate   the Steamer is not expected till Friday so an express is to be sent down by Canoe. The O'Reillys are expected back tomorrow.

Oct 6th – Recd a letter from Papa a few lines from Mama, and the long looked for letter from Algy in answer to the one I sent in July, I cant tell yet whether our engagement will be broken off or not. I have asked Mama's advice on the subject. Mr. Walker came down on route to Victoria   Isabel left for England accompanied by Charley Hankin on Saturday Sep 24th. Philip has let his house to the Creeses and gone to live with the Philippo's, what changes take place, I wonder if we shall ever see her again, I sometimes think not

Oct 7th – Wrote to Mama   Mrs. Trutch went down this morning to meet her son Joseph who is expected by the next mail. The prizes were given today at the School. Josephine took the 1st   Willy McKay 2nd   James McEntee & Sarah Jaine Bailey   the other two Baileys it seems are greatly aggreved at the Elder children not getting one and wont let Sarah keep her prize, so one of the others will reap the benefit.

11th – Recd a letter from Philip, the Express & Mail came by Canoe   the Steamer is not expected until Thursday, weather very fine

Oct 14th – Steamer came up today no letters for me. Mr. Henry Cornwall came by her. He came to see us & brought the gloves he lost, after stopping about an hour he went over to the O'Reillys; we were not thinking of having any other visitors when about 1/2 past 9. OC a knock came to the door, upon its being opened in walked Mr. & Mrs. OR. & Mr. C. again, we had been sitting in the dining room but adjourned now to the Parlour, and Mrs. O'Reilly delighted us with a succession of songs. it was past twelve when they left, & nearly one before we got to bed;

Oct 15th – Wrote to Mama & Jessie. Mr. O'Reilly & Mr. Cornwall started for up the country at 8 this morning   The weather is lovely, beginning to be cold tho' in the morning and evenings, nothing new nothing to write about, I wish there was more

17th – Recd letter from Mama enclosing others from Mr. Patten & Fred. She advises me to break off my engagement and I have quite made up my mind to do so, it seems very evident that he has lost a great part of his interest in the matter so I wont keep him to it. He fancied I wished to break it off with the intention of marrying someone else, this certainly is not the case & had he been working and showing that he was doing the best he could I would have waited any number of years for him, but as it is it is better at an end. We have all bad colds.

Thursday 20th – Aunts box has come at last and she is very pleased with her things. I am very poorly again my chest has been very painful   I put a mustard plaster on it which has been a little relief. It was just this time last year that I had the same kind of an attack and Mr. McKay put on the famous plaster. I dare say had he been here this year I would have had another infliction.

28th – Wrote to Mama, got up today have been ill since the 20th and little better today, but far from well.

Nov. 1st – Am getting better gradually my head troubles me a great deal. I get up in the morning feeling quite well with the exception of weakness. I am no sooner dressed tho' than I begin to feel faint then a buzzing begins in my head which goes on till it commences to ache, then I am obliged to lie down. About 5 OC it gradually gets better & I am able to sit up again & join the family, this has happened for three days now, if it does not mend by the [time the] Steamer comes, I have great thoughts of going to Victoria for advice for it is useless attempting to begin school with my present feelings.

7th – Began school today. with only 10 pupils it seems that I am to have rather a small school, for some reason or other more than half the children have left. Recd letters from Mama & Jessie by canoe   the Steamer did not get up.

10th – Recd box of Apples & letters from Papa Mama Jessie & Philip – Jessie has recd the app[ointmen]t of Teacher at the Esquimalt School, I hope she will get along with the people better than I do here. Wrote this evening to Papa & Harry.

17th – Recd a letter from Mama enclosing one she had recd from Isabel – Papa had been very unwell with face ache and Mama herself has had another attack of Rheumatism. Jessie was to begin her duties today. A Young man came up 'on route' up the Country belonging to the H[udson's] B[ay] Co named Hamilton, he is to stop here till the stage goes up. Have written to Mama Jessie & Mr. Patten

24th – Recd two letters from Papa   Mama is much better Nellie heard today that Mr. McKay would be down very soon, the Capt of the Steamer says she will only make two more trips. The weather is very changable, rain & fine but most of the former. Mr. Holmes entertainment is to come off tomorrow night. Mrs. O'Reilly and family went down on the 18th   J. Trutch's wedding is to come off on the 7th so Mr. O'Reilly will soon be going down also, I suppose, to be away till after Xmas. The School question is not yet settled   there's no saying how long I may keep it on, or it will keep me perhaps wd. be more to the point. Have written to Papa and Philip. We keep very late hours for country people, it is now nearly 12 O.C. and I dont think we have been in bed earlier one day this week. We dont rise very early tho' 1/4 to eight being my usual time and I dont think many of them are up before that unless it is the children. I practised [all] of the accompanyments to the songs that are to be sung at the entertainment last night as I was to have performed had Mr. Robinson not returned which I am glad to think he did, so I shall not distinguish myself in that way. Raining very hard tonight and blowing   'Pray for those at Sea.'

Nov 28th – Steamer came up this morning and started again at 2 O'C and as there was great doubts expressed as to her making another trip Nellie made up her mind to go by her. Everything was in a great scuffle for a little time, she got off tho,' and it really seems as tho' the winter had begun in earnest. I fancy the Steamer will be up again tho.' Mr. Walker also went down so she will have company on the way. The weather is very fine again, tho beginning to be cold, there was a thick white frost this morning on every thing. I cant help wondering what changes the end of the year or the beginning of next may bring – perhaps no, perhaps things may just go on as they are. I have great fears that I may be obliged to give up the School, if I am obliged to do so, no doubt it will be for the best, there may be something else in store for me who knows.

Dec. 12th – Wrote to Papa Mama Nelly & Mrs. Cridge, sent the latter $5. $3 of which were for the Sermons. Sent Mama $30. The weather continues cold about a foot of snow on the ground. Mr. Kimble took us to Church in his sleigh yesterday. The School Meeting took place on Saturday, resulted in Messrs Holmes, Church & McQuarrie being elected Local Board for the coming year, the Gov. Tax has been done away with and great doubts are entertained whether the School can be kept on.

Dec. 15th – Recd letters from Jessie & Ella, by a [illegible] the regular express is not due until Sunday. The weather continues bright and cold. The Thom. at 30   the snow is hard and crisp on the ground. The numbers at the School continue very small   more may come after the holidays   it is very annoying when one is doing the best they can to meet with so much discouragement when least expected. It is no use complaining tho' we must all look for trials of one sort or another, and no doubt they are useful showing us how little really we are able to do of ourselves. Mr. Holmes has again asked me to re-consider my decission but altho I feel he is a good man and no doubt wd. do his best to make me happy, still I cant bring myself to say I will marry him. I often wonder how Algernon is getting on and whether he is still in Belize. I am anxious to hear from him again, poor fellow, things turned out very differently to what we planed and looked forward to. It is the case all through life 'Man proposes.' God disposes. How foolish then are we to go on thinking and working only for the present day forgetting how soon it all passes away.

NOTES

Jessie Melville Nagle Diary, 1867–1871, British Columbia Archives and Records Service (BCARS), and Susan Abercrombie (Nagle) Holmes Diary, 1865–1911, BCARS, both MS-2576.

1 In all, eight of the Nagles' children survived infancy and childhood. The others were Kate, Harry, Isabella (Isabel or Belle), Fred, Ella, and Eddie, all of whom are mentioned in the excerpts.
2 See Ellen M. Thomas Gee, 'Marriage in Nineteenth-Century Canada,' *Canadian Review of Sociology and Anthropology* 19, no. 3 (1982): 320.
3 See Margo Culley, *A Day at a Time: The Diary Literature of American Women from 1764 to the Present* (New York: Feminist Press, 1985), 4 and 7.
4 Graham Hankin was the brother of Jessie and Susan's brother-in-law, Philip. From her early diary entries, it seems that Jessie considered him a good friend. He had left Victoria for England the previous summer, having suffered for some time with 'liver complaint and inflamation of the lungs' (Jessie Nagle, Diary, 22 December 1867).
5 Arthur Bushby was registrar of the Supreme Court until 1870, when he became postmaster general. He was married to Agnes Douglas, one of former governor James Douglas's daughters.
6 Henry Crease was the attorney general of the colony of British Colum-

bia, and later a Supreme Court justice. Jessie had stayed in the Crease home while she was teaching in New Westminster. See also the diary excerpts in the next section, by his wife and daughter, Sarah and Susan Crease.

7   The San Juan Islands lie between Vancouver Island and the mainland of Washington. During the mid-nineteenth century, jurisdiction over the islands was in dispute, with hostilities escalating during the 1859 incident called the Pig War. This resulted in a standoff, following which the largest of the islands, San Juan, was occupied by both British and American garrisons, until the German emperor arbitrated in favour of the U.S. claim in 1872.

8   Matthew Baillie Begbie was appointed judge of the colony of British Columbia in 1858, and became famous for his success in keeping order in the goldfields. He became chief justice of the British Columbia Mainland in 1869 and of all of British Columbia in 1870, and was knighted in 1874.

9   Charlotte Trutch, the mother of Joseph and John Trutch. Joseph Trutch was one of the negotiators of British Columbia's union with Canada, and the province's first lieutenant-governor.

10 Nellie McKay was a cousin of the Nagles. She was married to Joseph McKay, a Hudson's Bay Company official who had also served in the first House of Assembly on Vancouver Island.

11 Yale was the head of navigation on the Fraser River. As there were no roads from the coast, waterways provided the only passage.

12 Although Nagle gives the date as 10 April, it was probably a date between 3 and 9 April.

13 Edgar Dewdney was an engineer and surveyor contracted by the Royal Engineers during their construction of routes into the interior. He was later elected to both the Legislative Council of British Columbia and the House of Commons, and was lieutenant-governor of the province from 1892 to 1897.

Sarah Crease and Susan Crease
(1826–1922)   (1855–1947)

BARBARA POWELL

The Crease family of Victoria, British Columbia, fostered in its members a strong tradition of diary writing. Because several family members wrote over such a long period, the Crease family papers offer a comprehensive view of life in British Columbia from its settlement by British colonists to its early years as a Canadian province. These brief excerpts from 1878 show that the diaries of the women of the family also chronicle domestic life over time and through troubled changes. The Crease family emigrated from England in 1869 and helped to shape the government and society in colonial Victoria, a small city at the edge of the British Empire. The family was cultured and socially prominent, and its women were expected to maintain the family's position in social circles through cycles of entertaining other English emigrants, attending the Church of England, and engaging in good works and artistic projects.

This position was maintained with difficulty, for the Creases had suffered several financial setbacks, and their social position was not always backed up with financial security. As a young woman, Susan Crease wrote in her diaries about the effect of social and familial strictures on her dreams for the future. Her diary entries contrast with mother Sarah's version of events, and reading their diaries together shows how a young woman and her mother struggled to find a balance between autonomy and propriety. Their views of the events of 1878 were filtered through what they hoped to find in life. Susan was looking for love, while her mother was more concerned with social and financial security. They wrote, sometimes obliquely, of their daily lives, the patterns of which become evident over long stretches of time. Sarah Crease in particular wrote with decorum, and interesting aspects of the stories both women tell emerge only through hints and even omissions.[1]

In 1878, Susan Reynolds Crease was a woman of twenty-two. Despite having reached the age of adulthood, she had little life of her own; her daily routine of activities was shared with and bound by her family, including her parents, Henry Pering Pellew Crease and Sarah Lindley Crease; her older sisters, Mary Maberly (Mab) and Barbara (Babs); and her younger siblings, sister Josephine (Zeffie or Zeph) and brothers Lindley and Arthur (Artie). The family lived in Pentrelew, the Crease's spacious home that claimed the top of the hill on what is now Fort Street. Susan's diary tells of daily life in Pentrelew and among the members of Victoria society. It was a life shaped by family and social expectation. Unlike her brothers, who were sent to school in England, Susan was educated at home and in Victoria schools. She had studied drawing, painting, and music, but had not been prepared for any kind of work; presumably her career was to make a good marriage so that she would not be a continuing burden on her family. Her sister Mary taught art lessons at a local school, but even that occupation was denied Susan, who was confined to a life of social obligation.

One of the obligations in the Crease family was to write, and all were indefatigable record-keepers. They may have done this because they wanted a complete record of the colonial experience; some of what they wrote and drew they mailed to family members in England to explain what their life in Victoria was like. They appear to have been motivated just as much by the sense of personal and cultural justification that writing provides. They were well educated and saw themselves as authors and preservers of history, signing the covers of their diaries with names and dates to claim authorship and authority. The diaries also served several immediate purposes: the Crease women at different times used their diaries as account books, calendars of events, records of social occasions, and private confessionals. The Creases also all kept correspondence, sketches, watercolours, photographs, letterbooks, scrapbooks, and miscellaneous collections and documents.[2]

The overlapping detail in these diaries, written at the same time from different points of view, demonstrates the common concerns of a close, interdependent family and their social circle. Among other things, we can read accounts of the family's medical problems: toothache, erysipelas, eczema, and Mary's frightening bouts of hysteria. We can appreciate the importance of the naval presence in Victoria, with officers such as Captains Machell, Robinson, and Layton from such ships as the *Opal*, the *Shah*, and the *Turquoise* forming the core of many of the Creases' social activities. And we can follow the rounds of Victoria's elite, in daytime activities that included riding, lawn tennis, boating, picnics, and making calls, and in evening entertainments, such as the recitations of Mrs Siddons, or parlour games like vingt-et-un, backgammon, bezique, and consequences. But this shared background of lively social activities is filtered in the diaries through different emotional lenses. In each diary, we read of the individual concerns of each woman at a particular age and stage of her life.

Susan's diary for 1878 records her emotional state during her young adulthood. At the time when she begins the diary, she is and has been in love with several young men, including William Boyle, referred to in the diaries as Billy, WB, BB, and Bibi. During 1877, Susan and her older sister Mary had fought over the affections of Billy, who was several years younger than both women. In the diary transcribed here, Susan describes how she struggled with her feelings about Billy and found herself drawn to Lancelot Denman. Complicating her romantic life was a proposal of marriage from George Findlay, which was made through a letter to her mother. Despite her genuine affection for Mary, Susan was also jealous of her older sister, and angry with her mother, whom Susan thought thwarted her at every turn and criticized her unreasonably.

Susan's diaries for 1878 took two forms. One was a small (five-by-eight-inch) black leather book for the years 1875–8, in the back of which she listed her accounts for 1876–7. The other was a much larger book she made herself by stitching together odd-sized sheets of paper. The larger book gave her more room for reflection and to express her hopes, fears, and desires, sometimes regarding men. Susan, like her mother, always wrote in pen and ink, except for a brief period on a camping trip when she wrote in pencil.

Conflict arose in the family during 1878 because Sarah wanted Susan to resist the amorous attentions of eager young men, particularly those with uncertain futures or careers travelling in the naval service. Her own early married years with Henry Crease were strained, marred by financial crises and long separations for business reasons.[3] As a result, Sarah controlled her young adult daughters' affairs to the extent that she screened marriage proposals on their behalf.

At the same time as Susan was railing against her, Sarah was recording in her diary the ordered events of her busy social life. Sarah, at the beginning of 1878, was fifty-one years old and a matriarch in Victoria society. Her diary, calm and reserved next to Susan's, contains lists of names and events. She entertained and was a guest of the prominent families in Victoria; her diaries mention Sir Matthew Baillie Begbie, judge and later Supreme Court justice of British Columbia; Dean Mason, assistant rector at Christ Church in Victoria; Lieutenant-Governor A.N. Richards; and Benjamin Pearse, colonial surveyor. These men and their families were the builders of the physical, social, and cultural environment of British Columbia. Sarah's diaries are often terse, far less emotional than Susan's. One reason might be that Sarah did not have room for much elaboration in her chosen books. Her diary for 1878 was a tiny (2½-by-4-inch) Colonial Almanac of the Standard Life Assurance Company. This little book, published in Edinburgh, gave the diarist just one double page per month, with one side being taken up with 'Sundays and Remarkable Days,' and one blank page labelled 'Memoranda' on which Sarah did her writing.

Read together, these diary excerpts offer a tantalizing slice of the complexities of daily life as a mother and daughter sought to record it. Their stories continue, of course, in many more years of diaries, so the thread of narratives that appear in these accounts of late 1878 reappears in subsequent years. A calendar year imposes a form of closure on the diaries that is not borne out in fact, since both of these women wrote in their diaries almost to the day they died – Sarah for most years from 1875 to 1913 and Susan from 1865 to 1943.

Sarah and Susan Crease on the verandah of Pentrelew, in Victoria, 1912.

DIARIES, BRITISH COLUMBIA, SEPTEMBER – DECEMBER 1878

September 1878

Sarah

1st   S   Dean Mason[4]

4th   W   H.M.S. Daring left Esquimalt Harbor for Valpo [Valparaiso]   Capt Hammer

5th   Th   Last sight of father, mother, brother, sister & native land 19 years ago!!

7th – 14th   [crosswise:] smoky and foggy

8th   S   Mogg

12th   Th   The Machells return to Victoria

13th F   Mr & Mrs Price from Eng. Brought us an introduction fr Mr Booker –

14th   Sa   took them to Beaver Lake

15th   S Mason

17th   Tu   Lindley's holidays end   Chinese strike,[5] on Poll tax – 'Yang' & all other chinamen leave their places

18th – 23rd   Mary, Susy, & Babs cooked. self in bed two days with bad cold –

20th   F   Mr Findlay dined with us alone

22nd   S   Mogg

23rd   M   Chinese strike over. Mr Findlay & Mr Boyle dined with us alone

24th – 29th   [crosswise:] changing chinamen

29th   S   *Harvest Thanksgiving services.* A little too late in the season. Decorations very pretty – Services hearty & sermons from Dean Mason – splendid –

30th   M   Mr Findlay left for England. Gave me his pony 'Kitty' – & lent me his quilt and little piano

Susan

1st   *Sunday* – Mr Findlay came home with us – but had a bad headache and did not go to church in the evening   Billy stayed to dinner – went to see Mr F in afternoon – gave me his gloves to mend. I went to evening Services   Mama angry – because she thinks GF will think I am running after him! She is *quite* mistaken – I shall do no such thing – Billy at tea – and Mr Preston Bennett

2nd   Mama went to see the invalids Miss Musgrave, Willy Beaven & the Martin family – also Mrs Richards who has lately lost a brother, a Mr Chislett – Feeling too miserable to go out. Mary and Barbara went round the Hill before dinner –

3rd   Provincial Assembly prorogued   Capt Robinson (Turquoise) Dr Cree and Japanese mid Zendo called   At home till 5 when Vernon drove me in Papa's buggy to meet Barbara – went with her to enquire for Edith Carr. Capt Layton in evening – played Backgammon with him

4th   Mama and Papa went to Masons after dinner. Preston Bennett in eveg. played Bezique   Barbara went to lunch and for a row after with the Croasdailes   Zeffie to Stadacona for croquet Took [?] Florry Jones and Lidy – Mr Bennett did not leave till 12 o'clock

5th   Went to see Mrs Richards with B then to Fairfield – abt pears and apples   met Mrs O'Reilly there, who drove me into town – Papa and Mama went to Govt House aft dinner – Mary and I had a famous practise of duets – learning one ('Autumn') of Mendelssohn's – no Mr F – declare I won't trouble myself about him – I'm sure he can't care for me – Met Dr Ash in town, was so abominably affect: What *can* the man mean? it is so bad of him –

6th   Mrs Richards, Mama and Billy drove out to Beaver Lake. I rode 'Sherry' – left Victoria 10:30 returned 7:30. When mounting to come home some wasps stung poor Sherry and made him plunge and rear so that I might have been thrown if Billy had not seized my rein – Mrs Richards was very brave in trying to hold the black horse as she did till Perkins could do so for her – Had a very pleasant day – one of the very nicest this summer – all made sketches – Billy and I had our tea in the boat – Mama and Mrs Richards on the rocks still sketching

7th   Small Picnic at Macauley's Point – 2 Grays and Mrs J. Gray

Miss Macauley, Mr and Mrs Croasdaile, Mr Eberts, Mr Findlay
Geo: Wake, Mr P Bennett and Billy – Went in our boat – Mr
Croasdaile took his also – We stayed at M. Pt. till about 9 p.m. and
sat round a bonfire – singing – Mr Croasdaile sang 'Ten Thousand
miles away'   Mr Bennett – 'Canadian Boat Song' and 'Simon
the Cellarer' and 'When Ye gang awa Jamie' – Went off pretty well
I think –

8th   *Sunday* – As usual – No one at dinner or tea – Mr Nedham &
Capt Layton in afternoon –

9th   Had the buggy for a little while before dinner – drove with
Barbara to see Lettie – and round Beacon Hill – Mama and Mary
went to town – Mr Findlay wrote to Mama offering to give her
'Kitty' and also to lend his piano while he is away in England.

10th   Mr Croasdaile, Billy, and Capt Layton after dinner –
poor 'Yip'[6] very ill – Mama wrote to Mr Findlay accepting the
horse   also about other things – 'Yip' died –

11th   Little picnic arranged for Mrs Richards' benefit, not come
off owing to the dense smoke about every where – Mama spent the
day with Mrs Richards – Mary went by herself to Foul Bay. Lettie
came to spend the afternoon with me   Billy at lunch – also
Maggie & Hugo Beaven – Billy went to Foul Bay – where Mary
rode his horse in the most absurd way

12th   Mama at Government House all day – Mary also in
morning   Lettie came to make me go back with her to dinner –
went to Govt House to ask Mama   Met Mr Dawson of Montreal (junior) there – Dined with the Hetts, Lettie went with me to
Sunday School meeting – Mr Hett and she walked home with me –
Capt and Mrs Machell returned from Saanich

13th   Mr Mogg's Birthday – school supplies[?] went after 3 ho[urs]
sort Sunday school book – Capt and Mrs Price called with introduction from Mr Booker – came by [unclear] after dinner. They
seem *very* nice English people – I like her especially though she
seems to despise me – Mary went to choir practise –

14th   Capt and Mrs Price went with me to Beacon Hill and come
home to lunch – Mr P Bennett also – Papa, Mama, and our visitors

drove to Beaver Lake Mary and Mr Bennett rode – Barbara and I did some copying for Papa, – at 4 p.m. went to finish sorting SS Books – Arthur spending the day with little Willie Beaven – Zeffie at Stadacona – Billy came in evening and went to Driard with me – asked him to lunch could not come as he had promised to go on shooting expedition with Capt Machell

15th *Sunday* – Was in a horrible temper with Mr Findlay and would not walk with him – Went to Sunday School but not to church – with children went to Mrs Machell and made her come home with me. Billy at lunch – took Mr Findlay for drive afterwards – Capt and Mrs Price came in afternoon – also Capt Layton and Geo Wake – Mr Findlay and Billy at tea also Mr P Bennett

16th Mary went to dinner at Govt. House the other guests were Mr & Mrs Price, Mr Potter (another English politician) Miss M Gray and Mr Keith – Mr Bennett spent the evening with us as it is his last – stayed till past 12 o'clock – I was so sleepy I left the room just before he turned [?] to say 'goodbye' I was spared the affecting farewell – Packed two carpet bags for Arthur and self, as Mama has promised to let us stay with Mrs O'Reilly for a little while –

17th *Strike among the Chinamen* – Yang told me this morning all chinamen were ordered to leave their employers *today* after cooking breakfast – had arranged to go with Mrs Mogg to Harvest Festival in Highland District and then to be left at Point Ellice, was obliged to give up the longer visit but Barbara and I went to Highland and spent a very pleasant day there – Mrs Machell also of the party – came home about half past four – *very smoky* and *dusty* – Mr Findlay came in to compare notes – after dinner – which Mary cooked – Mr and Mrs Pierce went to New Westminster

18th Got up this morning to *see about breakfast* – arranged with the others to do this every day and to take the dinner-cooking in turns Barbara today – Mama in bed with bad cold – got up to dinner – Capt Layton after – Mary and I sang the duett 'Breathe not of Parting' played game of Backgammon with him – beaten of course –

19th   Papa asked Mr. Findlay to come to dinner – I had a great quarrel with Mary just before about the washing up. She would not let me help – Mary cooked – Mr and Mrs Price after dinner – a quiet evening – was so jealous of Mr Findlay's talking so much to Mary   I really have suffered more this week about this miserable affair than ever in my life before – He is so noble minded and generous I cannot help liking him very much – and it annoys me to think he knows it

20th   *Mrs Machell's Birthday* – She came to see Mary this morning and went to town with her – Feeling wretchedly blue I went for walk to rocks opposite Stadacona – (alone) and tried to make [pencil?] sketch but being very tired fell asleep instead and awoke to find a strange man staring at me who asked me all sorts of questions   Flurried and only half awake I answered most questions, but did not tell him my name or where I lived, when he asked. Thoroughly indignant, I enquired why he wanted to know about me – and he said 'he had the oversight' of the place and didn't know *what I might be after!!!* Resolved never to go alone again to such places – cooked dinner   Mary could not go to choir practice   [written crosswise next to entry:] Mr and Mrs Price left for England via Portland

21st   Went to Mrs Jones for my first singing lesson – to town and afterwards to Mrs Machell where Mama met me and we went home together   Repacked Aunt Emily's box of winter clothes – Mary went for ride on 'Darcy' – Billy drove Capt Machell to call on ships at Esquimalt. A heavy shower of rain cleared the sky and blue showed for the first time for many weeks

22nd   Billy drove Mr Findlay to Metchosin in morning where they dined with a Mrs Fisher who ordered her husband and children in one breath – peeled the potatoes at the table with her fingers and passed the spoons in a manner peculiar to herself – They (B & Mr F) came to tea – and amused us immensely with their account of their days proceedings – Billy made friends with Mrs Fisher and tried on some of her wearing apparel which he wanted

for acting – Things did not fit but they all went into howls of
laughter at her attempts and *suggestions*!! Resolved not to do anything to spoil Mr F's last week in Victoria – and went to bed with
the happy consciousness of having kept my resolution – for tonight
23rd   A hard day for all of us – I did kitchen work as usual – Mary
and Barbara the usual Monday house cleaning   Cooked dinner
– which fortunately (as Mr F and Billy dined with us) turned out
well – great fun a laughing about the puddings (one Mary's and one
mine)   Before either was produced they promised to take some
of that made by the one he liked best – but Mary's turning out *very*
hot with mustard – it was a cheese pudding. They both preferred
mine – castle pudding with wine sauce – saying however as they
did so, that they would have to break their resolution – played
Polka – after – A very nice evening – no fusses or quarrels –
24th   Mary went out with Mrs Machell and also dined with her
and went to practise – choir – Capt Layton in evening –
25th   *New chinaman came* (Sing)   Mary spent the day with
Mrs M.   went with her to Highland District for berries
etc.   poured with rain all the aftenoon
26th   Nothing in particular – borrowed 'Darcy' and went for a
ride in morning with Lidy   in afternoon we rode round to see
dear Lettie who gave us a tintype of Sibbald – Then round Beacon
Hill – and home – saw Billy twice today. G.J.F. and Mr Nedham
after dinner   We all made a mutual exchange of 'tin-types' – a
tremendous display! – Played 'Polka' – G.F. left about half past
eleven   Mr Nedham not till twelve –
27th   Went to town in the morning and bought a new hat ($1.75)
– also umbrella $4.50 – shoes $3.00 and other things – Met G.F.
at [Dengs?]   he screamed at my hat – 'it is so ugly' he said
I laughed till I was ashamed – Took it to show Lettie who began to
abuse it too – till at last we fairly danced and shouted   Mr F
went to Govt House in afternoon and to Dinner at the Jackson's – Mary dined with Mrs Machell and went to choir
practise

28th   Mary went to music lesson (Mrs Jones) and then to church
to assist at Harvest decorations – Barbara at home – I went to
church, where I again met Mr Deeding of Turquoise but he was not
introduced – I feel that I made a fool of myself in some way – was
very rude to Mr Offerhouse – brought a quantity of flowers home
from the surplus –
29th   *Sunday* – Mama, Mary, Billy and I stayed for Communion
after morning Service – G. F. in church – but we did not see him
till tea time – Billy would not stay to dinner but came in evening –
I could not help it. I was almost afraid to speak lest they should
hear my voice tremble – I *am* sorry he is going – Heighho! *What* a
fool I am!
30th   *Monday* – G.J.F left in the 'Panama' for England to be away
six or seven months he thinks – of course I cried my eyes out last
night and again this morning idiot that I am! He sent Kitty to us –
and Billy who is going to New Westminster with Capt Machell
tomorrow left Poacher – raining all day but not much wind –
31st   Mary desperately tired with her Monday work. They would
not let me do the Diningroom as usual – ~~Billy came for a few min-~~
~~utes in the afternoon I could not help his seeing my red eyes how-~~
~~ever this is better than anyone else~~   Billy went to New Westminster – Capt Layton in the evening   I won 3 games of
Backgammon

October 1878

Sarah

1st   Tu   'Fun' came to cook & make bread $25
5th Sa   Ah Hoy came. I called on Mrs Pearse   left card.
9th   W   Ah Hoy returned   Posted letters to Engd
10th   Th   Sent for Dr Helmcken to see Mary & Babs
15th   Tu   Susy & Babs heard Mrs Siddons from the Govt's box –
16th   W   Henry, self & Mary heard Mrs Scott Siddons recite at
the theatre. a *great* treat

18th Fr Darling Artie bitten by the Beaven's dog. Dr. Helmcken put a stitch in the worst wound in his head. the darling child
was very brave
21st – 31st [crosswise:] gardening weather lovely

Susan

1st Billy sent some game to the Richards Mrs Machell, Grays and
ourselves – *very* good – Mary and Barbara went for a ride – Mary
had 'Kitty' and Barbara 'Darcie' – with Mrs Croasdailes saddle and
bridle – I groomed and saddled little Kitty because I wanted always
to be able to feel that *no one* had done so before myself   Now
everybody is gone, it does feel eerie – I am going to try and do something with the singing so as to able to be of a *little* use when we
have to entertain people   Mrs Jones says my voice is worth cul-
tivating – so I am going to do it if I can – Went for a drive with Mrs
Machell   Mary riding Dixie which Billy left for her to use – a
very nice drive –
3rd Nothing whatseover worth the ink to record it–
4th Chinaman left without giving warning ('Fun') had to get
breakfast –
5th Second singing lesson – Mrs Jones says my voice is very good,
or will be if exercised – Another chinaman engaged – Hoy – Went
to see Lettie and stayed to lunch – Fuss at home at my absence –
6th *Sunday* – Hoy left – Awoke this morning feeling that we had
to live through the day *somehow* – Mary very poorly   *would* go to
church but had to leave abt the middle of the Service – The Dean
preached a most wonderful sermon on 'The Cross' – he made me
feel how difficult it is to live as a Christian should   Mrs Machell
and Walter came home with me – We discussed the sermon but I
could not – I cannot speak of those things to anyone who does not
sympathize with my peculiar vein of thought. There has been a
most unpleasant feeling of 'desolation' and anxiety in the air today
– Dinner was miserable – everyone being more or less anxious about
Mary who would neither come down nor have anything taken to

her – Alone at teatime for the first time for many weeks –
7th   Mary not better – Mama made Barbara promise not to do any
extra housework this morning – got breakfast – After lunch
groomed Kitty – asked Mrs Croasdaile to ride with me. She, not
caring to do so, I asked Lidy – we went round by Point Ellice to see
Mrs O'Reilly – Barbara cooked dinner –
8th   Arranged that Mrs Machell should drive Mama wherever she
liked. Mary and Lidy to follow on 'Dixie' and 'Sherry' respectively
– Mary put on her habit – Lidy brought hers here to change – Mrs
Machell came up fully equipped – I was busy in the back kitchen
plucking ducks! and watching for the start when it began to pour.
So she suggested that we should have a waltz – which we did
careering madly round both kitchens – I was really *very* tired; still I
felt less miserable after it –
9th   Mrs Machell and Mary went for drive. I rode Kitty – tried to
keep in their wake but had to give it up, as the rain came down in
sheets and I found some thickly branched trees under whose
friendly shelter I took refuge – and when the showers abated rode
home alone – Capt Machell and Billy came home from New West:
– Mary complains of not feeling well. [written crosswise next to
entry:] 'Hoy' came back
10th   Mary worse – The Doctor came to see her but of course she
did not tell him anything – she says she always forgets when she
sees him – Capt Layton and Mr Wake after dinner –
11th   Very uneasy about Mary who did not sleep at all well last
night   In the afternoon Papa sent for the Doctor again – I saw
him and told him everything I could think of   He made her go
to bed and examined her thoroughly. He still says she is
not seriously ill – and had ordered her tonics – Billy came in abt
dinnertime and seemed shocked when he heard she was ill – The
Doctor called quickly to ask for her in the evening –
12th   Mary a little better   I went to Mrs Jones and to town –
coming back a very heavy shower began to fall so I took refuge at
Dr Ash's – He opened the door and almost before I was aware had

taken me to the Drawing room and kept me there while he said
such things to me and at last took me in his arms, turned up my face
and kissed me passionately on the lips twice!! I don't know what to
make of him   I am sure it can't be right and I feel afraid and *so*
ashamed and disgusted – I could hardly help crying all the afternoon – it is too horrid – all my secret triumph that no one had ever
kissed me except Lancelot is gone now – Oh dear! what *can* I do – I
told Mary all about it & she thought it very queer –
13th   *Sunday* – Mrs Jones came home with B & self to see Mary
and stayed to lunch as did likewise V. Spalding – I met the two Mr
Grays when coming home from S School – who walked with me to
our gate where I met Capt Layton and brought him in – No one at
tea – Somehow or other there has been a most uncompromisingly
dull feeling pervading the Sundays of late –
14th   Rode Kitty to Highland District with Lidy – Received a
charming letter from Lancelot (fr. Honolulu) which happy event
sent me into an extacy of delight – He enclosed it in one to Mama
– Dear old boy! Really our friendship with him is the only comfortable one I had ever had – may it long continue! The first evening of
Mrs Scott Siddons recitations – [written crosswise next to entry:]
Mabel Charles returned fr Eveg: with Mr & Mrs Jones – BBC[7]
15th   Mary rode with Billy – to Cadboro' Bay. I went to town in
the morning and again met Dr Ash or rather as he popped out of a
doorway as I passed I was obliged to speak to him – much as I fear
him – Capt Layton after dinner – We played Backgammon – beat
me 4 games out of 5
16th   Barbara and I went with the Govt House party to the
Theatre to hear Mrs Siddons – We all thought it most excellent –
during the recitation of the 'Maniac' and the 'Faithful Soul' there
was a noticeable dimmness about the general vision and not a few
pktchfs[8] were put into requisition   Billy clapped most enthusi-
asticaly and threw a bouquet to her –
17th   Mary and Barbara went to see Mrs Jackson – Mabel Charles,
Annie Harvey, Mary Mason and a few others – Mary also lunched

with Mrs Machell – Mama and I busy mending mats etc – Mrs
Richards and Maggie came to see Mama
17th   [second entry for that date] Mrs Machell with us in the
morning. Mr Isaac Fisher called to say goodbye before going to
New Westminster to open a Branch of the B.C. Bank. Mrs Mowat
also called – I went with Mrs Machell to call on Mrs Mogg. found
Alice Wright there in a most hostile humour towards ourselves –
Papa, Mama and Mary went to the Theatre and were as much
charmed as B and I were   Zeffie went with Govt H party –
[written crosswise next to entry:] Mary rode with Billy again
18th   Went to lunch with Mrs Richards and stayed all the afternoon (by invitation) to help her receive her visitors of whom
there were a great many – though only three of the masculine
gender – The great Mrs Siddons came with the Macdonalds –
She is decidedly pretty and most exquisitely dressed – speaks
rapidly   chiefly however of herself and her doings – Arthur
went to see Willie Beaven and while there was badly bitten by a
dog (since killed) which he provoked by snatching away a stick he
had previously thrown at him and which he (the dog) mistook for
the bone in his mouth   Mrs Beaven kindly did all she could for
him and was bringing him home when they were met by Papa and
Capt Layton coming to look for him – Papa went for Dr Helmcken
and Capt Layton delivered him to me – I bathed his head in the
side of which were several deep punctures and made him comfortable – He did not cry either then or when the Dr came and put a
stick in the worst place – my brave little man! Afterwards – the Dr
having told us there was no danger and nothing else we could do
for him Barbara and I went to hear Mrs Siddons again with Capt
Layton and Papa – There we met Mary who had been dining with
Mrs Fellows and brought her home with us –
19th   Went to town to return songs – and to get the signet ring for
Mary from Rudolphs – then to Mrs Jones for singing lesson – who
by the way kept me waiting an hour as usual – Mr Dawson (geolo-
gist) dined with us – and always happens when he is our guest left a
very pleasant recollection of himself behind him – certainly *his*

head is worth half a dozen of most men's and the largeness of his intellect quite compensates for the smallness of his body – I wish more of our frequent visitors were as amusing as he! Mama spoke to me about monopolizing people and not letting Barbara have a chance – I dare say she is right, but it is so difficult to know exactly how to divide one person's attention among half a dozen – She spoke kindly, giving me full credit for the best motives so I suppose I must try and keep more out of the way – This sort of thing however is not conducive to general hilarity – [written crosswise next to entry:] Mary went to Theatre with Govt House party –

20th   Another Sunday to be lived through, somehow, however oppressive the atmosphere may be – as it certainly is today – Mary, Barbara, and I came home in solitary state – Billy having gone off with Charley Brodie – who is staying with him – and there being no one more lively than Vernon Spalding that we cared to ask to lunch – so we didn't ask him – Billy came in to tea – We did not quarrel as usual – I am afraid I miss someone at teatime a good deal. The sight of his place always gives me a horrid sick feeling   I do hope he will not come out again – it would be so hateful meeting him again –

22nd   Capt Machell went to Mud Bay with Mr Drake – duck shooting – Mr M came for German – Mary went out with her after Drawing – Capt Layton in the evening – Barbara had to be victimised – by going into the Dining room – Mary and I suffering from indigestion – the effect of eating pears –

23rd   A most lovely day – Mama not very well. Mary out all day with Mrs Machell from 10 a.m. to six p.m. Barbara went to see Mrs Croasdaile I to dear Lettie's where I encounted Dr Ash again – When I saw him coming I rushed out of the house and only went in when she came to tell me he was waiting to see me and would not go away – Persuaded her to come to town with me. Went to Mr Hett's new office in Langley St & found it a nice cozy place

24th   Asked Capt Layton to ride with me tomorrow – he promised to do so – Barbara, he, and I played 'Go Bay' on Lancelot's Board which I have nearly finished painting till 11:30 o'clock.

Papa and Mary returned, the first from Choral Meeting the last from Mrs Machells where she had waited for him   Billy ill with erysipilas in the foot   rode to see the Doctor (Ash) and also with Mary –

25th   Took Billy some books Mary had promised to lend him – rode to the Lodge with them but did not go in – Rode with Capt Layton up the Richmond road, round by Mt Tolmie – then up a road which seemed to go no where but to a large fenced-in piece of wild ground – these we explored by following a trail which led us to a sheep pen – out of this there was no other way of getting but by pulling down part of the fence – This my cavalier managed very nicely – till we found ourselves in an embryo road which took us to the highway and so home

26th   Papa and Mama busy in the garden   Mary with Mrs Machell and Mrs Jones sorting Ch: music etc. (in morning)   *afternoon* – Football at Beacon Hill Collegiate – boys marched there to receive ~~their~~ muskets – Barbara riding with Lidy – Mary driving with Mrs Macell – Zeff at home practising, nearly all afternoon – Mama proposed going to see Billy Sunday. Mary threw cold water on the scheme by refusing to go – She said he was much better and had been riding with Mabel Charles –

27th   Mama went to St John's and brought Mrs Miles home to lunch – I drove with Mrs Richards – Mary walked with Clara Dupont – *Afternoon* – Mrs Machell came to see Mary – also Mary Mason and Mabel Gray and her brother Scott who were not heard however so did not get in – Capt Layton as usual – Mr Wake came in to tea – We had a tremendously long and serious discussion on religious subjects – Mama went to see Billy before Eveg: Service and asked him to tea. Said he should come, but went to 5 o'clock dinner at the Charles' so did not go to church and consequently failed to appear at 9.

28th   Monday work as usual. Gardening with Mama all afternoon – Billy went for ride with Mary – after Drawing – Zeffie and Lidy from 2:30 to 4 o'clock – Vernon Spalding came to say goodbye as he goes to New Westminster tomorrow to join Mr Fisher in the New Branch of the B.C. bank.

29th   Dinner at Stadacona. Papa went. Billy rode with Mary
after drawing   Papa's face somewhat clouded in consequence   Told M in the evening abt Billy's saying she is jealous
of Mabel Charles – She is angry of course – declares
she will have nothing to do with him etc all of which I say is
ridiculous   I tell her to speak to him about the reports which
concern them both and stop there – Did not say anything of what
Mrs Machell told me of his doings –
30th   Mary spent the day with Mrs Machell   went out driving
with her – coming home met Billy – and spoke about his talking of
her supposed jealousy – He asked how she had heard of it – To keep
her promise of secrecy to Mrs Machell, she said I had told her – He
said 'I had no business to do so' – and was not appeased   When
she remarked that she 'did not agree with him and thought I had
every right to do so and she was glad I had – etc.' After squabbling for
some time he said – 'She did not care for him a bit' – 'Other people
say' was her answer, 'that I care for you so much that I am apt to forget what is due to myself'   'But you do *not* care a bit' he persisted
– 'I am told' she said again 'that I am being pitied for liking you so
much better than you do me' and I do not choose to become public
talk in this way – 'Oh very well' he said and went off in a huff – He is
very angry with me of course and thinks I am a horrid sneak a 'med-
dlesome Mabby' and every thing else detestable – I cannot help it –
he must not talk of Mary in that way if he wishes to be friendly with
me – Mr Cran after dinner – a most *horribly* slow evening –
31st   [Susan here begins writing in a handmade book of blue
paper tied with a string at the top and labelled on the cover *Diary
November 1878*.] Mama busy in the garden – Capt Layton in the
evening – gt fun chaffing abt the early dinner on Sat:

November 1878

Sarah

2nd   Sa   Mary & self dined at the Joe Pembertons – in the afternoon

4th   M   called on the Forsters at Driard House

5th   Tu   Din[ner] 12 – Had Dinner party for the Forsters & Sir
M. B. Begbie   12 after dinner   Mrs Sullivan cook. Mrs Winter waitress

6th   W   Admirable lecture   Dean Mason on Dickens's works –

7th   Th   Henry, self, Mary & Babs went to nice little dance at
the Wards

8th   F   Mr Rhodes died   Mrs Forster came to lunch & spent
quiet afternoon with me alone

11th   M   Mr Rhodes buried

13th   W   The 'Turquoise' gave theatrical entertainment at Theatre for Hospital – B.B. Farce, very good. B. Boyle made lovely girl

14th   Th   Mr. alias Bishop Cridges lecture on Nature well
attended – carefully studied but unsatisfactory

18th   M   Mary dined at the Marvins – Tremendous dinner
5 hours – Charlie Brodies farewell

20th   W   [Read?] Mr Cridge's lecture on 'Nature'

22nd   F   Made calls – Mrs J. Pemberton & Mrs Richards – Mrs
Fellows

25th   M   Made calls   Mrs Rhodes – Jenns.

26th – 30th   [crosswise:] Victoria Assizes   dear Henry on Bench

26th   Tu   Made calls   Mrs Roscoe – Johnston –

28th   Th   Choral Club – went into town with Zef. after music
lesson –

29th   F   Dear Henry not out of court till near midnight – Capt
Layton with us on his return –

30th   Sa   Self 52 years old today – & what can I say for myself!!   Alas! Alas! that I should be such a Xtian dwarf – Wrote
10 Xmas letters with cards

Susan

1st   Mama gardening – Barbara went to Govt House in the afternoon and found Mrs Beaven and Lettie there –

2nd Early dinner at Mr Joe Pembertons   guests Mr and Mrs

Mogg, Mrs [?] Wards and Macdonalds – Capt Layton, Mama and
Mary. invitations for —— past 2 – dinner announced at —— to 3.
Table and dishes without any ornaments whatever – menu
most extraordinary   three dishes of chickens – enormous
joints – inskewered tongue do [ditto] apple pie enough for fifty
etc   Everybody intensely bored –
3rd   Papa and Mama went to Esquimalt to be present at the chris-
tening of one of Mr Pooleys children. Papa godfather. After the
Service they went to lunch with the Fishers   We persuaded the
Machells to stay to lunch with us – After school went to Mrs
Machells & there met Mrs Forster, who seems very nice. Billy came
in to tea. he and I most distant!
4th Thick foggy day – Very tired after Monday work. Mama went to
call on Mrs Forster at Mrs Machells request. also to ask people to
come after dinner tomorrow – Mary out all the morning on
Kitty   I took her immediately after lunch and engaged Margaret
Winter to wait, also got flowers from Johnstons – (very poor) –
Mabel Charles and Billy came –
5th   *Dinner for the Forsters* – guests – Mrs Forster (Mr F declined
on score of no clothes & illness) Mrs Charles & Mabel (Mr
C[unclear]) Sir Matt: Begbie, Mr Bruce, the Dean & Mrs Mason
Capt Layton &   After dinner Billy came in looking like a suffering martyr – the Machells Mr Wake (in evening dress) Florry &
Mabel Gray – Mr Eberts – Mary Mason   considering the enormous preponderance of the womenkind – it went off pretty well –
singing first – then dancing. Mrs Mason and Mrs Machell *very* kind
in playing
6th   Very tired and stiff. have caught cold I think. Mama in her
room all day – Lettie came to see me. went with her to see Mrs
Croasdaile & to Johnstons nursery to find out the name of a
flower   All but self went to hear Mr Mason lecture on Dickens
works and came home at 11 o'clock delighted –
7th   *Dance at Homewood* – Had such a bad cold I could not go. all
the others but Zeffie went and enjoyed it *immensely*. Mr Keith
showed Mama a good deal of attention – the assurance of the man!

Did not come home till —— past 3 in the morning   amused
myself during their absence by practising accompaniment and
doing lace work – [written crosswise next to and over entry:] Had
to refuse a drive with Mrs Machell & ride with the Croasdailes &
Grays   Recd a nice letter from Mrs Robinson
8th   Mrs Forster came to lunch – I went for short ride with Mrs
Croasdaile – *Mr Rhodes died*   Mama, Mary and Barbara went to
church – Capt Layton came in evening   Played Backgammon
with him – Papa kept us on the [gui reve?] by going to sleep and
suddenly waking up – [written crosswise next to entry:] Had grand
scene with Mama abt Mrs R's letter
9th   Second day of Mary's senior class   Mrs Pope & Emma
Newton Barbara & Mary went to town in morning – Billy came
into lunch. rode with Mary after & they lost themselves near Prospect Lake and did not come in till past six. Billy stayed to dinner –
etc – he is most rude to me. I shall not stand it. Did not go down
after dinner as I do not wish to have a scene before all the family –
Barbara went to lunch and for ride with Mrs Croasdaile
10th   Answered Mrs Robinson's letter   Billy and Mrs Machell
walked home with us. Billy and I did not speak at dinner – sat side
by side – he would not have brussels sprouts because I helped it. I
would take nothing he passed   At the afternoon Service a child
was immersed by Mr Mogg instead of being sprinkled at its Baptism
– the first time I ever saw it done – Billy came home with them to
tea at which mention was made of our impending row with Mr
Mogg for the belief he expressed in his sermon this morning on the
efficacy of prayers for the dead –
11th   *Mr Rhodes buried* – Papa and Mama went to St Johns church
– a large crowd followed to the cemetary but by his (Mr R's) particular wish neither the Odd Fellows nor Free Masons (of both which
companies he was a member) made any demonstration on the
occasion – Billy came in morning with a message from Mrs Richards – Mrs Machell with Mary – Charley Brodie called and stayed
to lunch – Mrs Croasdaile asked me to go to lunch and for drive
after – Mama would not let me on account of my detestable cold

12th   Mama in bed all the morning   Mrs Machell asked me
to drive with her. had to decline for same reason as yesterday –
Mama drove with Mrs Richards   Capt Layton in the
evening   We all went into the Dining room and *endured*
the hours!
13th   Mary drove with Mrs Machell in morning –
14th   Mary went to town at 9 a.m. met Billy at Mrs M's and went
to town with him to see about his acting 'get up' – did some visiting also [written crosswise next to entry:] Papa and Mary went to
Choral meeting
15th   Took Kitty and rode to Stadacona to take Clara some
'Harper's' – Met Mr & Mrs Croasdaile and rode with them – Went
to lunch with them – came home about 3 o'clock – had scolding –
and went into drawing room to make myself agreeable to Mrs Bob
Ward & later to Alice Wright – Barbara went to dinner at Govt
House. The Captains of the Turquoise & Osprey there. also the
Hetts – Mrs Richards never asks me when they are there   I
wonder if I did not behave well the last time we were together –
Ch: Brodie & Mr Roper called the former to say goodbye –
16th   Two little Robertsons came to play with Arthur – *dreadful*
little fellow the younger is! –
17th   *Sunday* – I had such a bad cold I had to stay at home all day
– Stormy – Mary stayed with Mrs Machell and took my class at the
Sunday School – no Billy –
18th   My Birthday – Wet & showery – Dear Father & Mother
gave me black Lynx set – muff & boa & Papa a clever letter with it
– Barbara a vest pktchf   Mary a drawing block – Zeffie, a piece
of frilling, and Aunt Emily a knitted [unclear] – very nice – Billy
came in to dinner & to dress for rehearsal – Mary and Mama
helped him – he scarcely spoke to me & I was equally silent –
19th   Nothing –
20th   Very wet. Mrs Machell came up intending to drive but
could not on acct. of the rain – fuss about the horse – Billy – dear
fellow! Came to dinner and after, dressed for theatricals   acted
as Dorothey – maid at inn – in 'B.B.' a farce – Everyone said he

looked *very* well and did his part equally so. That piece went off *beautifully* – but the sailor's just before, was very coarse – All but Barbara went to see it. We all drove in Winter's carriage with Billy – A full house notwithstanding the rain – Charley Brodie left in the 'Alaska' for England –

21st   *Mr Cridge's lecture.* All but self went to hear it – Mr Cran came just after they left – had to entertain him till 10 o'clock till they returned – talked of improvement of talents – want of energy etc. ungentlemanly occupations for young gentlemen etc. Played Backgammon. Draughts

22nd   Went to lunch at Govt House   Lettie there – stayed to dinner – Capt Robinson and Dr Ash there also – Capt Robinson & self stayed the night – Lidy & Jenny Munro went to Mr Drakes to a children's party – spent one of the pleasantest days I have had for a long time

23rd   *Barbara's Birthday* – Mama gave her a gold brooch with turquoises – Papa, a new umbrella   Mary, a piece of patent lace   I, three pocketkchfs marked with B   Came home from Govt Ho in the morning   Football at Beacon Hill – Barbara drove with Mrs Machell   Mary rode with Mr Dudding & Billy – They both came in on their return & Billy spoke to me most bitterly about telling Mary of his calling her jealous – said I had been dishonest abt it – 'thought the end justified the means' – that I laughed when he said that – (abt the jealousy) & so made him believe I half agreed with him – would never trust me again etc etc   Certainly he has more reason on his side than I had before thought – I cannot exculpate myself without telling him of all Mrs Machell said and that she has made me promise not to do – as her husband told her in confidence – Florry & Connie Jones came to stay with us till Monday – Lidy spent the day with Zeffie – Arthur with Maggie – Mr Richards in the evening –

24th   *Sunday.* No one but the children at lunch – Quite alone at tea – Felt very blue all day – Thought over my quarrel with Billy during Service and came to the conclusion that in the main I could not have done otherwise – but had given him cause to despise me

for my weakness in not telling him at the time, of my true thoughts
about wht he said of Mary – Felt worse than ever how almost
impossible it is to live as a Christian should – I do not wish for a
long life – is it wicked I wonder to think such things?
25th   Did Monday work as usual – *very* tired – Mrs Machell asked
me to lunch and to drive with her. Mama made no objection,
so went. Came home at 4 p.m. At dinner Mama scolded me for
doing so & said many hard things both to, and of, me – (this at
dinner)   Mary fought valiantly for me – After we three went to
the workroom & there I exploded. Mary agreed – got excited then
went into hysterics – Mr Nedham after dinner   Barbara and I
went down – a most dismal evening.
26th   Barbara drove with Mrs Machell in morning. *Skating Club
started again*
27th   Spent a very pleasant day with Mrs Ward. Mary went to
Highwood to dinner. Mr and Mrs Fellows, Miss Martineau, Mr &
Mrs Thomson – Mr C Jones there also – *perfectly* informal. Left
about 11 o'clock
28th   At home all day. In the evening went with dear Padre &
Mary to Choral practise in room over Bagnall's music shop. about
50 members present.
29th   At home all day. Barbara drove with Mrs Machell in morning. went to town in afternoon – Billy came to lunch. did not see
him – Mary went to dinner at Govt House   Capt Layton in the
evening – Papa did not come home from Supreme Court till nearly
midnight   Cut out new serge suit for Arthur.
30th   *Dearest Mother's Birthday* – Mary gave her a handscreen of
her own painting – buff ground with wreath of forgetmenots – Barbara Letter tray – Zeffie card – Papa, a cheque for several $ – I did
not give her anything, or even wish her 'Many happy returns of the
Day' I *could* not – I thought she would thank me, and perhaps kiss
me, because she felt she ought to, and not because anything I did
could give her pleasure – It is most *miserable* feeling like this – Try
to think it all my fault – but want of sympathy & then my whole
heart rises in rebellion at the thought & I say 'she is so unjust' 'She

does not care for me' She never can *really*. I will not trouble her to
put on the appearance of affection – It was always so – always will
be I suppose – I am twenty three now, & I cannot remember a single day on which she seemed to care for me as much as Barbara or
Mary – [written crosswise next to entry:] Went to town for Mama –
to see Lettie, for myself – told her some of my home troubles. Did
not blame Mama

> Sadly, drearily, hopelessly
> Passes this life for me
> Can it indeed be possible
> I am but twenty-three?
>
> Conscience whispereth loudly
> Art not thou to blame?
> Think – if *thou* wer't not so proud, girl
> Would it be *quite* the same?
>
> 'I know it is wrong' I answer
> Sweet Spirit help thou me
> But I feel so *very* wicked
> Can *this* be forgiven me
>
> 'List!' Though thy sins be as scarlet
> They shall be white as snow
> Child! Twas a faithful promise
> Given many years ago'   SRC

December 1878

Sarah

1st   S   Pouring Rain till eveg. Went to St John's with Henry &
recd Holy Com. In eveg. Henry went to Cathedral   1st time for
18 months   Mr Mason gave a most pleasing impressive sermon
on the Prodigal Son.

4th   W   Mr Mogg's lecture on *Water*
9th   M   Hoy got a boy ('Wen') to help him in the kitchen –
wages the same $25 pr. month
12th   Th   Choral Club –
18th   W   Archdeacon Wright's lecture on Cyprus – very good –
but not well attended –
20th   F   Angela College breaks up for the holidays   Mr
Roscoe committed suicide (a Unitarian)
22nd   S   Mr Roscoe buried by Revd P. Jenns of St John's
ch.   attended with military honors –
25th   W   a large party at dinner – & a merry eveg – with charade
– music – singing & dancing
30th   M   Dean Mason's lecture for Sund. Sch. – 'Hamlet' – most
beautiful & excellent

Susan

1st   *Sunday* – A pleasant day though pouring with rain. Billy
walked home with Mary and Barbara. I went to the Parsonage. Mr
& Mrs Mogg so *very* kind to me   Billy & Mr Wake came to tea
– Papa went to the Cathedral in eveg!
2nd   Our first rehearsal of 'Antecedents' – Mrs Machell: the
young lady, Elizabeth Sinclair – Mary, the Aunt. Capt Layton Mr
Clarendon, Billy, The Lover. William Brown & the same in dis-
guise as Mons: de Fourbes [?] – Barbara, 'Kitty' Dr Cree (Turquoise)
came in the middle and formed, with Capt Machell & Zeffie, the
audience – at home – not very satisfactory –
3rd   Wet – Mary went to town in morning   came home after
lunch – attended to drawing class. then to dressmakers & town
again with Mama – Very busy in eveg: making dresses for children's
theatricals – at Angela College   Papa & Mama went to Govt
House after dinner – at home all day
4th   *Public holiday* – Thanksgiving Day   Papa and Mama went
to Service at the Cathedral – Mama and I gardened after
lunch   Mrs Croasdaile and Dr Cree found us in the garden. The
latter came to say – goodbye – Mrs Machell & Mary went for ride –

exchanged horses – 'Dick' very obstinate and   unmanageable
Mr Mogg's lecture on 'Water'   all but self went to hear
him   Practised till ½ past 10 when they returned
5th   Went to town in morning. Took Arthur who was very troublesome – and Mrs O'Reilly who asked me to stay with her till Monday. Thanked her, but said it was impossible – 2nd Rehearsal
in aft: Billy frightfully cross with me – Mr Dudding came to say
goodbye. very lame from an accident – Papa went to Gentleman's
dinner at Homewood – Capt Layton after dinner –
6th   Mama Mary & Barbara went to church & stayed to practise
as usual
7th   Mary, Zeffie, Billy & Capt Machell went for short ride – Barbara to town in the morning –
8th   *Sunday* – stormy – alone at dinner   Edgar Marvin, Mrs
Machell & Capt Layton in aft: – Billy and Mr Dudding came to tea
– Papa & Mr Dudding had a long talk abt Greek etc. Papa much
impressed with him   Billy and I had a gt sparring – he declared
before everyone that he didn't mind some people's laughing at him
but he did *hate* me to do so. He thinks me such an inferior being I
suppose –
9th   At home – Mama & Mary called on Mrs. Marvin after
drawing
11th   Mrs. Machell & Mary rode in the morning   Kitty &
Davie Keyser: – private rehearsal in the afternoon – Barbara rode
Darcie in aft: Mary dined at Highwood. Mama & I went to
Sunday School meeting   Mr. Cran in eveg –
10th[9]   Vestry meeting – Mama out all day – Mary went to meeting after drawing – Barbara to [unclear]   Lettie came to see me.
Walked down with her. went to meet Mary. Capt Layton after
dinner.
12th   Took Kitty and rode into town, then to all the nurseries I
knew of to bespeak flowers for Xmas Decorations – none to be had.
Went to Lettie for lunch – there Kitty slipped out of her bridle –
lost the bit three times during the day –

Dec 15th 1878. *Sunday*   Went to church in the morning
Mr. Mason preached a sermon on besetting sins which raised many
doubts in me and made me very unhappy – going to S.S. it
occurred to me to ask him abt it – So went to the College but
found he was at Metchosin – Mrs. Mason seeing my distress tried to
make me wait to see him after school – told her I *could* not – she
then advised me to write – which I did when I got home – thus

Dear Mr. Mason
May I ask you a question or two which I cannot answer for myself?

You said in your sermon this morning that *everyone* has a *besetting sin* and also that unless that sin is truly repented of – no sacra-
ments, no services are of avail to purify our hearts – You said did
you not that many are not aware that they *have* a besetting sin –
that it required much thought and self-inspection to find it –
What I want to ask you is the very question you suggested in your
sermon – How am I to know what is a besetting sin?

The more carefully I examine myself the more I find how little
goodness there is in me but no *one* sin seems to stand out more
prominently than many others –

I know well that others see faults in us which we do not see in
ourselves – but I also know my motives have often been misjudged
by those who know me well – and I do not doubt that I am equally
ready to misjudge others – how then could I believe anyone who
might tell me such & such a thing is your besetting sin – if I did not
feel in my inmost soul that they were right – And yet if I cannot
answer this thing to myself must I never come to the Holy Communion

I *do* enjoy the church & Services especially the Prayers and
Psalms – and often something in them has comforted me in per-
plexities & troubles more that I can say – Can it have been a false
peace I have enjoyed?

These are no new thoughts though awakened by your sermon of
today but this is the first time I have ventured to put them into

words & I thought that as you knew the difficulty you would know the remedy.

I feel just like a child always *questioning* never *knowing* what is right and what is wrong.

Pardon me if I am troubling you with these difficulties of mine – Mrs. Mason assured me when I saw her this afternoon that you would kindly answer me if I wrote to you therefore I have done so – Yours very truly

Susan R. Crease

This is not a faithful copy only the substance of what I wrote

Dec 16th   Zeffie took my note to school and delivered it to Mr. Mason – not without many remarks about it beforehand

17th   Mr. Mason sent me a most kind and satisfactory answer to my letter – urging me to a more regular nightly self-examination – Oh! I will try. I will try – He lent me Goulburn's 'Thoughts on Personal Religion'

21st   Mary very busy painting panels for Rood screen – Barbara cooking   Mama out with the chinaman taking bottles of cordial to friends

20th   Mr. Roscoe in an insane moment committed suicide by shooting himself. Mrs. Fellows very kind to his family who are in great grief – Breaking up party Angela College in the afternoon   Everyone much depressed in consequence of this disaster – Mr. Mason's voice almost inaudible –

22nd   Billy at tea –

23rd   All *very* busy with Ch: decorations at the Collegiate-School nearly all day. Mrs. Machell came to dinner and went down with us to school after – Mr. Wake saw us home – Last Rehearsal of 'Antecedents'

24th   Same as yesterday as to decorations but chiefly in the church – Mr. Offerhaus very good natured in helping – Mrs. Charles and Mabel did the pulpit (Did not go to bed till 2 am)

25th   *Xmas Day*   All went to church in the morning –

Mary to the early service – Barbara and I stayed after morning
service   *Very* solemn and impressive   Mrs. Moggs second
child born (a girl)   *Dinner guests –*
3 Machells   2 Boyles
3 Duponts   7 Selves
2 Croasdailes –
1 Eberts
1 Layton   18 in all –

After dinner Charades. Went off splendidly, so they say
Singing, dancing, and supper filled up the time till 2 a.m. when
they all departed – Recd. Such a number of Xmas cards for the first
time   Billy gave us all something – Mama and Mary blue velvet
picture frames – Barbara ink bottle – Papa letter weight – Zeffie –
box – Arthur book, me 2 pictures –   Lettie gave me a nice likeness of herself & a Xmas card, and a very loving note with them –
Mary gave Billy a gold signet ring with bloodstone – and three *very*
good sketches of Govt House –
      My darling Mother and I made a tacit peace with each other –
Goodbye Old year! Well ended for me and I trust not less well
for my dear ones at home and those far away

NOTES

Sara Crease Diary, British Columbia Archives and Records Service
(BCARS), AEC86 C861; Susan Crease Diary, BCARS, AEC86
C864.

1 See Barbara Powell, 'The Diaries of the Crease Family Women,' *BC
  Studies* nos. 105–6 (1995): 45–58, for a discussion of the 'spaces' in the
  diaries, especially the spaces between mother and daughters and the
  silent spaces of untold stories.
2 For an account of the Crease family papers, see Christina B. Johnson-
  Dean, *The Crease Family Archives: A Record of Settlement and Service in*

British Columbia (Victoria: Provincial Archives of British Columbia 1981).

3 See Kathryn Bridge, *Henry and Self: The Private Life of Sarah Crease, 1826–1922* (Victoria: Sono Nis Press, 1996) for a discussion of the financial difficulties in the early years of the marriage of Henry and Sarah Crease.

4 Appearing in Sunday entries the names Mogg and Mason refer to who preached the sermon.

5 In 1878 the British Columbia Provincial Legislature passed an act to regulate 'the evils of Chinese labour,' which resulted in the imposition of an annual tax of forty dollars on each Chinese male (Victoria *Colonist*, 19 September 1878, 3). The resulting strike meant that 250 situations were vacant in Victoria, and women like the Creases became responsible for their own housework and cooking.

6 Yip is the family's Chinese servant.

7 The Bank of British Columbia.

8 Pocket handkerchiefs.

9 Susan reverses the days, writing the 11th before the 10th. No explanation is given for the error, which occurs again later in the diary.

Constance Kerr Sissons
(1875–1973)

ROSALIND KERR

My maternal grandmother, Constance Kerr Sissons, practised the gentlewomanly art of domestic journal keeping from the early 1900s until shortly before her death three-quarters of a century later.[1] In the heavily coded, impersonal Victorian style that her mother taught her, she set out to create a private record of her family's affairs – including records itemizing household expenses, shopping lists, types of gifts received and sent, and, lengthiest of all, letters sent and received. The meticulous accounts of such 'trivial' matters offer a testimony to just how seriously she believed in performing her duties – as young teacher, bride, and mother-to-be. Entries from the first years of this century are full of the minutiae of everyday life; they leave the impression that her sense of self depended on paying close attention to taking care of the demands that filled her busy life. She described everything from the weather to household chores, teaching, sewing, reading, biking, and socializing. When she moved from civilized Ottawa to wild northern Ontario, the diary served her well by providing a record of her past experiences, and thereby offered a chance to reflect on questions about who she had become.

Kerr Sissons's journals include observations that help us penetrate her thick shield of propriety, but these are never too obvious. Conventions established several centuries earlier, at the beginning of early modern culture, when women took up the literary subgenre of journal writing, required that this private form of record keeping remain non-threatening to masculine dominance in major literary forms.[2] As a result, when female journal-keepers stray into the larger world of public events, they generally confine themselves to descriptions of their families' involvement. This is certainly the case with Kerr Sissons. She filters her record of national and world events through her own response – the Ottawa fire and the help she gave to its victims, the Boer War and her cheering the brave troops on, and the arrival of the railway and its impact on her life.

Expected to enhance the public reputation of the family of the writer, women's journals were supposed to censor scandalous family secrets. Because the records aimed at objectivity, expressions of strong personal feeling were avoided by such practices as the infrequent use of the pronoun 'I.' Deep unhappiness of any kind, financial embarrassments, bankruptcy, marital strife, adulteries, and misfortunes had to be glossed over so as not to allow any whisper of scandal to sully the family's reputation. Kerr Sissons maintained the required silence by keeping her journals relatively 'objective' and only occasionally letting a strong opinion or emotion slip out.[3] As such, they were safe enough to keep and to pass down to her daughters and granddaughters, unlike her voluminous correspondence, which had to be burned (including over seventeen hundred letters to her fiancé Henry Sissons). However, Kerr Sissons's journals do have secrets to tell. Sometime after my grandmother's death I was handed an unpublished manuscript of a novel that she had written about her experiences as a young bride in Fort Frances. Entitled 'Law in a Lean-to: Pioneer Days on the Rainy,' it is a curious mixture of autobiographical material drawn largely from the journals, and fictional characters she has invented to tell a story she could not name as her own. My research into the intertextual relations between the novel, the journals, and historical events occurring both in Fort Frances and across Canada has led me to believe that, by reading between the lines of the journals and through their marginalia, gaps, silences, apologies, ripped out pages, one can uncover an unsettling and sad story.[4] Diary entries reveal that Kerr Sissons saw herself as a dutiful imperial daughter whose main purpose in life was to marry and produce heirs to civilize 'empty' Canadian spaces. The excerpt here begins with exuberant entries anticipating her wedding on 25 September 1901, a time when she was still earning her living and enjoying a rich and varied social life among girl friends and loving family members; however, her engaged status acts as a counterweight – evident in the constant pull of letter writing to Harry as they negotiate their wedding arrangements. Once the flurry of preparations is over and married life is beginning, entries seem less enthusiastic. The increasingly mechanical nature of the entries as she plunges ever deeper into a domestic mode testifies to her acceptance of social roles in the name of respectability and motherhood. Her first daughter, Muriel Helena, arrived on 12 January 1903, and she describes it in the following entry: 'In bed all day. Dr. here after lunch. Had good night but much pain in morning also in middle of afternoon. Tried to read volume of short stories by W. D. Howells. Very ill about 6:30. Muriel came about 11.P.M. Dr. & Miss Buchanan there.' In some ways, this event – the successful entry of a white child into the world – represents Kerr Sissons's vindication of herself as a woman who had done her duty to her less-than-perfect partner.

Readers will discern in her journal the enormous adjustment she is required to make once she is married. What may be less easy to gather is why she reached a point on her twenty-sixth birthday, 5 November 1901, where she confessed to some unhappiness: 'it has been a lonely evening for my birthday. Harry went to a meeting and now is playing cards – He got me some candy.' More baffling, the 6 November heading which follows is blank, as is the rest of the year, except for a few empty pages which have obviously been torn in half. When she resumes her entries at the beginning of a new book, another change has taken place: she apologizes for not keeping up with the journal, possibly an admission that she is forcing

herself to carry on. Pencilled-in marginalia, added in 1942, tells us
that something had gone gravely wrong during the rest of that year,
including a miscarriage on 4 December. Her reticence in announc-
ing such a fact could be dismissed as Victorian modesty, but cou-
pled with her veiled expressions of discontent, and many other
clues gathered by me from her autofiction, I believe that she may
have miscarried when she discovered that Harry had filled in those
long, lonely years from 1898 by entering into a 'country-wife' relationship with a young Metis woman who was still living in town –
who may indeed have been the Mrs MacDonald slated to clean
windows, as mentioned in the entry of 9 May.[5] After Harry's
drowning seven years later in a reckless boating accident, Kerr
Sissons would wait years before she let some of her rage and
despair surface in 'Law in a Lean-to ...' Knowing how much the
journals are not telling us makes what they are telling us even more
significant.[6]

The diaries of 1901 are written in brown notepads. One is called
a 'Collegiate Notebook' with an a 8½-by-4-inch format; the other
is a 'Library notebook' with a picture of a library building on the
cover. Both of these covers have now come loose. The rest of the
diaries for that year are black record books with blue lines. They
measured 6.5 by 4 inches and were so thin that she needed three
to record a full year. She continued to write her diary until the
1960s.

CKS, as she liked to be known, had an active life and kept up
with family and friends. She lived to be ninety-seven, remaining
alert up until the last year. I sat with her in her last days and talked
about the past. She brought out locks of hair, one from Harry, one
from her, cut when they were about to be married. He had warned
her that he would die young and admonished her to remain faithful
to him after death. On the day he drowned, 14 September 1908,
she remembered how the telephone lines to her house had been
cut, and no one could call her to tell her the bad news. The women
at her house that day making bread kept whispering behind her
back, but she did not know what they were saying. She recalled

clearly the minister coming up the hill to tell her about the accident. For ever after, our family lived in the shadow of his death in the Rainy River whirlpool. My grandmother, widowed at thirty-three, moved to Toronto to raise her little girls, my aunt Muriel and mother Sheila.

Constance Kerr Sissons, 1898.

DIARY, ONTARIO, JULY 1901–JUNE 1902

1901: Diary – Constance Kerr 56 Gilmour St.

Thursday, July 18th
Letter from Harry asking news about Wedding. Mamma got one
from him too. Went out on errands. Cut out skirt, (navy blue
serge.) Ray came for his lesson. We both did sweet peas in a vase
(crayon)   He and 'Bob'[7] and I went through the new houses.
Evening called at Annie Johnson's. She has been sick.

Friday, July 19th
Cooler! There is quite a murder mystery on just now, a girl whose
body was found in the river – I cut out the rest of the skirt, basted
and fitted it. Afternoon went over and paid Miss Traveller, forgot
to say that she sent the dress and I tried it on last night. Also forgot
to say that I closed my account at the Savings Bank yesterday.

Friday, August 2nd
Kirks Ferry. A great deal to do to get off, pack and leave house
tolerably neat. Bea and I – out. I had to do things in such a hurry,
forgot jacket. Mamma took train. Got note from Margaret asking
what she could bring me, wrote card and said shoes. Card to Harry.
Left about four, arrived just a few minutes after Mamma at 'Temperance House.' Had a short ride, tea, a ramble, then there was a
big bonfire.

Friday, August 16th
Margaret left by the 11 o'clock train. I saw her off. We paid a short
call on Mrs. Walkley first, and on the way to the station M. bought
a lot of lovely flowers for Mamma, mauve sweet peas, mignonette,
asters and gladioli. I swept our room and moved things back –
Mother is very anxious about Maidie who is sick and low spirited.
It is decided that Mother will go to Toronto for the Winter. Aunty
Ray's and Mary's present came ($25)   Samples of lovely fur and
a note came from Paul for the cape Maidie and he are giving me.
Mrs. Walkley called in evening. Mr. – for rent. I finished letter to
Frank and wrote a long one to Harry.

Thursday, August 22nd
Went over to Bea's – she has consented to be bridesmaid. We talked over plans, took blouse to Mattie's, bicycle to have puncture mended, etc. Got felt shoes, corsets, lace. Bea came over in afternoon. We sewed. Sew. Sew. Sew.

Friday, August 23rd
Mamma and I went out and changed silk. Ray came for drawing lesson.[8] Rainy and quite impossible to wheel to the Ridgeways.' Mamma was asked to wheel to Hog's Back to tea but of course could not go. I am so glad Mamma will have a handsome dress now – $2.00 a yard – It is very pretty with a moiré stripe. Got bicycle. Got laundry also, and paid ridiculous price for some skirts.

Tuesday, August 27th
Did almost all ironing, Gave Ray a lesson at same time. He drew in crayon potatoes, knife and bowl. It was not hot in kitchen, I used charcoal iron. Called at Miss Traveller's gave order for wedding-dress. Decided to get white china silk with taffeta finish, and have gold spangled net – Very pretty. Sent card to Frank offering to send copy of 'Elizabeth and her German Garden' which I bought. Ev'g sewing. At my bathrobe now. It is green and pink. Letter from Harry.

Saturday, August 31st
Finished the bath-robe. Fitted waist of navy-blue suit. Went to Miss Ryan's was fitted for travelling-gown. Evening altered pretty shirt waist Margaret gave me, turning in neck, and making fancy tie of muslin, beading, lace, and black velvet baby ribbon. Got slippers (tan kid) for Harry to-day. Fitted at Miss Traveller's. Sent book to Frank. Maidie is very sick with inflammation of breast. Better now. Note from Frank. Better.

Tuesday, September 3rd
School opens to-day, but I am not there. Miss Dwinnell here till 5 P.M. She is a hustler. The girls' dresses are done. Daisy came to be

fitted. There is a little more finishing to the waists. Miss D. also cut
out fichus, half made one, and helped me fit my Eton jacket.
Evening Mamma and I took a lovely walk accompanied by 'Bob'
out the Archvale Road along Canal. I finished my fancy white tie.
Took a short nap in evening, did some machining,[9] drying of
dishes. Mr. Walkley's anti-imperialistic speech at Boston is still
exciting a great deal of comment. Daisy is now helping in a Kinder-
garten (First Av. School) pro tem.

Friday, September 6th
Very warm. Morning swept kitchen. Finished D's fichu, and made
hair-bows for both and a pointed belt with long streamers for D.
Afternoon. Shopped with Minnie, Got Marjorie's dress. White
divinity over yellow, with yellow satin ties. Also changed dirty
white gloves, inquired at C.P.R. am afraid Annie cannot get cheap
rates – Gave notice at Electric Light Co. of expiration of lease.
Ordered two of panel pictures from Topley. He asked me to be
taken again, (in wedding gown). Came home found Miss L. Ridgeway here. Her Sister could not come. Had tea of tomatoes, tongue
and peaches and cake. She left early to wheel home. I put lace in
girls' things evening. (After dishwashing) also nearly finished
Annie's belt and streamers.

Saturday, September 7th
Such a queer day, warm and close in morning, and a cold dust
storm all evening. Pres. McKinley was assassinated yesterday. It is
not known whether he will live or not. My tire burst again to-day. I
think I will sell my wheel for what I can get for it. I finished
Annie's belt etc. Made out bills for girls, neither amounted to quite
$6.00. Went uptown with Mother. Chose bridesmaid pins for
Harry. Got wedding gloves, two wrappers etc. Also took K.D. doll
over to Mrs. Gibson's said Goodbye to her. Mrs. Bott will make my
winter wrapper. It is red cashmere. Evg made Mamma's fichu. It is
in the cream and maize shades and very pretty. Maidie is better.
Mamma heard from Aunt Eleanor, Frank still very poorly. I don't

know how I came to forget to say that yesterday evening Ray came over with a lovely present from Mattie and Jack, a soft pink umbrella shawl and $10 in gold!

Tuesday, September 10th
At breakfast got registered letter from Harry with Accident Policy for $2000 and another note from him. Mamma got a letter from Aunt Bell. Ironed all morning. Presents came from Vancouver. Card received from Aunt Bell, little Chinese pins from Norah, a lovely Japanese silk parasol from Garda, a white silk tie from Hazel, and a dozen silver coffee-spoons from Mr. Cotton (Freda's young man). Afternoon Mr. Bryce and Maud called. He is installing her at the Pres – Ladies College here. They visited Toronto and the Pan-American[10] on the way from Winnipeg. I went on with navy blue dress   finished skirt, and partly finished jacket. Mattie and Ida called in evening. Ida is to have an operation performed on her ears by Dr. Courtenay next Saturday morning at St. Luke's. Wrote notes to Daisy Lil and Harry. Mamma heard from Mr. Harper. He will soon be home. The president is quite recovering. I was ill in evening and had to go to bed early with splitting head-ache.

– Friday, September 13th
Up-town twice to-day. Had wedding-dress tried on – Ordered picture for Harry's present. Got trunk etc. Mamma helped me choose picture, it is a lovely Corot. They mount Corots in such pretty shades of brown. Called at Mattie's afternoon. She will come to Topley's with me. Ev'g – Mrs. and Gertie Blanchet called in evening. I wrote notes to Aunt Bell, Mr. Cotton, Margaret, Lillian, Mrs. McGill, Card to Aunt Martha. Ida Brown had operation performed to-day, she was back at Mattie's but looked very tired. The President took a turn for the worse.

Saturday, September 14th
The President died about 2.A.M. All the flags are half masted. If

the mob could get hold of Czolgosz there is no saying what would happen to him. Buffalo's great Pan-American has a terrible blot on it. Shopped in morning, got fitted for silk waist, bought a pretty Persian flannel blouse. After dinner went on with planning, counted up expenses. Wrote note to Miss Waddell inviting her to wedding. Made navy-blue silk pompon trimmed with gold braid to furbish up my hat and make it match suit. Evening Mr. Harper called   [Inserted later as long marginalia running up side of page:] If 'Bert' and I had known Harry was to die exactly 7 years later and he (BH) had only (not quite) 12 weeks to live! I entirely finished coat. Got handkerchief, corset cover and chatelaine from Margaret, also tea cosey in white embroidered with violets from Gertie Blanchet.

– ~~Monday~~ Tuesday, September 24th
Harry came in morning. We went up-town. I got hair shampoo – then went to see Duke in procession going past; then I went and got fitted. paid Miss Ryan's bill. Aft Looked at presents Harry came – He and Annie and I went out – called at Mattie's. came here to tea. More presents. Harry brought $100 in gold from his father. Note from Helen. Crumb tray in silver from Minerva and Fred tea-cosey from Miss Webster who called, brush and comb from Daisy and Claire, sugar spoon and gravy ladle from Mrs. Baxter, cushion from Miss Potter. Ev'g – Harry and I went for stroll. Lovely moon-light. Uncle Will, Bea, Mr. Harper called –

– Wednesday, September 25th
Harry and I went out – Got bridesmaid pins etc. Went to station. His grip had not come. Later went to Mattie's. She measured us – I was 5 ft 4″ and Harry 5 ft 7″ in our stocking feet. Home to dinner – Note from Margaret. ~ Afternoon went in packing, laying out wed-ding things etc. Everything came- (I am writing this long after.) The girls all looked lovely. The bouquets were Uncle John's present excepting mine. Wedding cake was a pretty one. The man who drove Mother to Church in Quebec to be married (old Mr.

Buckley) drove Harry and me home. Dr. Glashan was quite in his element at the wedding. Several people went down to see us off, the Shakespeare girls and all our own party. We had a most luxurious state room. [Newspaper clippings describing the wedding are placed at this page.]

– Thursday, September 26th
Breakfast at ~~Russell~~ the Queen's. Went up to Maidie's, saw Baby & children wrote notes to Mamma and Mr. Sissons (thanking him). Jean Murray met us just as we were leaving the house. She had come over to see me. gave me a spoon. (Saw Miss Balmer at 12 o'clock, also Mr. Cox, coming down from school). Harry and I went out on King St car – wandered round. Had dinner at Queen's – Evg went to station met Charlie S. Harry had a talk with him. I rec'd a telegram of congratulation from Una who had another son on my Wedding day – also got pretty rose from Ida Parker.

– Friday, September 27th
Annie and Charlie called. Harry and I set off for the Falls. We read on the way over, magazine stories. Just got fruit for lunch. Spent afternoon around the Falls, after taking Gorge Route from Lewiston. Visited Three Sister Islands and went down 'Cave of the Winds.' Then took car to Buffalo. Arrived in time to see a big fire on the corner next our hotel. It was the largest hotel in the world. Shatler's Pan-American Hotel. (Temporary) our room was 1123. Saw illuminations. They were grand. We just walked through Midway and looked at a few mutascopes.[11]

– Saturday, September 28th
Railroad day at Pan.Am. We spent a good while at the Arts Building – also went through U.S. Gov. Building, Manufacturers, Canadian Building, Ordnance etc. Took lunch on grounds. Left late in Afternoon for Falls. Harry went to sleep in St. Car. Then we had some trouble about Hotels. Took tea at the Falls House, did not like it, went to Imperial. Strolled around by Falls – lost my clasps

off chatelaine-bag. Went to theatre – the Bostonians in Robin Hood, the same company I saw last spring in O_____.

– Sunday, September 29th
Got up rather late. Harry bought an umbrella. It was drizzling and windy. Went over to Canadian side and sat in park a while. After ~~dinner~~ lunch at 'Imperial' we read a while, went for a walk at dusk. Had ~~supper~~ dinner- Wrote to Mother and Mattie. Harry wrote to Mother and Bert Harper. We went early to bed.

– Monday, September 30th
Got up at 5.30 or thereabouts. Gorge Route to Lewiston. Got on 'Corona' (again) had breakfast. It had turned very cold. I slept so badly night before. I slept on Corona nearly all the way over. Went up to Maidie's and out to High park taking grapes and crab-apples along, of which we made a lunch. Saw Paul's new house, spoke through speaking-tubes. Took car over to Parlt Bldgs, then down to City Hall. Went up tower. A good day for a view. Bought some things – Up to Maidie's to tea, and they had a delicious one – the dear Baby sat in his high chair next his father. Angela and Hilda were opposite Harry and me. I got them each a little note paper. Mrs. Thompson had left a pretty lace d'oiley for me, her own work I am sure. We had a delightful visit with them all. Evening, Harry and I went to see Blanche Walsh in 'Joan of the Sword-Hand' at the Princess. I enjoyed it ever so much, it was a pretty faithful representation of book. We also enjoyed looking at the people. Went back to Queen's where we had a truly palatial room, a parlor bedroom. Harry read Saturday Night aloud to me. Letter from Mother.

– Tuesday, October 1st
Such a rush to get off. I got my hair shampooed and dressed at Dorenwends.' We bought caps, then I went to Eaton's and bought wool etc. Got a veil, paid for it and left it there. Had no time to run up to 430 to say Goodbye. Rushed down to station, wrote note to Eaton's from Station. After all train did not leave at 1.30. It was

delayed till 2. Harry wired Mr. Mcbush to meet him at Orangeville, but Mr. Mcb did not turn up at station. We got Strand and another magazine. Read – made lunch of bananas. Got to Owen Sd and stepped right off train into steamer 'Alberta.' Got stateroom 37. soon had dinner. Interested in studying fellow passengers. Walked upper deck.

– Wednesday, October 2nd
Pretty Cold. Walked around a good deal. It got very cold. Passed through Sault at a little after noon. Boat began to pitch and toss. About dinner time I was pretty sick. Read novel – of adventure. Took no dinner but Harry did. Walked deck at intervals.

– Thursday, October 3rd
All day on Lake Superior (we had to lie up in night it got so rough). Very Cold. Walked and read at intervals. A little squea-mish all day, but had three meals both of us. Fort William late at night – Hotel Kaministiqua, very tired. Took bath for $.50.

– Friday, October 4th
Spent a little while looking around Fort William. I burned off a piece of hair before going out in A.M. I did not like F.W. Took car to Port Arthur. Had lunch there. Harry did several strokes of busi-ness judging from the time he was away. Saw station and town. Met Mr. Mills, lawyer, and Mr. Marks, also a Mr. Burk. Read in Hotel parlor part of afternoon. Port Arthur has a pretty view – Across Thunder Bay to Sleeping Giant. Took C.P.R. train about 6 or 7. Got dinner, read a little, went to bed. Up at 5.

– Saturday, October 5th
Got up at 5 into Rat Portage at 5.30. Went to Hilliard House, rested a little on sofa. Had breakfast. Took long walk along C.P.R. track to Norman; through tunnel and over bridges – Saw power-dam. There are lovely falls on Winnipeg River. I took a great fancy to Rat Portage. Home, had dinner, wrote long letter to Mother and

Mattie, short ones to Bea, Maud LeSueur and Maidie. Harry
brought over Mr. Bird – Mrs. B could not call, so I went to see her.
Had afternoon tea with her and a Mrs. Earnsly, in her room. Mrs. E.
stays at H. House. Went to Mr. B.'s office for Harry, but he was
gone. Walked around town met Harry. Shopped – back to dinner.
Got a lovely present of silver tray with 'S' on it from Mr. and Mrs.
Bird. Ev'g – Harry brought in Mr. Draper lawyer – and others- Got
boat at 9 P.M. Mr. Bird came over to see us off. Waited a long time
on deck for Keenora to go, but there was some delay. However I
stayed up to see Devil's Gap. Very, very tired. Berth pretty comfortable.

– Sunday, October 6th
All Forenoon on Keenora. Got up in time to see bridge at Beaver
Mills. Met Mr. Horne and several others including Capt. Thorn-
son. Lovely warm day sat on deck and read 'Madness of David
Baring' – talked over school days . Enjoyed watching shore of river.
After dinner we changed to Agwinde for the river was low for
Keenora to finish trip. Read up in Wheel-house of A— Watched
boat going through rapids. Ev'g sat on deck and talked over trip.
State-room stuffy.

– Monday, October 7th
Got to Fort Frances at 4. A.M. Raining, we did not leave boat till
7 A.M. Went up stairs to Hudson's Bay House, avoiding front way.
The 'Angels' had a stove up for us and fire laid. Went to breakfast
at Albertan, met Mrs. Hanning, the Bishops, several friends. It was
too chilly and rainy to be out much but went to Harry's office and
to Post Office with him for mail. Got letter from Mamma and Margaret, also papers, sample of wedding-cake cards. Spent good part of
day unpacking and getting things into shape in our bed-room.
Wrote to Mamma but did not finish. Met all the Angels – had
some difficulty in hearing them. Evg – Harry held a skein for me
and I began umbrella shawl for Aunt Martha, hers is to be grey and
mauve.

– Tuesday, October 8th

Saw our house for first time. Rather discouraged and nervous about deafness which seems worse just now. Weather continues damp. Went on with crocheting. Finished letter to Mamma & note to Mrs. Bird thanking latter for my gift. Did a fine lot of sweeping and cleaning around, also some mending. Harry and I had several shopping tours over to H.B. Stores just across yard. Did some fixing to room. Harry played cards with the boys in evening. I very tired. Read a little.

– Wednesday, October 9th

Cold but not altogether unpleasant, it rains and shines at intervals. Got veil from Eaton's, they are very prompt, even sent me back 1 cent stamp. Got another silver salver from Fossie. Had a walk up grade with Harry, the first train came into Fort Frances this morning, we watched them laying nails and ties. Met Mr. Crandall (the Skipper) the middle aged and married Angel. Not well, and took no dinner. Crocheted and helped in arrangements for Reception to us. I put by a card for a souvenir. The boys are very generous. I made a lamp-shade for hall, arranged our room, beds were taken down, stove put up in kitchen, dishes, carpet rugs, curtains, lamps & piano brought in. Mrs. McCaffrey catered, (she does rooms and our washing, only now I have taken over our room). It rained again in evening, but a good many came enough for 8 tables of Pedro. Had a fine supper and songs. I met about all the nice people of F.F. After they went Mr. Crandall made speech, Harry replied, and we went up to Mr. Brenner's room which was buffet and had our healths drink. They put up our bed and we retired at 2 A.M. Then they sang songs for our entertainment.

– Thursday, October 10th

Nothing much happened, ~~but managed to see our house~~. Wrote a few business letters for Harry, also went around town a little. Bad weather. Started letter to Annie but did not finish. Wrote note to

Mr. Sissons [this] on 12th. Harry played cards with boys in evening, I looked on a while.

– Friday, October 11th
They had a nice little supper for us in the evening, just the Angels and ourselves, in Mr. Baker's room, presented us with a fine Morris chair, upholstered in green velvet. We had songs galore.

– Saturday, October 12th
Bad cough, doctored it up. Read, looked over old letters – took bath. Harry out in evening, but came in pretty early. Did some mending, brushing out furs, put fur collar on H's coat, etc.

– Sunday, October 13th
Harry got some biscuits, marmalade, and coffee, also short bread. Had breakfast in our room. Dressed, went to dinner. Afterwards borrowed Mr. B's canoe and paddled up to Pither's Point, walked around there, over to Rainy Lake. Paddled home, tea, church in Presbyterian Ch. Mr. Skea preached on 'Temptations'   Pretty good congregation. After Church the Angels came in and we had some coffee. I wear my red wrapper sometimes in evenings.

– Thursday, October 17th
Mrs. Hanning called in A.M. Lovely day. I finished shawl for Aunt M. Letter to Mother. Mrs. Hanning is the young married lady who knew Ethel Ellis well in T——. We have quite a few acquaintances in common. [The rest of the entry is written down the margin as if an afterthought.] Afternoon very warm. I wore my green striped dress. H & I went to see house. Evg. He read some of Don Juan to me. Beautiful sunset. Recited poetry to each other.

– Friday, October 18th
Very long letter from Mother, enclosing freight bills etc. They were not so high, thought the packer's wages mounted up a good deal. It took me all breakfast to read Mother's letter. I think we went round

to see house this day – or no – Harry was at court nearly all day. I
went for a walk in afternoon, met a man coming back who evidently knew me   any way accompanied me home. I cannot
remember all the faces. Beautiful day and oh the sun-set. I forgot to
mention the moon last night, I never saw it glitter so. The air here
is very clear, and last night it was soft and warm. H. had longing for
some fruit. We got some very poor plums and apples. But to continue for Friday. It was cooler but the air lovely – and such a sky. I
had to go out again to see it, and met Mrs. Smith and Mrs. Hanning, we walked a little way along shore together, Mrs. Smith is a
very jolly little Yankee, with a terror of a boy of four – young
Walter.

Ev'g Reading – I think this was the evening we read Don Juan. I
must keep my diary up and not get things missed, but it was a nice
evening anyway.

– Saturday, October 19th
Mrs. S. and Mrs. H. called. I am going to show Mrs. S. how to make
umbrella shawl. Afternoon, worked hard at Harry's office, I painted
two doors – helped other ways. We got oil cloth & linenette for
tables. Helped with office work in evening. Harry finished the
partition this afternoon. Discovered some poetry H. wrote. He
promptly burned it. [Her handwriting undergoes a change becoming more erratic in the following entries.]

– Friday October 25th
Seven years ago to-day, Harry and I first met. Colder weather. We
got a letter from Annie who is at Hamilton Conservatory of Music.
Was in office early this morning and did some letters for Harry. I
went again to see Mrs. Fetter bought stove for $15, also kettle &
stove pipes thrown in, a screen door for $1.00 and refrigerator for
$9. They were all new in May, and the stove cost $20 and the
refrigerator $10.50 (wholesale) when new. Harry and I went to see
house – the plastering is being done – Evening, Mrs. Hanning and I
took a stroll in moonlight. Harry slept, he was worn out, and the

room got too hot heating water for his bath. Tea. [Lovely?] oysters
for tea. Mr. Chandler's veal.

– Saturday October 26th
Our things were at the wharf. We went to see them, pretty badly
battered. Was at office a good deal, we were trying to plan about
house. Read in ev'g. H. played cards.

~~Wednesday~~ Thursday October ~~30~~ 31st
[Wednesday entry added below with note saying (Left out above)]
Colder. I stayed all morning in office and tried to do some book
keeping for Harry, also did quite a little copying (writs) and some
figuring. After dinner came in and did up room, I must not leave it
again that way. Then Harry came up and hurried off to train, was
going to Barwick. I went to station (it is getting on towards completion now.) Then over to our house to give some directions to
painter, then to look up man to send stoves over, and finally to
office where I did some copying, and entered some letters in books
and pasted them. Finally I went round to house again and found
the man had left all the truck on the verandah. He said the
workmen would not let him put it in. Very cold by this time and
pitch dark   went to tea – Came home [by] aid of Mr. B's
lantern   made crochet-hook out of a piece of kindling and knife
and sandpaper – Cut out a pair of pyjamas for Harry, and then he
came back saying there was a wreck and he had come back instead
of walking on to Emo. The two stoves were going and the house got
very hot.

~~Thursday Oct~~ Friday, November 1st
Harry left on morning's boat as he woke too late to catch 6 o'clock
train. I got letters from Annie and Mother. I took up carpet in our
room, swept it, washed oil cloth –, shook all carpet and Turkish rug
out side, then spent afternoon and part of Evening sweeping
H.'s office and laying carpet (which I carried over in installments),
dusted and arranged and oh what a job it all was – came home after

it was all done a little while after supper, did some writing, attended to fires, polished shoes and dusted. It is Baby's birthday, he is one year old. Wrote to Alice. Read some of Pax Vobiscum by Drummond – I forgot to say that shortly after we arrived here I got 5 photos from Mr. Topley – acknowledged them. They are very good.

– Saturday, November 2nd
Very rainy and windy and cold. A.M. saw to various things. Went over to house, the things had been taken indoors. Got 2 pr baby mitts to send to Friedel for his birthday. Mrs. Hanning came over after dinner. I worked on H's pyjamas. Evening when I was coming home it was desperately dark. I ran into Harry near the door, he had just arrived on train. He went over and got supper – I worked till he came back. Then he took bath – he was pleased with carpet.

– Sunday, November 3rd
The pleasure about the carpet somewhat evaporated. I cut it too much. Most of day in office. Wrote to Margaret, Beatrice, tried typewriting – We read a little at home – I went to sleep when I ought to have been going to church. Took bath ev'g –

– Monday, November 4th
Mail did not come in till late in afternoon so I got more time at Margaret's letter. When it did arrive I got nothing. In Harry's office a great deal. Went over to house, tried to get one floor ready for staining but it will all need scrubbing. H. & I called at Mr. Hollands' office. Ev'g reading papers.

– Tuesday, November 5th
My birthday (26), but it has not seemed much like it. At office nearly all day, but did not do much. We went to house, bought boiler and stain, engaged some one to scrub. Evening – did my washing – ~~two~~ Harry's woolen underwear, my woolen shirt, 2 prs stockings, 6 towels, gloves, my blue flannel nightgown, and pink

flannel undershirt. Sewed on pyjamas what time was left – it has
been a lonely evening for my birthday. Harry went to a meeting
and now is playing cards – He got me some candy.

– Wednesday November 6
[No entry. Rest of empty pages ripped across. At the end of the two
similar larger notebooks used for the wedding year, there is a list of
all the letters received and answered, carefully divided into columns. She includes a note saying that her August correspondence
was not kept count of so it is not quite right. In the second notebook where the pages are ripped after November 6th, the correspondence is recorded only between September and November 3.
This unusual lacuna is not explained by her.]

Wed. January First – 1902
These little books are often useful so I am going to keep one regularly for every day matters. My last, I see, in the old notebook was
written Nov 5th. We soon after began settling and in the process
my diary was neglected. I got a good many letters, especially about
Christmas. Among my friends not many changes have taken place
excepting the announcement of Margaret's engagement to Mr.
Roland McWilliams, and our poor best man's death on Dec 6th, by
drowning – his effort to save Miss Blair has made him one of our
heroes. I see also that Jean Adair Murray's father died on Christmas
Day – he was comparatively old. (75) They are all well at Indian
Rd. and dear Mother busy as usual (helping to wean Friedel.) The
LeSueurs are in Montreal, and Bea may go to Europe in the Spring.
– Mattie is her usual little self in Ottawa and seems to write me
more or less extensively for the 'common-wealth' and perform
many charitable acts in connection with the Unitarian crowd.
I heard from Mrs. Walkley, they are leaving Ottawa. – Jean Maclaren sent me many particulars of Bert Harper's death and funeral,
and I kept many clippings. It was very sad. [An arrow points up
to the top margin to a pencilled-in note added in 1942:] – I do
not say as I might have that it was also very sad that on Dec 4,

I lost my first hopes of motherhood.) – I spent New Year's morning doing the downstairs sweeping and so on. Prepared a dinner for a good many people as Harry had invited the Hollands' and Hannings. He hoped the Hon E.J. Davis would pass through and wanted to have him also, but there was no stopover. The Hon is to lay the last spike on the new railroad. The Hannings left unexpectedly, and Mrs. Hollands was ill so Harry and I had dinner alone, not till 7, as he was curling. Wrote letters to Angela and Sheila Pennock my old pupil who was always so good to me. Worked at illumination of address for old Mr. Thompson's relatives. He died on Dec 24th, but they did not put off the ball which took place on 27th.

Thurs. January Second 1902.
Ironed in Morning – Finished illuminating address afternoon. Ev'g, read and went for a skate, then to Harry's office and we came home together.

Friday January 3rd.
A great day changing stoves. Took down Queen and put up Bank Stove. Clear cold day. Afternoon – two men came to put hot-air shaft into my bedroom. Lots of dirt and muss to clear. went out shopping to Hudson's Bay Stores. Mr. Gebbie said his wife would send over some winter vegetables. Harry left in evening for Port Arthur. I wrote to his father after he left and stayed in the office book-keeping. Came home and read 'American wives and English husbands' one of the books Aunt Martha sent. In aft. I posted book to little Sheila Pennock.

Saturday – Jan 4th.
The new stove smokes. I discovered pipes were coming apart in H's room. Mrs. Gebbie sent over carrots, celery & beets. I did usual work, made three pies and pastry cakes, went up town swept and dusted Harry's office got mail, indexed in letter book. Ev'g read, darned Harry's sweater & stockings. Letters from Maidie, Hilda,

Angela, Mamma, Aunt Eleanor, Helen – Got tel. from H- said he would leave at 7 a.m. Mon.

Monday, January 6th.
A great day cleaning and C. mended H's coat, brought in piles of wood[,] made kindling, mended darning bag etc., washed oilcloth, swept all upstairs, oiled all stained floors, shook rugs, changed bed-linen, and put up pictures, tidied and arranged little sewing room. Went up to office, finished indexing and book-keeping as far as marked, bought oilcloth, came home and did Harry's washstand, made curtains for it. Wrote letter to Mother, card to Aunt Eleanor. Steam saw here all afternoon. 12 P.M. Have been out posting letters and card – Two men called to see Harry. If he does not get back in five minutes I must go to bed.

– Wednesday , Jan 15 –
Downstairs sweeping, and arranged furniture differently. Made two kinds of jelly, after lunch made custard. Went up to office, called at Mrs. Gebbie's for a minute. Mrs. Keating came after dinner and gave me a first lesson in bread making. Stayed and talked. After that I did some book keeping H. had brought home. He is not well, went early to bed.

– Friday. Jan 17 –
H and I walked out to see our lots, where some underbrushing was done at his orders – Came home did usual housework. Aft. Swept upstairs, cleaned doz silver spoons ready for the 'Assembly', made ham sandwiches, went up town and got meat for dinner, came home did dusting, brushed H.'s clothes, got dinner, got dressed and went to dance. Wore wedding dress again, with yellow. It was too cold there to be thoroughly enjoyable. I enjoyed the dancing better than the Masonic Ball.

– Friday, Jan. 24th –
Did all upstairs sweeping, finished attending to carnival costumes –

While I was dressing H. came and said no other married ladies were there, so I did not go in costume; went to look on, came home, wrote letter to Mattie, read.

– Wednesday, January 29th –
Did downstairs sweeping. Aft. Called on Mrs. Paul and Miss Atkins. I found Mrs. P— out, she was at Miss Atkins' (The Koochiching) when I went there. did shopping (got 3 doz new laid eggs at H.B.Co.'s) called at H's office, got pup, and called again at Mrs. Pauls' on way back, as I promised. Came in got dinner, then went to Rink where H. was curling in a match game. His rink (Mr. Floyd's) lost. It was very cold so I wore fur cap, skated around at intervals and talked to Mrs. Baker and Mrs. Gillon who has a cousin, Mrs. Campbell visiting her.

– Friday, February 7th –
Did baking today instead of tomorrow. Made one marmalade pie – two cranberry and one apricot, and got soup and ham ready for H's birthday dinner. At 3.30 called for Mrs. Gebbie and we called on the brides Mrs. Ireland and Mrs. Canniff, both were in, was at H's office also. Then ran over to H.B.Co and to ask the Keatings and Hollandses to come. The K's said they would. Ev'g The Phairs' party which was very enjoyable. H played whist with two other men and Mrs. Keating – I played Pedro with the Gebbie's and Mr. Brenner. Singing afterwards. I wore my white woollen blouse, tho' it is rather shabby, my silk ones are all splitting.

– Saturday, February 8th –
Mother's and Harry's B.D. All day getting ready for dinner tidying etc, & soaking wash for Mrs. Y. The K's and H's came & the dinner went off fairly well. We had meat tomato soup, ham, lamb, potatoes, peas, apricot and cranberry pies, fruit fill containing lemons, oranges, dates and almonds, graham wafers and coffee. Lemonade in Ev'g – the men smoked upstairs as usual. Very unsociable. Pup created a good deal of diversion. I was up-town in afternoon.

– Winnipeg –
Tuesday Feb.11th.
Got up at 4 a.m. Got breakfast etc. Train started at 6 A.M. –
arrived here at 6 P.M-after an uneventful journey, the other curlers
had hampers so we had plenty of grub, cold chicken, duck etc. I
read Canadian Magazine. Arrived at Aunt Martha's when they
were at tea. Then as they were going to theatre H went out and got
tickets. 'The Parish Priest' was very good – Our seats were not far
from Aunt M's. I just wore a muslim blouse and Hazel's white silk
scarf. Came home had talk & supper.

– Monday, Feb 17th –
Went early to a curling match at Granite. Another glorious day
The F.F. men lost again, to Birch of Alexandria. Came home did
room and then went shopping with Aunt Martha, then went over
to Fossie's meeting Lawrence on the way. He was just out of school.
I started a dinner mat for Fossie and worked at it after lunch. F. is a
very strict Methodist, wears no jewelry not even a wedding ring.
Aunt K. called and took me to a musicale in such a pretty little
auditorium in Y.M.C.A. very good soloists took part, a great many
ladies brought fancy work, it was a meeting of the women's Musical
Club. Afterwards we looked through the YMCA which is grandly
furnished, then back to concert room where we found two or three
people listening to Mrs. Evans (Irene Gurney) playing divinely.
She played two very different pieces   she is to give a concert
next week. Then we went to a green house on Portage Ave. I
bought some daffodils and white carnations for Fossie, and Aunt
Katie and I walked through the greenhouses then went to Fossie's
to dinner. Spent the evening doing mat, talking to Fossie & playing. Three men called on Aunt M. who is up to her eyes in all sorts
of 'good works.'[12] I came home by myself in glorious moonlight,
Mr. C. having left town. Stayed up reading very interesting book,
'A Self-denying Ordinance' by M. Hamilton and talking to Aunt
Martha.

– Tuesday, Feb 18th –
Did a little sweeping and dusting A.M. and reading. Aunt K.

called to take me for a drive after dinner. It was glorious and such
a day. We drove all around banks of Assiniboine and crossed the
Red – Mr. Bryce drove and the two little girls also came. Came
home about four, then Aunt Martha and I went shopping   I
got quite a few kitchen utensils. Home about 6.30 when I got a
note from Fossie asking me to go to the Elocution contest for
Diamond medal and take dinner at their house. It was late so
I went at once. Dinner was over but F—— got some out for me.
Aunt Minnie and I went half an hour early but the hall was full,
we sat on steps leading up to platform. Seven young ladies competed   the best won it. Miss Edith Miller sang solo also a Mr.
Handscomb. There was an orchestra. It was all very nice. Home
and had supper of crackers cheese and ginger ale with Aunt
Martha.

– Monday Feb 24th –
Got off with eggs and everything. Very mild yet. Almost all the
snow gone. All day on train. Mr. Johnson (tinsmith) was on, also
several other F.F. people. Dr. on board wanted to vaccinate us. I
read and finished 'The Awakening of Mary Fenwick.' Harry met
me at station. Just took cold wash and went to bed, after turning it
out and putting on clean linen. House in awful state and only a little water.

– Tues. Feb. 25 –
Spent all day cleaning, dishes, lamps, – etc. etc. Swept and oiled all
upstairs, it is now beautifully clean. H. got two pails of water from
river. He went to Koochiching and got a terrible black eye. Some
drunken wretch struck him for nothing at all. Pup was found and
was here on my return but is very lame. H. hit him by accident. I
went up town got supplies. After dinner H. worked at home. I tried
to help but could not keep awake.

– Wednesday Mar 19 –
Morning up late. H. came in at 3. Did downstairs sweeping in a
hustle. Aft. went up-town -shopping- came home fixed things to
wear to party – mended, patched navy blue skirt (where Parson

chewed it) sponged – etc. – but it will have to be all refaced. Put
valenciennes lace in black velvet evening waist and trimmed with
blue bows wore cream fichu & pearls. made new chiffon rosette
(black) for hair. Went to dance about 9.30 – Had pretty good time.
It was the Bank's affair & held in the new block of buildings – nice
big hall & fine supper. H. at office after he took me there but he
came back to the ball just before the end. Miss Atkins in pale pink
danced beautifully and was quite the belle.

– Tuesday- April 8 –
Mrs. Young sent over wash before we were out of bed – so I did all my
ironing and hers to-day, it was a small one altogether. The freight
came. H. came home early at noon to unpack it. There were blan-
kets, photos, 2 dozen bottles of pickles, and 1 ½ doz of fruit, the fruit
seem perfectly fresh, we had some delicious red plum for lunch.
There are besides greenpeppers, cherries, apples, raspberries, strawberries, tomatoes, peaches, pears, so we are rich. Annie must have
the art down to a fine point. After lunch I put away all the freight,
I ironed a little and went up-town where I did some typewriting very
badly. Home again to get dinner, at 5.30 while it was on the stove,
(I had lobster soup, roast beef, potatoes and tomatoes on) I ran over
to Mrs. Young's with a blouse she sent by mistake. I found she would
take old clothes, and she says Mrs. MacDonald will wash windows
for me. I was only gone ten minutes by the clock, but the fire got very
hot and I found the tomatoes burned. I did some fresh and did
'angel's food' for dessert. H. came home about on time, ev'g he went
to a banquet to Mr. McLeod, who is leaving. I spent the evening
having a good newspaper read. Then went to bed and fell asleep over
an article on 'Political Turning-Point of Germany.' H. came in and
woke me up. He left early so got in at a reasonable hour.
[Marginalia] Mattie sent me pamphlet on 'Norman'

– Sat. May 3rd –
Sorting and listing the by wash of curtains, drapes, etc. etc., I am
giving Mrs. Young everything this time. On with list of sewing &
mending. There always is something to do! Letters from Miss Cook
and Una. I am making cushions. Finished the green coverings of

rocking chair, put black buttons on. Ev'g, reading & both of us took baths. It rained very hard and I couldn't get waterman, so H. brought a pail from River, and I had 14 saucepans out to catch water (we have no eaves). H. gathered water from vacant lot for baths. Such a steady deluge. Poor Parson had a chill. I made cranberry & custard-coconut pies, late in aft. I wasted a good deal of day wandering around with pails etc.

– Friday- May 9 –
Mrs. McDonald did not come so I went over to find why – She has moved to Wpg! She might have let me know. I had the water all ready and now the double windows are off it had turned awfully cold. Pup very naughty. I left him alone a few minutes and he worried my best green velvet hat, the wing of cock's feathers is useless and it was so pretty. I whipped him and locked him up. I started my new cotton blouses. It froze last night, quite hard. Pup ran away so I had to go up-town without him, cleaned office thoroughly, went for mail, saw various people, a man called for Harry's mail, & said he didn't know when he'd be back. I did one long and very bothersome job of the typewriting, and then went home thinking it must be about 10 – It was just 12 when I got in and no puppy! I had almost been afraid to leave the office on account of the fire there, I made a far bigger one than I needed. Letter from Mamma.

– Tuesday May 27 –
Useless all day, feel so fagged – Took 'a day off' – went wild flowering with Parson the whole afternoon – also read up newspapers, arranged jardinieres etc. The fields behind our house are a veritable mine of violets, (white, and blue) ferns, strawberry blossoms and hundreds of 'Jack-in-the-Pulpits,' which we used to think so rare as children. There are numbers of wild lilies-of-the-valley in bud. H. very busy about Elections. Terrible mining catastrophe at Fernie B.C. 150 men killed.

– Thursday May 29 –
Had a bad nervous attack about 1.30 A.M. after dozing a while,

first I have had in a long time, and I do not know cause. H. not home till 2. Up at 7.15 – I rested after making him breakfast then went out to pick violets awhile. Glorious day. H. will not come home to lunch   I swept, dusted and tidied all the house, filled a screen for parlor with artsilk and scrim and then H. came home to tea. Afterwards he went out at once to hear returns. I planted the whole of the big bed outside, put in sweet peas, 'fairy pinks,' candytuft, dwarf nasturtium, and verbenas. Also planted two little pots with pansies in. Then took Parson and went out for a walk, came back and sat on verandah for awhile with shoes off my feet were so hot and sore. Read afterwards. Poor H. came home after I had fallen asleep, he was very tired and – . A close win for Govt.

– Tuesday- June 3rd.
Morning finished 'Her Majesty's Minister' – painted the three window boxes, and soaked the paper off a lot of coffee tins which I punched and also painted green, they make nice sized pots. Then I did the housework and began cooking, made a cake with cocoa icing and a mold of Spanish Cream. Dressed and went up town Called for mail, & got a letter from Mrs. Ridgeway. Miss Stone was in office, I told her she could go home. I stayed there a little, did up Harry's mail, and put up one of the new magazines for him to read on boat. (The 'Success' & other papers I brought home.) I handed mail to Mr. Guy, who was promised to take it to 'Keenora,' then I went and got bread and salmon, called and asked Miss Atkins to tea, stayed while she dressed. Then we came home together. We had an awfully pleasant evening, her father called for her. We looked over photos & those [English] water colors – I read papers & went to bed.

[End of first little black book for 1902.]

NOTES

Constance Kerr Sisson's Diary is held privately by Rosalind Kerr.

1 I have written about Constance Kerr Sissons's literary works elsewhere:
   'Reading My Grandmother's Life from Her Letters: Constance Kerr Sissons from Adolescence to Engagement,' in *Working Women's Archives*,
   ed. Helen M. Buss and Marlene Kadar (North York, ON: York University Press, Robarts Centre for Canadian Studies, 1995), 48–55 and 'The
   Flag in Her Flesh: A White Bride's Life in Fort Frances, 1901–1908,'
   Tessera 18 (1995): 20–30, but this is the first time that an extended
   excerpt from her journals has been published. I wish to thank my graduate research assistant, Kyna Hamill, for her help in transcribing and
   advising me on what to include.

2 See Sidonie Smith, A *Poetics of Women's Autobiography: Marginality and
   the Fictions of Self-Representation* (Bloomington: Indiana University
   Press, 1987), 42, where she traces the difficulties that women writers
   continued to experience after they began to write in the fifteenth century. The public silence that good women had been encouraged to
   maintain could still be served if they avoided writing about important
   matters of selfhood or state and stayed with the '"amateur" letters, diaries, and journals, [and possibly] ... their own stories [if] appropriately
   confin[ed] to a domestic setting.'

3 Smith, *Poetics*, 19, argues that since the autobiographical component
   was kept at a minimum, these domestic forms of life writing could pass
   as serving the private needs of the family and, in any case, were ever
   intended to reach only the eyes of other female relatives, who would
   also maintain the required silences.

4 Marlene Kadar, 'Coming to Terms: Life Writing – from Genre to Criti
   cal Practice,' in *Essays on Life Writing: From Genre to Critical Practice*, ed.
   Marlene Kadar (Toronto: University of Toronto Press, 1992), 12, refers
   to journal and letter writing as being part of the 'original (literary)
   genre' that women have had to base their literary works on. Sometime
   after Kerr Sissons left Fort Frances, she decided to move beyond the
   approved domestic forms of writing. First she wrote a biography of her
   uncle, *John Kerr* (Toronto: Oxford University Press, 1946) describing his
   adventures with Louis Riel and Gabriel Dumont. Later, as I have mentioned, she told a story closer to her own.

5 In Kerr Sissons's unpublished novel, the Metis girl, Madge MacNeil, is
   called on by various people in town to do chores. The alter ego for Kerr

Sissons, who undergoes the experience of finding out about her husband's affair, actually presents a pair of gloves to Madge as a gift in appreciation for her service. The Madge character disappears to Winnipeg at the suggestion of one of the town matrons, who sets out to get rid of her.

6 Smith, *Poetics*, 42, talks about women writers who move away from approved domestic forms, withdrawing their 'textual support' from the 'phallic order' so that they can write stories with themselves at the centre, 'thereby wresting significance and, with it, autobiographical authority out of cultural silence.' Kerr Sissons found a way to speak over the cultural silence, and I hope that in the near future 'Law in a Lean-To: Pioneer Days on the Rainy' will be available in some published form.

7 Bob was the neighbour's dog.

8 Sissons was herself taking drawing lessons at the time and passing on her knowledge to others, like this young boy.

9 Used her sewing machine.

10 The Pan-American Exposition was held in Buffalo, New York, in 1901.

11 Manufactured from 1895, mutoscopes wre an amusement and an early forerunner of motion pictures. A series of images on cards were mounted on a rotating drum that, when spun, created the illusion of moving pictures. http://www.mutoscope.co.uk/what1.htm

12 Aunt Minnie is Dr Amelia Yeomans, her mother's favourite sister, who was born in 1842 and died in 1913. Amelia and her daughter Lilian became medical doctors in 1885 and 1882, respectively, graduating from Ann Arbor, Michigan. Amelia's 'good works' included her interest in getting the vote for women, fighting against the sex trade, and promoting temperance. The good works that her niece refers to may have been connected with the preparations she was making to deliver her groundbreaking (males only) lecture on the evils of prostitution and venereal disease. See Carlotta Hacker, *The Indomitable Lady Doctors* (Toronto: Clarke Irwin, 1974), 86–93.

PART THREE:
HESITATION AND PAUSE

Phoebe McInnes
(1878–1938)

K. JANE WATT

The diary of twenty-three-year-old Phoebe McInnes describes eight months in the life of a teacher in the Fernridge district of Langley, British Columbia, at the beginning of the twentieth century. In an area of logging, landclearing, and mixed farming, and in an era of mud, gravel, and corduroy roads, McInnes relies on her 'wheel,' for transportation, travelling astonishing distances in the course of her ordinary day. Her bicycle, her status as a single woman earning a decent salary, and the particularities of her domestic situation (her mother died two years before, leaving the family in a loose affiliation minus some of the strictures that would be expected in a more nuclear Victorian family) allow her unprecedented freedoms. She moves at will, travelling by bike in fine weather, and by foot, by horseback, or in the family wagon at night or in poor weather. Although in her entry of 12 February she articulates her boredom with a short, almost peevish, note indicating 'nothing much happened,' much does happen in her community and in her life as she teaches her last term in public school: she entertains at home; she courts and is courted by a man referred to only as 'C,' who lives some distance away in Vancouver; she cycles the roads of the Fraser Valley on her wheel; she chronicles the ups and downs of her family's coping with her mother's death and with her father's retreat from responsibility.

McInnes's diary, surprisingly, says comparatively little about her working life as a teacher in the one-room East Kensington school approximately two and a half miles from her home. She writes her diary at school, presumably in the moments that her class is engaged with work. She seems to spend little time on it; consequently, the entries are closely written, short, impressionistic, and in some cases, a bit mysterious. She writes as if anticipating a reader, and leaves questions and gaps of information that she promises she will fill in due course – after a holiday in Vancouver, or after a weekend of parties. In one case, she directly addresses her diary in an apologetic tone, laments her neglect of it, and then proceeds to fill in her summertime activities in a long entry that spans the space of five pages and includes the birth of her sister's baby, her own engagement, and many outings she is a part of during her time as a substitute teacher in Chilliwack.

In its references to world events, both in the substance of the entries and in the materiality of the document itself, Phoebe McInnes's diary connects her home, her work, and her life in rural Langley to a vital international community focused on Canada's role in the British Empire. On 10 February, for example, she writes that seventy people filled the local church to participate in a memorial service for Queen Victoria. Her entries are written in a notebook supplied by 'Thomson Stationery Co, 325 Hastings Street, Vancouver,' a company that offers special promotions during April 1900: '10% off School and Teachers' Text Books, Dictionaries, Educational Books, Paper and Cloth Books of recent fiction, Works on the Transvaal and South Africa, War Maps, Battle Pictures, GOLDWIN'S UNITED EMPIRE, Bryce's Impressions of South Africa, Souvenirs of Vancouver.' Yet even as it registers imperial events and national debates, Phoebe McInnes's diary records the minutiae of a woman's life. A careful list-maker, McInnes records the letters she writes; details how much money she owes on her watch bought on credit at her uncle's store; catalogues her most recent reads (including Harriet Beecher Stowe's Uncle Tom's Cabin and Arthur Conan Doyle's The Sign of Four); and, under the headings 'Regularity and Irregularity' and the subheadings of 'Began' and 'Ended,' she chronicles her menstrual cycle in the spring of 1901.

Her diary also records her rides around the environs of Langley. East of Vancouver, in British Columbia's Lower Mainland, the Township of Langley is bounded on the north by the Fraser River, and on the south by the 49th parallel. In McInnes's day, Langley remained isolated from the metropolis of Vancouver by virtue of the curve of the Fraser River, a physical barrier not bridged until 1904. Incorporated in 1873 and sporting grand municipal aspira- tions, Langley had its growth limited by its lack of transportation infrastructure: the decision by the Canadian Pacific Railway to run its transcontinental line on the other side of the Fraser in the 1880s was one decisive blow against 'progress.' The state of the roads, too, was a recurring problem for this municipality in attract- ing settlers (who would, in turn, assist in the development of the area through taxes levied and through statute labour).[1] Only six years before McInnes's diary was penned, a travelling minister laments the impassability of the roads: 'I travelled to services on week evenings at Ft Langley, Murrayville, and Biggar's Prairie ... and Glen Valley. My mode of motoring was Horseback. I remember estimating that in 1894 I rode ... over 3000 miles, many miles of which I rode in the ditch, as the ditch was better footing than the road.'[2] Given the deplorable state of the roads for a good part of the year, McInnes's wide-ranging travel – an eight-mile return trip to church, or a five-mile return trip to work – is indeed remarkable.

Phoebe McInnes's ability to travel as widely as she did was made possible in part by her determination to get out no matter what the road conditions might be, and in part by changes in fashion that made it increasingly comfortable for Canadian women to sit and to move around. Although the severity of late Victorian dress was beginning to soften by McInnes's time, it nevertheless featured 'a tall, queenly figure with a voluptuous hourglass shape, a long neck, and abundant upswept hair.'[3] But dress reform was on the way. The introduction of the shorter corset to allow for prolonged

sitting and for a more comfortable range of motion was one important change. The T. Eaton Company catalogue of 1901 registers
this shift in health and fashion ideals as it advertises a range of
biking and walking skirts slightly shorter than the everyday skirt.[4]
The biking craze of the nineties, of which Phoebe McInnes was a
part, began to change perceptions not only about appropriate dress
for women, but also about appropriate norms of conduct. The
Canadian medical establishment, for example, debated the suitability of the sport for women. Its members were divided in their
opinions: some issued a moral condemnation, stemming from their
concern that women might use cycling as 'a means of gratifying
unholy and bestial desire.'[5] Others optimistically endorsed the
bicycle as 'the most valuable addition to the therapeutics of
women of the age'[6] and a possible agent of dress reform.[7] Officially,
however, the medical community in Canada was cautious about
encouraging this new diversion and suggested that, to be safe,
women should consult with their doctors before taking up cycling.

Born on 2 February 1878, Phoebe McInnes moved with her
family to Langley from Ontario in 1890. Far from living out the
isolation particular to pioneering families, the McInnes family
came with an entourage of relatives, all seeking new lives in the
Canadian west. Two McInnes brothers, Fergus (Phoebe's father)
and Rod, married two sisters from the MacKinnon family, Margaret
and Isabella. In addition, two other sisters, Janet (who married
Robert Braden) and Catherine (who married Thomas Waterhouse), became Langley pioneers. The Braden home and the Rod
McInnes home are much featured in Phoebe's diary as she details
the comings and goings of her cousins (especially Kate, little Mag,
Sadie, and Angus, or Allie). The extended McInnes family lived
dispersed in a Township that 'was in essence bush country where
people had their clearings to grow enough to feed a horse or two
and a cow or two for milk and butter for the family.'[8]

Phoebe's mother, Margaret, died two years before the diary
opens. She was a young widow with a daughter, Janet MacDonald,
when she married Fergus McInnes and began to have his children,

one almost every two years: Johnny, called Jack (1867), Angus (1869), Janet Ann, called Jean (1871), Charles, called Little Charlie (1874), Sarah (1876), Phoebe (1878), Neil (1880), William (1882), Maggie (1884). These siblings are a regular part of Phoebe's diary entries. Sarah, Neil, Will, and Maggie live with Phoebe on the family farm. Angus has his own farm nearby. Janet and Charlie are frequent correspondents. Jean lives with her family in Vancouver – indeed, it is at her house that Phoebe stays when visiting with 'C' or 'Charlie Vancouver,' her future husband, Charles Fulton. They were a surprisingly healthy family, apart from complaints of sore teeth and minor ailments: Phoebe notes that in 1901, 'all living well ... Janet, Jack, & Jean married.'

McInnes never returned to teaching school; after marrying Charles, she raised their four children in Vancouver. Her diary continued to be an important document to her: entries indicate she returned to it periodically over the next thirty years, as if in gestures of completion, to record the deaths of people dear to her. Phoebe herself died on 7 September 1938. All that remains of Phoebe McInnes's diary is a collection of poorly photocopied pages. No original can be found.

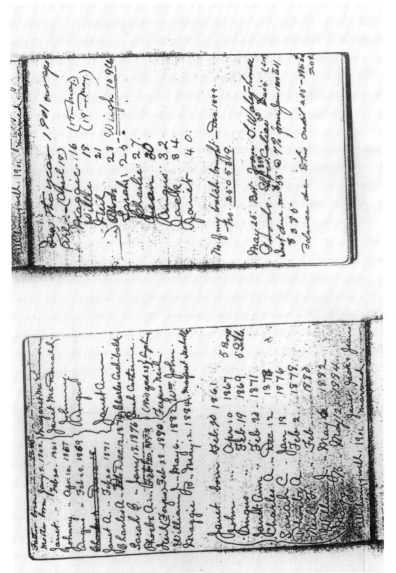

Adjoining pages in Phoebe McInnes's diary, 1901.

DIARY, BRITISH COLUMBIA,
MARCH–SEPTEMBER 1901

Mar. 1. School started at nine. Sarah's tooth ached all night and she went to Blaine to have it extracted. Little Mag stayed home from school 'cos' Big Mag didn't like to stay with [Mr.] Wag. Lovely afternoon. Wagg went away very much to our surprise and joy. More than half my hair has come out caused by my sickness in Nov. Wrote to C. Sarah missed the train & had to walk all the way from Blaine and didn't get her teeth pulled after all.

Mar 2. Drove S. down to Braden's. Visited there in afternoon. Saw lots of people and drove home alone. Awful lonesome road. Got home about six.

Mar 4. Mon. Didn't go to church yesterday. Didn't feel good. Lovely day. Stovepipe smoked all day so that we had to let the fire out and we were all about froze.

Mar 5. Went for a spin on my wheel after school. Went down near to Brown's and back about half a dozen times. Roads a little rough but riding exhilarating. Beautiful day just like summer. Mag took her first music lesson from Miss Lewis.

Mar. 6. A Knock came to the door today and when I opened it there stood Jean. Awfully surprised and glad to see her. Stayed till 11 o'clock and Little Mag drove her home in the buggy with old Nell.

Mar. 7. Had a bad dream last night   dreamt Kate was here & thought she had a letter from C. & I didn't like it one bit though I was trying not to let on. It made me feel silly in the morning. Didn't tell any one. Welcome to write to whoever he wants to. Raining. Rec'd a letter from Scholefield, Prov. Libr. Fred J. Came over and we arranged about exchanging Libraries tomorrow.

Mar 8. All dressed up to go to town. Fred Johnson came over with Lib 15 and took Lib. 5. away. Books are all right. Now 'Mr. Diary' as Peck's Bad Boy says, I won't write in you again until Monday. Then I'll tell you all about my trip to town and Grolo's party which is to be tonight and I will be away   Dreadful sorry. ~~also~~ glad.

Mar 11. Well diary here I am again. Went to town had a fair time, did not see C & was disappointed. Lent 50.[9]   Waited at Royal City Spur for train for 2 hrs   waited in Westminster for car for

1 hour. Went to bank Sat. morning. Jean & I took car & went to
Freeman's in the afternoon. Capt Freeman was home   had a
good time. Rained all the evening & didn't go down town. Went to
church alone Sunday morning to Princess St. Went for a short walk
in the afternoon and went to the S.A.[10] with Jean & Harry in the
evening. Pretty tame. Came home Monday (this morning) via
G.N.R.[11] Met Mary Corbett on the train going in. Mr Sharp (Rev)
called for a few minutes at recess. By what I hear Gr's party was
[rum?]. No girls but Nettie T. It rained so hard no one could go.
Mar 12. Rained.
Mar 13. A knock came to the door this afternoon & when I opened
it and saw Maggie & Kate & Sadie I was quite surprised. Uncle
Robert had come for Auntie Janet & the girls came with him. They
had to go right back with him that night as Kate was going to town
next day so they came down to the school & Mag & Kate & I
drove home & Little Mag & Sadie walked. Just when we were
through supper Mr Johnson came. The girls got him his tea & he
stayed till 8:30. He was looking for a housekeeper but Im afraid.
afraid. afraid. that he'll not find one.
Mar 14. Was very cross all day. Couldn't stand anything.
Mar 18.[12] Grace & Fred came up from S.S. & stayed for church.
Mar 18. Since I last wrote something has happened which I very
much dislike to record but as this diary is supposed to contain all
the events which have any bearing on my life I suppose I must
write every thing. Yesterday afternoon father went down towards
the H[alls] P[rairie] Road as we supposed merely for a stroll. By and
by Mr Griff. came along & wanted to see him so I told him that he
had gone out. He said he too would take a walk down that way &
perhaps he would overtake him. He did too. and on our way home
from church, when we were nearly home, we heard loud talking &
laughing and stood to listen when Willie said It's Father & old
Griffith dead drunk. and so it proved to be. Well we sat up a good
part of the night waiting for them but as they did not come in we
laid down. Finally about 3 o'clock in they came. We all went down
stairs & there was quite a time. S & I got them a cup of tea for that

seemed to be all they wanted. They came nearly fighting over old
Roger that Griff shot. but S made Griff go home & then W held
dad back Oh it was dreadful & on Sunday too. We were all very
angry & talked seriously of dissolution but I guess we will have to
try & stand it awhile yet for father's sake not our own for we are all
able to make as good or a better way for ourselves as we are getting
now. Oh it makes me sick to think of it all. We did not sleep for
more than half an hour all night last night.

Angus came home yesterday but of course he went back before
dark.

I intended going to the store Sat on my wheel. I wrote a letter to
Charlie Rock Bay & told him I was going out on my wheel. but it
poured rain in the afternoon & so I could not go. Tom F. came
along and took my letter to the office.

Went to church Sunday afternoon on my wheel. Grace & Fred
came up & stayed for preaching in the evening. Mr. C walked as far
as the corner with us after church. He wouldn't come up & when
we got home & saw the way things were we were very glad.

If I feel good this evening Im going to the store on my wheel, providing it does not rain. I think this is all of our Sat. & Sun. exploits.
Mar 19. Went to the office last night on my wheel. Roads a little
rough   Went in an hour and five min. Went to McCrimmon's &
stayed more than half an hour. Mrs McC. looks very much worse
but was still very bright. Got a letter for Maggie but none for myself.
Saw Rod. Met Mrs Armstrong moving home to her mother's.
Mar 20. Dad didn't do a thing yesterday but jump on Neil's horse
and to Blaine without so much a[s] saying he was going. Got back
at 2 o'clock in the morning. Came in & went to bed so quietly that
we scarcely heard him. Got up this morning after the boys went
away to work & began talking about them not working at home.
Sarah gave him fits but he held his own pretty well. Rode my bike
to school today. Dora brought me a bouquet of Daffodils. Lilies are
in full bloom. Forgot my lunch & didn't care much only Maggie
came down with it. Mrs Nelson came over today and asked me to

stop with her while George went to Wellington for a week. I said I would go.

Mar 21. Rode to school on my wheel again today. Roads a little rough but getting dry. Lovely weather. Sarah went to the store yesterday. Got a letter from Mrs Bond. Mrs. W Armstrong called at the door today. She found Grace Johnson's brooch that she had lost Sunday night while walking down to church with Neil.

Mar 22. No news. Rained last night & is windy to-day. Equinoctial gales I suppose. Am dreadfully cross these times. Girls gathered quite a nice bouquet of lilies, and gave them to me. Walked to school today because they have turned Nell out to graze & the roads were too muddy for wheeling.

Mar 25. This is Monday again and as I leave my diary at school I never get a chance to write anything between Friday and Monday. Wheeled to the Corners on Sat. afternoon. Intended going up to Charlie's but went over to McCrimmon's and found Mrs C. so bad that I came right home. She was very low. Got a letter from Janet and one from Charlie. Janet wants me to go East and stay a year but I guess not. It costs too much money for one that has none. Was glad to hear from C. Mag went for her lesson on Sat. Boys drove to church at the Corners on Sun. S. and Mag & Little Mag and boys went to S.S. Fred J came home with them. Went to church at night. Mr Whittaker preached. Only eight there. Rode down to school this morning on the hay rack. Rained awfully heavy.

Mar 26. Wrote a letter to C. also one to Jean. Sent a letter to Robinson to Hazelmere with the boys. Sent the other ones to the Corners with Sarah. She went to the store. Gus Johnson who used to be conductor on the old logging train called at the school today to see me. He only stayed during the last recess. He came down from Rock Bay some time ago and was in the hospital.

Mar 27. Drove to school this morning for the roads are dreadfully muddy again. Sarah went to the store yesterday   Mrs. McC. still living but very weak. Rec'd a letter from [Bk of M?].

April 1. As this is April Fool's Day I think I will tell my diary a few
things. It is raining hard. I am stopping at G. Nelson's just now,
while he is in Wellington. Mag & S. and Will went to Blaine yesterday Sun for Mag to have her teeth pulled. She got them pulled
too. Mr Robb is boarding at our place just now and working at a
contract. Just 8 at school today. Miss Lewis, Myrtle and Laing were
down Friday evening, but I was not 'to hum.' Got a letter from C
on Sat. very much to my surprise. He expected it would get here by
Good Friday but it came a little a head of time.

April 2. Didn't fool anyone yesterday because I was at Geo Nelson's.
Snowed quite a lot this morning but cleared off again and was a
fine day. Am anxiously waiting for Easter. Mr Jones, Trustee, came
bounding in today and expressed his deep regrets at the low attendance.

Apr [3]. Went home last night after school & went back to Geo.N.
Mag said she could not take me to the Fort. So I intend going to
town by train on Friday & coming back Mon. Will tell you all
about it when I come back.

Apr 9. Went to town Friday and came back today (Tuesday). Neil
drove me down to the station on Good Friday and we waited two
hours for the train. At last when it did come along it went away
past the Spur, and I had to walk up. The old conductor Mr Copeland was very nice as usual. talked to me nearly all the way there
carried my valise to the ferry, took me into the engine room
& secured a seat for me on the express wagon. Oh he's lovely.
Had a short chat with the little brakeman. He said that was his last
trip & this morning I see there is a new one on. Now for the news of
my trip. Went down town Sat. afternoon. Bought a sailor & veil.
Kate & Jean went with me. Went down town again at night. Kate,
Jean, Jennie, and I met C. on Cordova St. Turned around and
walked back with Jean & I. I had to go to Mason's for my chain so
he & Kate, Jennie & Jean stayed out and waited. Then Kate & Jean
& Jen went home & C & I walked up Granville & back again
home. Sile called around Sunday morning & he and Jean & I went
to Princess St. Jennie went to First Church & Kate wouldn't go

anywhere partly because we wouldn't go to the Catholic Church &
partly because she didn't feel well. Went to Sile's for dinner & to
the S.A. in the afternoon. Kate went to the park with Mike. C.
called & took me to church in the evening. We went to Reid's.
Went for a walk after church. Didn't go in till nearly eleven. Terrible dreadful. Don't think I shall go to town again   I forgot to say
that the ground was white with snow Good Friday morning, but it
soon went away & Easter was fine. [written along margin:] Bo't
sailors for S & M –

Apr 10. Wrote to C. because it was his birthday. Wrote to Janet,
Miss Bond & Mrs Deb. Rained this afternoon. Have no rain coat
nor umbrella at school.

Apr 11. Rained in the morning but turned out fine. Began table
mats. going to send them to Janet. Sadie drove S to McCrimmon's.

April 12. Am getting pretty tired teaching. Shall be glad when the
end of June comes. Mr. Robb is still at our place. Sarah is going to
stay at McCrimmon's till Saturday. Lovely day. Children are all
writing letters just now very busily.

April 15 Heard Friday night that Mary Thrift came home. Heard a
few weeks ago that Grolo's had a little baby. Put 2 and 2 together
and know it all. Went out to the Corners Sat & took Sarah home.
Went over to see Mrs McCrimmon. Got no letters. Will & I rode
to church at the corners on our wheels. Went in 50 minutes. Roads
pretty good. Intend wheeling to the Fort Friday night if its fine.
Grace & F & Miss P came up after S.S. Went to church in the
evening. Mr Campbell preached.
A. McKellar & H. Nelson came over at noon today & talked for a
while. Bad off.

April 17. Mr Carncross was around today taking the census. Had to
give him all the ages birthdays etc. etc.

April 19. Sadie has been at our place since Easter Monday. Sick &
they took her to see Dr. Sutherland today. Intended going to Langley tonight after school on my bike but it rained as usual. The
roads have been beautiful for wheeling.

April 22 Had a letter from C on Friday. Went to Lewis' with Mag-

gie on Sat. Went to church Sunday night. Mr Whittaker preached.
April 22. Wrote to C. today. Exacted a promise. Neil went to town
by rail. Sarah & little Maggie went over to see Sadie.
April 23. Wrote to Charlie Rock Bay. There was a big thunder &
lightning storm this afternoon. My pupils were very frightened. All
turned pale. It was the biggest storm I remember to have seen in
B.C. Lots of hail and rain. Lasted less than an hour.
April 25. Sarah went collecting for minister's salary yesterday stayed
at J's all night & came back today. Lent father $8 to buy grain. Tom
F. overtook us on the way home from school last night. We had a
great confab about things in general (old maids included).
April 28. Sunday. Went to Free Meth service in afternoon. Quite a
lot of shouting & laughing. T.F. came home with us & stayed for
tea & till ten. Dave Armstrong also spent the evening. Wheeled to
Charlie's Friday night & back Sat. Sadie all right. Went to see Mrs
McC. very weak.
April 29. Sarah went to town today to Van.
April 30. The train did not come till late last night so Sarah did not
go to town at all, but is going to day.
May 1. Allie came down from Rock Bay and Neil came home from
Van with him today. They both called at the school.
May 2. A letter from C.
May 4. Answered letter. Went to Blaine on my wheel, had it fixed
& bought Maggie a new dress. Had tea with Miss Boothroyd.
May 5. Sun. Father drove us to the Corners to Church. Went up to
Charlie's after church. Allie came home with us & we all went
down to school house to church. Mr Sharp preached. Beautiful
weather. Roads fine and dry.
May 8. Grace Johnson came up this evening on her wheel.
May 9. Neil & Allie left today on the train for Van. thence to Rock
Bay. Came to the school to say Good bye to Little Maggie and me.
Very sorry to see them go.
May 10 Mr Sterling (Scotty) formerly of Royal City Camp now
from Rock Bay came to see us yesterday and left today. Had a letter
from Charlie, Rock Bay, today also one from Miss Bond asking me

to act as substitute at Cheam while she attends Normal School in Aug. & Sept.

May 16. This is Thurs and it has rained every day since last Friday and it is still pouring down. Sarah is still in Van., Will At F's; and Little Mag & dad & Maggie & I alone. Had a letter from C. on Monday,

May 13 Answered it but have not got it posted yet. Too bad.

May 18. Kate & Sadie & Chas called in & had tea on their way from Blaine. Sent C's letter to post.

May 19. Geo & Nettie Thrift came up from S.S. & stayed for tea.

May 20. From this day to the end of the schoolterm I am not going to be cross. Frank Appell started to school today. Sarah still in Van. Expect her home every day.

May 21. Sarah came home yesterday. Maggie going to Vancouver tomorrow. Jean not very well.

May 22. Maggie went to Vancouver today to stay with Jean until Harry comes home from Atlin.

May 23. No school tomorrow. *Victoria Day 24th of May.*

May 24. Angus came home last night. He & I wheeled out as far as the Corners. He went to the picnic and I went to the Fort. Stayed until Sat evening. Hot day & good roads.

May 28. Got some ripe salmon berries. Heard of Mrs McCrimmon's death. dismissed school about 1:00 and went to the funeral with Father, Angus, and Sarah. Came home very tired.

June 3rd. Just 4 more weeks of school!

Went to the corners Sat. & went to see McCrimmon's. S & I called on Mrs Freeman. Very nice. Kate came home with us. Maggie & Mary Brown came up Sunday & we all went down to Church. They brought me a lovely bouquet. Expected a letter from C but didn't get one. Got one from Charlie, Rock Bay.

Monday – am going to send in my resignation today.

[June 6?]. Sent in my resignation on Monday June 3. Weather very wet not much wheeling. Wrote to Maggie and Supt. of Education.

June 7 Received a letter from Miss Bond, also one from C. Said he was coming up soon.

June 9   Kate went home.
June 11. Went to Blaine after school. Engaged for music lessons with Miss Frescohn. Bot a foulard dress. Posted a letter to Charlie, Rock Bay and one to Charlie. Vancouver.
12. Maggie came home from Van. today.
June 13   Had a meeting last night to make arrangements about a picnic. Not many present. Fred J. Chairman, myself secretary.
June 17. Mr & Mrs Boothroyd came over yesterday (Sunday). Enjoyed their visit. Weather turned very hot. Tom F. came in on Sat. morning and stayed all day. Cut up awfully.
June 18. Went to Mr D Brown's last night   Intended going home but they coaxed me to stay all night. I enjoyed myself very much. Mr. Brown lent me 'A Galloway Hero' a Scotch story.
June 19. Dressed to go to Blaine for my first music lesson from Miss Frescohn. Wheeled home for my lunch just for a *lark*. Ate for nearly half an hour. Got back to school just in time.
June 20 – Went to Blaine for my music lesson. Got along very well. Like Miss Frescohn. Grace went with me & we did our shopping after I got through with my lessons   We had lots of fun. Went to the Nicollet Restaurant and had our supper. Had more fun. Got home at dark. Wheeled from Blaine in an hour and ten minutes.
June 21. Expect a letter from C today. Will has gone for the mail. Had a meeting last night to make final arrangements about picnic on the 1st. Settled everything. Grace and I are on purchasing Committee. Raining a little today. Made out a report of Trav. Lib. 15 today. Allie came out on the train today. He came from Rock Bay to Van. on Mon. Went home for my lunch and Will had got back and as usual I didn't get the letter I expected.
June 22. Mrs. Grolo paid us a visit Sat. Didn't get much time to practice. Wheeled to the store in the evening. Called at McCrimmons. Got a letter from Mrs. DesBrisay Rock Bay. One from Charlie, Rock Bay and one from Charlie, Van.
June 25. Charlie came home from Rock Bay today. Called at the

school. Geo. Nelson, Trustee called at noon. Boys brought me in a cup of blackberries. Spent most of my spare time (which is very little) practising.

June 26. Went to Blaine for my lesson. Grace went too. Bo't a pair of shoes etc.

June 28 This is the morning of my Public Exam. It is to begin at ten and it lacks 20 minutes of the time. Don't expect many visitors. Am treating the children to straw berries and cream with cake. I expect this is my last Exam. Very glad and yet a little sorry. Just finished Rolls of Honour. One for Maggie one for Dora & one for George. Am going to Blaine this afternoon for the picnic 'goodies.'

Cheam Sept. 27, 1901

Well old diary I have forgotten you ever since the *last day* of school in June. Since then a great many things have happened. I spent a month in Vancouver on holidays at Jean's when baby came. had a good time while there. Went out a lot with C, to park & Bay. July 28 settled matters between us. Will not say much about it here for I shall always remember it anyway. Went home & stayed about two wks then came to Chilliwack to teach for Miss Bond. and here I am now.

I have had a most enjoyable time while here. Went fishing to Vedder Creek on Labour Day caught two trout. The fishing party consisted of : Mr. Hodges who drove us;
Mrs A. Gillanders
Mrs Ryder
Miss F Ryder
Edith Bayly
Cecil McEwan
Mr Joe Gillanders
and myself. We had a fine time.

Went to Sardis Church to hear Mrs McGillivary lecture on the Epworth League Convention. The party there consisted of
Mr Smedley who drove.
Mr. J. Gillanders
Mrs Ryder & Mrs A Gillanders
Miss Gooddell, Edith and myself. Got home about 12 o'clock

Joe Gillanders, Flossie & I wheeled out the see the dyke. Came back & had tea at Mrs. Gillanders. Mr. Joe G took me home.

Mr Hodges lent Flossie & I his horse & cart and we drove to Sardis to see the hop yard. Miss Tyron took us all thru the yard and kiln and then took us home with her for tea. Had a good time.

Flossie & I wheeled out to see the steam shovel at Camp Slough but it was not working. Came back around by East Chilliwack.

Attended a literary meeting of the E[pworth] League & recited Just One Glass.

Almost my only cause for worry since I came here has been Willie's illness, and he is yet in the hospital with typhoid fever but recovering slowly.

Get two letters every week from Charlie and that keeps me from getting lonesome.

Was at a corn supper at Mrs Ryder's: Flossie, Edith, Joe Gillanders, Mrs Warden & myself. Had a good time.

The places I visited since coming here are: –
Mrs Marss
Mrs A. Gillanders
Mrs M. Gillanders
Mrs Brown
Mrs Ryder

Old Mrs Gillanders and Miss Bayly
Mrs Proctor
Mrs J. Edmondson
Mrs A. Edmondson
Miss Tyson's
Mrs Navard (Eva Scott)

I take long rides on my wheel as the roads here are just beautiful.
Chilliwack Valley is altogether a beautiful place. The mountain
scenery is simply grand. This is a little valley entirely surrounded by
mountains.

Mother died July 5, 1899. Aged 57 years. Birthday Jany 7.
William John died Sept 10, 1899
Uncle Rory   "   Nov. 22, 1899
Aunt Bell   "   April 3, 1900
Brother Willie   "   January 17, 1902
Aunt Catherine Feby 6, 1912 Aged 70
Angus died June 29, 1917. Sullivan age 48 years
Father (Fergus McInnes) died Jan 1. 1929

Dear little Dick died Sept 25 1931 at Chilliwack following appen-
dix operation.[13]

NOTES

Phoebe Fulton (McInnes) Diary, photocopy of ms, Langley Centennial
Museum and National Exhibition Centre, 990.6, ms 198. I am indebted to
members of Phoebe McInnes's family who graciously shared their time and
their information with me. This project could not have gone forward without such help.

1 For more information on Langley's roads, see Maureen Pepin, *Roads and
   Other Place Names in Langley*, B.C. (Langley: Langley Centennial
   Museum and National Exhibition Centre, 1998).

2 Rev. Magee, letter to Rev. Grant, 14 September 1919, quoted in ibid., 7.

3 Caroline Routh, *In Style: 100 Years of Canadian Women's Fashion* (Toronto: Stoddart, 1993), 2.

4 *T. Eaton Co. Limited Catalogue: 1901*, ed. Jack Stoddart (Toronto: Musson, 1970), 7.

5 *Canadian Practitioner* 21 (November 1896): 848, quoted in Wendy Mitchinson, *The Nature of Their Bodies: Women and Their Doctors in Victorian Canada* (Toronto: University of Toronto Press, 1991), 114.

6 *Dominion Medical Monthly and Ontario Medical Journal* 11, no. 1 (1898): 27–30, quoted in Mitchinson, *Nature of Their Bodies*, 65.

7 Mitchinson, *Nature of Their Bodies*, 66.

8 A. Guinet, Handwritten notes, August 1998.

9 It's likely she lent money to her father.

10 The Salvation Army.

11 The Great Northern Railway.

12 McInnes writes the same date twice. This happens elsewhere in the diary as well (22 April and 13 May).

13 Phoebe McInnes added this note some thirty years after writing the diary. Dick was one of her four children.

Caroline Alice Porter
(1844–1934)

LILLIAN TUTTOSI

... this life is very short, changes and vacant chairs.　3 September 1927

It's hard to be old ...　6 September 1933

The epigraphs were written by Caroline Alice Porter, who recorded her long, eventful, and often sad life in ten diaries that are housed at the Saskatchewan Archives Board, in Regina.[1] Caroline Porter was born and raised in St Eleanors, Prince Edward Island, when that province was a colony of Britain. Despite the fact that she had twelve siblings, her birth family seems to have been well to do: she received her education from a select school for ladies in Nova Scotia. Her father, Nicholas Brown, who was born in New Brunswick, was an aggressive, self-educated, and affluent merchant/importer who operated a tin shop and two tanneries while serving as justice of the peace and member of the Health Board. Late in life, he established a marble quarry on Cape Breton Island, but in 1880, just as it became successful, he suffered a fatal stroke. Caroline's mother, Ann Brown, was born in Nova Scotia and died four years after her husband, in 1884.

On 10 April 1861 Caroline married James Porter, a trained tanner. They would eventually become parents to twelve children –

nine sons and three daughters. The boys were: John James (Jack), born 1 February 1863; William Ernest (Willie), born 3 September 1864; Justin Edwin (Jut), born 25 December 1866; Alvin George (Al), born 10 November 1868; Nathaniel Joseph (Nat), born 6 October 1872; Page Brown, born 1 January 1875; Thomas Henry (Harry/Hal), born 20 January 1878; Robert Alexander (Bob), born 11 October 1882; Frederick Arthur (Fred), born 21 May 1884. The girls were: Elizabeth Ann (Lizzie), born 25 October 1870; Mary Eva, born 3 November 1876; and Jennie Etta Davis, born 16 September 1887. After the death of Jut's wife, the Porters' grandson Waldo, Jut's son, came to live with them and became like a thirteenth child.

The family resided in St Eleanors until 1881. After that, James went to Ontario, where he was a farm worker, and to Winnipeg where he was a pumpman for the Canadian Pacific Railway (CPR). That year, Caroline Porter and their children joined her husband in Winnipeg. When the CPR tracks reached Moose Jaw, in what was then called the North West Territories, so did James Porter. After living in a tent in Moose Jaw, and still employed by the CPR, he bought some lots, built a house, and brought his family to their new home on Ominica Street in the summer of 1883. This house was destroyed by fire five years later. In October 1919, the Porters moved to Victoria, British Columbia, to be near their widowed daughter, Lizzie. Caroline remained in that city until late 1932 and thereafter divided her time between the homes of two sons, one in Cadillac and one in Shaunovan, Saskatchewan. Caroline outlived many members of her family, including all three of her daughters, one son, two sons-in-law, one daughter-in-law, three grandsons, and her husband.

Caroline began to keep diaries in 1907, after the marriage of her youngest child, Jennie. Her journal was her companion for about twenty-seven years. The ten volumes she filled record her many letters to her family, her loneliness, her anguish about having to accept money from her sons to pay expenses (especially after the death of her husband in 1922), her indomitable spirit and, above all, her love for her family, which was her life.

Caroline's personality and her motivations for writing inflect the content of her diary. She was a matriarch who described herself as too headstrong for her family and for God, but she was also given to worrying – about decisions involving the rental or sale of their home, or about her husband's naivety and generosity in business dealings, especially because these traits translated into financial problems. A devoutly religious woman, Caroline often reveals her impatience with her own shortcomings, and occasionally those of others. On 16 November 1918, she writes: 'I am afraid that I am a "Martha" wish I could be more of a "Mary" Jesus said she had chosen the better part.' She possessed an independent spirit and could not easily be docile and submissive.

In her ninety years, sadness and grief were so common that she had reason to think that 'life here is full of partings' (5 September 1913), and 'So much is slipping out of our lives here' (22 February 1919). The death of son Page in 1898 at the age of twenty-three must have been a very difficult blow for the family, but the death of the youngest child, Jennie, in 1910 (also aged twenty-three) left a rent in Caroline's heart that would never heal. In 1913 the complications of pregnancy left the second daughter, Eva, weak, ill, and blind. After giving birth, she lapsed into a fatal coma, barely aware that she had a frail son. The infant gave up his struggle three weeks later. Finally, in 1922, Lizzie Porter Green, the third and only remaining daughter, suffered a slow death from cancer. She became blind and was confined to bed. For some time before her death, she was tended by a nurse because she had lost her husband years before and because her mother was busy caring for Lizzie's father, who was also dying; indeed, James Porter would die a mere four days after Lizzie. Bereaved and lonely, Caroline had to help arrange for the care of her two orphaned granddaughters, the youngest of the Green family. Some of the most poignant diary writing conveys Caroline's grief and pain at this tragic time: 'I could scarcely hold

myself together. I thought I must give way to my grief, so I hurried
out, but when I got home and alone, I could just fall down and cry,
I tried to pray, but Oh I couldn't contain myself' (3 September
1922). In this and several other entries, Caroline wrestles emotionally and spiritually with her emptiness and loss.

For Caroline, her family was at the centre of all her endeavours.
Hers was the mentality of wife and mother. Her diary is a commen-
tary on and introspective reaction to events. Though her influence
appears limited to the microcosm of the family, she functioned in
the gendered value system that acted as a foundation for prairie
culture. As caregivers in the home, women were self-motivated
and self-directed individuals dedicated to carrying a significant
share of the responsibility for their family's survival. As custodians
of education and morality in both home and community, they
exercised a public voice in establishing and maintaining a network
of organizations such as church, school, and health-care facilities.
Helen Buss claims that women's lives revolved around participa-
tion in a 'dear domestic circle,'[2] and Caroline Porter's diaries testify
to her sense of familial duty: even in the most adverse circumstances she compelled herself to be strong for the family. Her diaries give us an extraordinary glimpse of a prairie family, its
tribulations and its achievements.

Caroline Porter wrote ten diaries in spare moments, sometimes
in pain and heartache. She speaks to the diary, at times saying
goodbye to it at the end of the book or the end of the year. On 26
August 1907, two weeks after the marriage of her youngest daughter, Caroline Porter begins her first diary in an ordinary old black
notebook of Jennie's, a book intended to be a recipe book; she continues erratically until November 1934. There are no entries for
1914, 1921, or 1926, possibly because she had no notebook in
which to write. The last diary begins with the dawn of a new year,
1930. Although by that time her writing is cramped and her hand
is unsteady, she continues to record events and correspondence,
her lifeline with family and friends. By mid-February 1934 she says,
'My hand will hardly hold the pen steady, how I will miss my diary

writing, if I get so I forget how to write, but I thank God that I am among good people.' In mid-July 1934 she decides that her son Jut should have the diaries. She writes: 'This is the last journal. I have been keeping a journal or many of them for some years. They are here with me in leather covered box or stool Annie [her daughter-in-law] gave me to put them in.'

Caroline Brown Porter, Diary No. 1, 1913.

DIARY, SASKATCHEWAN,
AUGUST–DECEMBER 1907

Moose Jaw

Fred passed his exams. Poor baby boy. how I would like to see him
tonight, he was home to Jenn'[3] wedding and was best man. he
could only stay one day. I scarcely got a word with him, but I saw
him which counts a lot to mothers ~ We hoped that he would see
his way clear to live with us, but God's ways are the best. We
believe that he directs all our ways. Eva and little Freddy and baby
were home for a couple days.

August 26 1907[4]: Jennie was married August 14th, 1907 at noon.
On Wednesday, and now its two weeks. I did not feel as if I could
write, or indeed settle to do anything. I have missed her more than
I can say. We have been in a hurry and busy for the summer. I
thought it might occupy some time of those lonely days to write
something each day, and call it my diary. Bob has been sick for
about 5 weeks. And we are anxious about him. Waldo has gone to
Nats for Annies milk. Pa away to the farm, and I am alone. Last
night the [two?] Miss Edwards called. We have heard three times
from Jenn.' When she arrived in Winnipeg, next day, and on Saturday, from Toronto. its fine today. I have been making Waldo a shirt.
Sitting in Jen's bedroom. I have left her pictures and things about
as she left them

Sept 1 Sunday
Went to the farm on Thursday and it rained so hard that I did not
get home till last night. Waldo was house keeper. had Fred Knight
in and Gordon Davidson for one afternoon. They made candy and
ate cake. We found a nice letter from Jenn' written from Chicago.
how we miss the child. Waldo is in [S?] School.[5] Pa and I did not
go to church this morning, it was so wet and muddy, but the sun is
bright. have not seen Bob, but hear that he is better. Wrote a letter
to Jenn' also one to Eva last night. Mr Speller preached a good sermon tonight. text was 'come unto me and find rest' Jesus says to
come and he will give rest. We are all looking for rest ~ and only

soul rest is satisfying. Bob and Ann came over just before we went to church. he looks some better. Tina [?] comes to their place today, is taking a school in Turtleford [?].

Moose Jaw

Sept 2. Nice and fine. Pa and Waldo bailing water out of cellar this morning. Seymour called with the baby, its a public holiday. Saturday [?] I am sewing at a shirt for Waldo   went out for a drive with pa. got two letters from Jenn,' both from Chicago, its nice of the dear to write so often. I do not feel so lonely when her letters come so often. Waldo had Fred Knight in for tea. Pa is going out to the farm in the morning. Miss Ferguson called. how busy I am. Time goes, and I do not seem to have time for reading, and

3 Tuesday Sept
Willies birth day.
Wrote him a letter. looking back ~ how short a time, and still its over fourty years. God has been good to us ~ and I trust we (pa and I) may be spared yet a while to the family ~ fine day   Pa gone to farm

4th Wednesday 1907
Another fine day. Did the upstairs. took poor Jenn' things out of her room and made it look as if she has left. Nat asked me if I would room one of his men for a time. So he can have her room, if he comes. I went down town this afternoon, ordered the paper 'Moose Jaw Times'   Sent to Jenn'   it will do for her birthday present. Bob and Annie went to the park. they seemed to enjoy it ~ Its rather lonely here just now, but I can have time to think   hope God will direct my thoughts, glad I can think. All these years He has helped me. I went [?] into Lizzie and got a cup of tea. Now I am going to [get?] bread and then go to bed. I am tired. My legs are sore and aching   Got a letter from Sister Jane Miss Banfour [?] was married this morning

Saturday 7th Moose Jaw 1907 Sept
Annie and Bob came home from our farm where they went on
Thursday. I got them a cup of tea [to?] make them warm   he
shot two prarie chicken and they ate them at the farm. the change
seems to have done Bob good. its cold and windy today. No letter
from Jenn' today. expect they are in Crawford by this. Pa and I
drove down town after six [?] this evening and saw Jenn' photo in
the Studio window all dressed in her bridal robes   she looks
nice but very ~~serious~~ sober

Sunday Morning
Its a cold windy morning half rainy so have not gone out to church.
the wind may go down and we can go in the evening. I have just
been reading that proverb 'The eyes of the Lord are in every place,
beholding the evil and the good 15.3.' Surely if we could realize as
we should, we would fear to do many things which we do ~ Went
to church text 'the rich young man'

~~8~~ 9 September   Pa went to the farm. fine today. Washed this
morning. Mrs Collin came and put the wash out on line. Lizzie sent
Munro with some green peas and celery for dinner. he stayed and
took dinner. then wanted to go home. I see the school children out
playing. What a flock, and all dressed, and kept with apparently so
much care, What a great thing is mother love. God knew that we
would all need that love. ~~For~~ See with what pride and pleasure the
mother toils for her children, giving strength, and time. And while
many of the mothers are at home working, those little ones go
shouting ~ and care free ~ not thinking. Such is life here. each sep-
erate home. and how much we need help and guidan[ce] from our
Father. Who gave all for us. So we parents here may be happy in
the families, and look forward to a brighter home in heaven

Sunday 15th Moose Jaw 1907
Cloudy and dull. We did not go to church this morning. Went in
the evening ~ and had a good sermon. 'We cannot fight our Chris-

tian fight alone.' God must be with us, or we fail. Surely our past experiences tell us that. Nat and the two little ones called. Earnest said that he would stay to tea, but had to go when he saw his father go ~

Monday 16th [September] : raw cold wind. looks like rain. Pa went to the farm. Answered an Ad in paper. think we best rent our house furnished, and let us get a room up town for the winter. Annie and Bob think its to far out of town to live with us. Bob is really not able to walk so far in winter. So I shall let things take their course. for God over rules all things. Seymour lost his position. I am so sorry for the family. poor Lizzie   And today is Jen ~ ~ 20th birthday [She adds at the top of the page: 'born in Moose Jaw 16th September 1887 born in the town M Jaw'] I wonder what she is doing. I can recall the little thing, just a wee mite, left on the sofa all day   and I wonder why Mrs. McDougall did not let me have [?] her ~ lots of changes since then, ~ and I can see dear Page coming in and looking at the baby, now he is gone home, & I guess it will only seem a little while till we see him. [In left margin of the page:] Died in Crawford Neb July 16 1910

Tuesday 17th
Beautiful bright day. Annie and Bob came over at dinner time and brought me some pie. they want to know if we got an answer from the ad in paper. just after they went out I was called up on the phone, and a lady, Mrs Mclean, she called herself, asked if she might come and see the house. So she did come, and is to let us know if they take it tomorrow at $40. per month, just as it is. We folks out and they folks in. She is very tiny [?] looking

Wednesday 18th September
I started to wash a down quilt today, and as soon as I got into the basement and a fire on, the door bell began to ring. the meter man, a music teacher, a blind pedler, a green grocer, Annie, Mrs Cock-

ran, then we went over to tea at Bob. pa came in from the farm about 5ock, this even[in]g, nice fine day, put add in paper to rent house ~

19th fine but cloudy seasonally [?]. Pa went to farm. Lizzie and Seymour came. poor things I am sorry for them. he has lost his situation, and has a big family, but Lizzie is the one who will feel it the most. I am praying for her, and God will open a way ~ and we have rented out house unfurnished for $35.00 per month to a lawyer, has one child. So I must hurry and get out, *dear me*

Novr 16.
A long time since writing in this book. We had to pack in a hurry. th as re [?] here taking Nats house with Bob's. We did not get our things unpacked for a long time. Stored them in tents, only now found my diary   and since the time we moved from our house till now ~ I seem to have been in a muddle. the Ominica house had to be cleaned and papered all through Our tenant left, and did not pay the rent. We worked there, Pa and I, and some days I almost felt like giving up, but we got through, with help, got it [illegible] again. then Eva phoned for me. She was not well. I hastened to her and stayed two weeks, had a rest and nice visit with her and Fred. ~~before~~ After the Ominica house affair, Lizzie and family left here to live in B.C. It seemed that I was so busy that I did not have time to miss her, until I returned from Eva's. Then it seemed some times that I could not bear it. All was so different without my girls. I think that I cried every day, and night too, for a long time ~ ~ but finaly I began to remember that it was as God wished it to be, and that I must think that our earthly props must fall one, by one, and although it seems hard, I have many blessings left. Still I feel that   Pa went to the farm today   its nice and fine, he will stay till after Sunday. Libb brought little Jim for me to mind ~ he was so good and sweet. Waldo and Fred Knight are making candy in the kitchen Ann has gone down town, its Saturday night ~ and the

streets and stores are bright ~ All lighted up ~ its raining some
too. Our house is let to a lawyer for the winter   hope to write
oftener [?] in this

Novr 17th
Sunday 3.30. Went to church *alone* this morning. pa is at the
farm. Bob and Annie [w]ere not up   its a most delightful
day. The pastor Rev. Speller, spoke on the 90 psalm, where Moses
is speaking to God. the great 'Majesty [of] the Master' our
lives   'teach us to Number our days'   how short life here is,
each day we have our work, and if we can feel that we are just
where He has put us ~ how tempted we are sometimes to rebel, but
if we can remember that 'He is my refuge and my fortress' how easy
it would be to bear up with little daily occurances. 'Under His
wings shalt thou take refuge.' All those beautiful psalms comfort
me. for He satisfieth the longing soul, and the hungry soul He fil-
leth with good things.

Decr 2 1907
Here I am again, after an illness of a little over a week ~ Dr
Radcliff has called in. Said it was acute indigestion, but I do
not think that was all ~ However I am up and able to be about
the house some. I am afraid that I let little things worry me, and
have not been quite as happy and contented as I ought to be.
While I have been laid up I have been seeing things differently.
I missed the daughters, and let myself fret. Waldo has chicken
pox, expects to go to school tomorrow ~ Got a letter from Jut
with $30 – enclosed   got the PO order cashed. Waldo and I
sent an order off to Eatons yesterday. And today Waldo sent one
off for $1.00 [?]   I mailed it for him. Got a letter from Mrs
Hopwood, Los Angeles today, also one from Lizzie, Victoria. We
have no snow yet. Lovely clear weather, pretty frosty nights. I was
out to the red [?] Store and got Waldo 2 suits of flannels. Wrote
to Eva & Fred Porter. 8 P.M. Pa gone to hear Cross[l]y &
Hunt[er].

Decr 23rd 1907
We have been attending the Crossly & Hunter meetings pretty
regularly ~ and have heard much preaching. Seems a number
of young people take their Stand for Jesus. Some older ones
too   it was a noble Stand to take. Among the younger boys
was Waldo ~ he knows what he is doing. and I believe God will,
and has accepted him. I pray that he, and all the others will look up
to 'the rock that is higher than I' and go on, and on, till at last we
shall meet at Jesus feet, saved from death. And God alone is able to
help us. The flesh is weak but the spirit is willing ~ I let the little
worries of home life bother me so. We surely should not have left
our house, and come to live in town. I miss my girls. I sometimes
wonder why it has to be that we must be seperated, its nice to think
of Eva being so near. Still its far for me ~ then, Lizzie and Jenn' so
far off

24th 1907: Here is Xmas eve, A little snow fell last night. Still its
fine. Not very cold. I am cooking a goose. got it from Jess [?]. I
believe its stale. So will see if he will exchange it.   have been
to see the butcher. And he has sent me a turkey. Ann is cooking
two [?] turkeys. We are having Nats family for dinner tomorrow
and we are looking for Fred. how we wish that more of our family
could be with us tomorrow   its the first Christmas for Jenn' to
be away. I have been looking back ~ back. All those fourty years
and more, and seeing pictures of our family at this time, Xmas eve,
how anxious the little ones were to get their stockings hung up.
alway[s] asked to go to bed earlier, and then the whispering, and
hiding of presents. holiday gifts. Now that stage of my life is over ~
I think it was my happiest time but I used to long, and wish that
they were grown up. Now they do not need mother, but O I need
them all. And I'm always thinking and never forget to pray every
day for them, likely we, Pa and I, will not be spared very much
longer but I am thankful that we were spared to them, till they all
can do without us, just got a letter from Wolseley. Eva had a son on

the 22nd ~ wish I could fly to her, if ever one needs a mother after she is married it is now. I can remember ~ how that was. I hope she will do well. All I can do now is pray for her, that is my comfort. Now I will stop. Waldo and Fred Knight are making candy, he just got a phone to go home but is asking to stay longer ~ Ann has her friend Tina [?], do not know how long she is going to stay   Mr and Mrs Speller called. Also Aggie Brice [?] from Rolo [?] was here to tea. Annie and Bob have gone to the rink. Pa is reading. he does not even notice that I am writing beside him ~ he loves reading so that he cannot be lonely. the girls write often, but I do miss them. And wish I could be near the girls. every one is kind, but I want to see the girls occasionally ~ When I get strong I won't fret so for them. I know its wrong, and I should be thankful ~ Fred just sent me a lovely box of nice stationery. also Alvin engraved some for me. Now I feel that I can write lots of letters while I am gaining up strength. I would write in this often ~ but I do not want the home folk to see it. I may burn all this some day ~ but just now its a comfort to me. And I shall keep on while I can. Now I am going to bed   am so tired   have been up a long while.

NOTES

Caroline Porter, Diaries, 1907–1934. Saskatchewan Archives, Regina, Collection R-89.

1 For a list of all the writing by the women of Saskatchewan housed in the Saskatchewan Archives, see Barbara Powell and Myrna Williams, *Piecing the Quilt: Sources for Women's History in the Saskatchewan Archives Board* (Regina: Canadian Plains Research Center, 1996).
2 See Helen Buss, *Canadian Women's Autobiography in English: An Introductory Guide for Researchers and Teachers* (Ottawa: CRIAW, 1991). Also see Buss ' "The Dear Domestic Circle": Frameworks for the Literary Study of Women's Personal Narratives in Archival Collections,' *Studies*

in *Canadian Literature* 14, no. 1 (1978): 1–17, and her *Mapping Our
Selves: Canadian Women's Autobiography in English* (Montreal: McGill-
Queen's University Press, 1993).

3 When Caroline Porter wrote her daughter's name, she rarely took time
to spell out the entire name Jennie; more frequently it appeared as Jenn,
with the final letters trailing off. In the excerpt, it appears as Jenn' for
this reason.

4 Although they begin in August, these are all of Caroline Porter's entries
for 1907.

5 Sunday school.

Sophie Alice Puckette
(1885–1971)

NANCI LANGFORD

This excerpt from Sophie Puckette's 1908 diary documents a turning point in her life. Twenty-two years old and far away from home for the first time, Sophie was teaching without qualifications on a temporary certificate in a rural community near Colfax, Washington at the time of these entries. Sophie and her brother and sister had contacted the authorities in Washington State when they heard there were teaching opportunities there. They had to pass a written examination, which they received in the mail and wrote at their kitchen table in Innisfree, Alberta, and they had to submit documentation of their formal education to obtain temporary teaching certificates for the state. None of them had attended normal school to earn a permanent teaching certificate – indeed, there were no normal schools in the new territory in which they lived – and it was difficult to secure teaching positions in Alberta without such qualifications.

Sophie had a dilemma to resolve: her beau, Jim Miles, who was farming on a homestead beside her parents' homestead in Innisfree, proposed to her before she left for Washington. Her family did not approve of Jim as a husband for Sophie. She had decided, in consultation with her mother, Alyce, to think over the proposal for six months. During that time, she was learning through her experiences in the Colfax district how difficult and unpleasant a teaching career could be. She was also learning how much she missed and cared for Jim (referred to in her diary as Jim, Jimmie, and J.G.), her family, and the life she had grown to enjoy in Alberta. Sophie's diaries record the emerging identity of a young woman struggling to decide her future and frustrated with the lack of opportunities to complete her education and obtain a teaching certificate.

Sophie began diary writing at the age of seven, providing sporadic accounts of life in an Oklahoma farm community and of brief attendance at Oklahoma Agricultural and Mechanical College in Stillwater after completing her basic schooling at Pleasantview School. But her five homesteading diaries, written when she was between eighteen and twenty-three – that is, during the years 1903 to 1908 – as she migrated with her family from Oklahoma to Alberta and built a new life there, are the most detailed and substantial. The first diary begins in October 1903, as her family prepares to migrate to Canada, and ends in January 1906, when Sophie arrives in Edmonton to attend Alberta College. She stopped diary writing for a whole year, from January 1906 to January 1907. When she began writing again in January 1907, she was working at the general store in Ranfurly, Alberta. The second diary covers the period of January to July 1907. The third chronicles the months between July 1907, when she is filled with despair about her future, and January 1908, when she is newly arrived in Colfax to teach. The fourth and fifth diaries cover Sophie's experience in Colfax and her return home to Alberta; they are written from 17 January to 16 April 1908 and 24 April to 31 July 1908, respectively. She wrote more detailed stories and more frequently in her last four diaries than in the first.

Sophie wrote in a reasonably neat, although sometimes cryptic, style of handwriting in two different types of booklets. The first two diaries are narrow bound books; the other three are larger booklets, more like school exercise books. She provides the dates and, where applicable, the locations of her writing at the top of each entry. For this time period, Sophie's diaries are unusual in how frankly she shares her opinions and feelings. In her first diary she is cautious and proper; as she matures, she becomes more open and more emotional. Like most women who regularly wrote in journals, Sophie described weather conditions, the chores she undertook each day, and the social encounters and activities of her family. The diaries reveal that she wrote letters almost every day; clearly, expressing herself in writing, either to her friends or to her diary, was a significant part of her life.

One noticeable difference over the years is that Sophie's handwriting changes. Her first diaries are written in half-page columns, and the writing is small and pinched. She makes use of every available space on the page. Later, as her personal confidence grows and a stronger sense of self emerges, her handwriting enlarges, becomes more sprawling and free, and she is less economical with space. The tone of her diaries also changes, suggesting a change in her relationship to them. When she is away from home in Ranfurly and Colfax, her letters and her diary are her only emotional outlet, and she relates to the pages of the diary as she would to a close friend. She confides in them in a way that is both revealing and charming.

In many ways Sophie's story is typical of young women who found themselves transplanted to the Canadian prairies in the early twentieth century. In an environment that offered few formal social structures or norms, and that was inhabited by a wide diversity of people from all over the world, Sophie found her character being tested as she was confronted with new experiences. Like most young women forced to move to Alberta with their families, she didn't want to be there, and resented the dramatic change in lifestyle the move brought. Homesteading offered her a limited life of farm and household work. At the age of eighteen, Sophie felt continuing her education was critical, yet attending school meant boarding in Edmonton. Because of her family's reduced financial circumstances, she was able to attend Alberta College for only one year, and the program did not qualify her for a teaching certificate. Gaining this certificate had been her cherished goal, and Sophie suffered terribly from this lost opportunity.

Sophie was not only an educated young woman with career aspirations, but she also belonged to an educated and very religious family. Her father, George Puckette, was a Christian church minister for thirty-one years in the United States before he brought the family to Canada. They brought their old-fashioned tall organ with them in 1903, crowding it and six people into the small sod-roofed house dug out of the hillside on the homestead owned by Troy, Sophie's brother. It wasn't long before the little soddy became a centre of worship and fellowship on Sundays as neighbours joined the family for a sermon and a hymn sing and stayed for dinner and a visit. This level of social interaction was unusual for homesteaders during this period, many of whom were isolated from neighbours for weeks at a time due to bad roads, weather, and sparse settlement.

By the spring of 1904, the men of the family had built a tiny log house for the Puckette family along the Barr Colony Trail in the middle of Sophie's father's homestead. This was the first real house – as opposed to dugout or soddy – in the district, and was also the first 'stopping house' in the district. Living in a 'stopping house' exposed the Puckette girls to all kinds of people who were travelling through the district, some staying just one night, others boarding for a while. Most were young bachelors. One distinguished visitor who stopped over was the Governor General of Canada, Earl Grey. Sophie wrote in her diary, 'Earl Grey came through and partook of a cup of tea in our humble abode. As he chatted with my mother, his aide stood stiffly behind his chair while the Northwest Mounted Police escorts in scarlet were clustered outside. The informants said they were riding from Edmonton to North Battleford.' When the Canadian National Railway cut through George Puckette's homestead in 1905, he donated the southern half of his homestead for a town site, and the village of Delnorte, later Innisfree, quickly sprang up a half mile from the Puckette farmhouse.

Sophie had four sisters and three brothers, although only two of the brothers survived to adulthood. Some of Sophie's married brothers and sisters lived as neighbours on adjacent homesteads.

This proximity fostered an exchange of goods, services, and social companionship that was constant and supportive to all the families. Sophie would often help her sister with the chores or the children after completing her own chores at home. Such sharing also provided a change of scene for the unmarried Puckette sisters, who could stay over at a brother's or sister's place for a night or two after arranging for someone to cover their home duties. Sophie was a good friend to her brothers and sisters, and when she decided to apply for a temporary teaching job near Colfax, her sister Alta and her brother Troy did the same. All three were successful in obtaining positions. As is clear in these entries, her frequent visits with Troy and Alta and the constant stream of correspondence between Sophie and her family and friends eased her loneliness in Colfax; they were essential aspects of her life. The excerpt printed here reveals the strong ties Sophie had to her siblings and their spouses.

Sophie had a strong sense of herself, and she reveals both intelligence and wit in her writing. Despite the evidence throughout her homesteading diaries of a strong drive to be educated and self-sufficient, the prospect of teaching seemed to dazzle her less and less, particularly after Jim began a serious courtship. Her six months boarding with a family in Colfax made her painfully aware of the importance of her attachments to her family. All of these considerations influenced her response when she finally realized what had been her dream – to be a teacher – during her six-month contract position near Colfax, and they converge at the turning point found in these excerpts.

In March 1908, Jim wrote Sophie to ask her to set 'the day' and to request her ring size. In May, Sophie received an engagement ring from Jim in the mail and, upon completing her teaching contract, returned to Alberta. Sophie married Jim Miles in August 1908 at Vermilion, Alberta. Over the course of their marriage they had six children, three boys and three girls, including a set of twins. One of the girls, the last, was stillborn. They lived at Innisfree until 1920, when they moved to Edmonton, where Jim worked in real estate and later joined the police force. Sophie ceased writing in her diary the week of her wedding. However, samples of her prolific correspondence during her married life remain to provide evidence that her spirited observations of life and of people continued, as did her strong ties to friends and family.

Sophie Puckette, in Washington State, 1908.

DIARY, ALBERTA, JANUARY–FEBRUARY 1908

Jan. 17th   Well, the first week of my second month of school is at last ended. I rec'd a letter from Cousin Valley this evening. And, as is usual with me, I was disappointed, for it wasn't the one I wanted! He wants me to send him my picture – humph – I guess if he could see me once, he'd not care for a likeness to remind him constantly.

I just do wonder why that boy Jim doesn't write to me? I wonder if he's just busy, and neglectful, or if something is the matter? His last letter was written Dec. 26 – and this is Jan. 17th! I wish he'd happen to remember that he has a 'little sister' away off down here who likes to hear from her 'big brother' once in awhile. Well, I haven't anything to write, and I may as well stop.

Jan. 19th   Another Sunday has rolled round at last. It is now 7 p.m. I started this about four, but Price Neely was here and he's such a kid to talk that I gave it up in despair. The long looked for letter came yesterday eve. It made me a little homesick when I read it. He told me not to get homesick but when this school was out to come along home right quick and be a good girl. Mama advised us to stay next summer if we could get something to do. O, well, I can't tell yet, what I will do. I may go back next spring, after all. I want to go to Colfax next Saturday and see the kids. Mrs. N. says maybe she'll go with me to Pullman. I hope she will. If we can get there Fri. eve. I'll run on out to Troy's Sat. morn, then bring Alta back Sat. p.m. to C-fax do a little running around together, stay at Perine's, and go our separate ways to our schools Sunday. I wish we could have our pictures taken. If we're in the mood, maybe we will. Valley wants my picture but I've written that, already.

One man down here described me to Neely's as a '*little* girl with light hair'! When Neely's were looking at my photos they tho't Alta's picture was mine! Said the expression was like mine. There's no accounting for ideas and tastes.

Jim Stephenson told Mr. Neely he was coming out today to see the School Ma'am; out he didn't come – I guess he changed his notion.

Price took my letter to 'Home' to mail. Bob mailed one for me last Sun. I wonder if Jim would notice it if I didn't answer his letter for a week? He says Mrs. Marshall and the three younger girls are keeping house for them. I guess they have pretty lively times if such is the case. Willa and her father are holding down the ranch I suppose. Well, I believe I'll stop for tonight.

Vic and Merl told Anita Alta & I came down here more to get a man than any thing else. Also that Maude tho't so much of E.N.[1] that he had to come down every Sun. for her to comb his hair for church! O, they are so mean. Why will girls degrade themselves so by envious backbiting? And to say such mean things to Babe, too – it just makes me boil – there, there – the room's hot enough without spending extra energy boiling. I think you'd better go to bed it you can't do better.

Jan. 20th
Well, when I got home this evening Mrs. N. asked if I went to the mailbox, and I said 'no, Did Mr. Neely?' She said she wasn't going to tell. Then walked back into the sitting room and said there's only *four*. Sure enough there were two from Alta, one from Alice, and one from the agent at Pullman – and the trains do make connections, too!

O, but I am glad – Alta is having an awful time with her ears, poor kid. She hadn't got my last letter yet when she wrote. Harold has slipped noiselessly out and knocked at the dining room door. I tho't he was up to something.

I've a notion to write and tell Jimmie 'yes.' It would be such a comfort to have it off my mind for good.

I think I'll write to Alta tonight.

Jan 21st   Well, I made two trips to the mail box today. This morn. I made the fire at the S.H. [schoolhouse] then went down and mailed the letter to Alta. This evening Floyd went over and bro't me one from Troy, and – the one I'd mailed! This is the second time that carrier has left letters for me, and I was so disappointed –

I want it to go. I wrote him a little note telling him of his short-comings and if he does it again, I'll just report him. He's no business being so careless. Troy says they've taken Opha to the hospital in Colfax, and don't think she'll live. The Diphtheria is all gone, but the pain in her head is, if anything, worse, and her eye is swelled shut and dreadfully inflamed. Her sister from KS. [Kansas] is expected. Or was, on Sat.

Little Geo. is having a cold and earache. Poor little chap – I do hope I'll get to go to Pullman Fri. eve., then I'll make them a flying visit on Sat. from ten till 1:30 – If we can't make P~ Fri. eve., then I won't get to C-fax till Sat. night and won't see any but Alta.

Jan 22n – I've not heard from Alta yet and this is Wed. I wonder why she doesn't write? I sent by Mrs. N. to Johnson today and nothing is just what I wanted. The stockings – O, dear me, they're great big ribbed things. I just can't bear ribbed sox.

The rubbers are great heavy rolled sole affairs – Still they're not so bad. The notebook is all right, and the pencil too, only the color. It has the stars and stripes on it. I like a plain one better.

My stomach hurt me this morning nearly all morn, just like it used to when my eyes hurt me so badly. I am sorry they are troubling me again. Mrs. N. said they were very red last night. They bother me quite a lot. If I'm in Pullman all day Sat., I'll have that eye Specialist to examine them and *Of* course, he'll say I must put on glasses again. I don't want to wear the horrid things. But I guess it *might* be better than going blind. Mrs. N. has just given me some maple sugar. I b'lieve I'll read the new Ladies Home Journal awhile.

Jan. 23rd   This is pretty regular writing *eh?* Every day.   Got the letter from Alta today. She wanted me to wait till next Sat., to come to Colfax, but we've made all our arrangements to go tomorrow eve., and I think I'll go. I'll make it a visit rather than business trip. I'll have to, the way the trains go.

I also got letters from Papa & Maude and one from Lena McCall. She signed her name *Helen* McCall. *And* the greatest joke on me,

too. I just had to laugh. I wrote that I had sent a note to the mail
carrier. Well, if I didn't send it in an envelope that I had some
stamps in! If that wasn't the brightest trick! He sent them back
with a little sarcastic note asking if they were meant as a reward for
his faithful discharge of his duties!! O, dear, dear! I have to laugh
whenever I think of it ~

It is now 9:25 p.m. and I am all ready for to retire. I have my
clean clothes all layed out for morning, have taken a bath, and O,
I hope & pray that that train will go up tomorrow eve – Good
night –

Jan. 28 – Well, I've waited quite a long time, but last night I had to
write home, to Allie & to Valley, and by that time didn't feel equal
to this. The train didn't go, after all, and we were so disappointed,
and at last we took the team and drove over. Harold drove till he
got careless, then I took the lines and as 'twas dark and a strange
road I tho't we'd never on earth get there. Peach got scared at an
engine beside the road, and backed us off into a little ditch. Harold
went and got a man to help us past it, and we were good and glad to
drive into the alley by Doris.

After we'd had supper, they played the phonograph till ten. I
took the 8:00 train next morn, waited fifteen minutes in Colfax
then went on out to Troy's.

They stopped away up at the end of warehouses, and when I
walked around, saw Alta in the yard, and Geo. standing in the
door. Troy & Beulah had gone to Colfax to have her teeth attended
to. She had nine filled and seventeen pulled! She wasn't able to
come home that eve. Horace was out with Kelso and didn't get in
till afternoon. He is as tall as I am now. I had a fine visit. Roy Lee
bro't the team out and told us the kids stayed in town. Alta & I
tried to phone to Troy for him to get me that history but couldn't
get Colfax. Horace flagged the train for me. When I got to Perine's,
Mr. and Mrs. P. had gone to church. T & B had gone to bed. The
man who came to the door didn't seem anxious to let me in, but I
went in anyway. I called Troy and that way found their room and

talked to them till Perines came home. Mrs. P. popped corn and we ate it with candy. When Mr. P. had given me a handshake he patted me on the cheek and said I was as nice as ever. I said I was as mean as ever. He said he tho't I was never mean, was as good as I could be. I remarked 'I hope so' where upon he agreed.

Mr. N. just gave me a big long letter from May R. Her letters always do me so much good. Still, I feel as I'd like to cry.

She tells of a man down there who thinks a lot of her. I believe she halfway likes him too, but 'her people' object. I just think people haven't any right to wet-blanket everything a girl does. It's not any of Ina's business, and she ought to keep out.

I can't write any more about my trip, we drove out in the afternoon got here at 5 p.m. Mr. N. wasn't here and it was an hour before we got the fire started to warm up. Bye bye for now.

O, dear, dear   I feel so lonesome. I wish I had the faculty of always being content, rather than as I am – never satisfied.

I never *do* know what I want.

Today, there were some fellows at the hall. One and his girl went past at recess and he said, 'O, what a pretty school ma'am! ain't she pretty?' I could have bitten a ten penny nail in two. I was watching the kids play ball. They all pretended not to hear but Harold, at least for one, did, for he told Mrs. N. about it this evening. He was disgusted and said that fellow tho't he was smart.

The kids want me to go down again next Sat., and be in town with them. I wish I could. If I find that the train will go Fri., I guess I'll go again. Well, I'll stop this time, for good (til next time).

[in margin:] Wednesday
Jan 29th   Well, well – Jan. is nearly gone. How time does fly. Still it seems to creep, too. Two months will soon be gone (I mean of school). Mrs. N. said we'd go over Friday p.m., and see if the train is going. Say, I hope it will – I'll have to not be disappointed tho,' if it doesn't.

Last night it snowed and again today. Mr. N. said there was about five or six inches. Floyd took my letters to the box today and didn't raise the flag, so they didn't go. We tho't we heard someone knock at the S.H. door, and when I went it was Nelson's dog! I suppose he got lonesome all alone.

Feb. 2nd   I guess I'll begin from where I stopped. Thurs. night Mrs. Neely coaxed me to go down with her to the dance to hear the music. There was to be musicians from Pullman. I didn't want to go, a bit, and the closer the time came, the less I cared to go, but they are always so good to me, and were going to take me to the train Friday, that I at last consented to go. Harold took a stubborn spell and didn't go, so we didn't stay long. I was glad to come back tho – I was so tired. I shouldn't care to dance – I don't see why people get so silly over it. I'll not like to be held quite so close to just any old fellow, for my part. Fri. I cut the noon twenty minutes short and didn't give any recess and finished by 2:30. The kids didn't like it very well, but I felt as if I wanted to please myself for once.

It was pretty good going to Johnson. We went in a homemade 'cutter.' The train was going, for a wonder, and I was O, so glad! Jimmie came into the store for awhile before train time. We didn't get in in time to catch the 4:35 for Colfax, so I went up to Davis.' Ola was going with her S.S. [Sunday School] class for a sleigh ride and asked me to go too. I went – There were three sleigh loads – over thirty. We went out two miles, and surprised some people. I had a fine time. They were all so nice. Not silly and sentimental, at all. Everyone seemed to have lots of fun too. We played games, ate apples and talked – After we started back. Next morn. I took the 8:05 train for C. – I found Alta at Perine's. She had come in Fri. eve. We had such a fine visit. Ran around all day. I got some shoes, got overshoes at Johnson and Mrs. N. bro't 'em out   side combs, Pompeiian cream, etc. We sent Maude four songs. I hope they'll prove to be pretty. And what else do you suppose we did? Had our pictures taken! Yes sir, we surely did. I always feel so silly that I usually succeed in looking the same charming way – Alta & the 'picture man' both said they tho't mine would be fine – I certainly do hope they will. Troy came into town but we didn't get to see him at all. We didn't know he was in till he was gone. Horace came up on the 7 train. When he got there we had gone to church with Perine's. He went with Roy Lee to the skating rink then came back again. He went out with Alta this morning.

How I did hate to come back again! I don't like my job overly much I'm afraid. Mrs. N. had a little 'card party' Sat. night. I'm really glad I wasn't here.

Well, I guess this is enough for this time.

Feb. 4th   It is nearly eight – Mr. & Mrs. N. have just got home from Moscow. She had her teeth worked on. It is drizzling rain. It began snowing about three this afternoon, and by dark turned to rain. I got up this morn. at 5:20 – After breakfast I fixed the school dinners and finished drying the dishes, swept the floors and helped Mrs. N. dress. She borrowed my Xmas scarf, and I made her put my golf jacket and overshoes on. When I got home I bro't in part of the clothes and folded them away. Was going to get supper but Harold said there wasn't any more wood, so we ate a cold lunch. I bro't a bucket of coal in and then he said one cow kicked and he was afraid to milk him so I went and milked him for him thus milked the other one too! I then made out some test questions in gram for my 6th & 7th graders and read McCall's magazine.

I feel better now but all this evening I have been feeling so lonesome – I did so want a letter from 'my boy' and it didn't come. Tomorrow, two weeks will have elapsed, since I wrote to him. I answered May's letter yesterday and told her about Jim. Poor kid I'm hardly fair to him. The proofs came yesterday, for my pictures. I ordered the full face view, as I liked it better than the other. I sent the other proof to May! There's to be a teacher's meeting in Colton Sat – I'd like to go but don't know yet – well so long for this time –

Feb. 7th ,   Friday Well, this ends my second month of school. O, say, just let me whisper, 'I'm glad, glad!' I don't see how I'm to stand

it all spring. I believe they'll drive me crazy. I just tho't they'd worry
me to death today. As soon as they finished the test in one subj.,
why then *they're 'figged'* and talk and *laugh* and *giggle*. I'd think
they'd get tired of laughing *all* the time. I'm easy   just dead
easy   I can't help giving them help when they tell me they
don't know this or that. O, they're so careless   don't seem to care
whether they remember or not. I get so sick of it all I want to pitch
'em all out into a snowbank and cool 'em off a bit. Today we had
speaking again and I made Elvin read when he didn't want to, and
he read a horrid one just to make them laugh. I must own that I was
mad. When he took his seat, I said I tho't it was a very poor selection – that I was surprised at him and I must have looked what I
felt for he looked so ashamed, and that put a stop to their laughing.
When they laughed so today, I looked at them and tho't: 'you stop
your laughing, you little heathen!' I really did, and tho't it so
strongly, I wonder they couldn't read it in my face. Harold & Elvin
were eating peanuts this morning too. I never saw the like & he is
lots worse since he went up to Davis.' I s'pose the kids up there
tho't I was easy and told him what to do. I just wish I had a good
strap. I'd wake them up some fine way.

  Got letters from Beulah and Clara Schroter this eve. Walked
down to the box and back after & came home. They're the first
'letters' I've had this week. I've not heard from home for over a
week. Mr. N. went to Pullman this eve. to see a play. Mrs. N. is
making her collar. Copying off my white ribbon one Allie started
and never finished. I believe I'll stop.

Sunday, Feb. 9 – 1908 ~ ~ ~
  Yesterday I finished up grading the kids' exam papers, then after
dinner, which we didn't have till two o'clock. I was going down for
the mail, but Mrs. N. said twas too sloppy for one to go out, so
Harold took Bob's pony and went. I was just sick I was so anxious
to know if there were letters from home. He came back and said
there wasn't any. I was reading in Uncle Tom's Cabins, and went
on with my reading but O, how I wanted to cry. I didn't know

whether he was telling the truth or not either – you never can tell. Pretty soon, sure enough, he hauled out two letters and held them to view. He said no, they weren't for me. Then walked straight over and gave them to me.

They were both JG's handwriting. One was a letter the other two valentines. One Old Maid, one pretty one. I was so glad to get the letter I heaved two or three great sighs – Then when I read it, for awhile I was mad. He said if I ever should dance, he *wouldn't want my answer.* He doesn't seem to think it might work both ways. That hurt me worse *than anything.* I looked so blue that Mrs. Neely tried to rally me after the men went out. Harold went home with Bob, and Mr. N. was about the chores, and I told her a lot. How we stood, and I felt better afterward. After hearing the case, she advised me to write and tell him, yes, and quit worrying about it.

I want to, too, but that about the dancing hurts. I should think he'd have more confidence in me than that if he really loves me. Whenever I think of it, in all its lights, I get back to the old muddle, and don't know what to do. It's plain to be seen I don't want to give him up.

Feb. 11th   It has snowed today, comparatively all day. Yest. too. Yest., I got letters from Laura, Kit, Alta, Maude   also a whisk broom holder from Laura. Mr. & Mrs. Neely went to a party last night, and I sat up and wrote till eleven. Answered Alta's, Maude's, and wrote a little short note to Jim, but didn't send it off.

My pictures should come – I wish I knew if they came today. I didn't get the mail. Eva said my eyes looked red today. A girl last night asked Mrs. N. if she was on the train a week ago Sun. She saw a tall 'slim girl' dressed in brown with Iva Davis. Queer ways people have of describing me – Eva says I remind her so very strongly of Edna Rolfe – a school teacher here on the flat – The only difference, she has black hair!

Feb. 12th   Well, those pictures didn't come again today. I wish he'd hurry – yesterday morning Neely's didn't get up till nearly eight. At a quarter past I couldn't stand it any longer, and after some opposition from Mrs. N. ate a dish of apples & cream, with a cold biscuit & butter and went on. I just had things in order when the children came. She never seems to have breakfast till nearly or quite eight of a morning. I never have time for a thing of a morning, as I don't get up till they do, and of an evening I am too tired usually to do much. I'll be glad when spring comes in reality. I wonder if Mrs. N. sent that warrant for Mr. Davis to sign – I told her I wished she would, and I want it.[2] I've not sent any home for my second month yet – O, I wish I could always tell what to do to get the kids to take an interest in their work.

Sunday, Feb. 16th ~ ~ ~
Drizzle, drazzle – hear the rain! It's bad enough to be cooped up all day with nothing to do, without a rain. Mr. N. and Bob went to Johnson today to see the horse buyer. They went to Pullman yesterday and Mr. N. took my warrant and had it signed up and cashed.

I wrote to J.G. the 12th and put in what I'd written the 10th. It kind of put a stop to my worrying, and I don't believe I'll regret it. At least, I hope not. He does lots of things I don't like but I'll have to look over them (or teach him better!) I wonder what he'll say? I wonder what the folks will think. They won't say much. I hope they won't be ugly about it, for if they are, twill just about kill me. I think so much of them all – I hope they'll be good to me.

I wrote to Troy, Kit, Clara, and Laura yesterday P.M., and home this morning. My pictures didn't come yet. I do wish they would. I'm so anxious to send one home – I wish I could be there myself – O, how I wish my school were out!

I dated my letter to Jim wrong the other day – and it all came of Troy dating one wrong to me!

On Fri. eve (St. Valentine's) Bob came over. He was here for supper and stayed till a little after eight. I had a regular streak on. We shelled and popped corn and I teased and laughed more than I have for a long time. He didn't seem to mind tho,' I believe he rather enjoyed it! Price is here today but I don't feel inclined to talk much so he and Harold are reading. He was here for supper last night and awhile after. He showed me a valentine he got at school then demanded to know if I was ashamed to show mine – So, of course, I let him see the old maid one – (Harold had told him I had it!) and you may be sure he didn't even know I had the other. O, my shoulders ache from sitting in one position so long. I must stop. I guess I'll read 'Common Sense Didactics' awhile. a little common sense won't hurt me, *eh?*

Feb. 17 – '08 Monday

Well to begin with, I asked Price to take my letters to the box, yesterday. Mr. N. bro't me a valentine from Johnson and Price was so anxious to see it that I wouldn't let him at all. I'm sure he sent it. He went off and forgot my letters. Mr. Davis came in the evening. This morning it was snowing and blustering so they concluded not to butcher. Bob came over any way, and was going on to Johnson. He said he doubted if I could get across the creek, and if I wanted to I might ride around with him. Mr. Davis & Harold went down and put a board across one place and thus managed to cross.

Floyd and Ernest didn't come, so I suppose that school started. Harold & Herman got to snapping matches again, and I asked him which one it was and Harold just sat there and wouldn't answer a word – I got mad and told him to answer me immediately. I heard Elvin ask why they didn't answer – when Herman spoke up and said it was both of them. I said 'very well, you may both come up here – bring your books!' My voice was 'very like a two edged sword.' Harold looked so scared – he's an awful coward and I know he put Herman up to it. He got Herman & Ernest at it awhile but I tho't I had it stopped. I made them stand on their knees and study. After ten minutes Herman got so pale and looked so appealing that I told him he might take his seat.

I let Harold stay for 2 min. yet, till his class – but he wasn't 'fazed' – the little sinner – and this eve just as he left, there was another pop. He popped one during the Geog. Class in his pocket, but I let it go as an accident. I have an awful notion to give him a tanning for that. If it happens again, I'll have to. I hate to tho' as long as I can keep from it. I got letters this eve from Mrs. Starry, Ida and Alta. She's been having trouble with her boys too. They're a bad lot any way.

Ida wrote a great long letter, and told about her work, their leap year parties, etc., etc., and O, dear me – I'd just give almost anything if I could be there with her, in school. She passed the civil service exam for Indian work, and got an appointment at Ft. Defiance, Arizona, but doesn't know yet whether she'll go or not – It is so dark I can't see the lines so I'll stop.

Tues. Feb. 18th ~ ~ ~ Well, I can't think of anything to write after getting my book out. Elvin & Roy went to the mailbox this eve. but I didn't know they were going, and consequently my letter to Alta didn't get taken away. Bob is here, helped butcher today, and if I can catch him I'll send it by him. No pictures again. No mail of any kind for me this eve. I wish I'd hear from home. I'm going to have to lay in another supply of stationery pretty soon. My stock is running low.

I guess I'll study some more Methods.

Feb. 19 – Had another letter from Alta this morn even. I sent one to her this morn., Bob took it to Pullman. I wish I had kept it now, then I could have written to her this eve. I've not had one from home yet this morn ~~week~~   what on earth ails me, anyway – I keep trying to write morning   Bob had just got back from Pullman. Mr. N. has gone to help him with the teams. We've had supper – Had ribs! They killed thirteen hogs yesterday. But took some to Pullman.

Today Eva and I played 'catch' in the house. Roy & Elvin came in and caught the ball right out of our hands. It was nip & tuck which ones had it. We didn't scuffle, only each tried to catch it. They weren't at all rough, so it was fun.

I wonder when 'my big boy' got my letter. I wonder when I'll get an answer? I had a dream last night. We seemed to be married and were starting away somewhere, when he got a message and was going to have to go somewhere else, alone. I felt so badly, and there were great tears in my eyes when I told him I'd be lonely while he was gone. My, how silly of me to write this down. I do think a lot of him tho' now that I have a right to.

Feb. 20 th   Thurs.

Letters from Maude, Alice and Beulah today. Maude sent Kodak pictures of Mary & Warren, Mama knitting, and a moonlight view of Anita Lake. The ones of the children isn't very plain but Warren does look so sweet! And Mama, so natural – O, wouldn't I like to be there for a while? Sometimes I think I won't be able to wait till school is out to see them all.

My, I'm glad tomorrow's Friday. I wrote to DuVall yesterday – I wish he'd send those pictures on. Elvin bro't my letters this eve. I like that kid – He is so much better since Floyd quit school, but Master Harold seems to be trying himself.

My old nerves seem to be trying themselves too. I have that old hurting in my stomach again. I'm not going to get glasses tho' as long as I can keep from it.

Feb. 22nd   12:20 p.m. I've written to Alta & Alice and as my envelopes are all gone I guess I'll wait till after dinner anyway to write more. I just heard the whistle of the train from Pullman. Wish Alta'd surprise me.

Got a letter from DuVall yesterday. The pictures have been finished since last Sat., 'awaiting our orders' – The idea – I hope Troy will see about them today – Alta said she & Beulah were going to town. She's going to keep the children – then she'll go next Sat. Her third month will be out then. My school is half finished. Only ten more weeks.

I've a bad taste in my mouth. This books seems to be all filled with complaints. That's rather a bad *record*. It's such a relief tho' to be able to write it out, then I don't have to worry someone with every ache and pain.

Sunday, Feb. 23, 1908 ~
Mrs. Neely and I have just got back from taking some letters to the
mail box. It is pretty muddy. It has been such a gloriously bright day
today.
I went to the box yesterday too, but didn't get any mail.
I feel tired, some way – I wonder what letters I'll get tomorrow.

Thurs. morn – Feb. 27 – before breakfast
Mon. I got letters from Maude & Mama, May Evans Dixon, King
bookstore, drawing books and two postcards from J.G. – I could
have just shaken him with pleasure. They were in an envelope –
and I tho't 'twas a letter. Horrid things too – perhaps he tho't them
expressive. Tues. a letter from Alta came. Yesterday there was
none.
Mrs. N. went to Pullman, and Mr. N. bro't Mrs. Wiley out.
Eva was disappointed because if Mrs. W. hadn't come she would
either have come with me, or I'd have gone with her.
Amy, Mrs. Wiley's two (I think about) year old and I had a big
romp. She's a cute little one, and talks a jot. Mr. N. is making biscuits for breakfast!
It snowed last night but is nearly clear this morn. Mrs. N. will be
back today.
O, say if Alta shouldn't get my letter! I sent it yesterday. It will
get there tomorrow, but she may not get the mail! I mustn't worry
tho.'
I hope I get a letter from J.G. today – surely his mind is settled by
now! breakfast. I must write home tonight. I go to C-fax Sat.

Feb. 28 – Friday – Well, yesterday eve when we got home from
School Mr. & Mrs. N. hadn't come yet. Harold gave me my letter
from J.G. and like the big baby that I am, when I read it, I had to
take a cry. I felt so lonesome and had been sick all day any way. I
was afraid to cry long for fear they'd get home and see my red eyes;
so I made the fire in the kitchen and had supper, in a manner ready
when they got home. I'm so nervous lately – This morn. I dreaded

to go to school, and at length told Mrs. N. about having a cry. She said: 'And when we got here you were all smiles!'

Yesterday morn. the creek was up, booming. In walking across a little plank on yon side, the water ran over our feet. I was kinder afraid. Like Miss G. 'my nerves nearly give out sometimes'!

Mrs. N. wants me to go to a Dr. and get some medicine for them. I hate to pour down drugs tho.'

I wrote to Perines last night to keep Alta in town tomorrow night in case she shouldn't get my letter. My heel has a big blister on it – and I'm afraid I'll not enjoy my long day's wait in Pullman.

I wish I could see Jim. I get so lonesome I can't hardly bear it sometimes. My eyes hurt tonight – kind of smart – I guess I'd better quit using them. bye bye – till I get back from Colfax.

NOTES

Sophie Alice Puckette diary, Glenbow Museum and Archives, M843.

1 E.N. is Elmer Nodwell, who married Sophie's sister Maude.
2 A warrant was a document that permitted the teacher to be paid. In this case, the school board treasurer, Mr Davis, needs to sign the warrant so Sophie can cash it.

PART FOUR:
EXPLORATION

Mina Wylie
(1888–1972)

MORGAN HOLMES[1]

On her winter journey in 1911 from the relatively sleepy city of Ottawa to the bustle of New York City and the major metropolises of Europe, Wilhelmina (Mina) Washington Wylie recorded the sights, sensations, and pleasures of a world that was soon after swept away by cataclysmic social upheaval. Travelling with her mother, father, and sister Ida, Mina is given to using exuberant adjectives such as 'jolly,' 'lovely,' 'dear,' 'darling,' and 'great fun.' This is the language of an adventurous person who, from her departure on 14 January until she broke off writing in Glasgow on 8 March, records a sincere delight in encountering new people and learning about foreign lands.[2] Like most diaries, Mina's is taken up with numerous mundane bits and trivial observations – the weather was sunny, the paintings were beautiful, dinner was superb. At the same time, though, the journal is possessed of an animated, forthright spirit that carries the reader into the heart and mind of a young woman capable of living each day to its fullest.

Mina was the third of four children born to William Washington Wylie and his wife, whose Christian name has been lost, but who is still remembered fondly by her grandson and others simply as 'Granny Dear.' Mina's parents were both Scots who arrived in Canada by chance. Intending to immigrate to Chile, where William had been born (and where his mother and father still lived), on the voyage out the Wylies were forced to disembark at Montreal because their young son Jack had become seriously ill. William soon found work as a carpenter, constructing the Canadian Pacific Railway's new sleeper cars, and eventually the family moved to Bell's Corners, outside Ottawa. Here, Mina and her two sisters, Nell and Ida, were born.

After several years on a farm in Bell's Corners, the family moved to Canada's capital, where, in 1893, William made his fortune as a founding partner of the Ottawa Car Manufacturing Company, a firm that made streetcars for the Ottawa Electric Railway and horse-drawn vehicles for the public.[3] Although Mina had been born into a solidly working-class immigrant family, by the time she set sail for Europe as a young woman, she and her siblings were enjoying the comforts of upper-middle-class life.

When Mina returned from her European journey she married her fiancé, William Young Denison, the man to whom she refers in the journal as 'Denny.' Her husband became a successful chartered accountant. In 1913, Mina gave birth to a son, Ainslie, and, in 1915, to Robert. A third son, Teddy, died in infancy. William predeceased his wife in the 1960s. Until her death, Mina and Ainslie lived in the family home at 189 Carling Avenue, Ottawa. Mother and son also continued to spend much of their time from Victoria Day to Labour Day at the Gables, a gracious summer home, at Portland on the Rideau River, that the Denisons acquired in 1929. Mina had a great love of family. During the Great Depression, when her nephew, his wife, and two children were much too poor to be able to afford holidays, Mina had them down to visit the Gables for two weeks every summer.

Mina came of age in a transforming economic and cultural environment, in which the forces of modernity were working to displace conventional Victorian attitudes and culture. In her diary, one can readily discern a questioning, confident mind that drew on this energetic atmosphere in an attempt to understand the greater world beyond. At the same time, though, Mina was the product of a privileged segment of society, and she took a keen delight in the trappings of that demi-monde. From about the time she was five, Mina's upbringing was typical for women of the upper-middle class. She learned to play the piano, do needlepoint, and paint in oils; a number of her canvases, depicting tranquil, umber-shaded woodland scenes, still survive. Drawn throughout her life to lovely clothes, she particularly fancied dresses that complemented her sparkling blue eyes. As a married woman, golf (at the Rivermead Club and the Ottawa Hunt Club), dancing, and cocktail and dinner parties were chief among her social activities. Mina prepared for these latter two activites while enrolled in the 'Diamond Ring' course[4] at Macdonald College, a sort of finishing school for well-off young ladies. In addition, Mina was an avid bridge player and met regularly with her friends Agnes, Nympha, Queenie, and Gladys for that purpose. The golden rule of Mina's bridge club was that a successful afternoon requires five players. This tenet came into being when, one day, Nympha suffered a heart attack and had to be rushed to the hospital by ambulance. Luckily, though, because a fifth lady was present, the game could continue.

Similar to her behaviour during this potentially upsetting episode, a seemingly imperturbable nature springs forth from the pages of Mina's diary; indeed, 'on with the show' seems to have been her life-long motto. Her great-niece Judy recalls the time that Mina very nearly lost her life in an automobile accident. When the family was at last permitted to visit her in hospital, Mina was sitting up in bed, hair and makeup perfect, attired in an elegant blue night gown. No one would have suspected that she was in any pain; she was the perfect hostess, making sure that her 'guests' were comfortable and amused.

Throughout her life Mina possessed a flair for drama and self-conscious performance. In her journal we occasionally catch sight of this penchant. Towards the end of her visit to Rome, for example, she paid a night-time visit to the Coliseum. Mina enthusiastically records that 'It was the most impressive sight I have ever witnessed – We stood in the centre of the Arena – watching the Moon climb – higher and higher – now and then peeping through

the ruins – till it was clear above and flooded the place with light –
The very stillness was grand – and all kinds of phantoms rose
before the mind.' Fortunately, Mina's sojourn in the Eternal City
ended much more happily than that of Daisy Miller, her Jamesian
literary progenitor, whose similarly enraptured visit to the Coliseum resulted in death by malaria.

Mina's diary is a compact, red-leather-bound notebook, 7½ by
4½ inches. Writing on its ruled sheets Mina used black ink to
record her thoughts and experiences in a ladylike, English back-
hand script. Her spelling is atrocious and must have caused her
teachers not a little grief. There is little consistency to the length
of Mina's daily entries, though on average she filled about one-and-
a-half to two pages per day; especially exciting or busy days (such as
25 January) could occupy almost six. The diary was evidently a gift
(purchased at an unidentified Ottawa bookstore) from Nell, who
inscribed the following prefatory note in her younger sister's voice:

> Ottawa Jan. 12th, 5911 [*sic*]
>
> I, Mina W. Wylie, of the City of Ottawa, County of Carleton, Prov-
> ince of Ontario, hereby make oath and say that this book was pur-
> chased by me this twelvth [*sic*] day of January in the year of our Lord
> nineteen hundred and eleven for the purpose of recording herein an
> accurate, full true and correct record of my first trip to New York City
> and to Europe which I contemplate starting on Saturday January 14th
> 1911.
>
> Of course, being of the female persuasion, I may change my mind
> and leave somethings out, but it is understood that will be permissable.
>
> Should this little book be so indiscreet as to desert me for another
> that other party is hereby requested to examine the date at the top of
> page one, box it well and send it to Mrs W^m McLaren Carling Ave.
> Ottawa, Ont.

it was such a treat - away from the sight of land - rather a pity the wind went down - dinner with father - nearly all the ladies had to leave the table on account?"

Friday June 20.
On Board -
A nice cool bright day.
Up up early and had a nice brush walk on deck before breakfast.
Mother was well enough to go down - I only stayed a short while - hurried back indeed, and rested in my steamer chair. Mrs Wilson and Mrs Pulitzer asked me to go to the upper deck with them. It was very pleasant up there, but I took ill about eleven o'clock, and had to go to my cabin.
It was very lovely for a while, when I was ill did I

thought of everyone at home and tried to picture what they would all be doing - Soon I fell asleep - woke up about 3 o'clock - feeling splendid - went out on deck - Had Afternoon tea in Mother's stateroom - The first biscuit cup tea since we left home.
The most amusing all the waiters are french and we had great times making ourselves understood.
Dressed and went down to dinner - just had to leave the dining room - Mrs Wilson - the stewardess brought up my dinner, but really I could not eat it. - I fell asleep very soon -
I always do rest so well in this dear little cabin.
Saw a shoal of porpoises this morning.
by a hair 410 steerage passengers on board

Excerpt from Mina Wylie's journal, 1911.

Mina and her husband, Denny, at Blue Sea Lake, QC, ca. 1925.

DIARY, ONTARIO,
JANUARY–FEBRUARY 1911

Tuesday Jan. 17 – 1911
New York.

A Bright pleasant day, shopping again – We went – to all the uptown stores today   Gimbals is very ~~pretty~~ beautiful. I saw so many things I would dearly love to buy – but alas – allready are [our] trunks are bulged – as Father has limited us to one suit case – and one steamer-trunk each. Had the most delicious choclate and listened to a pianola Recital

Then we went over to Macy's   did a little shopping but had to hurry back to Hotel by 3. o'clock to meet Father.[6] – we took the heaviest suit-case and went over to the Dock to see our Steamer – The barges were thick around coal – they have an immense cargo and were as busy as Bee's

Going over to the Brooklyn, Docks. – we took the subway to South Ferry then ferried across.

It was very pretty – to watch ~~all~~ the sea Gulls swarming around the Boats.

Coming back, New York was lighting up – it was just one mass of little lights

We took the elevated home from the Ferry – Oh it was awful – looking into dirty-dingy rooms, where people were all huddled together eating.

We had dinner, tonight at a restaurant uptown, then went to the 'Hippodrome' after

It was certainly, the most wonderful performance I have ever seen, – Most spectacular and the Music was lovely.[7]
The Niagra was, very wonderful and weird.

Wednesday Jan 18th.
Lying in Harbor Brooklyn.

We have had such glorious weather since our arrival in New York – a little windy but very bright + bracing

Today is exceptionally pleasant and we would like to have a few days longer in New York among the wonderful stores and to see a few of the Theatres

Mother and Ida went out to see Mrs Mandle this morning so
Father and I walked down Broadway and around the Bowery –
thank goodness it was a bright cheerful day – it must be the most
deplorable sight on a dark day.

Father treated me to a nice pair of tan shoes – at Wanamakers on
our way home.

We all met at the Hotel at 12.30 had lunch – and came over to
our Steamer – to find that on account of being delayed in Dry
Dock – the cargo was late in loading so we wouldn't sail till 10
o'clock, in the morning

However everyone got settled nicely and we had a very pleasant
dinner and evening.

I was delighted to find letters and telegrams for us on board –
when we went down for Afternoon tea.

Got a lovely newsy letter from Denny   it was such a pleasant
surprise.

Retired quite early.

On board. S.S Sant'Anna,
Thursday Jan 19 – 1911.

We were all up bright and early this morning – all the cargo was
loaded and everything was quiet.

Sailed sharp at 10. o'clock. it was very bright and pleasant but a
little too misty to get a good view of New York.

After we were out a while the mist cleared up – slowly we saw
New York fading away from Veiw – leaving our own dear land far
behind.

We enjoyed everything to the utmost – a huge flock of Sea Gulls
folling [following] us all along.

Went down for Afternoon Tea and just about Dinner time I felt
rather shaky so sought the seclusion of my Cabin and off to the
land of Dreams.

At half past five I was delighted at getting a wireless from
Mr Edwards   it was such a treat, away from the sight of
land –

Mother and Ida went down to Dinner with Father – nearly all the ladies had to leave the 'Salle au Mangê'

Friday Jan 20 –
On Board –
A nice cool Bright day. Got up early and had a nice brisk walk on Deck before Breakfast.

Mother was well enough to go down – I only stayed a short while – hurried back on deck, and rested in my steamer chair

Mrs Nelson and Miss Pelletier asked me to go to the Upper deck with them – It was very pleasant up there, but I took ill about eleven o'clock, and had to go to my cabin

It was very lonely for a while when I was ill but I thought of everyone at home and tried to picture what they would all be doing – Soon I fell asleep – woke up about 3 o'clock – feeling splendid – Went out on Deck – Had Afternoon tea in Mother's stateroom – The first descent cup of tea since we left home.

Its most amusing all the Waiters are french and we have great times making ourselves understood.

Dressed and went down for dinner – but had to leave the dinnigroom. Louise – the Stewardess – brought up my dinner, but I really couldn't eat it. – I fell asleep very soon –

I always do rest so well in this dear little cabin.

Saw a shoal of porpoise this morning.

We have 470 Steerage Passengers on board

Saturday Jan 21.
Was up at seven o'clock feeling like a new Girl

Its very much warmer this morning – we came into the Gulf Stream – there's a good brisk breeze blowing

Mr Nelson and Mother were the only ones on Deck when I got out   Father and Ida came along shortly and we went down to Breakfast. Had quite a nice Breakfast.

We sighted a vessael and watched it through the glasses till it came quite near – It was an Italian Vessael bound for South America.

Played Bean Bags with Dr Crane – then Shuffle Board.

Chicken Broth was served on Deck about eleven.

I felt rather shaky at lunch time, so Ida and I had lunch in Mothers Stateroom

Have been siting out on Upper Deck all afternoon – We were watching the big waves with the lovely spray flying off each one. The Captain came along and told us – that meant a storm

About five o'clock a fierce wind started to blow – it was gloriously warm but made everything rattle so – we had gthe Gards on the table at Dinner – tonight.

Dressed and went down for Dinner – only stayed four courses as Afternoon tea took away my appetite

Mrs Crane and I had a fast walk on Deck in spite of the fact that we were almost blown away

Had Coffee with Father and Dr Crane in the Café upstairs.

The Salt water Baths are perfectly delightful.

Retired to the Land of Dreams at 8.30

Sunday Jan 22.

A lovely warm day – just like a summer's day at home with a delightful breeze.

Up early as usual – sat out on Deck – starting letters home.

We have to change our Watches forward, 30 min – each day – at eleven o'clock the Stewart comes out on Deck with the time

Read and snoozed on Deck all afternoon

After dinner we had a pleasant few hours of Music. – Mrs Crane is a great pianist and Mrs Pratt and the Captain sang.

Wonder what everyone's doing in dear old Ottawa tonight.

This has been our first Sunday on the Ocean – we couldn't possibly have had a more peaceful or Beautiful day.

Still – on – Board –

Monday Jan 23.

The Captain informed us that we have been in the 'Devils Hole' for three days. – and the weather has been exceptionally good for this place. – but now we will have better sailing

The 'Devil's Hole' is caused by the Gulf Stream and Atlantic Ocean meeting – it forms a sort of whirl pool – currents both ways.

We are in connection with the 'Roma' today another Fabre Vessell.

Have had a very pleasant day as usual – playing games – telling stories and reading

Back into the Atlantic again but the sun is so warm – it makes up for the warm water.

Tuesday Jan 24

Clear – warm. Bright day. Sat out on Deck. all morning

Wrote to Nell this afternoon   Everyone slept till afternoon tea was served.

One of our Artists was indisposed so our Concert was called off.

Walked Deck with Henrietta de Frank[en]stein – learning many interesting things about Rome.[8] and adding a few drops to that grey matter which is supposed to be floating around in my brain

Had a chat with Mr Raschaise after lunch – he offers to teach me french –

Wednesday Jan 25 – 1911

Another glorious day –

This has been the most exciting day – on board ship.

Everyone was up bright and early this morning – eager to catch the first sight of land.

It was great when away off in the distance – a few dim dark peaks – were descerned rising out of the water, – and soon we were along side of the first of the Azores, the island of Graciosa – then another one on our right, and finally, Treceira, came in sight.

These islands are so quaint – dear little white houses, seemed to be built all in a line along the centre of the island.

The fields a beautiful green were hedged off in small squares giving such a doll-land apperance,

We entered the Harbor about 12.30 – Such a perfect natural harbor

The quaint little city of Augra, ~~coming rig~~built right down to the waters edge –

The Harbor is well fortified – the old Portugesse forts standing out so plainly all around the Hills.

The Sea was very rough – and everyone wanted to go on shore – The Captain was very much against it -.

Eventually he gave in saying the Gentlemen might go for an hour. I was bound to go, but he was certain I would get killed.

However, Father was going and said I might go along

Oh it was exciting – we had to go, down a long flight of stairs at the side of the Boat – a little fishing smack – manned with six old men – were waiting at the bottom – Everytime the waves would come up it brought the Boat – level with the bottom step – then someone made a leap and away off – below – the boat would go again – coming up with the next wave –

Dad got in first then I got in next – Miss Isherwood an English girl was the only other lady to come but I was the first to land on Portugesse soil – Mr Raschais joined our party – and I don't know ~~wh~~however we could have managed without him – He could talk Spanish so well –

Such a jolly time as we had skipping along through this quaint little Village.

At the warf – there were several Yoke – of Oxen – pulling along carts with high Basket sides – little wooden wheels and wooden axles.

We passed through a narrow lane – stone wall on one side and tiny small white houses built high one above the other up on a cliff at the other side.

The main street was narrow Cobble-stone road and the side-walks made of small flat stones –

The buildings are all stone – little Iron railing balconys in front of the upstairs windows The women and Girls all ran out on these – to watch us passing along – beaming smiles at us –

A crowd of Chrildren pfollowed us greatly amused at our feet –
They wear wooden shoes – or just sandals that cover their toes only
– The women wear a very strange head gear – something like a nun,
　We bought post cards and a splendid view of the city
　I did want choclates so we had heaps of fun carring them around.
paid 10 centisimas each – (2¢)
　They didn't want to take American money – when Mr Raschais
way [was] buying cigars, – in fact they absolutely refused – but
accepted a Canadian Dollar Bill – as soon as they saw the Kings
head, – The Portugese have always been very fond of England –
The only nation that has not at some-time or other – gone to war
with England –
　We had to hurry back by three o'clock and were just in time
to see the Funeral of a steerage passenger who died during the
night – They were to bury him in Augra – It was very sad to see the
big black coffin being lowered over the side into a small boat
below.
　We sailed again, at four o'clock just in time for Afternoon tea –
we were all ravenuously hungry.
　Sat up on Deck with Mr + Miss Orme watching the Sunset.
　Oh such a delightful surprise as I got this evening –
　After dinner Mr Raschaise asked me to walk for a while.
　I did but felt so restless and a little lonely. – I just wanted to be
alone – so came to my cabin – very early – on a plea of being very
tired
　Mother came and presented me with a lovely big envelope – to
be opened on the 25th of Jan –
　It was just the dearest – most interesting letter from Denny –
Such a happy thought of his and gave me such pleasure.
　I have longed – several times since coming on board for some
news or message – from the dear world behind but never dreamt of
this delightful idea of Denny's –
　So now I am off to the land of Dreams – a very happy-tired little
girl.
　I know I will rest so well.

Thursday Jan 246
A lovely, warm, bright day, – played Shuffle board – with, Monsieur Reschaise all morning –

Sat up on Deck all afternoon   Had a very jolly, afternoon tea – Wrote a few notes till the dinner bell rang – Walked on deck all evening with Henriette Frankenstein

We sighted the lights of a steamer away off in the distance tonight

Friday January 27
This has been a beautiful day   Warm and Bright with a very calm sea.

We had a little Musicale this morning.

While sitting upon the Upper deck read the dearest little story 'The wheels of Time' by Florence Barclay. It is about – Dereck Brand and Flower, – two of The Rosary characters and most intensly interesting after reading The Rosary – and all the sweet memories that surround it.[9]

Had a little snap after lunch. Played Shuffle Board with Mr Raschaise, and beat him.

We had the most marveluous sunset tonight – The sea was like Ma Mirror – and the sky one mass of the most georguous oplescent colors.

Walked on Deck this evening
Dined with Henrietta Frankenstein.

Saturday Jan 298 – 1911
Still – on – board –
In the Mediterrean

Well dear diary this has been a most eventful day – And very pleasant weather but a little colder than usual.

We were up moderately early and as lunch was to be an hour soon – took a very light Breakfast.

Everyone was on Deck – Steamers were passing on all sides of us – I sighted 15, altogether today

Was away up on BThe Bridge with Mr Raschaise and was the first to see the dim outlines of the Spanish Coast, – rising in the distance – Then on our right soon the coast of Africa was descerned

We were in the Str of Gibralter and it was a strange feeling – land on both sides – and Ocean Steamers to be seen everywhere,

First of all we could see the City of Cadix on the Spanish Coast where all the beautiful ladies are supposed to be.

Then the City of Tarifa – an old mMoorish city with the old moorish Towers, all along the Coast.

The word Tarriff comes from Tarifa theylt areis just around the corner from Giberalter and they used to impose a fine or demand something from every vessal passing by.

On the African Coast we could dimly see the city of Ceuta.

We were soon passing through the Pillars of Hercules – The Rock of Giberalter and an equally Huge Rock on the Africian Coast

It is seven miles between them but didn't seem that far.

The City of Algercerias lies just at the base of Giberalter – famous for the great European Conference held in connection with Morocco –

Our dance tonight was very jolly   'Mr' Snider making himself exceedingly agreeable.

Sunday Jan 29 –

Our second Sunday on the dear old briny Blue – but the Mediterrean is such a beautiful Blue – just enough ripple to make the sunea pretty – The sky is very clear and Blue –

Walked – and Read this morning – wrote a little more to my letters.

The days are all so lovely and peaceful that Sunday deffers very little from every other day –

We were sitting out on the top deck underneath the Stars telling stories – when we all seemed to be growing lonely – so played Hide and seek – It was great fun – but very hot work.

Had lenenade [lemonade] in the Dinning rom at nine.

Went down a second time with Mr Raschaise – He gave me a very serious talking to.[10]

Monday Jan 30 – 1911

Another glorious day – We were passing very close to the island of Sardinea ~~thall~~ morning –

It has beautiful craggy mountains – small villages all along – tiny fishing vessels sailing back and forth –

All along the Sardinea cost are old towers built at high points on the mountains. These are built of dry stone and have been there since a thousand years before Christ – built by an unknown race.

We are due in Naples at 6 o'clock tomorrow morning – Everyone feels very sad – The party will be all broken up – Twelve embarking at Naples.

The Captains dinner was a great success

Won my final game of ShuffleBoard.

Italy
Naples,
Tuesday Jan 31

Well dear diary – here we are in dear Sunny Italy – but we got a very cold – breezey Reception –

When we woke up – on the Sant'Anna this morning – she was lying – just out of The Bay of Naples – and Oh it was cold – Everyone was up hustling around at six o'clock – I did try to sleep later as we were in no hurry – but there was too much going on.

Said Good-Bye to all our fellow – passengers – we were leaving behind –

Had no trouble whatever getting through the customs – and our Party of Ten – meant a lot of trunks and Valises – They opened only one trunk of Mrs Crane

Our Party consists of Dr + Mrs Frank Crane – Mrs James Crane – Col McNutt – Hen~~Mr~~ Doten – Mr Kavanagh – ~~and ourselves~~ We all boarded the Hotel Buss which was waiting and they piled every solitary bit of Baggage on the top – Till we were almost frightened stiff for fear it would either fall through or tip over –

However we arrived safe and sound at the Hotel Hassler. It's a very beautiful Hotel – directly on the Bay – The view from our Window is supurb – w~~the~~ Bright – warm sun streams in through long – glass doors and there is a little iron railed Balcony – we can step out on.

The Gardens in connection with the Hotel, are very beautiful   Its so lovely to see all the tropicial trees and plants.

A big wide esplanade – seperates the Gardens and Verendas from the Bay – All the fine carreages and Auto pass here and the Soldiers drill just in front of here – Well we all had lunch here together –

Ida and I started out after lunch for the Post Office – We were talked into hiring a Cabby and overcharged just a little bit – However we saw a lot of most interesting things   Came back to the Hotel and Father and Mother came out walking with us – We walked around the Bay – it was very pretty and we got back just in time to dress for dinner.

We went to the Beautiful San Carlo – Theatre tonight to hear the grand Opera – La Tosca – It was really lovely – The Solists were really wonderful and altho the play was very tradgic – I was in a delightful dream – it seemed all the time.

They had almost three hundred in the Orchestra – so the Music was the finest I have ever heard –

The Opera – started at nine so it was after twelve when it was over –

After the Opera finished they had – four Ballad Dances which didn't amount to much –

The San Carlo Theatre is the finest in Italy – It is very beautiful – The seats are on the floor of the House   Then six-tiers of Boxes all around the Theatre – The Royal Box – in the centre – directly facing the stage –

The paintings are very beautiful and away up at the top of the stage a beautiful Bronze statue points to the time on a dial – The Arm moves around.[11]

Naples. *Wednesday Feb 1* – 1911
    This has been a most glorious day – its impossible to express the vast amount of pleasure we have had – so many new thrills of delight
    Truely this is 'Naples the Beautiful'   Our party was all up bright and early – breakfast over and ready to start at eleven o'clock –
    The Aquarium – was our first goal – The others riding down on the car – Father and I had a delightful walk, along the broad Via Carácciola – next the sea –
    The marine life in the Aquarium is vastly interesting – we spent an hour here – then out on the – broad walk by the sea – all around the Bay to the Grand Hotel – Here we took the tramcar – back to the centre of the City – Had our lunch at a most unique German Ps.[12] It was so jolly – Crossing over to the Palazzo Reale or Royal Palace – we registered then obtained tickets of admission for tomorrow.
    We all boared [boarded] a tramcar to find our way up to Parker House on the Heights to see the sun-set   · This was very funny   we took a car which went all around the Outskirts of the City – finally landing us at the Museum where we got another car – Everyone was in splendid humor and no hurry – We were pleased with the Parker House and had such a delightful Afternoon Tea –
    From here we strolled out and took the lift up to Bertolni's Palace Hotel – such a georgeous veiw, as we witnessed – from the look-out – will long be remembered by every one of us –
    The Sun was just sinking behind the Mountains – The air was clear and cool – All over the sky was that beautiful rich glow – Blue – merging into a soft pink – The snow on the top of the Mountains on the left – was a most lovely pink shaded from the

sky – and the smoke – curling up from Vesuvius – turned many
different hues as it slowly – rose into the heavens – This glow
lasted a over half an hour then slowly died away – and settled
into a deep blue – quickly growing black – Little merrids [myri-
ads?] of lights – started to shoot out all over the great white city –
lying at our feet – and the beautiful bOlue of the Bay of Naples –
was lost.

Our thoughts now turned to the Hotel and it is well named a
'Palace' I can't imagine anything more lovely – We knew we simply
coudn't leave so ordered our Dinner to be served in an hour – We
strolled around the Hotel – The writing-room looking so cosy and
nice   I sat down and scribbled a few lines – to the dear ones
away off in Canada – I am so happy and everything is so beautiful
and fascinating – I wish they were here to share the delights.

The Dinning-Room – was perfectly beautiful – A Dome shaped
Room – glasse Bevelled Glass on three sides and top, – overlooking
Naples – All woodwork and Silk Draping – white – and – Huge
Crystal Candalaberies [candelabras] hanging from the ceiling.

The orchestra – rendered very sweet music – Their uniforms
were the style worn by the first King of Italy – 180 years ago –

There was a huge Orange tree growing in the centre of the
Dinning-room – and a Pineapple growing on a tree also.

The King of Saxony and Party had the Table next to us – so we
were honored guests – He has the most amusing Voice – We came
home the, Funicorlari [funicular] railway.

Naples Thursday Feb 2 –
Bright but a little cooler.
After breakfast Ida and I went down to the Post Office but had to
wait so long for a car both ways – that when we got back to the
Hotel Our party had started off, but Dr Crane was waiting for us, as
jolly and good-natured as usual.

We met at the Church of San Francesco di Páola – This is very
beautiful, an imatation of the Roman Pantheon – The marble

columns are superb and the Alter inlaid with Jasper and lapisla-
zuli   The Huge Dome, with marvelous pai[n]tings seems to
reach to the sky.

Crossing over to the Royal Palace – (Palazzo Reale) We were
guided, through – The roof gardens were beautiful – and the interior – one georgeously furnished room after the other – We glided
over the Ball Room – knelt on the Kings stool in the Chapel – The
Grand Staircase built entirely of Marble, (pure white) with statues
and releifs. But oh it was so cold and is seldom used – The whole
palace has that cold, severe, atmosphere, which is anything but
homelike.

The San Carlo Theatre is in the centre of the Palace.

When leaving the Palace – we went through the Galleria to Pilsner's for lunch – it wasn't half as nice as yesterday but still its
always jolly when we're all together.

The Palace of Capidemonte was very beautiful – and interesting containing a large collection of of Modern paintings and
sculptures   Porcelian from the old factory of Capidemonte –
One huge room is full of all the differents armors and weapons.

We had Afternoon Tea in the Galleria   Dinner at the Hassler. Pleasant evening all together at home.

NOTES

Mina Wylie's diary is in the private collection of Morgan Holmes.

1 The research and writing of this introduction, as well as the procure-
  ment and reproduction of Mina's photograph, was carried out with the
  kind assistance of Judith MacLaren Holmes.
2 Mina disembarked in Naples and then travelled northward, visiting
  Rome, Lausanne, Paris, London, and Glasgow.
3 For information on the Ottawa Car Manufacturing Company, see Shirley E. Woods, Jr., *Ottawa: The Capital of Canada* (Toronto: Doubleday,
  1980), 240–1.

4 The 'Diamond Ring course' was a colloquial name for what was officially known as the 'Homemaker's Course' at Macdonald College in Ste-Anne-de-Bellevue, Quebec. Macdonald College was affiliated with McGill University. See Margaret Gillett, *We Walked Very Warily: A History of Women at McGill* (Montreal: Eden Press, 1981).

5 Nell's affectionate acronym, 'S.W. / A.K.,' signifies 'Sealed with a Kiss.' A hand-drawn circle surrounds the letters. Unlike her sister, Nell wrote in a regular North American hand, slanting to the right.

6 While in New York, the Wylies stayed at the Union Square Hotel.

7 The Hippodrome Theater was an enormous venue (5,200 seated, 800 standees) located on Sixth Avenue between Forty-Third and Forty-Fourth Streets. It opened in 1905 and, for the next seventeen years, lavish, spectacular shows (including choruses of over 500 members, and horses that dove into a huge tank of water) were mounted on its stage. Vaudeville appeared between the major spectacles and eventually became the staple fare. After being converted into a cinema, the Hippodrome was demolished in 1939. See Gerald Bordman, 'Hippodrome Theatre,' *The Oxford Companion to American Theatre* (Oxford: Oxford University Press, 1984), 344.

8 On Valentine's Day in Rome, Henrietta and her mother, the Countess de Frankenstein, held a tea party at their home for Mina and her sister Ida. According to Mina's diary, Henrietta could 'converse ... beautifully in Four languages.' Mina was so impressed by this ability that she 'firmly resolved to study French till I have mastered it.'

9 I have not been able to locate a copy of 'The Wheels of Time'; however, I have found Florence Louisa Charlesworth Barclay's (1862–1921) novel *The Rosary* (New York: Putnam, 1909), a romantic story set amidst the homes and gardens of Britain's Edwardian elite. It tells the affecting tale of the unlikely love between an independent-minded woman, Jane Champion, and a Scots aesthetic painter, Garth Dalmain. Barclay's title is drawn from the 1894 poem of the same name by Robert Cameron Rogers, a text that became the basis of a popular turn-of-the-century song (sung in the novel by Jane); see James J. Fuld, *The Book of World-Famous Music: Classical, Popular and Folk*, rev. ed. (New York: Crown, 1971).

10 One can only speculate on the nature of Monsieur Raschaise's admonishment. Perhaps the overheated game of hide and seek had come perilously close to certain social indiscretions. Certainly, throughout the voyage to Europe, Monsieur Raschaise repeatedly appears as a paternal guide for enthusiastic Mina.

11 The Teatro San Carlo was built in 1737 by King Charles III, monarch of a newly independent Neapolitan state. Michael Robinson notes that eighteenth-century visitors tended to be more impressed by the theatre's spectacular architecture and decorative features than by the operas presented on its stage (*Naples and Neapolitan Opera* [Oxford: Clarendon, 1972], esp. 7–11). Judging from Mina's diary, the horseshoe-shaped auditorium's visual splendour remained a focal point for travellers to the city into the twentieth century.

12 A reference to Pilsner's, where they also dined the following day.

Miriam Green Ellis
(1881–1964)

LISA LAFRAMBOISE

'Since I went to school and was taught that the world was round and that each end was flattened out a little like an apple, I have wanted to go to the place where it started to flatten. This year I went ...'[1] Thus Miriam Green Ellis begins three of the newspaper articles she wrote about her 1922 journey to Aklavik, on the delta of the Mackenzie River in the Northwest Territories. The articles and lectures that Ellis produced about her trip were themselves based on material she recorded in the daily entries of the diary she kept that summer. Her diary not only offers readers an enthusiastically detailed and vivid account of the places and people she met along the Mackenzie River, but also provides a glimpse into the character and information-gathering practices of one of Canada's important early journalists.

Miriam Green Ellis was born in Ogdensburg, New York, to Canadian parents who returned to Canada while she was still a small child. She grew up on her grandfather's farm in Brockville, Ontario. Although she studied at the Royal Conservatory of Music in Toronto, she taught music for only a short time before, in 1914, she found a job reporting at the *Prince Albert Herald* in Saskatchewan. From there she moved to the *Regina Post*, and by 1917 she was working on the *Edmonton Bulletin*, where she quickly established herself as the agricultural reporter.[2] Her choice of farm reporting was rare for a woman in the early twentieth century; even fifteen years later, the *Canadian Magazine* described her as 'a lone woman in a great crowd of agriculturists and agrarian experts, talking the language that is common to them.'[3] Her specialization in agricultural journalism may have seemed eccentric, but it allowed Ellis to travel to rural communities, fairs, and shows throughout the Canadian west. She reported on the new settlements of the Peace River country in 1919, and spent the summer of 1922 travelling the small settlements of the Mackenzie River.[4]

Although Ellis was still a reporter with the *Bulletin* in 1922, her editor refused to finance her northern journey. Ellis was convinced, however, that Canadians wanted to hear about the exciting developments in the North: the expansion of settlement, the opening of the new mineral and oil discoveries, the progress of the fur trade, and the lives of indigenous peoples in the opening decades of the twentieth century. She took a leave of absence from the *Bulletin* and made the trip at her own expense, travelling with relatives Mary Ellis Conlin and John and Ethel Carley; they appear frequently in her diary, and more frequently than she herself does in the collection of photographs contained in her papers.

The party left Edmonton by train on 19 June, travelling to the northern terminus of the Alberta and Great Waterways Railway at Waterways, just south of Fort McMurray on the Athabasca River. There, they boarded the wood-burning river-steamer *Slave River*, owned by the Lamson and Hubbard trading company's subsidiary, the Alberta and Arctic Transportation Company (AATC). With stops at Fort McMurray and Fort Chipewyan, the *Slave River* travelled north down the Athabasca River, across Lake Athabasca, down the Rivière des Rochers to its junction with the Slave River, and then north to Fort Fitzgerald. There, a series of impassible rapids (including the Cassette Rapids, which Ellis visited on 23 June) prevented the steamer from proceeding farther northward; Ellis's party crossed the Smith Portage by automobile, and arrived at Fort Smith in the Northwest Territories, where another AATC steamer, the *Distributor*, waited to carry them to the Mackenzie delta. The

Distributor left Fort Smith on 25 June, travelling down the Slave River to Great Slave Lake, and entering the Mackenzie River four days later. The boat proceeded northward to the junction of the Mackenzie and Peel rivers, stopping at several settlements en route. On 4 July, the steamer entered the Peel River, travelling upriver as far as Fort McPherson, before returning to the Mackenzie and steaming northward to Aklavik, arriving the next morning at the northern terminus of the journey. They left the same day, retracing their route southward up the Mackenzie. The *Distributor* reached Fort Smith on 16 July, where they had a five-day wait. Ellis took advantage of the time to extend her travels, making a two-day journey by horseback to visit the salt deposits at Salt River. Then the party embarked on the *Slave River* at Fort Fitzgerald for the return journey to Waterways on 25 July. They reached Edmonton three days later.

This journey marked a turning point in Ellis's career. It gave her the material for a series of ten lectures, illustrated with glass slides, which she gave in New York, and then across eastern Canada, speaking at venues such as Canadian Club meetings and the University Women's Club in Toronto.[5] Her articles about the Canadian Arctic were in such great demand that she left the *Edmonton Bulletin* and freelanced for several years before finally accepting a position as western editor of the Montreal *Family Herald and Weekly Star*. She remained with the Montreal paper for twenty-four years, basing herself in Winnipeg and travelling throughout western Canada, reporting on farm life and agricultural concerns, and lecturing throughout the region until her retirement in 1952. Although today she is not as well known as other early women journalists such as Cora Hind and Kit Coleman, Ellis was a celebrity in western Canada. She was a pioneer member of the Canadian Women's Press Club, serving on both provincial and national executives,[6] and she was among the first generation of women journalists to centre her professional life around a specialty other than the women's page.

Ellis's diary of her 1922 trip 'To [the] Midnight Sun,' as she called it, offers not only a glimpse of the working life and travels of an important early Canadian woman journalist, but also reveals the first impressions and personal reactions of one of the journalists who represented the North to the Canadian public during this early period of northern development. Like most travel diaries, her writing exhibits a strong documentary impulse, recording facts and figures, describing communities, landscapes, and people, and relating stories and events that would later appear in her articles and lectures about the Canadian Arctic.[7] Her interest in the women of the North is particularly clear from her diary, where she notes earlier northern travellers such as Emma Shaw Colcleugh (19 June) and Agnes Deans Cameron (25 July), and also describes in detail the lives of Ada Conibear and Christine Gordon (25 July), both women making a living as traders in the north, independent of the male-dominated trading companies.

In her diary, Ellis exhibits a keen interest in the progress of agricultural enterprise in the northern communities she visited, as well as industrial developments in oil and gas prospecting, newsworthy events, and the lives of the people who lived in the North: her diary records ethnographic descriptions of the First Nations and Inuit peoples she met at each community, as well as more detailed portraits of specific individuals such as the indigenous wife and son of the famous explorer Vilhjalmur Stefansson. Her interest, as a reporter, both in the romance of northern history and in the region's modern development results in a detailed portrait of the North, despite the brevity of her five-week journey. Her diary records a range of items, from the characteristics of northern flora and landscapes to labour relations on board the steamer (25 June), from Soeur Ste Rose du Lima's agricultural struggles on Great Slave Lake (29 June, 12 July) to the 'Eskimo murders' that rivetted the attention of southern audiences and bespoke the clash of cultures in the North (4 July). The trade rivalry between Lamson and Hubbard, the Northern Trading Company, and the Hudson's Bay Company (HBC), appears in Ellis's record of the constant race between the *Distributor*, owned by a Lamson and Hubbard subsidiary, and the Northern Trading Company's *Pioneer*, as the two steamers leap-frogged each other up and down the river (1, 2, 5, 15 July). This rivalry had the passengers betting on their ships' arrival times and the ships looting each other's woodpiles, and it resulted over the next two years in the commercial failure of Lamson and Hubbard and the sale of their subsidiary, the AATC, to the HBC.[8] Ellis's conversations with prospectors, traders, Mounties, and missionaries reveal how these figures, through their contact with journalists and travellers, perceived the Canadian North and, through their contact with journalists and travellers, represented it to a southern audience. Her information about First Nations and Inuit peoples of the Mackenzie River was gathered largely from the white authorities she met, confirmed by her own limited observations, and reproduced in the many articles and lectures she produced about the North and its peoples. Ellis's diary reveals, in part, how information about the North was gathered and disseminated in the early part of the twentieth century.

Most entries in the diary are typewritten, although there are frequent annotations in black ink that (judging by their content) were made during the journey as Ellis verified facts or spelling; later sections of the diary also contain marginalia in pencil that were written at a later date. Occasionally a short entry is made in pen. The entries made during the trip to Salt River are all in pen. Ellis clearly did not bring her typewriter along on horseback; instead, she wrote entries by hand in her tent during the journey, and, after the party returned to Fort Smith, she recorded (by typewriter) additional entries for those days. Most of her entries, however, were typewritten daily.

Ellis recorded her diary on six-holed, unlined, machine-made paper measuring 3½ by 6 inches. The loose-leaf pages are edged in red and held between brown cardboard covers by two metal rings. The pages are numbered on both sides (by hand or typewriter, depending on how that day's entry was written). The diary itself is 176 pages long, and is followed by an index, handwritten by Ellis, on tabbed pages originally intended for recording addresses. Ellis frequently ran off the right margin of the page when typing her diary; word endings have been added in square brackets where necessary. No other corrections (Ellis frequently substitutes commas for periods) have been made, although illegible words that have been crossed out have been omitted. Pencil corrections of the manuscript are also omitted, but portions of the diary that appear in Ellis's handwriting are reproduced in italics.

The following excerpt of the diary describes an early part of the journey, from 22 June, when the party reached Fort Chipewyan on Lake Athabasca, to 29 June, when they arrived at Fort Providence.

Miriam Green Ellis and unidentified Native woman, taken during Ellis's trip to Aklavik, NWT.

DIARY NORTHWEST TERRITORIES, JUNE 1922

June 22

Down in the delta of the Athabasca when we wakened
We took the stream farthest to th[e] East which is the largest.
When we got to the mouth of the river, it was too rough to start
across the lake, so tied up for about three hours. and we are now
crossing the lake to Chipewyan.

The river channel goes out for miles into the lake, so that the
boat picks its steps as carefully as it did in the river.

When we were tied up, a man 'George' came rowing down
strea[m] on his way to chipewyan. He said he had caught ten
fish.

Uncle John and his pal the red coated young mountie have
struck up quite a friendship and went fishing off the end of a
Norther Transportation Scow that was hitched to this island. It
had been used earlier in the season for transportation of horses. We
have a team of horses down stairs too.

I went out for a tramp along th[e] shore. It was all very low and
the island looked as though it had been washed over with ice and
water when the river was higher. A few little willows and some wild
rice. I looked for nests but saw none.

Several camp fires where othe[r] voyageurs have camped waiting
for Lake Athabasca to calm. All the land on this side of the lake is
low and lots of ducks flying around.

When the wind is off the lake it makes the water in the delta
higher and vice versa

Took pictures of the boat tied up, of Uncle John and the Mountie fishing.

Dr McDonald tells of a Dr Richardson who is down at Fort Norman. He used to be in B.C.   follows the outposts.

A new word is Snye, meaning a channel away from the main
channel used in connection with the outlets of the delta. *corruption
of 'chenal.' or snythe*

Chipewyan
Cloudy till six o'clock.

Reached Chipewyan about 3.30 and unloaded the horses for Colin Fraser first and then went back and unloaded flour for Lamson and Hubbard. All the sacks unloaded by lines of boys with hundred pound sack on his back.

Heard that as many as 19000 rat pelts had been baled in one day at Chipewyan.

As we walked aroung from the Colin Fraser landing to the Lamson Hubbard, passed the Catholic buildings, the orphanage, the church and priests house. In front of the church was an evergreen arch with lots of flags, especially French flags, and letters said, Pauperes Evangelizautur, 1862–1922.

Saw Bishop Gerard at Chipewyan, Took his picture with some Indian boys at the landing. Also took picture of the black sail and going to take the dining room boys now.

At Fort Smith, Dr. McDonald told us to look up Father Manzsoz. Bishop Brenat is bishop

Before we came to Chipewyan, saw an island where the Catholic mission had a house where they came to fish in winter. Lots of fish there. There was a little herd of cattl[e] with poor shorthorn bull at Chipewyan belonging to the mission.

Mr, Card,, Dr, McDonald left us at Chipewyan to pay the treaty money. They pay the Cree first down at the Fraser landing and then pull up camp and go over to the other side to pay the Chipewyans.

Fraser said there were so many had died with the Flue he did no[t] know how many inhabitants there were.

It is beautiful rocky location altogether different from the South side of the lake where we waited this morning.

There are heaps of islands in the lake and we are now loading the Canadusa for Fond du Lac. The doctor and Mr Card are going over to pay traty there by this boat.

12.30 P.M.

We have just wooded up and started again for Fitzgerald. It is quite light – just dusk. I piloted the boat for 30 miles tonight up the Rochérs

River till the Peace came in and after an hour down the Peace or Slave River as it is called stopped for the wood.

Sergeant Anderton tells me they are going to centralize the RNWMP,[9] *at Aklavik. Cut out the posts at Herschell Id and several other places and put up regular barracks at Aklavik. There will probably be a force of 4 or 5 men there this year and more next year.*

A fur dealer Seigler on board estimates that 50.000 worth of furs went out of Chipewyan last year. It has been a lovely day.

Beautiful scenery. Lots of islands all heavily wooded in this Lake off Athabasca Lake. and afterwards in the River des Rochers where the channel was deeper. This river runs sometimes one way + sometimes another

June 23

Arrived Fitzgerald early morning   Packed trunks and then went for walk out to rapids. beautiful walk through the woods and took two pictures of upper and two of lower rapids, ~~Pelican~~ *Cassette* rapids   Brought back bouquet of blue co[l]umbine.

Had lunch and came over in the big red car to Fort Smith. Portage is sixteen miles or more long and they are doing considerable work on the road. It is roug[h] in spots, but on the whole very good. Met a big caterpillar dragging several wagons and several smaller tractors and teams. Those going towards Smith all heavily laden. Coming the other way empty. The bull dogs are bad and the horses all have boudoir caps of bright colored calico.

At Fitzgerald saw a few very poor cattle badly eaten with flies. They belonged to the Metis. Man by the name of Burns came and spoke to me. Said he had seen me at the Spring Show in Edmonton.

Coming over we saw considerable of the Indian Paint brush.[10] As we got towards Fort Smith the road was very sandy and jack pine on each side. All timber all the way.

Walked down the big hill at Smith, as the sand is feet deep and cars cannot make it. In fact even the empty tractor brings up only one empty wagon at a time.

Met Ray Ross and gave him his letters. Later met Ken Purdy and gave him his. They were also glad to get Edmonton papers.

The Distributor which was waiting, is a beautiful boat with complete appointments. Red carpet on staterooms. Big dining saloon. Doc, *Griffin* who has one year in University of Chicago for medicine is the cook and a real good one. Captain ~~Busy~~ *Bucey* took me over the boat. He was delighted to see Miss Conlin, who was an old friend from a trip on the Peace last year. She made the walk down the hill all right.

The trunks were teamed over and got in about midnight.

Captain Bucy gave us the run of the pilot house. He is a dear.

Met Jack Ransford, who is working on the boat. B, Byer who is manager of Union bank here. Mr, West, inspector of Lamson and Hubbard posts, and several others who came down to eat. It is such a treat to get fresh beef that all the men who can do so, come down for meals to the boat. They run a regular restraurant while they are in port.

Went for a walk up town with Rae Ross.

June 24

This is Saturday, but I had to look up my calender to find out Have lost all track of the days and it seems hardly credible that I have seen so much since I left home on Monday morning.

Very hot today and hard to get up energy to go up the hill to see the mission garden.

Uncle John made me a type writer table that is as neat as a pocket in a shirt. Just the very thing,

Went up the hill after lunch with Uncle John and as it started to shower, we went into the Northern Trading post to wait. As the manager, talked to us, Uncle John went asleep. and snored, 3 times.

He told us that he wanted to get back to the MacKenzie River as he considered that his home. He said that his wife was content to make her home where ever he was.

We saw thermos bottles in this store and he told us that the Indians used them quite a lot.

The Indian that is to pi-ot the N.T. boat was in there.

We walked over to the new buildings of the dominion government. There is a beautiful office building a large house and barns, all of logs. and all quite luxurious looking.

O.S. Finney, is the director of the North West territories, with headquarters at Ottawa. Major L,T, Burwash, the mining recorder lives here. His wife is coming in to visit him this summer. In the interim, the staf[f] of which there are 6 besides Burwash have been living at the residence.

They record the mining leases, and generally represent the dominiogovernment in the North West territories. The line between the territories and Alberta is about a mile and a half from here.

Burwash and J,Fm Moran, chief clerk in Finney's office at Ottawa is going down with us to Aklavik for a trip.

G,H, Blanchette down in charge of a survey party of 18 to make the channels in and out of Great Slave Lake. *and also survey Great Slave Lake*   He is not going with us.

Mr Byer tells me that the government took in over $100.000 in oil lease fees here last year. This year there will be the rentals to collect. The rentals are $1.00 an acre and the filing fees, 50¢ an acre.

The trade in fur was about $60.000 last year.

There is great scandal about the graft in building the Dominion governmrnt buildings here, They claim it cost as much to build these houses as it would palaces in town.

Called on Mr, Byer manager of the Union Bank. He was sent in to establish a post at Fort Norman last year but just got this far and was told to stay here. He opened in a tent and later built a little log house with the bank in front. He boards at a sort of restrurant in the summer and in the winter batches. Has moose meat, ducks, chicken, ptarmigan and so on. The ptarmiga[n] come down this far from the Artic in the winter and are good eating.

He has a neat little office and living quarters at the back.

Next door is Mrs, Conibear wi h her little trading post. She has everything from a clothes wringer to fancy combs, oranges, lemons, cocoanuts and said that last year she had brought in plums, the first that had ever come in. They were the first she had seen in ten year[s.] She has never been out in that time. Her husband mushed into Norman last year.[11] He is an engineer and she does all the housework and the trading. She is known about the settlement for having things at the store that no one else had. She has cake pans, and snow shoes, fancy hair pins and moccasins, bacon. At first the store was about eight feet square. Then they enlarged it to about three times that size and now are building another addition. She is said to be the only one that is really making money in the place.

She has a complete house. They came in there about four years ago and cleared a home righ[t] right out of the woods. Now has quite a clearing, with a a vegetab[le] garden, a flower garden and a nice lawn. The lawn they have made bit by bit bringing in a little piece of sod as they found it her[e] and there.

She had iceland poppies, stocks, sweet william, geraniums forget me not, pansies etc. The poppies were in bloom and the geraniums and the pansies.

During all the time they have been making a home have also made their living.

They are English people.

She has a complete house. Litt[le] cupboards, even for the men's shaving tackle. Had an open cupboard for the dishes with plate rail with blue rimmed plates.

She had a large organ – the first brought into the country also a gramophone.

Back of the lot had three little pigs, Percival, Reginald and Belina and the pup was Selina.

She has one daughter Mabel, a pretty girl of seventeen and a son. *2 Sons.*

She has a well under the house with a pump and an attachment for watering the garden. Also has a tap in the kitchen from the soft water barrel.

She has quite a collection of Eskimo and Indian work.

Daughter has an Artic or silver rat fur, that is light grey with quite a sheen and very pretty and soft.

Has a 'tea bag' of an unborn moose hide in which the Eskimos carry their stuff. also boots and moccasins made by the Eskimo. centre piece make of squares of mink, silver rat, a little carribo[o] and edged with white fox.

There was also a strap made of goose quills, dyed same as porcupine quills. in which the women carry the babies on their backs. She had some suspenders and belts in the porcupine quil[l] work also and an Eskimo babische bag make of fancily woven strips of leather that looked like twine and trimmed with coarse bright colored wools and at the top a piece of leather ornamented with quill work. There was also a rug of sealski[n] and polar bear, made into squares.

Called on Mrs, Card wife of th[e] Indian agent who is also the post mistress and had just sent out seventy sacks of mail for the North. All the people in the North regret that Mr, Oliver was not elected and made minister of the Interior.

The mail comes in on the H.B and the N.T. boats,[12] arriving about once in ten days in the summer and about every two months in the winter. Even in the summer the papers come only once a month

They have a beautiful field of winter rye that came breast high and is all in head.

It was a late spring here too. They have some wheat and oat[s] in too. She has a charming house and fireplace.

They tell me that out at the Catholic Mission some sixteen miles out they are working into a purebred Shorthorn herd of cattle, have four hundre[d] hens and had f esh eggs all last winter. Also, I think they raise pigs, I understand.

Pelicans nest on rocks by rapid

June 25, Sunday.

Most beautiful day. When I got up found we were well on our way having left Fort Smith about four o'clock.

Talking with J,F, Moran of Dom govt branch and he tells me that B.H. Segre is going to complete the transverse of the MacKanzie River this year. He will stay in all winter and make survey from a point below the Norman Oil fields through the delta. He has a party of 9 or 10 men but not sure these will all stay in for the winter.

The yellow jacket [wasp] managed to get on again and is the shunned of all shunners.

The passengers on board now are:

John Carley, Sharon, Pen[n]

Ethel Carley, Sharon, Penn.

Mary Ellis Conlin, nurse, Edmonton,

Harry Ransford, banker, Edmont[on]

Sergeant Anderton, going to Aklavik to organize and centralize R.N.W.M.P. barracks,

J,F, Moran, of ~~of the mining recorder's office.~~ *Finnie's office Ottawa*

Major L,T, Burwash, mining recorder from Fort Smith. and crown timber lands agent.

Roland Holroyd, university of Pennslyvania, instructor in botany

A,H, Shurer, White Beaver Oil Company.

W,J, West, manager A, and A Co,

Ken Purdy, with Lamson and Hubbar[d]

V W West, inspector for   "   "

F.R. Ross, Lamson and Hubbard expecting to take charge of a post at far end of Great Bear Lake.

P, Seigler, furbuyer, Edmonton,

Major Gooch, Mrs, Gooch British Columbia

Father Lecuyer, going in to Eskimos at Aklavik,

Sergeant Anderton, going into establish post of Can M,P, at Aklavik

F,E, Jones.

Mrs, McDonald is stewardess,

Miss Giles, maid

Mr Mcdonald, *steward*

Beautiful day but very hot. had a sleep in the afternoon. Just as I woke up struck a sand bar. Had no trouble however, backed up and went other side of island.

Some labor trouble on boat   This afternoon two fresh kids that are chopping wood for the company got fresh and West put them off at the next stop.

Three frenchmen who are going down the McKenzie to chop wood are raising trouble on boat and may be put off before they get down.

Stopped about six o'clock for several hours to take on thirty cords of wood, Gang of a dozen men carrying.

Wild roses are in full bloom few buds left.

Heard Canada birds when we stopped.

Saw Pioneer, the N.T. boat in distance on ret rn from Fort Rae, presumably,

12.30. P.M. Could read without artificial light, about same as after sundown.

12.30 P.M. could hear Canada bird singing.

Red glow in East looks like sun up.

Monday June 26

Beautiful day, to be stuck on sandbank, practically no wind During early morning we started out through the delta of the Slave River into the Slave Lake, but the lake looked rough so Captain took boat back into the River. Later we came out and stuck on sand bar for about eight hours. Got off one to get on another and all the business of putting out anchor and winding ourselves off.

Arrived at Resolution at five in afternoon instead of four in morning as expected.

Resolution is in a bay that is so shallow that the boat has to stand off and unload freight into scow. It looks quite picturesque with the white and other buildings perched on bank. The Hudson Bay has a big post here and Fairweathers have had a post but since the failure of the firm, these posts are being closed up and man by name of Boucher who was up here for this purpose got on here.

We also saw Dave McAlpine who is in here for Lamson and Hubbard and stays here the summer.

Mr, Bassett, manager of Lamson and Hubbard got on here as did also three sisters and Bishop Brenat.

We went on shore and only had time to visit the Catholic orphanage. They had a nice flower garden and a herd of about a dozen cattle.

It was getting rough before we left here and the capt hurried across to Burnt Islands for shelter. There was a high wind and the flat boat rolled considerable but we made the harbor alright.

Played a game of bridge with Mary Ellis, Rae Ross and Ken Purdy.

Sister Augenie is the mother [S]uperior at the couvent at Resolution and Seour McQuillan, who has been the teacher there for nineteen years and founded that school was down to New Brunswick for holiday   There are about ten sisters. *including Sister Honorine who came with Sister McQuillan to found Resolution*

Tuesday June 27.

Still windy and still anchored off Burnt Islands. There is some timber, looks like Jackpin[e] but not heavily timbered. Seems to be a lot of undergrowth.

The captain says that the trees on this island are bastard spruce, 'aint nothin,' he says, sort of cross between spruce and balsam,

Spent the afternoon sleeping. and the evening reading of the Grey Nuns in the Far North. The passengers who got on at Resolution were:

Bishop Gabriel Breynat of Mackenzie;

A Bassett, manager of Lamson and Hubbard,

~~Rameau~~ Romanet inspector of all H.B. posts,

F, Johnson, Lamson and Hubbard,

Sister provincial, Sister Girouard of Divine providence

Sister Lussier
Sister Champoux.
and three Indian children.
for Fort Providence.

Wednesday June 28
 Still at anchor at Burnt Islands Went with Mr West and Mr Ransford to shore and had a lomg walk.
 Big feature of the day was the finding of wild orchids in most beautiful shades of orchid. They are about inch and half long and half an inch wide. Delicate beautiful things. Found only one little clump in the morning but in the afternoon when I went for a walk with Ray Ross and Ken Purdy found lots of them. Several beds [f]our feet long and three wide.
 They are the most beautiful flowers I ever saw and when we brought them home and put them on the table they lasted for several days. We also got another pretty delicate pink flower that looks like some sort of heath. There was any amount of it. The orchids grew in the moss but it was quite dry. They have a little bulbous root and one leaf to a flower.
 There was a nice sandy beach in one place on the island but we did not go for a swim as the day was rather windy and cold. In the afternoon we heard the boat whistle and hurried home. They rafted in wood here for engin[e]
 The lake had become quite calm and we arrived at Hay River about 11.15, The sun went down about 10.30
 We visited the Anglican mission Mr and Mrs, Vale in charge, Miss Samwell, the teacher. She came on with us later to go to her home in Fort Norman for the holidays.
 The Vales are hopeless bromides, but they had a nice school with about fifty or sixty students, mostly Louchoux, Eskimos and Slavis. The children were all in bed.
 Storkerson's Eskimo wife has been at this school for three years with her three children. She finds it very difficult to leard the English language. He is expected to come in this summer to get

her. Steffansen also has an Eskimo wife in the North. She is not being educated.

Storkerson's wife is a littl[e] above the average, her father having been

It was difficult to see much difference in the appearance of the different tribes of Indians and Eskimos.

The ice has only been out of the lake a week or so, and the night got real cold and getting very chilled looking over the mission there it was hard to get to sleep.

The mission was very tidy and they had nice gardens started there, but the seeds are just coming up. Mrs, Vale had asters and nasturtiums and popies and most every kind of flower and vegetable.

They all have their gardens closely fenced with poles like baricaded forts, to keep out the dogs.

There were two very cunning pups at the rectory, which was also the post office.

We are well into the fish eating country now and when I got back to the boat they had taken on some inconnu, caught in a net. They have bodies like a salmon, but mouths rather like a *whitefish*. They say they bite at a hook however. They grow to be thirty or forty pounds. *They have no teeth*

Children soon forget their own language. One little four year old Louchoux and her mither came down to the Hay River Mission and at first the child readily learned English and acted as interpreter for her mother. In a few months she had forgotten the Indian dialect altogether.

Children only remember thei[r] own language about a year.

In the Hay River church is a beass [brass?] tablet to the honor of Pte Frank H, Minchin, a lay reader. There was also a colored window and lectern put in in his honor. The baptismal font had been his last gift to the church before he had gone to the front. He had made it himself.

The chancel chair was home made, the seat being of babiche, leather thongs interwoven to look like cane. Very comfortable.

Mission heated by furnace
Slave Lake is about 520 feet above sea level,
In the girls dormitories little Eskimos sleeping under spreads made by
children in Montreal

Providence
June 29. Thursday
    I was tired and slept in, We arrived at Providence about 2.P.M.
and the children from the Catholic Mission came running along
with the nuns to meet the bishop and the mother provincial.
    We are well into the MacKenzie River here and the bank[s] are
high. solid clay with scarce ly any soil on top. Sister St, Rose, told
me it was h art breaking to try to grow things in the garden.
    We went up the hill, took pictures of the Slavi Indians in groups
etc.
    Saw Hudson Bay post and went on to the Mission where they
put on drills, songs etc for us. Later had regular tea, with big cake
and everything.
    Sister St Rose gave me some cakes and cookies with red sugar for
my birthday and a piec[e] for Uncle John.
    We stopped a few minutes afterwards for wood and Uncle John
gathered some beautiful roses.
    The three sisters and Mr, V.W. West got off at Providence.
    Albert Lebeau who was tried and convicted of Murder of his wife
and child last year, was the hunter for the mission at Providence
and his little shack is right beside their buildings,
    They need 20.000 to 25 000 fish for winter
    There was the most beautiful sunset tonight I ever saw. It was
particularly magnificent over the Mills Lake or Willow Lake as it
used to be called.
    The sut set at 10.30 and although the night never got dark, rain
across the lake made heavy clouds.
    The lake looks like ink at 12. midnight.
    Sun dial at Providence which was reported to have been left by Frank-
lin was dated 1887.

NOTES

Miriam Green Ellis's diary is part of the Miriam Green Ellis Collection, held by the Bruce Peel Special Collections Library at the University of Alberta, 96–91, File 3–1. This excerpt from Ellis's 1922 'Diary of Trip to Midnight Sun' is reproduced here with their permission. Other materials in the collection relating to Ellis's northern journey include an album containing 240 black-and-white photographs and a collection of 168 hand-painted glass slides, which Ellis had prepared to illustrate her lectures. The photos and the slide collection document the vegetation, landscape, people, and communities of the Mackenzie Valley, as well as incidents from Ellis's trip.

1 Miriam Green Ellis, 'The Capital of Esquimo Land,' *Manitoba Free Press*, 11 November 1922, 32; 'Natives in Canada's North Are Learning Value of Money –Able to Drive Shrewd Bargain with Whites,' *Vancouver Daily Province*, 18 November 1922, 27; 'When the Eskimo Celebrates at Aklavik,' *Toronto Sunday World Magazine*, 7 January 1923, 2.

2 Grant MacEwan, ... *And Mighty Women Too: Stories of Notable Western Canadian Women* (Saskatoon: Western Producer Prairie Books, 1975).

3 Bev Struan, 'It's a Neighborly Land,' *Canadian Magazine* 77 (March 1932), 20.

4 MacEwan, ... *And Mighty Women Too*.

5 Cornelia, 'Magic Journey North to Land of Midnight Sun,' *Toronto Telegram*, 28 November 1923, 8; MacEwan, ... *And Mighty Women Too*.

6 Miriam Green Ellis, *Pathfinders* (n.p.: Canadian Women's Press Club, 1956).

7 For instance, Ellis's trek to the Salt River resulted in an article in *The Outing Magazine*, and her descriptions of Ada Mary Conibear in the excerpt printed here (24 June) clearly form the basis for articles that later appeared in the *Vancouver Province* and in *Canadian Countryman*.

8 Arthur J. Ray, *The Canadian Fur Trade in the Industrial Age* (Toronto: University of Toronto Press, 1990).

9 The Royal North-West Mounted Police – the Mounties.

10 A bright orange or red wildflower.

11 'Norman' refers to Norman Wells, a settlement in the Northwest Territories. Interest in oil and mineral prospecting in the western Arctic
increased markedly after the First World War, and the precedent set by
the Klondike gold rush of the preceding century ensured that any discovery received eager attention in the south. The first major oil strike
occurred at Norman Wells in 1920; refining operations began the following year. Lead zinc claims at Pine Point, originally discovered in
1909, were also restaked in 1920 (Morris Zaslow, *The Northward
Expansion of Canada, 1914–1967* [Toronto: McClelland and Stewart,
1988], 22). Ellis was only one of many journalists who responded to
public interest in northern resource exploitation.

12 That is, the Hudson's Bay Company and Northern Trading Company
boats.

Mary Dulhanty
(1909–1999)

JANNE CLEVELAND AND MARGARET CONRAD

'I love to write in you diary. It is such a consolation. I suppose some people will think me silly. But no one loves me and understands me like you do.' These words were written on 17 January 1927 by seventeen-year-old Mary Dulhanty, a student enrolled in the Commercial program at Mount Saint Vincent Academy in Halifax, Nova Scotia. Her diary, kept sporadically between 7 December 1926 and 10 June 1927, provides a fascinating glimpse of student life at a Roman Catholic girls' school in the 1920s.

Marked 'P[r]ivate S.W.A.K,' the hard-covered notebook in which Mary chronicled her adolescent musings includes entries of varying length written in pen, pencil, and, on one occasion, in indelible ink. Her usually legible script and reasonably accurate spelling testify to the fact that Nova Scotia schools in the early twentieth century taught handwriting and spelling. Discovered between walls during house renovations in 1987, the diary was passed along to Toni Laidlaw, who, together with Margaret Conrad and Donna Smyth, were engaged in collecting the life writing of Maritime women.[1] To our great delight, we discovered that Mary herself was still alive, and we have been able to learn directly from the diarist and her daughter, Beth Powell, more of the context that frames this extraordinary document.

Mary Dulhanty was born in Springhill, Nova Scotia, in 1909,

and three years later moved with her family to Bridgewater. Her father, Richard Dulhanty, who worked as a track master for the Canadian National Railways, died in 1923. Sustained by insurance and savings, Mary's mother, Hannah (commonly called Mamie), was not compelled, as were many widows in this period, to enter the paid labour force to survive. Nor was Mary denied the opportunity to follow in the footsteps of her older sisters who had previously 'taken Commercial' at Mount Saint Vincent Academy. Founded by the Sisters of Charity in 1873, the Academy – like Mount Saint Vincent College, which received its provincial charter in 1925 – specialized in programs tailored for 'young ladies.'[2]

Mary was not always happy as a Mount student. She chafed at the discipline imposed by the Sisters of Charity and desperately missed her family. Her sisters, Jane Marie (b. 1900) and Margaret Theresa (b. 1903), were working in New York, while her brother, Richard Francis, called Frank (b. 1906), was attempting to qualify as a telegrapher. Although Mrs Dulhanty visited her homesick daughter on at least one occasion during the academic year, Mary was on her own for the first time in her life. Her diary speaks eloquently to the conflicting pressures and emotional swings that most people experience in their adolescent years. It also captures in remarkable detail the interwar context that framed Mary's life choices.

The period from 1919 to 1939 witnessed the triumph of corporate capitalism, the bureaucratic state, and mass consumer culture in North America.[3] While Nova Scotia was on the margins of these developments, its citizens were no less influenced by them than people elsewhere. A prolonged economic crisis, emigration to the United States, social unrest, and nostalgia for a 'golden age' all testify to the impact of the new corporate culture on the province.[4] Indeed, if Mary's diary is any indication, the cultural issues that were debated in the larger North American society – gender roles, prohibition, and fashion, to name only three – deeply touched the lives of ordinary Nova Scotians.[5]

The difficulty of combining family, work, and individual fulfilment was particularly acute for young women.[6] In the 1920s, the 'working girl' replaced the self-sacrificing mother as the predominant image of womanhood. While spinsters were still scorned, lesbian relationships discouraged, and pay scales for women in the paid labour force blatantly unfair, working women in the interwar years had a freedom and mobility that contrasted dramatically with the limited options available to their mothers. Not surprisingly, large urban centres held special attractions for young women. Cities offered entertainment, unchaperoned friendships, and a host of consumer delights. Although most women who grew up in the interwar years eventually married, popular culture filled their heads with visions of a companionate relationship with their husbands, fewer children, and access to the material possessions hitherto available only to the most affluent members of society.[7]

People living through this period of Nova Scotia history, of course, had no such analysis upon which to base their life choices. Instead, older family, church, and community traditions rubbed uneasily against new values invading society on a daily basis through movies, magazines, newspapers, catalogues, shop windows, radio programs, and popular songs. Mary's diary reveals just how deeply mass consumer culture had penetrated Nova Scotia society. Not only is Mary preoccupied by trips to downtown Halifax, the purchase of new clothes, the length of her hair, and the state of her finances and friendships, she also spoke a new language. 'To-day is the seventh day of December. Two weeks from tomorrow [I will be going home]. Hot dawg,' she announced on 7 December 1926. Many sentences are prefaced with 'Gee,' a slang expression that would have been considered blasphemous in an earlier era and was no doubt frowned upon by the good Sisters of Charity. From Mary's perspective, the Sisters of Charity continued to live by impossibly old-fashioned standards. For their part, the Sisters did their best to keep up with the times, to the point of including a beauty contest among the activities provided during one of the Mount's social occasions.

In her diary, Mary tracks the course of her emotional life, which is fraught with ambiguous longing. She describes in some detail the

crushes – Mary called them 'cases' – that she had on other classmates as well as on her favourite Sisters. Although the latter were
usually careful to discourage such feelings, the girls apparently had
ways of attracting the attention they craved, including 'doing a
grand,' or fainting, at strategic moments. We must be careful not to
read too much, or too little, into Mary's 'cases.' As Carroll Smith-
Rosenberg has revealed in the American context, women in the
nineteenth century could express their affection for each other in
ways that in the post-Freudian world became pathologized and pro-
scribed.[8] Mary's romantic yearnings for other women would have
attracted less attention in Victorian times when the 'female world
of love and ritual' had been developed to a high art.

Affective relationships among women were not new to the
twentieth century, but the way they were articulated and the alarm
expressed about them warrant our attention. In the interwar years,
as sentimentality gave way to sexuality in defining close human
relationships, heterosexual marriage was emphasized to the exclu-
sion of other emotional bonds. Friendships between people of the
same sex, and even platonic relationships between women and
men, were discounted; romantic interactions between women and
men became the predominant narrative line in novels, movies,
popular songs, advertising, and family life itself.[9]

The mention of 'cases' disappears abruptly after Mary and her
Roman Catholic classmates attended a three-day retreat early in
February. Conducted by Father Knox, an itinerant mission priest, it
was an occasion to impart lessons on Catholic girlhood to the cap-
tive audience.[10] The retreat put Mary on the defensive emotionally
and intellectually. Her description of Father Knox's teachings on
the perils of mass consumer culture, the high point of the diary, is a
powerful mix of reportage and reaction to issues that preoccupied
students – and teachers – at the Mount.

While mired in the ambiguities of modern womanhood, Mary
struggled with bookkeeping, typing, shorthand, and Christian doctrine, at times despairing that she would ever graduate. The diary
entries for the last ten weeks of term, which are not included here,

suggest that sports, especially basketball and tennis, and trips to town continued to be more appealing to the fun-loving Mary than the discipline of the study hall. In the yearbook, *Folio Montana*, Mary's classmates expressed the hope that she would return to the Mount to continue her education, but Mary's ambition, they reported, was 'to seek her fortune in the "States" next year.' As it turned out, she did neither, but was obliged to spend two years at home in Bridgewater marking time with her mother before emigrating to New York in 1929. Despite the onset of the Great Depression, she had little difficulty finding work and eventually landed a job as a machine operator with Elizabeth Arden, another Canadian lured by the opportunities available to women in North America's greatest metropolis.

On 11 June 1932, Mary married William Swift in a Roman Catholic ceremony at the Church of Joan of Arc, Jackson Heights, New York. The marriage quickly broke down. After a Reno divorce in 1936, an attempted reconciliation ended in a second divorce under New York State laws in 1938. Mary followed her sister Jane to California and then to Hawaii, where she worked for a general contractor. Her timing always impeccable, Mary was in Pearl Harbor when it was bombed by the Japanese in 1941. Shortly thereafter, she married Alexander Kirkland McKendrick (1916–68), a man seven years her junior. They had two children, Mary Elizabeth (called Beth, b. 1942) and James (called Jim, b. 1944), and lived for most of their married life in Belmont, California. Following Al's death in 1968, Mary took a trip around the world. When we approached her to allow her diary to be made available for research purposes, she had the courage and good sense to become a 'public woman.' Mary lived the final years of her life in a senior citizens' apartment in Redwood City, California, where she died on 29 April 1999. In ways too numerous to discuss here, her life represents the pain and the possibilities open to the 'working girl' of the 1920s.

In our telephone interview with Mary in July 1997, she indicated that, as a teenager, she considered Nova Scotia to be a boring place and found the Mount too strict for her liking. She remembered almost nothing of the events described in her diary, thus confirming the elusiveness of human memory and the value of diaries such as this one that capture narrative and meaning in the making. Mary kept diaries for most of her life but destroyed most of them. This one, it seems, was destined to survive. As she noted in her entry of 9 June 1927, 'I was just reading what I wrote [in] you Diary during Retreat and wonder had I better leave them in here for I would hate to have someone else read it but I know this is bound to be read sometime.'[11]

Mary Dulhanty, ca. 1927.

DIARY, NOVA SCOTIA, DECEMBER 1926–FEBRUARY 1927

[Cover:] Property of Mary Dulhanty, Commercial Class, 1926–27, Mount Saint Vincent (P[r]ivate S.W.A.K.)

To-day is the seventh day of December. Two weeks from to-morrow [I will be going home]. Hot dawg. We had a very interesting English Class to-day. The Commercials are having the Ice Cream booth. Sister Assissium has a cake which we have to sell tickets, five each. The back window of the Commercial Class is banked almost to the top. I wish I would get a letter from someone. We practised the cer[e]monies for the Reception to-morrow. Six are being received Children of Mary and about thirty I imagine are being received in the Sodality.

Wensday   Dec. 8

To-day is the Feast of the Immaculate Conception. Two novices were professed to-day. We had high mass. All the lights were on, it was gorgeous. A sister of Sister Aneta Gertrude's and Helen Copeland's aunt were the sisters. I had a letter from Frank. He seems kind of lonesome. Poor Kid. Sez he thinks he can arrange to go home the same day. We had pork and mashed potatoes to-day for dinner. We are having supper at five or half past I guess. Gee I wish Mom would hurry and come home. Norah has gone to town to see her Mother. I've only fifteen cents, don't know what I'll do at the sale. So long.

Monday   Dec. 13

My mother arrived at last. Friday night. Called me Saturday morning. Of course I went to Town. Had to wait for half an hour for the bus. I had to borrow 15 cents to get in on the bus from my ticket money. Poor me. It was beastly raining and snowing. Mother went home at 2:30. I went to the Orpheus. Wild West show. Went to bed early. Jan's in Amherst. Margaret's still in New York. Sister de Chantall said that Harriet Hebb could go home Wednesday afternoon and asked if I was going too. We the Commercials are going to Town next Monday. Three cheers. We got our club pins.

They are rather nice. Mom didn't bring me anything much. This
pen I'm writing with. Bot a new pair of shoes. Black patent.

Tuesday   December 14, 1926
    Fine. But rather wet at times. Harriet Hebb is watching every
letter I write. But such is life in a large city. Life just drizzles on at
M.S.V. Havn't had a letter. But expect Mom will write later. Gee a
week from to-day and I'll be jumping around. I have rather a busy
week starting to-morrow.
Wednesday. Baskit Ball   I hear we are not playing.
Thursday.
Friday – Exam Shorthand
Saturday – Bookkeeping
Monday. Christian Doctrine Exam and last but not least Town.
D.V.[12]

Wednesdnesday
    Fine. We have decided to go to Town Saturday, hope its fine.

Sunday   December 19
    Time is drawing nearer. I was in Town yesterday from eight until
five. We left M.S.V. at 8 o'clock. Eighteen girls and Sister Assissium. First we went to the Infirmary, saw Rose Orlando and the
Hospital. We were in the operating room. Gee its nice. Then we
proceeded to the office Specialty office. A fellow showed us the
working of the files. When we were coming from there I met Mrs.
C.J. Cragg and Mrs. Dunny Campbell. Then we went to the customs office and post office. Got some stamps and so forth. Then we
disbanded then I went with Ruby Bell and Harriette but I lost them
in the five and ten   met Mary Riley, Grace Amerault and
Helen Lavers. We had dinner at the Green. Clam chowder, fish
and vegetables and ice-cream hot chocolate sauce and chocolate.
Kind of good. Then we met at the Parade and went to Moirs! Moirs
have a wonderful office. We were all thru the office   they
showed us all the offices and gave us a box of chocolates. Then I

met Mr. Dulhanty. Can you imagine that? Well I was rather taken back. He says that his sister is some relation, is a sister at Saint Patrick's. Sister Marie Agnus. I'd like to see her. From that we proceed down stairs and one of the men showed us some of the cakes and things. I spent the rest of the afternoon in the five and ten. We are getting lectures by the dozen. One at Prime to-day. Just the sixth for me. Gee I'm just dying to get home but – Mom sent me five dollars to go home on. Poor me. I'm having a hard time getting there. Harriett Hebb owes me one dollar.

Monday   December 20

Another day has passed. Just two or rather one and a half more days. Life is becoming more interesting. We don't have to come back until the tenth. Three cheers. Gee I'm glad. Well we had our Christian Doctrine and Bookkeeping exames to-day. Thats that. Typed from two hours and a half. Guess I'll have to start sitting straight. Sister Angnus Eucharia is having study to-night. Gee she's a pet. I like to know what Jane and Frank and Margaret are doing but I suppose time will tell. Gee I'm just on edge. Filing tomorrow. But such is life. I'm knee deep in daisys and head over heals in love.

Tuesday   January 11, 1927

I've been home and am back her[e] again. It's a wonderful feeling. I left Wednesday at 2:30. Left the commercial room about ten to. Ruby Bell & I did some shopping and got the thirty past two train home. Frank had gone Tuesday. He met me. How crant [?] when I arrived their. Time passed rapidly on for two weeks and five days. Went to the movies every chance almost. Fred B. was home with his radio. And I was down there several nights. Got a new coat and blue marvella with seal collar and cuffs, also pocket. A black satin dress trimmed in metallic. Scarf, overshoes, 2 pair of stockings, powder, vanity case, note paper (green), sterling pen, silk shirt, step-ins, photo and various other articals. Midnight Mass was very nice but the congre[g]ation was certainly differ[ent] from

that at the Mount. Jane is in New York with Margaret. Mom, Frank
& I were the only people home for Xmas. Kay was up for tea one
night. I got a pain and it hurts. Ouch. I went to Mass Monday
morning before I came. There were a dozen Mount girls on the
train. Catherine Davison & Avery Gelling were on the train too.
Arrived back on the seven o'clock bus. It's an awful life. Mildred's
Edna is back. And Pearl Southeland is going to room with me.
She's a College girl. I wish we didn't have to change, its a nuisance.
Bluebell Comefort is back. Most of them are back. Mary K.
McDougal is back too. Poor Mom. I'm just dying to hear had [how]
she is getting along. We have to write our letters on the typewriter
now. It makes me sick.

Wednesday   Jan. 12
    Sister Agnus Camilla woke us up this morning and there on the
dress[er] was a calendar of Kitty there and she turned it face down
and said 'Who ever owns this put it away.['] Then she went out and
left the door open. She must live on a raft. Nice way to start the
day. Then we went to Mass. Everybody or at least practically all the
girls had to sit down. Mildred had to go out before Mass started.
Helen Stokes has the mumps. She has Helen Keddy's room where
Mildred and Edna were going. I don't know what they'll do about
it. Gee there's an awful lot of cats around the building. We had
marmalade and toast for breakfast and cocoa for dinner last night.
Gee it was good. Our gym classes are changed. I go Tuesdays and
Fridays now. Gee I must get my money changed and pay my lawful
debts payed. Gee I wonder how Kay is. The poor girl she has an
awful time of it. I wonder if Jean will write me. I hope she does. My
poor Kitty I hope Mom found it. Mrs. Morris will have no one to
argue religion with her now. She's awful bigoted I fear. Sister Aneta
Gertrude has gone to Boston. I wonder if Jane got my letter. Everything is I wonder in the book. Life is an awful trial. I made 75.5 on
filing and 76 on bookkeeping 80 on shorthand. Believe my [me] I
shall have some time catching up on typewriting. Took a bath and
went to bed early Kitty and I. Pearl hasn't moved in yet. But she is

going to to-morrow. Some of the kids were skating from 7 until 8 with Sister Marie Agnus.

Thursday   January 13
   Fine. Very slow day. Pearl & Mildred are moving in and out. Got a letter from Mom. Said she wasn't lonely. Nobody loves ~~my~~ (corrected by Caddy Doran) me.

Saturday   January 15/27
   I just finished the Green Lantern. It was really good. Gee a week ago to-day I can remember what I did all last week. I went down to Michells anyway after supper. I hav[e]n't my first chapter written for to-morrow yet. I don't know what I'll do. I suppose mom will get my letter to-night. Gee she must find it lonesome. I hope she writes.

Sunday   January 16/27
   Gee Sundays are dull here. We were on the road for an hour. Everybody is telling me how nice my coat is. That's nice isn't it diary? Gee I knocked a chair over last night about ten o'clock. It made a terrific noise. I wish someone would come to see me. But no such good luck. I took a Shorthand Test Friday. I wonder how much I made. Helen Lavers has left I think. Went yesterday morning. It is a shame. She is some kid. This is Bea's pen. It certainly is nice to write with. That door bell keeps ringing and ringing. It makes me cross, never for me. Lillian Romkey, Frances Lockart, Grace Amereau, and Mildred MacDonald got the honors for this month in the Commercials. A week ago to-day I had come downstairs after a bath & was playing the piano. It is just three. Oh dear! I walked with Margaret Romkey and Harriett Hebb. Behind Kitty and Mary Shannon. Mary Shannon was telling us this morning about playing in the theatre. She has played in the Imperial, Orpheus & the Majestic. Some kid believe me. Gee she is a nice kid tho. We had a very interesting lecture this morning. Well to-morrow is Wednesday or Monday (I guess I'm sleepy). Starting the

new month or week. I think I could write for years not saying
a thing. Like I am now. I got an awful surprise Friday night. I
received a visitor after I got in bed. We typewrote instead of having
Business Tycology [?] Saturday. I have an awful lot of typewriting to
do. Also I have to pick up on my bookkeeping. I suppose I have to
pay out some more money to-morrow. Mite box. Mary Comerfort
is going to Town to spend the night. Her father is coming in the
morning. I have a picture of dad with me. Gee I wish I could have
him. It makes me miss him so, hearing all the girls talking about
their fathers. The birch trees are very pretty in front of the Mount.
Everybody is studying hard and I can't. I was talking to Sister
Agnus Theresa to-day. Giving her Father Penny's message. About
time I guess. Gee I certainly get enough about cases now. Kitty and
Pearl. I wonder what Mom is doing. It will be a week to-morrow
since my return. Oh! Oh! Oh! Oh!!! Life is just one darn thing
after another.

Monday   Jan. 17
    Monday the day every [one] does not like, at school anyway. Sis-
ter read our first chapters. Norah Welphey's was choosen for the
first one. It is about a dope fiend. I have a cold. It certainly is very
pleasant. Walked with Margaret Romkey. Everybody is talking
about Retreat. At least the non-Catholics mostly. They are going
home. Madeline had a box of chocolates to-day. I think I must
have had about ten. I'm an awful hog. I was teaching Madeline &
Jean to say 'I am right in the pink' last night and when Sister de
Chantall asked them how they were they said Right in the pink.
She said don't say that it is very common, and she asked who told
them that & they said Mary Dulhanty. Poor sister she will think I
am an awful wretch. Gee I was interrupted in a wonderful visit to
the Chapel to-night. The old Bell rang. I love the Chapel at night.
I could have spent hours there to-night. I had a nice talk to my
sister this morning. But of course the third party was there. She
always is. I love to write to you diary. It is such a consolation. I suppose some people will think me silly. But no one loves me and

understands like you do. I saw Mother to-night. She never smiles. I
always do. I suppose I am too insignificant not in size but importance. I wish I would hear from Jane or Margaret or Frank or Mom,
diary, I really have lost connection with the world in one short
night, (not that sudden) week. The moon is wonderful tonight.
Diary, I am sitting in the front part of the study, by the window, the
third desk. There is a lovely [view] of [the] shrine of Our Lady at
the front   there are twelve girls outside of myself here and the
sister are walking up and down in the corridor or rather passing.
There is a train shunting up and down, up and down. The moon is
glorious. Everybody is studying but myself. Sister Columbia has the
lov[el]iest ferns around the Shrine. Gee the Grot[t]o looked nice
this afternoon. The sun was setting and the sky was lovely it made
a perfect background for the Groto. The statues are covered now.
In the spring I must make my stations there. I have never. I wonder
what mother is doing. I shall see my sister again to night. I wonder
what she would say if she could read you diary? You are the only
one who knows about her in regard to my relation to her. If other
people read this they would not believe I wrote it. But never the
less I did. Sister Agnus Camilla has an awful cold so has Sister
Assissium. Rachel Hogan has been rushed to the Hospital for an
operation. That certainly sounds serious. We offered our Rosary for
her to night. She has one, the oldest child about a year and a half
and another two or three months. It would be awful if she did not
get better. I suppose not awful if God willed it. But it seems so to
me now. As I grow old I suppose I shall realize it is not so awful as it
seems now. If only I can be good. Oh that God will give me
strength to live a good holy and pure life.

Tuesday   January 18
      Had a nice talk this morning. It was real exciting. I asked her to
write something in my album and she [said] that I wouldn't want
her to write anything in that book and I said 'I'd like *anything you'd*
do.['] Thrills Diary. Home was never like this. Diary please don't

think me silly and sentimental really she's the a darling. Not mushy like the other sisters. We had Christian Doctrine in the 'A' Classroom. Sister Marie Agnus is sick. Sister Francis is a dear. I love her truly. X,Y,Z nix.

Sunday   January 23
Diary Dear, almost a week since I have last spoken to you. And such a week. I've had a reched cold. Was in bed Friday afternoon from three until tea time. And Saturday from half past ten until twelve thirty. And this afternoon from one thirty until tea time. I did not even half [have] to ask Saturday either. Wasn't that wonderful? I am getting teased awfully diary. I can't decide who to have a case on. Pearl fell and hurt her ankle Wednesday night. After Meditation. It was really very exciting. But it did not last long. I guess it was not very serious. She went [to] Mass this morning. We are going on Retreat two weeks from to-day. I forgot to say I had a long sleep Saturday morning too! Sister Columbia had us for Decoration Friday night before Benediction and Saturday night for polit[e]ness class. Gee! Mrs. Telfer, Mrs. Rathburn, Capt. & Mrs. Innis were up to [see] me. We were in both Parlours, Chaple, Libary, Music Hall, Class Rooms up stairs, Studio, and up and down the sisters stairs. Dear! I wonder if I shall get my vocation on a plate. Also I got a box of candy. Which was needed very much. Mrs. Telfer saw Frank. I forgot to ask her when she was going home. Captain Innis reminds me of Frank Cushing. Marie H. had her brother in the Parlour. My he's odd looking. Not a very handsome chap like all brothers. Some of the kids were swimming. Oh, Diary I'm nutty I mean skating.

Monday   January 24
I havn't had any thrills today at all. It is real mean. I knew it was too good to be true. Such an ordinary person like myself. But such is life in a large city. No letter for Me to-day. Both Jane and Margaret owe me one but –

Tuesday   January 25
   Nothing exciting at all to-day. I guess my case is off. But oh hot dog something exciting happened. S.A.C. sowed [sewed] our skirts to our blouses. Mildred McDougal, Joyce Roop, Marion Embreys, Mary McSween & Myself. Gee mine is almost an inch too long. We had silence for Dinner to-day. Gee it was good. A man's cleaning the typewriters. The college kids are taking exams. Everybody is so cranky I mean the sisters. But such is life. I made eighty on my Eleventh Lesson. Not so bad. I bet I'll make thirty on the next ones. They are awful hard. But such is life. I wish would get some notice of me taken by my loved one. Guess I'm just a fly upon the wall. Oh, Gee Pond   I havn't a partner.

Wednesday   Jan. 26
   I've just come from off the Pond and I havn't any strength in my fingers to write. Nothing exciting. She turned off our light last night   just say the prayer. Poor Mary, she is broken hearted, I havn't spoken to her since Monday. Imagine that diary. Life isn't worth living. I havn't had letters all week. Guess my honorable relations & friends have forgotten me. Oh Diary, Diary, I have an awful case and she doesn't even know it. I wish I knew more about cases so I could find my way around. Oh Diary I love, love, love her. Kitty is in bed. She did the grand at breakfast this morning. Last night too I guess. Gee she is lucky in a way. She had someone exceptionally nice love her. Of course it couldn't be me. I think I will have to learn to faint. Gee that sounds awful heartless. But I'm getting desperate. Surely she can see my loving glances. But I suppose she is too busy to notice me. Oh Boo hoo Boo hoo, Diary I am a sentimental fool. But – Sister Assissium sez we should not check all or [of] our imagination. Gee Kitty is up. She must be dying to study. I know I am. I havn't looked at a book all day. I did fourteen letters to-day. Sister Francis gave us a lecture on vocations to-day. Gee I get tired of her. I'd hate to have her for classes every day. Eva Barbara is here. Visiting. She is rather cuty. But she doesn't come up to my expectations. She was so well heralded.

Monday   January 31

Diary dear, I have not written to you for five whole days. Dear, Oh, Dear. Had a most thrilling talk last night at supper. Got a box of cookies from Mom. Gee they were good. Sister De Chantall was ripping. But such is life. I was in Town Saturday. Went to the Orpheus. The picture was rotten. It rained pi[t]chforks all the time I was in Town. My coat is all out of press & the fur raty. Pearl did the Grand at Mass this morning. Kitty did it Thursday night and Friday morning at breakfast. She went in Town Saturday to see the doctor. Said there was nothing wrong with her. Went to the Green for lu[n]ch. The girls and men were smoking away. Seems queer. Not seeing things like that all the time. Gee Prime was wild Sunday. Got Hail Columbia all around. But such is life. Got a letter from Mom Saturday. Sez Frank is coming home this week. Going to take his exams soon. I hope he calls on me. If he doesn't I'll pass out. Got a new collar in Town. Sported around by myself all afternoon. Finished my letters in typing. Gee Retreat I don't know whether we go on Thursday & Friday. I wish it was this time next week. Walked with Kitty. I got a letter from Margaret. Sez she is very busy. Jane hasn't a job. Too bad. They think she will not stay because she is a Canadian. She is sort of getting back what she gave. Rather true to life. Got special mention at Prime for my Catechism. Oh Yes! Special Mention. I am sitting with Jean La Fevre. She is studying so hard she will kill herself. I suppose she enjoys it. I do. Oh yes! I wonder what we will have for supper to-night. Something Good nix. The darn fried potatoes gave me integestion. Gee we are stud[y]ing Law now and it is beastly. Sis Lochart got the Honor Medal for the Commercial Class. Mildred for the 'A' and she turned her back to them when she came back. Oh! Gee! It was awful. Annie MacSeen got it for the 'B' Annie Mantin for 'C' and Mary Hashe for 'D.' Sister de Chantall was down at our class this morning at shorthand time but the girls were taking tests so that's all right. S.A.C. gave us an awful lecture Saturday night. Nobody seems to quite get the drift of it yet. Time will tell I suppose.
Irene [?] Commo comes to the Mount for piano lessons I guess.

Mary Shannon isn't back yet. She had rehumitism awful bad.
Sister Agnus Eucharia had Pond to-day.

Tuesday   Feb. 1st/27
   Diary dear! Life is rather slow. Nothing exciting at all. Had a
long talk with Sister Columbia to-day. Just now. Got a letter from
Jean Walsh. Imagine that, rather a surprise I guess. One from
Margaret yesterday. I'm lucky. Oh Boy!

Wednesday   Feb 2/27
   We didn't have a long sleep this morning because it was the
Feast of the Presentation. But we will have one to-morrow, and a
bath to-night, imagine! Father Brady said Mass and he is so slow.
Kitty got two letters I didn't get any. We still don't know when we
are going on Retreat. Time will tell I suppose. Sister Roselsten has
study to-night. I havn't seen my sweet hardly at all to-day. But such
is life. Gee Retreat! I wouldn't mind it if it wasn't for a General
Confession. I have never made one before and I don't know how.
My other case has blown off. Sad but true. I only made fifty-five on
my twel[f]th lesson. Gee that is rotten. I am taking it over tomorrow. We didn't have to go on the Pond. I went to my room and
Sister Marie Geneva came up and sent me down. I went to the
Commercial radiator and Sister Assissium came in & I was sitting
on the radiator. Trust me. She just laughed. We had mashed potatoes for dinner and Washington pie with marshmallows on top for
dinner. Wonder what we will have for supper. I wish it would be
baked potatoes but no such good luck. We had scalloped potatoes
for supper last night. Jean says we will have Stew. Gee I wonder
where Frank is. I hope he comes to see me. Mildred McDonald &
two French girls went to Town for the opening of Parliament. I
wish I could have But – I wonder what Mom is doing all by her
ownsum. We are getting or rather our diplomas have come for filing & the English Correspondence course have come too. But I
don't get one of them.

J[esus]M[ary]J[oseph]
Retreat Thursday   February 3/26[7]
   Diary dear nothing very exciting. But we are going on Retreat
to-night. Holy Hour this after noon. We are having Father Knox.
Said Good Bye to all the sisters. The two most important ones at
any rate. Went to the Chapel at seven o'clock to have our throats
blessed. Then to Lecture at 7:30. Just the opening one. Our Retreat
is based on the new feast 'Jesus Christ King.'
   Bot some Holy Cards also received some. Gee going to bed was
funny   no one would look at the other. Mass at half past seven,
breakfast at eight. Sister Marie Agnus read during breakfast. Sister
Marie Jeneva for dinner and Sister Agnus de Chantall for supper.
The lectures are good. I can't at this moment remember the subject. But I shall tell you as I proceed. It is half past eight and I am
going to retire.

JMJ
We went to bed this afternoon from one thirty until three. It
snowed so much last night that we could not go on the Pond to-day
and I was going to walk with Kitty too. But Thy will not my way. I
have the Life of a Modern Marter [Martyr] to read. Sister Columbia gave it to me. I am walking with Yvonne to-morrow. I saw Sister Anita Gertrude yesterday and Sister Regina just now also Sister
Columbia. Father Knox is some speaker. Spoke on or rather the
main subject to-night was Liquor. Sez Kathleen Norris is one of the
good Catholic writers. First time I knew it. But I shall take more
notice of her books now. I do not like them much. Our programme
by the way runs like this. Mass seven thirty and eight on Sunday.
Nine thirty lecture afterward we go to the Chapel. Lecture eleven
fifteen. Dinner twelve thirty. Rest until three. Pond at three. Lecture at four. Rosary at five, supper at six. Benediction at seven.
Seven fifteen lecture. Then Chapel for our night prayers & bed.
The lecture Friday morning was about disobeying parents and our
superiors. Sez parents are more than half to blame. But there are

two sides to every question. [Here a line has been thoroughly scratched out] The poor kids, but – May Jesus, Mary and Joseph help me. Gee it is cold. I don't mind it but I suppose we will on the road. Father Knox sez we cannot follow to [two] masters or serve them   when you are choosing say 'God or this.' Father has a wonderful voice. He speaks always as tho he doesn't know what to say next but believe me he does. Has a voice something like Jack Smiths only used for a different purpose. The girls say he [studied] for an English minister before he became a priest. I don't know. Maybe he was. But he certainly is a Catholic now. He seems to have a limp. Gee he must be over six feet. Speaks very slowly but with a meaning to every word. Says if he could parade some of the Sisters 'Dear girls' before them during vacation the sisters would not know them. He sez he *knows* what Catholic girls and women are doing. You can not belong to the Catholic church and do or live as the women of to-day live *now*. Sez there are more pitfalls in the world for girls now than there ever was, just as there is in traffic. 'A man respects a girl if she respects her self. Always.' We can command the love of a man so that he will respect us, he will do anything for her, and, he will never by word, look, or action do anything or utter any unpure thing. That when we choose a man who is not Catholic we choose Barabus instead of Christ. When a girl says with a lift of her nose, 'I can take care of myself,' she is like Peter. We can not win glory in God's sight by a disobedient act. He was asked by a woman Does the end gratify the means   he says in some cases. But not enough to kill a person. [Several words are heavily scratched out here] what I have. It certainly gave me a [text scratched out] so many many things to [text scratched out]. Well I suppose time will help me. But Oh Gee it is hard. If ever I am a [scratched out] I shall tell my [scratched out] the truth, please God, and they will not get it from outside means as I did. When I think of the stuff I have [scratched out] about to other [scratched out] I makes me feel like, I don't know. Father sezs that he wishes that people could say 'You could[n't] take liberties with that girl' 'Why' [']She is Catholic.' I have heard that said but not in all cases.

Please God that it will be in this case. He DO NOT PUT ON PIOUSNESS
ONLY ON SUNDAY. There is so much to be done home. The kids have
never been taught and not only the kids but the youths. It is a
crime. I hope Father Penny gets some kind of a Sunday School
organized. I have just come from another lecture. About bobbed
hair and short dresses. He sez it is not the bobbed hair that is the
sin   it is the cutting and where it is cut that is the sin. If you
must have your hair cut have it done but [by] one of your own sex.
He sez girls are very delicate about people touching their necks or
bodies but the[y] let *any* barbar maul all over their necks. If when
you meet a priest you are ashamed of your short skirts why are you
not ashamed and embarresed before other people. We also had a
short lecture on confession. We are to go to confession at four and
if we are not thru by then we are to go after lecture to-night. He sez
it is not necessary to make a General Confession unless the[re] is
some real cause. I want to make one but I suppose maybe I had better not. We are to go to him to-morrow in the Confessional to ask
advice if we wish. His morning lectures are always the best. Diary I
spend much of my spare time with you. I hope that these notes will
some day be of use to me. I wish Margaret and Jane and Mom were
here to make the Retreat with me. I wonder if Mom has ever made
one. He sez dancing in itself is not a sin but that more than one
half of the dances of to-day cannot be executed without the ocas-
sion of sin. When a girl goes to a public dance in a damndable
one piece dress with practically nothing else on, it is the essence
of nudity and a sure occassion of sin. [Marginal notation: He
sez you cannot judge a person by what she has on but you can by
what she has not.] I just seem to begin to realize what life is
and what is it doing or what the people of the present day are doing.
The sisters all tell us not to judge our past by our present. If I did
God help me. But Oh God that You will give me the strength to
live a good Catholic girls life, that God I am not worthy of your
notice. I seem just to begin to notice what I am and what I have
been doing. Oh how I wish that Jean could come here. She has
such an influence over boys if only it is the right kind   Jesus,

Mary and Joseph pray for her. Our Lecture was based on the fall of
our first parents. Father said that Eve was not temp[t]ed all at once
but she was coaxed and told things and led on as we are likely to
do. The lecture at eleven fifteen was based on baptizm. By his lecture I know now that he was an Anglican Minister. Certainly some
change. It does seem funny because you see Knox's Prespeterian
[Presbyterian] church. He sez it seems strange the Catholics do not
seem eager to bring more Catholics into the church. They do not
ask has he been baptised. I wonder if we will get a lecture on what
Father O'Riley lectures on. We have to go on the road this afternoon. I suppose we will freeze. I'm going to put on all the extra
clothes I have around. Retreat certainly is taking stock. I just begin
to realize what I have been doing. I wonder where and when I shall
make my next retreat. Confession this afternoon. Well I've been to
Confession it wasn't much. I mean I did not make a real general
confession just a sort of one. Our lecture this morning the first was
about society. He said that Queen Mary & King George may come
over here for the celebration of Confederation, the fiftieth [sixti-
eth] anniversary I guess. Sez the Queen is no fool and she will
know what's what and who is who. He sez he wonders what she will
think of Montreal or Ottawa, Toronto society. He sez she is a lady.
[Marginal notation: He sez bobbed hair is not allowed in Court.]
Our eleven o'clock lecture was on I can't remember I'll think of it
later. He certainly gives you a different outlook on life. It seems
that this school does all around. He sez trouble with this world is
that no body thinks. In every action or thing that is being done
people do not think. He sez that bobbed hair is not allowed at the
English Court now. I wonder if my hair would be long enoug[h] to
go up by June. I am expecting to be present at Court you see Diary.
Our lecture this afternoon was on the Catholic religion. I really
cannot put it under a heading I suppose I am not bright but never
the less. Gee I wish the Retreat was not over or almost. I love it.
We had exposition to-day. And Holy Hour tonight. We had a very
pressing lecture on vocations. He sez in everything else but religion
there are more than enough but in the Catholic religion – He sez

there are more men with vocation than there are women. Why?
Because of the condition of the Catholic homes. A mother prays
that her first-born will be anything but a priest a sister or nun. It
[the] lecture was certainly good. I am a selfish prig. I can not give
up the world. Jesus, Mary and Joseph help me. I wonder if there is a
letter from Mom. I wonder how she is. It worries me having her all
alone. But I suppose she is all right. I wonder what she would say if
I said I was going to enter. Gee I wonder. It does not seem to me I
could do much good here when I think of what should be done
home. If I had only the strength and constitution to carry on the
work. JMJ give me light.

Monday   February 6/27
Well diary it is all over. Father Knox is gone. He went this morning. He gave us a short address and the papal blessing. Gee I like
him. I wish we had him always but such is life. We came off Retreat
at breakfast. And talk about noise there sure was some din. We had
congi [?] all morning but not much if you ask me. Kitty & I went up
in Connie' room and Sister A.C. put us out. Pearl has the blues,
her brother has gone to California. Mary Comerfort is in Town.
Kitty had a box of choc[ol]ates. (But the[y]'re all gone now.)

Tuesday   February 7/27
Time is passing slowly onward. I forgot to tell you diary that we had
beaf steak apples for breakfast and browned potatoes (Gee, they
were luscious), fresh pork, carrots for dinner and cold pork and
baked potatoes for supper which surely was a treat. I had a letter
from Mom today. She sez she likes the typewritten letter very much
better than the hand writing. Sez I had better take a course in hand
writing. I do not know where I could get it. Mildred McDonald was
sent out Christian Doctrine class this morning because she was eating candy. Sister S.C. said she was perfectly discusting and oh bless
us. Sister M.A. cap on the side   part of it got stuck up and oh,
oh, oh she looked funny. I thot that I would die. She was telling
some joke at the time and we just roared and she thot we were

laughing at it and she laughed too. I did not dare look at her or I would have burst out laughing. Such exciting things do happen. Oh yes! Madge is back with curl. About everyone is back now I guess. Everyone is quoting Father Knox. I suppose he is giving a Retreat somewhere else now. Mildred ask me what I am always writing in here. I say it is law. It is isn't it Diary.

Wednesday   February 9, 1926[7]

Time slowly drifts on. It is a gorgous day. I walked with Margaret Romkey, she gives me the willies she talks so slow. We are not going to have the concert until a week from to-morrow. We didn't have a long sleep this morning and we had beads in the hall at dinner time. The days are beginning to get longer, it is half past five now and it is still light, the sun is just going down.

Thursday   February 10, 1926[7]

Another day has drifted slowly by. I took a bath last night and did odds and ends. Was down for Meditation this morning imagine.

Friday

Another day! And Kitty has gone to the parlor imagine that! I hope it is something good. Gee I'm awful, I'm sort of an animal I guess, always want something to eat. Oh well. Lillian Romkey is back. Did not get my thirty words, a letter either but such is life. Was with Sister all during Adoration [?] didn't get much kick out of it tho. Walked with Helen Copland. Gee she is a funny kid some days I like and some days I – – her. Party Monday that is something to look forward to. Also the play Thursday and the conje Friday. But I suppose I shall or rather we will have to have fish for our bankuet [banquet]. Oh well such is life. I guess I'll go to the Chapel to say my Office.

Sunday   Feb. 13/1927

Two days and I have had no letters, everybody is getting the measels [measles]. There are nine now I think. Walked with Kitty to-day and Helen Copland to-day. About the measels. Margaret

Lauder has had them for three weeks, then Bluebell, Lucy Fletcher
Friday and Mildred Marsh, Anna McLean, Madeline Borotra, and
Catherine Burgess and Marion Emberee to-day. And Marjorie
O'Brien to-day too. I was playing cards with Marjorie O'Brien last
night and Marion Emberee took my place and she sat with us all
evening. Oh well I suppose everyone will have them. Sister Regina
will have her hands full. Kitty got three pounds of chocolates, she
and I finished one box Friday night. Pearl isn't eating candy. Too
bad. I wish someone would come to see me but – . To-morrow is the
day of the big party. I wonder when Frank is coming up, I hope it
will be soon. I wrote to Mom for Money. I have not one black cent
to my name now. I don't need any now so I am not worrying. Kitty
and I said our beads and office. I wish this was last Sunday. Oh boo!

Tuesday   Feb. 15
    Time is drifting on. It snowed last night and we didn't go on the
Pond this afternoon. I was out for a while with Helen Copland.
Well the party has come and gone. Connie McGrath had a darling
dress. Had supper with Pearl. Had a nice time. We had rather punk
eats. Fox berry sandwitches & deviled ham, cheese and ice cream,
animal cookies. Florence Archibald has the measles, had them last
night. You would never know it. The kids with the measles are all
in Saint Joseph's dormitory. Had a letter from Marjorie. Nothing in
it. The party was called Mother Goose's. There were some girls
from Town, not many. I made eighty six on my fourteenth lesson.
Sister said that was good! 'Twas too. Marjorie O'Brien and Marion
Embree didn't have measles at all. The Sydney girls have gone to
town. Dr. Sullivan is here. I'd love to have a letter from Mom to
find out about Frank. The play is put off until Madeline gets over
the measles. Poor kid. I suspect we will never have it at the rate
they are going now. Kitty got another pound of chocolates Sunday,
that is four pounds in two days.

Sunday   February 27, 1927
    But to-day is Monday. I have been in bed it will be two weeks
Thursday with the measels. Imagine! I had a marvelous time. First

there was Kay Owen, Kay Burgess, Ealnor Moore and Ruby, Irene McQuillen, Rosela Belliveau, Alice Como, Grace Amirault and myself there then. The four left and Alice Dowd came. We had a marvelous time again I say. We had a table up there and we washed our dishes there. Made as much racket as we could. Got up Saturday to see the play. I don't feel like writing diary. This old pen is the dickens. Got a letter from Jane to-day. See you later.

NOTES

Mary Dulhanty's diary is housed in the Mount Saint Vincent University Archives. We are indebted to Mary Dulhanty McKendrick, Redwood City, California, and her daughter Beth Powell, Eureka, California, for giving us permission to publish excerpts from the diary and for answering our persistent questions.

1 See Margaret Conrad, Toni Laidlaw, and Donna Smyth, *No Place Like Home: The Diaries and Letters of Nova Scotia Women, 1771–1938* (Halifax: Formac, 1988).
2 Sister Maura, *The Sisters of Charity, Halifax* (Toronto: Ryerson Press, 1956); Sister Marie Agnes White, 'Early Beginnings: Mount Saint Vincent College, 1925–1951,' *Insight* 4, no. 2 (1975): 2–13; Theresa Corcoran, sc, *Mount Saint Vincent University: A Vision Unfolding, 1873–1988* (Lanham, MD: University Press of America, 1999).
3 J.T. Jackson Lears, *No Place of Grace: Antimodernism and the Transformation of American Culture, 1880–1920* (New York: Pantheon Books, 1983), and idem, *Fables of Abundance: A Cultural History of Advertising in America* (New York: Basic Book, 1994).
4 These developments are summarized in the chapters 'The 1920s' by David Frank and 'The 1930s' by E.R. Forbes in *The Atlantic Provinces in Confederation*, ed. E.R. Forbes and D.A. Muise (Toronto: University of Toronto Press, 1993). See also E.R. Forbes, *Challenging the Regional Stereotype: Essays on the 20th Century Maritimes* (Fredericton: Acadiensis Press, 1989).

5 The most sophisticated analysis of cultural developments in this period
   can be found in Ian McKay, *The Quest of the Folk: Antimodernism and
   Cultural Selection in Twentieth-Century Nova Scotia* (Montreal: McGill-
   Queen's University Press, 1994).

6 See Suzanne Morton, *Ideal Surroundings: Domestic Life in a Working
   Class Suburb in the 1920s* (Toronto: University of Toronto Press, 1995),
   ch. 7 for an analysis of young womanhood in Halifax in this period.
   See also Veronica Strong-Boag, *The New Day Recalled: Lives of Girls
   and Women in English Canada, 1919–1939* (Toronto: Copp Clark Pit-
   man, 1988), and her earlier article 'The Girl of the New Day: Cana-
   dian Working Women in the 1920s,' *Labour/Le Travailleur* 4
   (1979):131–64; Andrée Lévesque, *Making and Breaking the Rules:
   Women in Quebec, 1919–1939*, trans. Yvonne M. Klein (Toronto:
   McClelland and Stewart, 1994); Ruth Roach Pierson, *'They're Still
   Women After All': The Second World War and Canadian Womanhood*
   (Toronto: McClelland and Stewart, 1986).

7 For a lucid summary of these developments in the context of the
   United States, see Nancy Cott, 'The Modern Woman of the 1920s,
   American Style,' in *A History of Women in the West*, vol. 5, *Toward a
   Cultural Identity in the Twentieth Century*, ed. Françoise Thebaud
   (Cambridge, MA: Belknap, 1994), 76–91.

8 Carroll Smith-Rosenberg, 'The Female World of Love and Ritual:
   Relations between Women in Nineteenth-Century America,' *Signs* 1,
   no. 1 (1975), reprinted in Carroll Smith-Rosenberg, ed., *Disorderly
   Conduct: Visions of Gender in Victorian America* (New York: Oxford
   University Press, 1985), 53–76.

9 For a general discussion of relationships between women see Lillian
   Faderman, *Surpassing the Love of Men: Romantic Friendship and Love
   between Women from the Renaissance to the Present Day* (London:
   Women's Press, 1981).

10 We want to thank the Sisters at Mount Saint Vincent Motherhouse for
   their assistance in filling the many gaps in our knowledge of academy
   life, including the identity of Father Knox, whose visit to the Mount is
   also described in *Folio Montana* 9 (June 1927): 13.

11 For a discussion of Mary Dulhanty's diary in the Nova Scotia context,

see Margaret Conrad, '"But Such Is Life": Growing Up in Nova Scotia in the Interwar Years,' *Journal of the Royal Nova Scotia Historical Society* 2 (1999): 1–26.

12 Deo volente – God willing.

PART FIVE:
LOVE, LOSS, AND WORK

Dorothy Choate Herriman
(1901–1978)

ALBERT BRAZ

Dorothy Choate Herriman's great ambition in life was to be a poet, to join the hallowed ranks of those who can capture a country's human and natural essence. Ironically, her foremost achievement as a writer is not her poetry, in which she invested so much hope and energy, but her incidental writings, her diaries. Born in 1901, in Lindsay, Ontario, Herriman was the only child of Nellie J. Williams and Dr William Choate Herriman. Her father was a physician 'specializing in mental diseases' as well as a hospital administrator, and she was raised in a series of central and eastern Ontario towns. In her words, the reason she became a 'lover of nature and the wild woods' was that she was fortunate to have spent her childhood 'in the park-like surroundings of various public institutions where spacious lawns and sparkling waters formed the background of every day's occurrences.'[1] Herriman's upbringing was not always idyllic, though. Her relationship with her mother, as the excerpt from her diaries suggests, was troubled. In contrast, her relationship with her father was much more amicable. A third-generation medical doctor, Herriman's father believed in the therapeutic power of literature and advised his patients to read. He shared his substantial library with his daughter, whom he encouraged to write.[2] It is not surprising that, after attending Toronto's exclusive Havergal College and the Ontario College of Art, Herriman would emerge not just as a budding graphic artist but also as a poet.

In 1926, at the age of twenty-five, Herriman became the youngest contributor to the revised edition of John Garvin's influential anthology *Canadian Poets*. Garvin himself praised her as a 'genuine talent' from whom 'we may expect much good verse in the future,'[3] a prediction that seemed to be realized three years later when she published a collection of poems entitled *Mater Silva*.[4] Yet Herriman's self-illustrated volume, which the critic William Arthur Deacon asserted had taken the author out of 'the junior ranks,'[5] did not mark the beginning of her public career as a writer but rather its end. Even though she would live until 1978, working for some time as the (unpaid) secretary of the Toronto branch of the Canadian Authors' Association,[6] she would not publish another book. Her most substantial body of work after the late 1920s was not her poetry, or her book illustrations, but her diaries.

Comprising eleven volumes, Herriman's diaries were written between 1926 and 1944. Their dominant theme is her conflicting sense of self, an emotional confusion reflected in her perpetual search for a purpose. As she states late in 1927, 'I seem to crave an impetus of some sort to feel any vital interest in life. I must be suffering from ennui – or the modern craze for excitement & stimulation.'[7] Another significant concern in her diaries is an aesthetic/ moral one, her wilful attempt if not to completely ignore the negative side of life at least to approach it from the most pleasant angle possible. As she praises her idol Bliss Carman, the 'bard of the sea,' in one of the works included in *Canadian Poems*:

> Yours is the youthful heart tuned to life's melody.
> Minstrel of morning-time, lover of dream,
> Lead us to a fairy-land softly, beguilingly,
> Tell us of sorrow and pathos, but smilingly
> Teach us life's woes are but half what they seem.[8]

Or as she describes herself in a short autobiographical sketch she sent to the anthology's editor, she '[p]refers the romanticists to the realists, Tennyson to Walt Whitman, and Dürer's line to Turner's color.'[9] Herriman's preference for romanticism over realism is certainly discernible in much of her work, both her poetry and her visual art. For instance, the drawings she did for the illuminated manuscript of her unpublished ten-stanza poem 'Alack I Loved' are indisputably lush. However, the seemingly unalloyed sweetness of the sketches is tempered by the irony she injects into the tale they are designed to illustrate. That Herriman possesses a strong sense of irony, or perhaps self-deprecation, is also apparent in her diaries. On the inside cover of her first diary, begun in 1926, when she was not yet twenty-five years old, she writes under age: 'Spinster!!' She then describes her complexion as 'Sallow!'[10] In the next diary, the following year, she characterizes herself 'as old as I feel!' and her complexion as 'Not too good!'[11] By 1938, she opens her eighth diary with a note entitled '(The frail and fond confessions of a fool).' In it she warns 'whoever peruses the pages of the enclosed journal' to beware not only of 'the variety and convolutions of the handwriting' but also of the author's motives and even her state of mind. To quote her, 'The style is affected and bombastic – The morals of the writer are more than dubious – although they undergo a slight improvement and steadying of purpose; the phrasing & imagery are sentimental & poetical – straining for "individuality" – .'[12]

Herriman's irony aside, though, there is no denying that she invariably favours the ideal over the real, the sublime over the mundane – or, using her metaphor, gardens over deserts. This aspect of her work is never more evident than in the segment of her diaries excerpted here. Written in 1933, it was composed in Toronto and Orillia, a resort community best known as the model for Stephen Leacock's Mariposa and as Gordon Lightfoot's hometown. The year 1933, of course, marked a moment in the midst of the Great Depression, a socio-economic crisis that she characteristically does her best to avoid mentioning. Yet, at times, the cataclysm that was shaking the foundations of her society manages to penetrate her somewhat hermetic world and, when it does, she succeeds in capturing it with considerable verve.

The handwriting in Herriman's eleven diaries is generally clear, if occasionally a bit crowded. Although all the manuscripts have hard covers, they vary considerably in format. The fifth volume is written in a medium-sized blank book. Like the other volumes, it shows evidence of revisions by the author, mostly stylistic or grammatical. Like them, too, it has virtually no illustrations.

Excerpt from Dorothy Herriman's Diary No. 5, 1933.

DIARY, ONTARIO, 1932–3

Reminiscent of 1932

December 29. 1932
Surely I have gathered something from the grinding wheels of
experience as the hours and days have passed inevitably through
the mill of Time and made another year. – A little patience perhaps, at least a little more of *wishing* for forbearance. I still mistrust
myself and fling barbed words that tear, sharp words that sting. Better to cower beneath a glancing shield? be like a tortoise in himself
concealed? Not yet for me the all defenseless, meek and humble
spirit of the martyr who turns the other cheek.

I realize (being now a year past 30) that I have during that past,
grown more in spirit thro experiences of Joy than of Anguish.
When I have had great Joy of Love – I have then lived in rare tran-
scendence of the soul for long days after. I seemed then better able
to exercise my latent powers of sympathy. I practised patience. But
experiences most intense endure the shortest – and the exaspera-
tions of the world were too insistent always for my frail defenses of
romance, built upon sands of hope and dream.

But I shall dwell in memory on the gardens and eschew the
deserts. There have been blossoms of some Angel's planting that
blessed my life. I will not hold that all the tares and thistles are of a
Devil's sowing sent to curse me. I shall forget them.

But I shall remember the roses and the lilies forever. The red
roses and the white roses: the blues iris and the white arum: and
the green fern-fiddlehead and pretty fern-frond: and the fat blowzy
peonies and the thin, prim holly hocks – and the skunk cabbage
and the sundew plant and the stinkhorn – For a pungent odour is
not always unhealthy – but a thorn of hatred can tear the spirit and
a thistle of malice may wound the foot of the soul. The desires of
the flesh may fail – but the heart that seeketh its vengeance is not
satisfied until all hell be turned upside down.

Sun January 1st. 1933.
W.C.H[13] & I to Orillia last night. Weather turned from rain on

Friday and a little colder Sat. to 21° below zero here Sat. eve. Some
snow here – & cold & clear. D.[14] to a party late last p.m. We heard
the 'Old Year out' etc over the radio. D & I to church this morning.
The old familiar church and many familiar faces.
    Margaret Graham[15] here for dinner & the night.
    D. had a party in evening – for her school chums on their holi-
day from university – including Corinne, Jean F., Eliz. B., Margaret,
– & boys – Bruce, 'Nip' Tissy & Gordon. They played bridge &
then had 'eats,' – & dancing was expected but two of the girls left
early and the party 'broke up – [']

January 28th. 1933
    Still at Orillia. Doris seized with appendicitis two weeks ago &
had the operation at 12.20 A.M. Dr. S. diagnosed it quickly –
before it became a 'pus' case and her recovery has been rapid. She
came home on Thursday – 2 nights ago and now sits up in a chair
every day for awhile. We did a jig-saw puzzle this evening – They
are all the 'rage' at present.
    The 'depression' is being felt on all sides – and among ones
friends & acquaintances.
    Mr Roy Brillinger former railway ticket agent & insurance man
– a 'pillar' of ST. Paul's United Church – walked into the Narrows
near Atherley a couple of days ago – leaving his coat & hat upon
the shore. His family will receive the life insurance. He had looked
over his mail at the office and then hired a taxi which let him out
at the Bridge shortly after 9 A.M. (He was very lame and wore a
'large boot' on one foot but had always exhibited a cheerful disposi-
tion). Financial trouble seems the apparent cause.
    Mr. D. has also lost his position as manager of the branch of
Northway's store here. He suffers from sinus trouble of a long
standing, chronic type – which is horribly painful. His son is
teaching. Daughter in her third year honours course at Vic.[16]
Unless Mrs. D. can obtain a teaching position they will soon be up
against it.

Nottawasaga St. Orillia by Victoria Park
– *Jan. 28. 1933*

The evening sky is now a pale, cool yellow in the lowest west blending above to icy green and so to blue – that indescribable translucent blue – the blue that roofs the palaces of dream – the blue that blessed the dome of Zanadu; a starless blue; all undistracted in a trancéd calm; an evening sky as innocent as dawn – and too, prophetic of eternity and messianic hope's millenial peace.

And in the west three-parts above the pale horizon rides a silver crescent-rimming a disc of [illegible]. Fine as a fillet binding a maiden's hair! or slender as the shining coronet a weeping queen on her sad brow might wear mourning for Arthur on the shadowy barge that bore him unto Avalon, and peace.

The new moon pays allegiance to the old – The phases of the moon like generations shine and fade: passing the light of life to one-another: ever the same, made manifest anew by the sun's hidden splendour and god's grace.

The pine trees tower like columns under the blue dome of heaven, their strong stems stand starkly against the paling yellow of the west, their branches overshadowing the earth like sombre lintels of some pagan temple, brooding in mystery upon the sacred moon.

Hearken to the voice of the oracle, like the music of silver cymbals clashed melodiously in a marble shrine; Lo, from the peaceful heart of the pine grove the still small voice of the unfailing spring issues perpetually in blessing from the calm bosom of the mothering hill; nourishing the attentive spirit with melody.

A voice that in the breathless heat of summer is vocal of coolness, carrying in its clear chime a keen suggestion of icy freshness; that in the frozen chillness of mid-January sings hopefully to all young hearts melting snow in its fleeting birdsong. It chants here without lyra a glad doxology to the God of the waters under the earth! Waters that break forth freshly forever into moonlight or into the brilliance of the sun. It sings forever, with wild wood-birds – a part-song praising a forgotten deity.

And I who walk, worshipping in the evening, join with immortal yearning in the praise of Being for the service of Beauty. I taste and drink a sweet communion of the spirit; I *learn a new Beatitude*.

Feb. 4. 1933
The sunset is beautiful, but not self or being. The bird is beautiful, and feeling the influence of the sunset retires to rest – but knows not beauty except the rapture of weaving a bright ribbon with colourless grasses to make its insignificant nest.

Man is rarely beautiful to the casual sight: he is one of a monotonous ant-like multitude – and yet the call of Beauty sounds for him alone: the sunset bids him pause upon his doorstep in spite perhaps of hunger and sheer weariness after the long day's work: the bird too singing in the morning, takes his ear & eye, flaunting its dainty feathers vividly on a budding twig: Beauty of human form & face he worships blindly – seeking some hidden meaning in it of godlike grace – as did the Greeks in Athens.

They only see & know the inner beauty of the life of truth: for truth is beauty: the seeing of beauty breaks the blinding spell of all things hideous: sets the vision free to view perfection – possible to all, – perpetual sunrise; – birds of paradise, a city set upon a holy hill; where dwell the blest – frail men somehow perfected.

Feb. 21. 1933
(On train leaving Orillia after visit of nearly two *months* in the 'old home town')

I remember that land as I saw it last
Half-hidden in smoke and snow.
Smoke of the hurrying train that flew,
And snow that eddied and whirled and blew,
Fogging with mist the fading view
That glimmered dreamlike as it passed,
From the tear-blurred vision too swift; too fast;

Lone and beautiful; snowbound, vast.
I remember that land as I saw it last.

Orillia to Toronto. Feb. 21. 1933
C.N.R. leaving 3.25 p.m. Not cold but a blizzard of soft snow.

At *Barrie and Allandale* – a colony of more than fifty fishing shacks in groups on Kempenfeldt. Cars run back & forth – the snow is packed quite firmly on the ice. The men look lost and tiny on the vastness suggesting arctic travellers.

Lefroy – There is snow here only in patches – in the furrows and fence-corners, remaining from deeper drifts. There is ice on the ponds. Passed a gray barn, quite large, with two red doors.

Gilford – more snow here thinly covering the ground.

Bradford – less again. The wine-red alder (-) bushes seem alive with colour between the dark thicket and the frozen marsh.

Newmarket (Delivery truck at station marked 'H.M. Gladman.') Snow on the level stretches but not deep. Sky clearing.

South of Aurora. A blizzard blowing. Some snow already on the ground ... Now a golden sunset gleams suddenly through the flurries and the sky grows clear. The East is pale blue-green above horizon clouds of violet-gray.

Maple – Bare ground again with snowy furrows. The sun goes down behind a level cloud-bank leaving for a moment stray wisps of vapour to glow in crimson splendour.

Snow less and less.

At *Concord* – six o'clock. Passed north bound train.

The trainsmoke rolling low over the brown fields is grimly reminiscent of war-time – of poison gases and muddy trenches. And now we pass the 'Home of Moth Aeroplanes' – a somewhat forlorn and unsubstantial structure in ridiculous proximity to Shacktown. Now comes an isolated tile-factory and soon the city closes on the right of way: – houses push and crowd & rush to the fences; factories too, elbow their way and stand akimbo, taking up space and craning their tall chimneys and spindling water-tanks. Their blank windows stare like bleared eyes looking from vacant minds.

The sky still glows but here must be no twilight – no time for
folding hands and idly dreaming – the lamps are lit, they shine in
every street and park and avenue.
St. Clair – the homeward traffic halts for us. The bells of street-
cars jangle and the horns of motors bleat.
The ground is like a bone, – dry, frozen. There is no sign of snow.
Six passengers perhaps or nine get off. I put my coat and gloves on
– *Parkdale* next.

March 1. 1933
After seeing the 'sensational' movie 'The Sign of the Cross'[17] – a
pageant-picture of the early Christian martyrs and the debasement
of the Roman scene.
It seems somehow particularly apt that Hollywood – standing as
it does for the principle of sacrificing morals and manners to give
the public what it wants – should so ably portray that period of history when a great Empire slaughtered its most enthusiastic idealists
to make, Roman holidays.
The obscene satiety and deluded egotism of Nero were particularly unforgetable. – quite like an optical translation of Gibbon in
fact![18]
There was much flashing of armour of course – and a surfeit of
chariots & horse in the street scenes (as in Ben Hur) – the glimpse
of the domestic arrangements was good – (obtained from excava-
tions at Pompeii no doubt) – but did ladies in 64 AD wear rows of
ornamental buttons down the back of high necked frocks?
The Empress' bath in a swimming pool full of asse's milk was a
bit on too grand a scale surely –
The arena scene was splendid – gladiators, bull-wrestlers, boxers
with brass knuckles – & the comic scene with clowns and dwarfs.
The early christian episodes were a great strain on the emotions
of course – (and I *always* get maudlin – and look like a wet rag
afterwards) But the impressiveness of them gave me a realization or
two.
1) 'Faith of our fathers,' etc

holy faith.' –

2) Rome eventually fell –

(and Jerusalem also.)

3) We are not early Christians and nothing much worse than imprisonment for ransom by Chinese bandits (with possibility of a stray bullet) awaits the most zealous –

4) The martyrs of to-day are the 'Early Socialists' 'Young Pioneers' etc. whose zeal certainly appears fiery – quite a 'purging flame' in fact.

5) Not those who call 'Lord Lord' – but those who do the will of their Father which is in Heaven – '

Cavalcade[19] – reviewing British war history (1899 to Present time) – had in reality more of a *gospel* than the 'Christian' film described above. As a Christian civilization we must awaken to our international responsibilities – and the true value of human life – Hindu & hottentot life: German life: Japanese life: Better that the entity of an Empire should pass away than that one innocent life should be sacrificed. – one small Siamese or Scythian perish in poison gas.

The fear of the nations is just this – they dare not shelve old loyalties without a clearer vision of the newer loyalty.

But as in the days of early christianity forswearing the old gods did not mean that the Goths lost their sacred evergreens or the Druids their mistletoe, or the Jews their decalogue, – Even So must the flags of the nations be sanctified and transmuted into precious symbols of brotherhood.

The Ark of this the newest covenant rests upon the mountains: The spires of the latest of God's temples rise up by the cold blue waters of Lake Geneva.

Neither shall the French lose their Napoleon or the Germans their Frederick the Great or the Japanese their General Togo. There is one glory of the soldier and there is another glory of the civilian: but the greatest glory will be of those civilians who keep their standing army in serried ranks on their library shelves – who beat their swords – not into implements of competitive agriculture only – but also into pens.

March 25. 1933

The Green Pastures[20] – A strangely significant creation in this sophisticated age. The 'intelligentsia' may pronounce it 'quaint' and anthropomorphic etc. forgetting the dictum: 'Unless ye become as little children' –

This play realizes the childlike beauty of all primitive things – the '*saving*' grace of such simplicity – Yet also realizing the most modern aspect of the evolution of ideals – even in the Absolute!

Miracles here seem to be self explanatory – appearing as natural acts. – quite in accord with the milieu of the negro interpretation.

There is a sort of Alice-in-Wonderland inevitability about it all. The language of both is the language of dreams – or rather that of visions which in the highest sense are dreams of the intellect – i.e. symbolic interpretations of human experience – of more than personal application.

The real miracle is, That Truth is still and ever Truth, whether the Lord God Jehovah wears the garb of a simple-hearted negro preacher – as here, or the richly embroidered rob[e] of a Chinese Mandarin, as perhaps he could to some – or the distorted features of an Epstein statue.

The lessons to be learned are unchanged: the moral goal is a fixed one – and inevitably fallen short of.

Few of us can so take leave of our material senses as to desire communion of soul with an omnipotent ghost. We know our human nature through the interpretation of our own senses and may not conceive a creator having no contact by means of like senses with his own environment – and with us.

There may be some so lost in theosophistries and spiritual transcendentalism that they prefer the undiluted ether for their godhead – a sort of plasmic presence, an all-pervading goodness and almighty will: such tend to cast all the moral responsibility of the

race upon the social organization of it. They seem at times imper-
sonalized – institutionalized – the fatal dehumanizing influence of
the purely scientific mind (as seen in the Symposium of Religion –
Darrow, Russell & Eisenradth[21] – Massey Hall. Mar 9./33.

The greatest teacher taught his truths by parable – deriving the
infinity of truth from a fig-tree; a lost penny, a grain of mustard
seed. He lived as a peasant among the humble people of Palestine –
but lived as God himself would have lived –

Therefore are all things holy in the righteous using thereof:
Wherefore 'Ol' Man Adam and His Chillum' are 'All God's Chillum'[22] and God, their father

March 25. 1933
Personal (Same date as above)

The echo of another message has come from the 'Prophet' A.
who was with me at 'The Green Pastures' informed me that she
had attended a meeting of the Graphic Arts Club (Thursday, I
think.) C.[23] was there. She told him she had received one of the
pictures from his & T's 'Portfolio of Lithographs' for Christmas –
and had him guessing who the donor was; – and said what a pleasant time they must have had sketching at *Tobermory* (where hers
was made). When she told him I was the donor – he asked the
name of the picture (Tony's – 'Fishing Boat') – He then said he was
glad I had *kept his!*

As usual the perfection of ambiguity! – As A. herself remarked.
She had wondered whether she had better tell me or not; but of
course I would miss *any* remark of his – no matter how cryptic. He
knows I have the portfolio anyway.

Strange that I should have had such 'white nights' (or rather,
purple ones) of late. The last two to be precise. Is there anything in
being psychic, I wonder? or in mental telepathy? It is certainly too
wearing on a lone mortal to crave emotional sustenance from
another – at long distance – Never having read that masterpiece of
Du Maurier's 'Peter Ibbotson'[24] – I have no guaranteed directions
for 'dreaming true' – and am rapidly becoming a Mad Spinster –

psychopathic. In other words, if I ever go quite 'off' – I know what the symptoms will be – I will act the part of C. and make long speeches in his character – all about Art and teaching etc. – and pretend to be in love with my actual self!

Mother still refers to the affair contemptuously as a 'crush' – (*She* can certainly crush one in the saying, also. All attempt to realize an ideal in an individual is beyond her powers.) Whatever name, the condition has lasted nearly ten years – nourished by crumbs of momentary conversation – of terrific significance to me – and of little beyond casual interest to the other party. But would I change my place with *any* one? Not I.

If, as he said to me so *emphatically*, at the Tech. Sketch Exhibition in November (when I told him how much I admired his *line* work – & that I liked the things he did with lines etc etc, if he is *perfectly* happy when he is doing it – I have no rival but the abstract one of Art, alluring Goddess.

He walks, *apparently*, unscathed among such shoals of feminine attraction & intelligence. Still keeping a *very* warm spot for M. – (now a buxom matron, many miles away.) – and always asks for news of her – she being a mutual friend.

I could at least *act* sensibly if I had a regular full-time job. I'd have less time for *Star(r)*-gazing [Herriman draws a star].

I *have* gone after 'strange gods' several times – being a hopelessly 'volatile' person and easily flattered – (and despising myself simultaneously) (Well, Dante didn't *marry* his Beatrice, either!)

Since knowing C. there have been J. and D.R. & E. who each inspired his share of 'tender verse.'

I deliberately withdrew. If this was some medieval period doubtless I would 'hie me to a nunnery' or die outright – Elaine, exactly. Decidedly, I am *not* 'modern'!

I *could* not stand the strain of meeting C. more frequently than twice or four times a year, at *most*! It takes so much control not to go 'jittery' – that I become a 'total loss' in other respects.

We did get on in studies at that Exhibition, I will admit – but that was too good – Staged for the benefit of any bankrupt mem-

ory – that is well set up for a long lifetime as the immediate result.
But there was plenty of crowd and, moving about and much-
needed distraction. It wasn't concentrated contact – I *couldn't*
have stood *that*. He sort of *focusses* my emotions – and, who
knows, I would likely disintegrate if exposed for very long! Burn
up, in other words

Instead of working it off in so-called 'poetry' this time I am trying to 'rationalize' the latest development by honest-to-good
prose.

I *must* be a fool – but of what *specific* variety? I have yet to find
out!

He's altogether too perfect to live, of course, that's the biggest
trouble. No one ever has hinted at any scandal, he is simply not
made that way. He is modelling himself (he would be the first too
admit it, too) on the lives and works of: Charles M. Manly & Robert Holmes[25] – two darling old fogies – both bachelor art teachers
who lived laboriously and died at their posts – and who live on in
the memories of former pupils!

And C. is himself one of those 'inspirational' teachers! Ye gods,
he may up & marry some prize pupil of his – when he is somewhere
in the feverish fifties – like Emmanuel H.[26] 23 forinstance. Better a
bachelor, perhaps, than that.

What I *must* do is be a female Pagliacchi,[27] which is much easier
to write – than say or do.

I'm not the marrying kind either. All my troubles would never
have existed if my father had only realized that fact about himself
long ago. – (and then to pick a frigid companion? They both
thought love was a figure of speech – one of those delightful Victorian metaphors – a literary thing with no thews or breasts to it, save
the mark!)

My own reactions are so penultimately intellectual, so subjective
in their emotional urge; so retroactive with relation to the 'men-
tally creative' instinct. I write things out of my system – or else
develop a bad temper – of which two evils: the first, is, believe me,
the lesser (I have tried both.)

NOTES

The diary is in Dorothy Choate Herriman's Papers, Trent University Archives (TUA), Peterborough, 94-019, box 1. I am extremely grateful to Dianne Choate not only for granting me permission to excerpt part of Herriman's Diary Number 5 but also for providing otherwise inaccessible information about her distant cousin's life and work.

1 Untitled biographical sketch, TUA 92–010, box 5, folder 15.
2 Author's interview with Dianne Choate, 20 November 1997.
3 John W. Garvin, ed., *Canadian Poets*, rev. ed. (Toronto: McClelland and Stewart, 1926), 527.
4 *Mater Silva* (Toronto: McClelland and Stewart, 1929).
5 William Arthur Deacon, Letter to Dorothy Choate Herriman, 12 December 1929, TUA 92-010, Box 5, File 13.
6 Author's interview with Dianne Choate.
7 Diary #2, 17 November 1927, TUA 94-019, Box 1.
8 'A Welcome to Bliss Carman,' in *Canadian Poets*, 530.
9 Untitled biographical sketch.
10 Diary #1, 1926, TUA 94-019, Box 1.
11 Diary #2, 1927, TUA 94-019, Box 1.
12 Diary #8, 1938, TUA 94-019, Box 1.
13 Dr William Choate Herriman, her father.
14 Her cousin Doris Gladman. According to Dianne Choate, interview with the author, it was at Gladman's house in Orangeville, Ontario, that Herriman died in 1978.
15 Margaret Graham was another cousin.
16 Victoria College, University of Toronto.
17 Cecil B. DeMille, dir., *The Sign of the Cross* (Paramount, 1932).
18 Edward Gibbon's *The Decline and Fall of the Roman Empire* (1776–83).
19 Frank Lloyd, dir., *Cavalcade* (Fox, 1933). The film was based on a play by Noël Coward.
20 Marc Connelly, *The Green Pastures: A Fable* (New York: Holt, Rinehart and Winston), 1932.
21 American attorney Clarence Darrow, United Church of Canada minis-

ter G. Stanley Russell, and Rabbi Maurice Eisenradth debated each other under the billing 'Agnostic, Christian, and Jew.' See Maurice Eisenradth, *Can Faith Survive? The Thoughts and Afterthoughts of an American Rabbi* (New York: McGraw-Hill, 1964), 293–4.

22 Roark Bradford, *Ol' Man Adam an' His Chillun: Being the Tales They Tell about the Time When the Lord Walked the Earth Like a Natural Man* (New York: Harper, 1928). Connelly's play, *Green Pastures*, is based on Bradford's tales.

23 Charles Goldhamer (1903–85) taught in the art department at Toronto's Central Technical School for over forty years, from 1927 to 1969, and was, at one point, Herriman's teacher. During the Second World War, Goldhamer was 'commissioned as one of Canada's official war artists, and his candidly observed charcoal drawings of burned Canadian airmen in an English hospital are some of the most horrific images' of the war. *The Canadian Encyclopedia* [Edmonton: Hurtig, 1985], 2:750.).

24 George Du Maurier, *Peter Ibbetson* (New York: Harper, 1891).

25 Manly and Holmes were instructors at the Ontario College of Art.

26 Emmanuel Horn, too, was an instructor at the Ontario College of Art. The information on Horn, like that on Goldhamer, Manly, and Holmes, was provided to the author by Dianne Choate, e-mail, 21 November 1997.

27 *I Pagliacci* is the title of an 1892 opera by the Italian composer Ruggero Leoncavallo about an actor who murders both his wife and her lover. See Michele Girardi, '*Pagliacci* (Players'),' in *The New Grove Dictionary of Opera*, ed. Stanley Slade (New York: Macmillan, 1992), 3: 819–22.

Elsie Rogstad Jones
(1918–)

MAXINE HANCOCK

Elsie Rogstad Jones was born in Robsart, Saskatchewan, on 14 January 1918, to Perry and Anna (nee Hansen) Rogstad. Her parents were both children of Norwegian immigrants. Drought and hail in southern Saskatchewan drove the young Rogstad family to Minneapolis in 1921, where Elsie's father did house painting and wall papering. Three other children were born there: brother Bob, sister Pat, and 'little brother' Jack. The youngest was just five months old when, in 1927, Perry Rogstad died of heart failure, leaving Elsie's mother with four small children. If economic necessity had brought the family to Minneapolis, it now drove them back to the land, this time to subsistence farming near Turtle Lake in west-central Saskatchewan. Elsie's mother remarried a local bachelor farmer, Geordie Ewen, and began a second family of six more children. From 1929 to 1935, Elsie endured the privations of depression-era farming. These years cost her the opportunity to finish high school. As the eldest child, she had to become an economic contributor as quickly as possible, 'working out' as a hired girl for five dollars a month, from 1932.

In 1936, Elsie returned to Minneapolis to work while she had her aching teeth replaced with dentures at the University of Minneapolis school of dentistry. She returned to Canada, taking a job in the spring of 1937 helping her step-father's brother, Sandy

Ewen, in his butcher shop in the raw new railway village of Dewberry, sixteen miles inside the Alberta border west and north of Lloydminster. At five foot eight, Elsie was strong and able to help with the hard and heavy work of butchering as well as serving at the counter. And the dark-haired nineteen-year-old, who was an excellent dancer, soon became a part of the Dewberry social scene, with the local twenty-three-year-old fuel merchant and machine agent, Neal Jones, her steady 'fellow.' She writes: 'December 21, 1937. Came to Dewberry in March & have had grand times since. Learned to play tennis, also drive a car. Bob worked here this fall too. This is our 1st Xmas from Home.' Elsie later found a position with the housekeeping staff of the University of Alberta Hospital in Edmonton, and worked for another year before marrying Neal on 5 June 1939. After an epic journey from the village of Dewberry to the New York World's Fair for a honeymoon, Elsie settled into the life of a village woman, taking up the role of businessman's wife and pillar of church and community for the next fifty-six years, raising a family of three children, all of whom took up professional careers far from the village. Only after Neal's death in 1995 would Elsie, by then in her late seventies, gather herself for one more move, working through the accumulated stuff of a long married life, holding an auction, and moving to Edmonton to be near some of her adult children – and, at the same time, to enjoy the amenities of city life.

Between 1937 and 1947, Elsie kept up regular entries in two small five-year diaries covering the important years between age twenty and thirty as she sought and found work, married, and bore her children – events that are central to Elsie's life story. The entries are cryptic, constrained both by the form of a five-year diary format (four-by-five-inch pages, each divided into five sections) and by the sheer pressure of urgent work that made up every day. The diary form allows only four lines per day on pages. What is amazing is how much energy and detail is somehow conveyed in the tight, hurried, lightly punctuated spaces.

Elsie's diaries are a record of activity, not emotion. To suggest from the laconic entries that Elsie was passive in the face of the demands of life is to fail to understand the woman, or the writing form of the diary. Elsie was an extremely emotional – even volatile – young woman, and lying behind the double exclamation points and the simple entries are ocean tides of emotions, for which a diary is far too small. The dailiness of the entries inhibits the tendency to 'write through' crises in order to gain understanding; Elsie's diaries, because of the very small but daily space, emphasize the dailiness of life – the 'usual round' is noted and emphasized more than its disruptions, which, at most, prompt a few empty spaces in these small records.

In the excerpt from the diary reproduced here, Elsie's quick notes sketch a life in which domestic duties are foremost but are carried out against a backdrop of an active village and family network. The women of the village form an informal but highly active society of their own, going frequently to each other's homes for 'tea,' attending the Ladies' Aid meetings, walking, and playing tennis. Her special friend was the 'Mrs E.' of her diary, wife of the Alberta Wheat Pool elevator agent Cecil Ennis. Several years older than Elsie, Mrs Ennis welcomed the new bride into a warm, mentoring friendship. Age-mate friends mentioned in this excerpt include Olga and Elsie, married to the cattle-buying Braithwaite brothers Joe and Fred, respectively, and Ariel, married to their cousin, farmer Bobby Braithwaite.

Elsie and Neal's first child, a red-haired son named James Perry Jones – 'Jimmy' in these entries – was born 17 April 1940 at the Islay Hospital. Three years later, in the spring of 1943, Elsie's mother and step-father and the flock of Ewens moved from Saskatchewan to Dewberry. Elsie's mother was still having babies of her own, two born after Elsie's own first child, and so the 'big-sister – little-sister' relationship she had treasured with her mother was resumed, although now Elsie assumed the 'big-sister' role. The names of Elsie's half-siblings occur frequently in this excerpt: Sandy, Wilford, Peggy, Glenn, Betty, and Ruth; in 1943 these children ranged in age from fourteen to one, with the two youngest being toddlers. Elsie's sister, Pat, lived with Neal and Elsie while she finished high school; Elsie's brother Jack was employed in the district; and in 1943 her brother Bob was in South Pacific with the United States Navy. Elsie's widowed grandfather also came to live with Elsie and Neal, taking over the care of garden, cow, and pig. Their family was extended in another direction, as well, when their second child, a girl named Phyllis, was born on 22 April 1943.

Elsie is a nursing mother as this part of the diary begins. The story is told in the context of the social world of the village, the weekly round of domestic work, and the seasonal imperatives of putting up food. The Second World War shadows the events recorded here: friends and family enlist or are already in the military service, and Neal's call-up is an impending possibility. This section of the diary takes Elsie's story through the heavy work of August and September through to the terrible rains of late fall, and beyond.[1] The terrible tragedy of this excerpt is that Elsie's baby dies from complications from a telescoping bowel. Although terrified that there was something wrong with her as a mother, Elsie went on to have two more healthy girls, Cheryl and Isabelle. Now in her eighties, she still lives a very full life. In the long winter of widowhood, she divides her time between her Edmonton apartment, near her daughter Isabelle, and Scottsdale, Arizona, where her daughter Cheryl lives.

Jones family portrait, 1943.

DIARY, ALBERTA, JULY–DECEMBER 1943

July 31, 1943 – Sat. Went to church, Verna & Myrt came too. We went picking saskatoons   took our supper   Mom went too   Jimmy feels tough looks like measles.

August 1, 1943 – Sun. missed a day. Up early   did work up we went to Doris's   picked raspberries   Mother, Gramp, Jimmy, Ruth, Betty & Peg. I took Mom home   did 18 qts of raspberries went to the show.[2]

August 2, 1943 – Glenn is sick too   Jimmy has a few spots. Up early again   washed B[aby] clothes and Mom's clothes cleaned house up   took clothes to Mothers   fitted my dress   did my ironing at nite.

August 3, 1943 – Wed. Jimmy is really sick to day   has the measles for sure   Gramp & I canned 7 qts peas and 5 of beans 2 pints greens. Was tired at nite.

August 4, 1943 – missed a day.

August 5, 1943 – Thurs. Up early   doesn't look nice is cold & windy   I baked short bread   made sandwiches   went to Aid in afternoon   Jimmy is sick has a fever   not many at Aid.

August 6, 1943 – Washed B. Clothes   let Jimmy up for a while   Ruth has the measles now   that's 4 of them & Peg is starting. Went down town paid my bills   we picked beans canned 10 qts.

August 7, 1943 – Sat. Started to rain at nite   Talk about warm!! We picked peas   Gramp J[ones] took Gramp H[ansen] up to pick raspberries. I canned 7 qts peas & carrots 12 qts raspberries and 10 of peaches.

August 8, 1943 – Sun. Ruth is one to day. Still raining and feels cold   Jimmy is much better   didn't go to Church   Had an easy day cooked a big dinner though   rained most of the day cistern is full again.

August 9, 1943 – Betty has the measles. Lovely warm day. Up early   put water on   washed mine & Moms clothes Mom came in for a couple of hrs. Did my ironing   Neal & I went to show at nite   Pat passed her exams.

August 10, 1943 – Up early again   we were busy all day

canned peas and beans   Sent a letter to Pat, Miss Smith & Bob.
August 11, 1943 – Did up house work this A.M.   washed out a
few B. Clothes   we went to Aunt Nellies in after noon
Neal fixed the tractor   we stayed all nite it rained so. Phyllis
slept in the trunk.
August 12, 1943 – Left Aunt Nellies at 7:30 AM. Roads were
terrible   got here 10 AM   went down town   had Mr &
Mrs Parker & sister & Mrs Loyd for dinner   canned 11 qts beets
baked ginger snaps and doughnuts   Mum came in to set her
hair   washed floor at midnite!!!
August 13, 1943 – Up early   got some things ready for
dinner   Mom Doris Elmer Jim & I went to Loyd with Gramp J.
I got a perm   saw the Dr.   have Geordie here for meals
they get their own supper.
August 14, 1943 – It rained last nite again. Gramp had a bunch of
beans cut   we picked peas too   did 17 [qts.] of beans & 9 of
peas. Made a pie   cleaned house up   got to bed at 1:00 A.M.
August 15, 1943 – Sun. Rained last nite but there was church
we didn't go   Neal was busy   I tidied house up. Got to bed at
11:00 p.m.
August 16, 1943 – Built fire at 4:30 AM.   washed clothes for us
& Mom. Peg, Betty & Ruth came too   we did our ironing &
canned 11 qts beets   we went to the show at nite   was
good   was the 'Mask of Zorro'   1:30 again when we retired.
August 17, 1943 – Glenn was in. Put clothes away   we picked
peas & shelled   canned 13 qts 2 qts beans. Made 8 qts dills
Didnt get finished till midnite   Churned at 11:00 p.m. Storm at
nite.
August 18, 1943 – Up early   we picked & cut beans   Made
dinner for men   Mrs Ennis & Sheila came in after noon. Made
16 qts dills 13 of beans have 60 of beans now   Gramp pulled a
tub of carrots   I cleaned & cut till midnite.
August 19, 1943 – Wilford is 11 to day   I washed B. clothes
canned 26 qts of carrots   we went to Moms in after noon. Got
to bed at 10:30 for a change.

August 20, 1943 – Friday. Didn't do any canning to day   Elsie was over   I cleaned sun porch windows etc. waxed in front rooms. Nice day quite warm though.

August 21, 1943 – Up early   washed my hair   did the shopping (took all A.M.)   Mrs Molohon picked beans   Elsie did last nite. Mrs McKay came up   I'm to be Sup.[erintendent] of S.[unday] School   I do hope Neal doesn't have to be drafted   I should quit worrying but I can't. Baked cookies & short Bread.

August 22, 1943 – Started to rain in A.M. but we went to church, went out to Moms in afternoon. Verna came home Friday nite   has enlisted in the Air Force.

August 23, 1943 – Phyllis is 4 mo. to day. Didn't wash in A.M. baked lemon tarts   had Verna & her mother for lunch   I washed some clothes at 6:00 P.M. McKays picked peas.

August 24, 1943 – Up early   washed clothes   such a day   hot, but still we got clothes sprinkled & 4 pints greens for Mom   Neal & I & the kids went with Fred & Elsie to Verm.[ilion] to see 'My Friend Flikka.'

August 25, 1943 – Tidied house up   made two puddings Mrs Garnier & Margie picked beans   gave them coffee started my ironing but didn't finish   had letter from Edith M.

August 26, 1943 – A lovely day so warm though   Mom & Glenn were in   got out new ration books. Phyllis weighs 16 lbs. 11 oz. Finished my ironing in the A.M.

August 27, 1943 – Up early   did a big B. wash   tidied house up   Jim has been down with Neal these last few days. Mrs Bob picked peas   Mrs McKay called for me at nite to say Goodbye to Verna. I baked short bread & snaps.

August 28, 1943 – Verna left for Ed.[monton] & the Service   is going to Rockliffe Ont. Jimmy got sick this A.M. I just nursed him all day   we took him in to Islay   a touch of pneumonia. Mom was in at nite made a slip for Phyllis.

August 29, 1943 – Sun. Beautiful day   I got up at 5:30 A.M.

baked buns & lemon tarts cooked spuds made breakfast then heard
the minister wasn't coming   we went in to hos. to see Jimmy –
he looks better.

August 30, 1943 – Washed clothes for 14 of us   the men are
cutting [wheat] at home   canned 12 qts plums   had George
Z & Pop for supper   canned 32 qts blueberries after supper.
The Armstrong family eye the country today. went to bed at
1:00 A.M.

August 31, 1943 – Put fruit down   tidied house up   ironed
clothes   scrubbed cellar steps   am getting the shelves
full. Heard from Marie   she is coming home for a month
or so.

September 1, 1943 – Did up work   made pudding & cookies
churned   we went out to Mom's   picked choke cherries.

September 2, 1943 – Got things tidied up. Jimmy went to the shop
with Neal   I left Phyllis with Gramp   I went to the Aid for a
while   not much business done   small crowd

September 3, 1943 – Was busy all day   did big baby wash
squeezed juice out of choke cherries & apples. Mrs G. came   I
made jelly & more dills. Went to the show   had Bobs for
lunch.

September 4, 1943 – Sat. Up early   baked buns and tarts, went
down town   did my shopping   got a locket from Pat.
Cleaned house up   shellaced floor.

September 5, 1943 – Up early   did work up   took Phyllis to
be christened   Brian, Beverly & Maureen were too. Had Mert
& Minister for dinner at noon   Mom & some of kids came in at
nite.

September 6, 1943 – Up early   did washing for 14 of us such a
day   so stormy   not nice out. Had Lyle & Mrs Martin for
supper   they slept here   Jack Mc. was here.

September 7, 1943 – Baked Pancakes   they left on train. Did
my ironing   tidied house up. Went with Neal to Polly Iserts
we played crocinole till midnite.

September 8, 1943 – It froze last nite   I washed all the curtains

in the house   ironed ones in front rooms   Went out to
R. Bowmans in evening.
September 9, 1943 – Canned 12 pints corn   did big baby wash
also sweaters   ironed some more curtains   finished them
up at nite   22 altogether.
September 10, 1943 – Waxed front room floors   cleaned sun-
porch windows   canned 3 pints corn   more dills   Toby
& Mrs Redman were in
September 11, 1943 – Sat. Did up dishes etc. went down town did
my shopping   Baked tarts & buns   churned 4 lbs butter.
Mom didn't get in.   Marie should be coming to see us soon.
Had Toby for supper.
September 12, 1943 – Up early   did up work   went to S.
School   Jim too   Neal came to church. Went to Bobs and to
Durwoods but they weren't home   lovely day   Les is home
on leave for 6 weeks   Mrs M. is nursing Baby.
September 13, 1943 – Mon. Cold & windy   did my washing
went out & got Moms   did hers   did some of my ironing.
Gramp has carrots & beets up   is digging spuds   Mom heard
from Bob. Mom came in, in the evening
September 14, 1943 – Tues. Did my ironing   had the auditor for
dinner   made 3 pumpkin pies   Went down town   over
to Machons   got S. School things   I am Sup. now.
awfully windy.
September 15, 1943 – Another windy day   cleaned house
up   made batch of ginger snaps   went to Ennis's in after
noon   got the S. School order off. Mrs McKay & Muriel H were
there.
September 16, 1943 – Gramp has all the potatoes in   just turnip
& parsnips left. I found some moths in my ski pants   hung
woolens out. Went to Moms   wrote out the Eatons order. Baked
bread & churned. Awfully windy.
September 17, 1943 – Friday. Did a big baby wash   cleaned
house good from top to Bottom   Turned so cold feels like snow.
The Russians are gaining on Germany. the Allies are fighting in

Italy. Had Elsie B & family for supper. looks a bit better. Went to
the show at nite   was good.
September 18, 1943 – The Gas trucker from Calgary woke us at
20 to 5: A.M. Neal had to go. So cold out. I canned 14 qts plums
have 230 qts fruit now. Phyllis has a bad cold   feels tough.
Mr Castle fell off the Anex   was killed.
September 19, 1943 – Taught S. School again & went to Church
thought A. Myrtle might come   Mrs Isert was in for a few min.
Finally got work done up!! Folks came in, in after noon we had
lunch.
September 20, 1943 – Up early   started machine at 6:00 A.M.
quit at 11:00 A.M.   just finished dishes & helped Gramp with
turnips when A. Myrtle, Edsel, Dorothy, Marnie,
Dot & Jim came   made supper for them   they left at 6:30
pm   Mrs E & Mrs Mc came before I had dishes done
finished about 11:00 p.m.
September 21, 1943 – Should have been up at 6:00 A.M. was so
tired though   I did some ironing   had a phone call from A.
Nellie   we left for her place at 7:00 p.m.   had supper & slept
there   A. Dora is here from Vancouver. Phyllis slept in Aunt
Nellies trunk
September 22, 1943 – Wed. Left A. Nellies at 7:30 A.M. got home
at 9:00 AM.   heavy frost last nite   Gramp J. came in
took A. Nellie & A. Dora up north   they came back here for
supper then left for home about 9: p.m. I made lemon pies
doughnuts   short bread and buns.
September 23, 1943 – Thurs. Phyllis was 5 mo. Should have
washed B. clothes but tried to tidy house up   took fuel to W.
Hodgsons   stopped at Moms   brought Peg & Glenn in
washed theirs & Jims heads   took them to the S. School Picnic.
September 24, 1943 – Fri. Milder out   washed B. clothes
cleaned house up   went down town   went over to Muriel
H.   her baby is teething   took Phyllis along   she was so
good. went to show at nite   saw a medical picture. Awfully
warm out

September 25, 1943 – Just like a summer day   so warm   I
waxed floors etc. baked some cookies   did some shopping
Mrs. R. was over   Fred & Hattie came   stayed till
1:30 A.M.
September 26, 1943 – Sunday S. again   beautiful day out
Neal came to church   he did books in afternoon
we went to Moms for afternoon. Went to bed fairly early.
September 27, 1943 – Mon. *Wash day*   such a miserable wind
but clothes dried fast   got the washing done and some of the
ironing   had Gramp J. & George Z for supper. Gramp J. held
Phyllis.
September 28, 1943 – Up early   did some ironing   got Parcel last nite so went out to Mothers   Material was grand.[3] came
home & finished the ironing at nite. We churned 5 lbs butter
baked bread.
September 29, 1943 – Wed. Another nice day   I mailed
parcel   cleaned up good in the basement – big job done. Roy
Smith is home for a few days.
September 30, 1943 – Washed my hair   big baby wash
canned 11 qts crabs and squeezed juice out of 2 baskets of grapes
went McKays in afternoon   Elsie too   Made jelly at nite –
14 pints
October 1, 1943 – Up early   tidied house up   took kids &
went to Moms   we had the threshers for lunch & supper   I
came home about 9:00 P.M. Folks got 1100 bu of wheat on K.
farm   Phyllis was good   sat in the chair to go out.
October 2, 1943 – Out to thresh again   they managed to
finish by nite   We got home about 9:00 P.M. I canned 8 qts
grapes into fruit   Mom & I did jelly & fruit besides threshers
Olive Walker & Joan Harrington were drowned in River at Ferry
last nite   Got to bed at 1:30 A.M.
October 3, 1943 – Sun. Taught S. School again   Neal came to
church   Gramp Jones was here for lunch & church   we
cleaned car good   went to Moms.

October 4, 1943 – Wash day again   nice day   Gramp J & George Z. put tombstone for Neal's mother up. They came here for supper at nite   Pat came home on the train   stayed here we went to the show at nite

October 5, 1943 – Got some ironing done   went down home in A.M. Went to the funeral in the afternoon   had to sit out side there was such a crowd.

October 6, 1943 – Finished my ironing   did some baking & went down town   put clothes away   nice day but so dirty & windy.

October 7, 1943 – Marie phoned this A.M. so I went to Islay for her   washed Baby clothes   stopped at Moms   went over to Olgas.

October 8, 1943 – Baked doughnuts & short bread   waxed front rooms   had Mrs McKay   Ennis   Elsie & Olga in for lunch took some fuel to Max M.   went out to Moms.

October 9, 1943 – Up early   baked some pumpkin pies Baked bread   we went down town   did the shopping Took Phyllis downtown too. went over to Elsie's in the evening. went to bed about 1:30 AM.

October 10, 1943 – Marie came to S. School & church   we took Marie home to Mannville   saw A. Nellie & U. Ed started to rain   saw Maries sisters etc   got back here at 12:00 P.M. sharp   Theresa [Marie's sister] would like to have kept Phyllis.

October 11, 1943 – Pat is with me to day but such a wash day it rained   tried to dry clothes in house   went to the show at nite   was good.

October 12, 1943 – First day of school   I baked pumpkin pies   ironed a bit   Elsie was in Olga too   had Olive & Ellis for supper   we played Crockinole & bridge till midnite. Still raining out

October 13, 1943 – Raining yet. Christina is to stay here till Nov. 1   work for her room & board.

October 14, 1943 – [No entry]

October 15, 1943 – [No entry]

October 16, 1943 – Phyllis sat on the kitchen floor by herself & watched me work.

October 17, 1943 – Sun. Phyllis was sick this A.M. I thought it was flu but we took her to Islay   Dr. Sweet had to operate. Started to rain.

October 18, 1943 – Phyllis passed away at noon, – oh why – she was so healthy, sweet & good   maybe someday we will understand.

October 19, 1943 – [No entry]

October 20, 1943 – [No entry]

October 21, 1943 – Has rained for days   Mom is with me to day. we washed clothes   Mrs Ennis was up. Jimmy has a terrible cold.

October 22, 1943 – Snowed last nite. It is so hard to take. It gets worse   I miss my baby so   Pat went to school to day   I had 3 kids for dinner at noon.

October 23, 1943 – Cold out feels like winter   Pat stayed over last nite. I was busy all day   baked 3 pumpkin pies   Roy Doris & Elmer came in in the evening.

October 24, 1943 – Didn't teach S. School   we went to Moms for dinner & supper. still miserable out   Pat came with us back.

October 25, 1943 – I washed clothes   not a bad day   did Moms too   Mrs Glaholt was up   she got a new coat. Pat stayed in again   Jimmy feels better.

October 26, 1943 – Have rec'd some lovely cards   got the latest pictures of Phyllis too   Mrs Bruce and Elsie were both here We churned   I made doughnuts & did the ironing.

October 27, 1943 – Lovely day so warm out. It is so hard without our little girl. I do hope we have another some time. Jimmy is such a man. Mrs McKay & Mrs Redman were in.

October 28, 1943 – Another nice day   had Pat & Christina for dinner again   Washed the sunporch windows & cleaned it up in general. We went to bed early.

October 29, 1943 – Friday. Rec'd some more letters & cards   I made Jimmy a shirt   took it along   sewed buttons & button holes in it at Bruces   Mrs E. & McKay were there. I bought a new congoleum.[4]

October 30, 1943 – Didn't get much done   a miserable day Miss Dunsmore was in   Mom, G & Ruth for supper & Olga came in after supper.

October 31, 1943 – [No entry]

November 1, 1943 – [No entry]

November 2, 1943 – [No entry]

November 3, 1943 – [No entry]

November 4, 1943 – Can't seem to keep my diary up   went to the Aid at Ennis's   such a miserable day   there weren't many out.

November 5, 1943 – Did up the work   went to Mrs McKays for the afternoon. Mrs Bruce & Ennis were there   we have snow on the ground   yet not much.

November 6, 1943 – Did some baking   Mom came in brought Ruth   she did her shopping   they stayed for supper.

November 7, 1943 – Taught S. School   Neal came to church we went out to Durwoods. I missed my little warm bundle so.

November 8, 1943 – Washed & ironed to day   not bad out   we intend to go to Ed[monton] on Wed. or Thurs.

November 9, 1943 – Didn't get my work done when Olga dropped in for a min then Mrs Lee came & spent the after noon.

November 10, 1943 – Packed   got ready   Neal went out for Mom   it was raining at nite   Mom slept here also Gramp J. Dance in town   Pat went.

November 11, 1943 – Left for Ed at 8:30 AM. arrived there around 2:30   went to Annes & Aunt Myrtles   went to the Capitol at nite.

November 12, 1943 – Up early   Mom & I went shopping Mom had her teeth started   beautiful weather   Went to see 'Yankee Doodle Dandy.'

November 13, 1943 – Marie met us in A.M. Went downtown

early   I bought a green coat, dress, shoes, hat & blouse. Took
Jimmy on the street car   went out to the Air Port.
November 14, 1943 – Sun. Slept in but Mom, Neal & I went to
Church, had dinner then went to see Air Port   Marie was with
us. left for home at 8:00 P.M.
November 15, 1943 – Such a terrible trip last nite   fog was so
thick   took us 9 1/2 hrs.   just put clothes away today
November 16, 1943 – Washed mine & Moms clothes   got mine
ironed   Neal stayed in at nite   went to bed early. He got his
call to go to the Army.
November 17, 1943 – I just feel sick about this new business   I
do hope Neal doesn't have to go. Mrs G. & Muriel H. were in for
the afternoon.
November 18, 1943 – Another lovely day out   I went down
town in AM   helped Mrs G. make fruit cake   did the
p[illow] cases for Aid.
November 19, 1943 – Started some more embroidery. Waxed floors
etc. Have rec'd so many cards & letters
November 20, 1943 – Was busy all day   went down town in the
A.M.   went to church   had our tea   Mom was in for the
evening
November 21, 1943 – Sun. Taught S. School   had minister for
dinner   we went skating   had supper at Moms   Ice was
grand.
November 22, 1943 – Washed & ironed to day   teachers came
in the evening   want me to help with concert   we tried
pieces till late. Rec'd a lovely picture from Mrs. Loy.
November 23, 1943 – Put clothes away. went out to Mums   she
brought kids   we cleaned & canned 21 chickens   got 21 qts.
November 24, 1943 – Another nice day   weather is holding so
good. J. & I went to Mrs Lee's did so [baking?]   Am to go to
school to morrow
November 25, 1943 – Did up work   baked some cookies
Mrs G came at 1:30 borrowed the camera   J. & I went to the
school   we went to Bob's at nite   came home 3:30 AM.

November 26, 1943 – Am I tired. I got a bunch of mail off
baked a Birthday cake for Pat   she is 18 today   she had Mary
up here for supper   Allen came up.
November 27, 1943 – Sat. Cleaned house up   baked a pie &
pudding   C. Ladies had a Bingo   we didn't go   Played
piano   studied S School lesson
November 28, 1943 – Sun. Neal & Gramp washed breakfast
dishes   I taught S. School   played for church too. We went
out to Pats B[irthday] Dinner then skating out at the Elliot place
took Miss Freehill.
November 29, 1943 – Up early   washed & ironed   quite a
nice drying day   washed curtains too.
November 30, 1943 – Expected the Auditor to day but Verna came
at noon   I went down town with her   just got back   did
the dishes   went to the school. came back   finished ironing.
Started to snow heavy at noon.
December 1, 1943 – Put clothes away   rec'd pictures of
Phyllis   they are good. Got all the curtains ironed and the floors
waxed.
December 2, 1943 – Had to go down town for meat   had baked
short bread. Auditor came   I had the L. Aid in afternoon.
December 3, 1943 – Cleaned house up good   made a shirt for
Jimmy also pair of overalls.   very mild out   ˙ went to school
again.
December 4, 1943 – Dr Sweet stopped in   didn't give me much
satisfaction[5]   did some baking   paid my store bills. Folks
were in at nite.
December 5, 1943 – Taught S. School   Jimmy has a cold so
Neal left us at Mothers   he took the rest down skating   Pat
came back with us.
December 6, 1943 – Washed clothes for all of us. (15) not bad drying day   went to the school with Mrs Porter   got
supper   listened to Lux [Radio Theatre] was Mrs Miniver
December 7, 1943 – Did my ironing in the A.M. Went to the
school again after dinner   I don't get a thing done these days.

December 8, 1943 – Did usual round   mended and put clothes
away   went to the school with Mrs. Porter in afternoon
stopped down town.

December 9, 1943 – Tidied up   made a pie   went to the
school to play after dinner   went up to Machons after for a few
mins. Wonderful weather so mild.

December 10, 1943 – Did some baking   Cleaned the house up
started the R[ed] Cross Pyjamas   Olga was in   had coffee.

December 11, 1943 – Sat. Tried to clean the house up   went
down town in afternoon. Mrs McKay was in at nite   Neal & I
went to Ed & Hilda's   got home 3:00 AM.

December 12, 1943 – Taught S. School   we all (Mom & Pat
too) went to the Unveiling in the hall. Neal, Jimmy & I went to
Ennis's for supper & evening.

December 13, 1943 – Washed clothes   Grandpa cut the pork up
about 60 pork chops. Did a little ironing   my gas iron won't
work. Edsel slept here at nite.

December 14, 1943 – Tried to get my ironing done   baked
bread   Grandpa made head cheese   fixed the pigs feet went
to the school in afternoon   rendered about 22 lbs lard.

December 15, 1943 – Trying to get ready for Xmas. Made a batch of
ginger snaps and a batch of over nite cookies   finally finished
my ironing   wrote out cards at nite. We churned & Grandpa
ground meat.

December 16, 1943 – Thurs. Another mild day   I made my
Xmas puddings and baked a batch of doughnuts. Wrote cards &
letters at nite   Rec'd some cards. Mrs McKay helped me fill S.
School candy bags

December 17, 1943 – Wrapped Xmas presents   got rest of my
cards off   did some shopping   went to the hall in the afternoon. We went to the show at nite   took Jimmy. Peggy Garnier
has twin girls.

December 18, 1943 – Sat. Talk about windy!! Cleaned whole
house up   finished wrapping presents   went down town
baked my white fruit cake   Jimmy was inoculated for whooping

cough   Mom & Geordie were in   we went to Elsie's in
evening   came home 1:30 A.M.
December 19, 1943 – Taught S. School   gave presents out had
20 children there   wonderful weather no snow just a little black
[soil showing through]. Neal took the boys to play hockey   I
stayed at Mom's.
December 20, 1943 – Washed clothes again   got some ironing
done in the afternoon   mailed more calendars. Girls came in
evening also Olga   I finished ironing at midnite.
December 2, 1943 – Put the clothes away   did some mending
went to the hall in the afternoon then out to Mom's   she sewed
R. Cross Pyjamas   I pressed pants for the kids.
December 22, 1943 – Baked mince meat tarts   went to the hall
at 1:00 p.m.   stayed till 3:00   came home   wrapped more
presents etc.
December 23, 1943 – Have received so many cards   had a picture & letter from Mrs Loy   was at the hall in A.M. then played
piano at the concert at nite. Rec'd a bottle of perfume from Verna
stationery from teachers.
December 24, 1943 – Made Norwegian Xmas bread and fixed the
turkey   decorated the house and tree   Neal didn't get home
till midnite. Grandpa Jones is here.
December 25, 1943 – Seems so hard to see why our 'little sister'
couldn't have been here but God knows best. Had folks &
Pinkie   16 of us. We rec'd so many lovely things. Neal gave me
a nice 64 piece set of dishes.
December 26, 1943 – Sun. Started to snow on Xmas Eve   we
really have sleighing now. We are all so tired   went to S. School
and also Church   not many out. Ennis's went to her home. We
all had a sleep in the afternoon.
December 27, 1943 – Washed clothes for all of us again   not a
bad day   about 20 above   Pat was in   also Olga.
December 28, 1943 – Did rest of the ironing   tidied house
up   we went over to Olga's for the evening   played bridge.
December 29, 1943 – Tidied house up   got meals etc. Elmer is

here again. Gramp J. went home yesterday. I walked out to Glenns
birthday party   pulled J. on his sled   got a ride home
December 30, 1943 – Did up usual round of work   went down-
town in the after noon   paid the bills & shopped   had Ed &
Hilda for the evening. Went to McKays for tea.
December 31, 1943 – Didn't do much   we went to the show at
nite also the dance   Bobby   Ariel, Muriel   Gerald, Fred &
Elsie all came up for supper in 1944   we had a nice time.

MEMORANDUM
July 4 – Have 20 qts rhubarb so far
Did 60 qts beans – had 6 left
60 qts peas – had 4 left
22 qts beets
26 qts carrots
8 pints greens
19 pints tomatoes
about 40 qts dills
Have 230 qts fruit as September 18, 1943

Ration Book No's
mine – 070201
Neal's – 070200
Jimmy – 070202

NOTES

Elsie Rogstad Jones's diary is in her possession.

1 A full version of the Elsie Rogstad Jones self-narrative is being prepared
   for publication, together with the stories of several other women of the
   Dewberry Valley in east-central Alberta.
2 Despite the economic hardship that the diaries reveal, the young people
   in Elsie Rogstad Jones's group attended movies often: first-run movies at

the Capitol Theatre on trips to Edmonton; reruns weekly in the village hall in Dewberry. The village show cost twenty-five cents per adult and fifteen cents per child and represented the only entertainment available. The projector was community-owned and run by volunteers. Elsie remembers the time when the show had to be stopped because a child got his hand caught in the reel. She also recalls the clicking of knitting needles as one of the village school teachers would continue with her knitting as the show ran.

3 The parcel noted here is from the Eaton's mail-order catalogue. The material was fabric for sewing. Both Elsie and her mother were expert seamstresses and made all their own clothes and those of the children.

4 A kind of flooring, like linoleum.

5 Dr Sweet, the McGill-trained physician who served Dewberry and other rural communities in the area, was unable to establish whether or not Elsie was at risk for a problematic pregnancy, given the recent death of her baby. Elsie sought the advice of a specialist in Edmonton.

Dorothy Duncan MacLennan
(1903–1957)

MARTHA SLOWE

No one ever keeps a diary who doesn't expect it to be read by someone else – unless it is purely a reference for his own future use.

The epigraph, inscribed by American-born writer and artist Dorothy Duncan MacLennan on a Montreal *Gazette* clipping, is inserted between two pages of her 1955 diary.[1] Beginning on New Year's Day 1953, and continuing through a long period of recurring illness that ended in her death on Easter Monday, 22 April 1957, Duncan kept a series of diaries.[2] At a time when painting had replaced writing as her mode of artistic expression, these personal journals offered her a private space in which to analyse her situation and attempt to come to terms with her physical and mental stress. Allowing her to express and examine her thoughts and emotions as well as the day-to-day events of her life, the diaries facilitated a dual process of self-knowledge and self-representation – in effect, a self-portrait. After her death, her husband, Hugh MacLennan, commented that 'during all that time of pain and weakness, with death an imminent certainty, she loved people and life and the world.'[3] In her final years, Duncan's life, like her increasingly abstract paintings, focused on essentials. Her priorities were marriage, art, and friendships.

Duncan seems never to have asked herself what she might have accomplished without her history of frail health that began in early childhood, but only what was possible in spite of it. Born to Dorothy and Edwin L. Duncan in East Orange, New Jersey, in 1903, she lived in St Louis and Denver before her family settled in the Chicago area. As a very young child, she suffered the first of four attacks of rheumatic fever – a disease that severely damaged both of her heart valves. All her life, Duncan experienced episodic chest pain and difficulty in walking long distances or climbing stairs. In spite of her physical limitations, however, she lived an active life. After graduating from high school, she attended Northwestern University, where she received a Bachelor of Science degree. An independent and energetic young woman, Duncan held various positions in the 1920s and early 1930s, working first for an advertising agency, then opening a small business of her own. She later managed a grammar school office in a poor section of Chicago. Her summers were spent 'traveling all over Europe.'[4] In the summer of 1932, on a trip to Europe that was part of her job with an American travel agency, she met Hugh MacLennan aboard a ship, the SS *Penfield*.[5] After a four-year courtship, during which the couple exchanged hundreds of letters,[6] they were married in 1936 in Wilmette, Illinois, a suburb of Chicago.

After the wedding, Duncan and MacLennan moved to Montreal, where MacLennan held a teaching position at Lower Canada College. For Duncan, the distance from Chicago to Montreal was cultural as well as geographical. Aware that, as an American, she was not well informed about Canadian culture, politics, history, and geography, she made an effort to learn as much as she could about Canada, travelling across the country and meeting with government officials in Ottawa to conduct her research. In the early years of her marriage, she began a writing career. Her first publication, in 1939, was a practical handbook entitled *You Can Live in an Apartment*.[7] Duncan's next book, *Here's to Canada*, published in 1941, was a well-received semi-autobiographical travel narrative that incorporated much of her earlier Canadian studies. Conscious of her insider/outsider perspective, she confided to her readers that, as an adjunct of the MacLennan family, she was automatically accepted by Canadians, but that Nova Scotians, in particular, still looked upon her as an American.[8] She published another successful personal memoir / travel narrative, *Bluenose: A Portrait of Nova Scotia*, in 1942. This book focused on Nova Scotia, Cape Breton, and MacLennan's Nova Scotian heritage, from Duncan's point of view. In 1945, she and MacLennan each won a Governor General's Award – MacLennan for his novel *Two Solitudes*, and Duncan for *Partner in Three Worlds*, her biography of a Czech-Canadian army soldier.

Although her resolve and formidable organizing skills sustained her through a demanding writing and domestic schedule, Duncan achieved her literary success at a high cost to her always precarious health. In the winter of 1947, following the aftermath of a severe bout with pneumonia that caused her damaged heart to fibrillate, she found herself too weak to endure the physical strain of another book-length project. A year later, she again became ill with pneumonia and the complication of a nearly fatal brain embolism, followed by two more embolisms.[9] By this time, she had turned her creative energies to occasional short magazine articles and to painting. On 1 January 1953, she began her diaries, writing in gold-lettered black leatherette yearbooks supplied by the MacLennans' insurer, F. Minden Cole & Co.[10] The entries continued until a few weeks before her death.

Duncan's 1953 diary extracts reveal that, despite her steadily declining reserves of strength, she kept a heroic schedule. She handled most of her own and her husband's personal correspondence, did her own housekeeping, worked with MacLennan on the gardens of their summer home in North Hatley, Quebec, and maintained an active social life there and in Montreal. We read – amidst records of her bouts of illness, physician calls, and visits to the hospital – guest lists and menus for dinner parties, as well as descriptions of various social, cultural, and academic events and gatherings, that she and MacLennan attended. Indeed, the stimulus of her interests and social activities appeared to revive Duncan. Dinners with friends at her home or theirs, dining out, and arts performances were particularly appealing.

By the 1950s, Hugh MacLennan was a celebrity, and the couple had a wide range of friends, including artists, writers, arts and university administrators, professors, journalists, politicians, and business and television executives. Reflecting the English Montreal cultural and social scene and the literary and artistic milieu, Duncan's diaries transmit a vivid impression of life in the 'Square Mile' area in which the MacLennan apartment was located.[11] Readers are given as well as a glimpse of the North Hatley summers, with their almost equally busy social calendars. The diaries chronicle the large and small events of Duncan's daily existence, describing her paintings in some detail, as well as her trips to the hairdresser, her dress for special occasions, her meetings, conversations, and lunches with friends and acquaintances, her thoughts afterwards, and her visits to the hospital. She does not omit her occasionally negative criticism of friends and acquaintances.

Always supportive, Duncan assisted MacLennan in his non-fictional work, serving as his proofreader and copy editor even as she attempted to develop herself as an artist and to cope with debilitating illness. Her efforts to be the perfect wife and yet to have an artistic life of her own in the midst of frequent medical emergencies were sometimes draining. One of her more acute internal conflicts was a concern that her art suffered from the fragmentation of her time and energy. One entry directly refers to her 'outspoken anger and resentment at being held to the service of his writing at a moment when I was trying to make a break toward outside interests and activities of my own, apart from a life of being always on call to act the silent, unacknowledged partner in his public work.' As if to convince herself of the propriety of such a role, however, she quickly adds, 'Every good wife does that of course' (5 March 1953). From the early years of their marriage, despite her independent spirit and her obvious competence in many areas, Duncan had always deferred to MacLennan as head of the household. In *Here's to Canada*, she asserted that in Canada, 'neither half of the household doubts who is master of the family. And make no mistake, Canadian women prefer it that way, and so do the American girls who marry Canadians'.[12] While in the privacy of her diaries, she questioned her position in the marriage, she seemed on the whole to accept it. Such passages as the one commenting on 'his remarkable character' (20 March 1953) and another on her resolve to preserve MacLennan's 'self-esteem' even if it meant her own self-effacement, suggest that she did not wish to disturb the status quo. The genuine pride and pleasure that she took in MacLennan's accomplishments, and the public admiration that he elicited, are evident in such entries as her Washington Memoranda (30 April 1953).

Next to human relationships, painting was a source of deep satisfaction for Duncan. In a passage describing the changing colours in the final version of her painting *Peggy's Cove*, she wonders whether a 'writer feel[s] the same happy excitement when a single paragraph, book, sentence, chapter is completed and good?' (17 April 1953). MacLennan believed that painting allowed Duncan to express herself more eloquently and affirmatively than her writing. He characterized her works as 'strong in form, vibrant and full of colour and a poetry that she never discovered when she wrote books.'[13] Painting offered her an mode of expression and a release for her creative impulses. It also gave her a sense of purpose, confirming the value of her daily struggle against despair. MacLennan attested that on a day in which she had written in her diary the words 'Low as a winter sky, Low as weeds in January. Low. Low,' her painting was 'an explosion of colour and joy.'[14] He also remarked in his eulogy that in the last days of her life Duncan was 'quietly happy,' preparing her paintings for a show at the Agnes Lefort Galleries.[15] The self-portrait projected through the 1953 diary extracts illuminates the darkness of depression with the writer's resilience and affirmation of life.

Dorothy Duncan MacLennan, Montreal, 1940.

DIARY, QUEBEC, FEBRUARY–MAY 1953

Sunday – February 1
A man committed suicide today by turning on the oven in his apartment three floors below. The smell of gas after the Super went in and opened to find the 44-yr-old man, was appalling and sickening. It rose straight up here of course. Hugh and I were too busy to let ourselves think much about it, but in bed at midnight, after the TV show,[16] the delayed reaction hit us both. How many times had we passed him in the halls, or ridden up with him in the elevator, never guessing what must had been his inner torment. For he had a wife and children, and it was a Sunday afternoon.

Monday – February 2
Now we learn from Cunningham that the gas was first smelled an hour before the time he went in to find the man dead. This earlier time he rang the bell, opened up when he got no answer, found the windows open and the man in the kitchen, explaining that everything was all right now. So Cunningham made a joke and left. An hour later the windows were closed and all the jets on the stove open. How many people change their minds after a first attempt and then return to finish the job?
Jim and Norma in – happy enough together, but barren of interests.

Tuesday – February 3
[No entry]

Wednesday – February 4
Spent the evening with Dr. Randles and his wife Katya. It can't be often that one puts a character in a book – even a sort of biography like my *Partner*, and then finds [one]self living under the same roof with said character.
He's a Yorkshire man – his wife with a rheumatic heart – and he's one of the Canadian VIP's of Cunard.

Thursday – February 5
Lunch at the St. James Club as guests of the Fergusons with Bob Fowler, the Parkins, Gerald Selion, and a guest of honour, Vera

Michaelis Dean, head of the Foreign Policy Assn. of the US.
Badura – Skoda at L.M.M.
Dio-oxocylin.

Friday – February 6
Rheumatism, nerves, curses.
Tennis at the Forum – Segura-MacGregor; Sedgeman-Kramer –
Beautiful!

Saturday – February 7
In and out of bed all day.

Sunday – February 8
Supper (Chop suey) – for Mary Ferguson
Jack Spector
Max Cohens
Houde[17] on TV show
Later, Brotts, Cohens, Stewart Griffiths, and Neil Morrison (CBC
TV Toronto) back with us for discussion.

Monday – February 9
Traded John Lyman's *Massawippi* (which we never wanted) for
Goodridge Roberts' *Georgian Bay* at Sterre's Dominion Gallery
($100 on the Lyman – a fair deal!)

Tuesday – February 10
John Gray with us to Indoor Tennis Club for drinks while
Hugh played. The man who committed suicide in the building
ten days ago was his cousin. Spoiled by his mother as a child,
John said, then too much drink, no success, no ability to face
reality.

Wednesday – February 11
Joan and Francis Allen's son born at 5:30 a.m. – after three days
and nights of intermittent labour.

'Revolting looking thing,' Droop said, 'red hair, and otherwise just like me.'
(What is a cold? I have one).

Thursday – February 12
Next day: – 'Isn't it amazing,' said F.A., 'what a single sperm could do!'

Friday – February 13
Admiring my new painting – *The Seedling* – I suddenly discovered that it was all phallic symbols – all of it! Hugh grinned and said 'why not – you're a fine healthy girl.' (But I've no need to paint them).

Saturday – February 14
How flat and empty and unproductive a cold can make one feel! Whereas a temperature – at least in the beginning – leads to fine feats of mental skill and acumen. I have no temperature and no elan.

Sunday – February 15
Ralph Cohens. To TV show and then to Desjardins for supper – back here afterwards. Best show yet, especially for Hugh.

Monday – February 16
A loathsome permanent and haircut by the same operator who gave me the best I've ever had last time. What is wrong? Do I trust those who are supposed to know their jobs too much? (I didn't doubt she knew her job as she worked). Am I afraid of being thought too fussy?

Tuesday – February 17
Harry Cramer has made an engagement for me at the Ross [Pavilion, Royal Victoria Hospital] for March 1 – a thorough Barium examination of my digestive system. Oh, well – it will be the first time I haven't been carried into the Ross on a stretcher.

Wednesday – February 18
My hair redone by Mildred – and with kindness & pleasure on her part. I have learned from Gwen; instead of pulling rank and authority, make those who serve you feel sorry for you and able to do something to help. Then all is well, your end accomplished, and their self-esteem left intact, if not heightened.

Thursday – February 19
Dr. Philpott – 4:00.
Di-oxocylin.
Larry Adler at the McGill Conservatorium – 8:00.

Friday – February 20
Well – I've made the spring show[18] at last. How big that objective has loomed on the horizon for years! But to be chosen one of 42 out of 758 entries for Jury II – and none of the three judges knowing my work – pleases me!

Saturday – February 21
Elmer Pairs at the C.I.I.A.[19] Then on to the Von Eichen's for drinks, plus Warwick Chipman, and the Bill Buddens – and finally to the University Club for dinner, less Warwick. A thoroughly satisfying man, exactly as he should be. He says that Joe McCarthy could be the next Republican nominee for President. Hugh has cold chills already – in fact, all the Canadians at the meeting were more eager to explore the subject of McCarthy than any other.

Sunday – February 22
Diarmid MacLennan, Lilias Newton & Mary Ferguson for tea and drinks, plus George [Ferguson] and Albert Trueman, Pres. of U.N.B. – Good fun for all.

Monday – February 23
I Confess- a Hitchcock movie of Quebec City. Very well done. (And moving).

Anne Baxter
Montgomerey Clift
Karl Malden
Brian Aherne

Wednesday – February 25
You must never again, Dorothy, talk to him about his work when
he asks direct questions which you may foolishly think are asked
because he wants a direct answer. He doesn't want an opinion – he
wants only confirmation of his opinion. If you will remember this,
it will be easy enough. The thing is to form a habit – then you
won't easily forget this resolution. What is one swallowed opinion
worth, compared with the preservation of his self-esteem? If you
can't do this for him, he'll find someone else who will –

Saturday – February 28
Dinner with Fred and Gertrude Katz.
Painted *The Yellow Cloth*.

Sunday – March 1
Into the Ross (R.V.H.) on my feet, rather than by stretcher – for
internal examinations – 3:00 p.m. Back on the third floor-with
Miss Reid, Miss Cooke, Mrs. Harvey, Miss Alison, Miss Gordon
and Miss Clarke.

Monday – March 2
Barium enema and fluoroscope, plus X- rays.

Tuesday – March 3
Barium to drink for breakfast – then up to my room and down
again five times, until 2:30 – while it was watched on its journey.
Blood tests, too.

Wednesday – March 4
Basal metabolism – and I got through it without misbehaving at all.
I'll never be afraid of it again.

Went out to dinner with Hugh, home for an hour, then bac again.

Thursday – March 5
This time – again without breakfast – an intravenous pylegram (to put metal into the kidneys) and more x-rays. They found what they were looking for, on my left kidney. More tests – but I went out to a movie with Hugh in the afternoon, my breath smelling like East Chicago.

Friday – March 6
To the operating room, this time for a cystoscopy – a light inserted through my bladder, into my kidney – but the x-rays showed the growth to be outside, pressing against the kidney.
Spent the day sleeping off the dope, then to Her Majesty's to see *The Fourposter.*

Saturday – March 7
Nothing will be done about the larger cyst, except watch it. Thank fortune the x-rays taken in 1951 show it to have been the same size then.
Dio-xocylin.
Spent the afternoon watching the filming of *Dr. Ainslee* by the N.F.B. [National Film Board].

Sunday – March 8
Resting still from the somewhat battered state of nerves left over from the week at the Vic.
Stump the Experts with Mary Ferguson as guest.

Monday – March 9
Oh, I am so tired!
Twenty years ago today Hugh and I found each other in New York –

Wednesday – March 11
Enough[–]better to paint a simple flower piece – yellow tulips and white narcissus – brought by Marian.

Thursday – March 12
An evening with the Parkins, also with Jacques and Zoe Bieler.
Eloise writes that George Homaus [Homans] is being spoken of as
the next president of Harvard!
Answer-my God!

Friday – March 13
Opening of the 70th Annual Spring Show at the Montreal
Museum of Fine Arts – preceded by a dinner à deux at Café Martin.
The show was a shambles; it angered Hugh and bored me irrepara-
bly.

Saturday – March 14
Took Norma (Wiken) to the Indoor to see Hugh and Jim in a
match with Brookline Tennis Club, and incidentally launch her
into Jim's world, now that his divorce is going through. Highly successful, said Jim. I didn't stay for cocktails – to see.

Sunday – March 15
How does anyone exist on phenobarb without committing either
murder or suicide? I disliked everything and everyone today after
taking phenobarb at 4 a.m. – and most of all myself.

Monday – March 16
Arts in Montreal – Council meeting at Ritz.

Tuesday – March 17
Dined with Norrice and Jim Conaut in Pointe Claire – plus Larry
Laybourne, Chief of U.S. correspondents of *Time*. Hugh says 'I've
never yet met anyone who works for Time that I didn't like and
respect.' We've known Larry before, but he wears exceedingly well.
Began painting *Baddeck Harbor* from photo –
Dio-xocyllin.
Sat on the roof in the sun today.

Wednesday – March 19
How difficult it is to convince me that I don't have a cancer –
Harry Cramer said, 'I don't know, but I don't think so.' The condition of my heart I take for granted. But I fear that which I dread
most of all – not for myself – but its cost to Hugh in personal suffering I mean.

Thursday – March 20
Hugh's 46th birthday.
I'm so accustomed to his remarkable character that I sometimes
forget to think about it – until another man behaves like most
other men, and then the contrast shows up as accute. I suppose
that's why it hurts me when he uses the term 'women' as a curse –
for if I am not thoroughly a woman, of what use am I to him?

Friday – March 21
Dinner at L'Abourd á Plouffe with the Scotts – père, Wendy, Ann,
John Scott and Tony Graham.
Watched television for the first time on a home set, got cold, chat-
tered with the infants, who find me more interesting than 'the
man' right now because they think they know him and want to discover what it is like being married to him.

Saturday March 22
Flu – damn!

Monday – March 23
Not too bad.
Hugh's back is of course giving him much trouble. It's the way his
body always behaves under the stress of his feeling too much
responsibility, not that he can help it.

Tuesday – March 24
Marian brought in a baked chicken, bless her.

Hugh now says that he, too, has been having a mild flu. But he's over it. Only his back continues weak.
When my temp. shot up to 102 at 10 p.m. he said 'Oh, well I expected trouble today!' (!!!)

Wednesday – March 25
Temp. 101 this morning, so Harry Cramer came in and insisted on Hugh's getting a trained attendant. The moment he connected with one (from Cape Breton of course) he began to relax and walk straighter. Poor guy.
The T.A. knew – they all do – all Hugh's aunts and cousins and – they all are valuable on the subject. This one, Margaret Mitchell by name, came in to ask me what we did with the Jori Smith nude when our minister called. I explained that we had no problem in that direction.

Thursday – March 26
'Some of your friends must be shocked. Of course it doesn't bother me.'
'We have no friends who are shockable,' I said.
'Oh. Is she a friend of yours?'
I realized she meant the model, and the overwhelming vulgarity of the idea convulsed me with amusement. I longed to say 'She's my husband's mistress.' When I get old enough I expect to be able to make such answers on impulse. Hugh thought it was a hilarious conversation when I told him, especially the part I repressed. 'It wouldn't have looked so well for you if you said it though.' Once again, I repressed an answer: 'I might have seemed too noble.'

Friday – March 27
It takes no great skill to characterize a man by showing his weaknesses – his lacks. There are an infinite variety of things any one human being is not, in a thousand combinations. But there are only a few things that he is, in a combination which makes him an

individual personality, and to find the special color, form and texture of those very few characteristics does take some skill, some understanding and much experience. To castigate a man for what he doesn't happen to be is, therefore, the easiest way to show the limitations of oneself.

No man is the sum of what he is not. For even if a certain lack seems of paramount importance, it is still meaningless except in relation to those qualities that are.

Saturday – March 28
Miss Margaret Mitchell Wi. 3576 (Nurses' Service).
What a lot of ideas fever induces in a muddled brain!

Sunday – March 29
Still in bed.
Terramycin has strange effects. For one thing it completely deodorizes the body and all bodily excretions, sweat, breath, etc. In other words, it must kill all bacteria, including the necessary ones for bodily functions –

Monday – March 30
More fever – but not high.

Thursday – March 31
Marian came in again – this time with a casserole she had made for our dinner. She studied my Baddeck landscape yet again – thinks it the best thing I have done (excepting Beer on the rocks) – and wondered if I had obtained the effects she admires consciously. The answer – sometimes, but always when they simply happen, I let them stand, knowing they are right. And so learn.

I am finishing 'Journey with Genius,' Brynner's study of D.H. Lawrence. At last I am old enough to face down the cult of Lawrence which I resisted with all the force of my instincts when Hugh found most to admire in him. I remember it as the first passion of Hugh's with which I refused to accede, and so disappointed

him in his desire to share his beliefs and enthusiasms.
Now he is revolted as by an old sin.

Wednesday – April 1
The earliest spring in Montreal since I first came, 16 1/2 years ago.
Still in bed. Lord, how it hangs on, in lowered vitality.

Thursday- April 2
Marian[20] and Peter in for drinks. Peter has suddenly become
entirely himself – not Frank's unwanted son or Marian's reason for
being. Women will love him greatly, and he will know how to
accept it and grow with it.

Friday – April 3
Good Friday –
Such a meaningless day in our lives. Hugh is still made uncomfortable by its undertones from his past, though much less than he used
to be.
In my past it only meant a day for smelling the earth and the sun
with Chart.[21]

Saturday – April 4
Hugh brought Jim home from the Indoor and Jim admired my Baddeck, so I admired Jim. Then Hugh insisted that we go out for dinner against my belief that I didn't have strength enough to dress.
Picked up Norma, went to the Pavilion at the La Salle, and all was
well again, between me and the world.

Sunday – April 5
Easter – and loud, clanging bells from all directions. I finished
Spring 53, and Hugh says it is my most original painting yet. Cer-
tainly it grew and grew in my mind before it ever went onto canvas.
When it was finished I knew it, and was mortally tired, spent, but
happy.

Monday – April 6
Deep depression from flu.

Tuesday – April 7
Hugh went to N[orth] H[atley] for the car. Filthy gray day.
Book Club. Every time I see this group of women I have known for
fifteen years – after not having been with them for awhile – I am
appalled at the signs & ravages of their age. And what do they
think of me?

Wednesday – April 8
We took ourselves to see *Call Me Madam*. Ethel Merman did us
both good.
Dio-oxocylin.

Thursday – April 9
Having the color of one's hair changed is the modern equivalent of
buying a new hat, as a morale booster. Better, too, because it can be
worn all the time –

Friday – April 10
Stump the Experts resumed. A notable performance because a)
Michael Pym – the Englishman-adventurer (from Toronto) producer hoped to please, and b) Max got sick in the middle of the
show, left it, returned and the audience never guessed. Good work
all around. The Brotts came back with us for coffee.

Saturday – April 11
Dined with Ned and Hazel Cleghorn. Pre-dinner with the
American consul and Virginian wife – Butrick – pro-McCarthy,
and Vice-Consul Scott. For dinner – Charles & Alice Stoppan,
of the consulate, Robin and Dodo Watt, and John Steegman[22] –
and the Montreal letter from *Saturday Night* re the Spring
Show! Never was Hugh so well in balance, so strong, so kind to

his irate opposition, or so effective in the 2-hr.-long-argument. We left with Steegman begging us to invite him to our home.

Sunday – April 12
Poor intrepid little man! He [Steegman]'s making a valiant fight for his principles against the Mount Royal Club mentality who hired him. And he was bitterly hurt by what he thought were Hugh's intentions in what he wrote. It can't be much fun, at his age, to go to a very strange country, into a hornet's nest, with almost no one wishing him well – no wife, no roots, no reputation (that Canadians care about) – 'and your husband has such power in what he writes. He's so respected. Everyone hears what he says.'

Monday – April 13
The depression is lifting at last. Yesterday we drove to Pointe Claire to the Jim Conaut's housewarming. Met Dr. James B. Conaut – and I said, 'But you're in Germany. I saw a picture of you there in the papers three days ago.' 'That's right.' he said, 'So I was.' A shy, quiet man who twinkled when Hugh suggested he had picked a good time to be in Germany, with the Russian peace offensive under way.

Tuesday – April 14
The Bill Buddens came in for drinks (because Diana came up on Arts Survey business first) and Bill went home at 9:00 sans supper. I'm still not too old to be impressed by the repetition of evidence that tells me that all sensitive men are less poised and self-assured and 'on top' than they seem. And so undeniably endearing.
I think I have a new category for dividing people – those who are sensitive (meaning aware, imaginative, feeling) and those who are not. It's so much [more] important to be sensitive than clever.

Wednesday – April 15
Come Back Little Sheba

Saw Dr. Rab about the pain in my left leg. Even if I did have a malignant growth, he'd make me feel that I could see it through with my chin up.

Thursday – April 16
Stanley Cup final – Hugh as Jim's guest –
Jim for supper –
Temperature up again.
Double damn!

Thursday – April 17
The final version of my *Peggy's Cove* – thoroughly satisfying – muted, subtle colors. But they change in night lights. Does a writer feel the same happy excitement when a single paragraph, book, sentence, chapter is completed and good?

Saturday – April 18
Cocktail party for Herbert & Mary Brita Langfelt, Eloise (Mason left at home with flu), Scotts, Thomsons – and Jim and Louis Robert by chance.
Dinner à deux later at Tour Eiffel.

Sunday – April 19
Di-oxocylin.
Dull, raw & cold.

Monday – April 20
What a weight I am on Hugh – most especially when I feel my own heaviness.

Tuesday – April 21
How does one learn to laugh all over again? I mean the physical act of laughing. I grew up too conscious of my teeth to laugh easily.
Then – then –

Wednesday – April 22
It's a matter of unused muscles, really it is. At least, most of the time.

Friday – April 24
Face treatment.

Saturday – April 25
Dinner at La tour Eiffel.
Leave for New York by *The Washingtonian*.
First time I had slept (no sleep) on a train since the return from California in 1948. Connecting bedrooms.

Sunday – April 26
New York
Barbizon Plaza – 17th floor overlooking the Park. What a lovely lift to face the smile of spring overnight – Flowering trees seen from afar in a sea of many greens.
Yankee Stadium by taxi through the park to watch the Senators beat the Yankees 5–4. Temperature 74°. Dinner at the Cripsholm, seated next to a Vogue model with a voice like a buzz-saw.
TV show – *What's My Line?*
Then exhaustion.

Monday – April 27
Shopping at Bloomingdales, not much.
Came unstuck just before dinner – enteritis. Hugh went alone to Shirley Booth in *The Time of the Cuckoo*.

Tuesday – April 28
Guggenheim Gallery of abstracts – exciting and satisfying. No other galleries seemed worth the effort after that.
Town and Country for dinner.
The Crucible – fine!
Then home with Grace Brynolsson and Jean Fraser, her guest for a week.

Wednesday – April 29

Mark Tobey show. Maybe I haven't gone far enough to see what there is to see. It left me both dry and cold. Lever Building – Hugh's new love.

To Washington on *The Congressional*, a super-train, and into a room at The Statler, a super-hotel. One wall all mirror, desk-dressing table, TV set, radio, armchairs, couch, air-conditioning. [A]ll beige, green & brown colors – space.

Thursday – April 30

The big day – in bed until noon. Luncheon in the South American Room. Guest of Ethel, plus Jad, Peggy Ross, and others.

Hugh's speech a smashing success. The Americans were incredulous – Who was this Canadian? How did he manage to move them so profoundly? Even Louis Bromfield left them bored when he followed Hugh. See Memoranda at end for further comments.

Washington Memoranda

At the luncheon, Sen. Alexander Wiley presided, Hugh at his right. Hugh said he (Wiley) obviously knew little and cared less about him. He began gulping at his grapefruit before half the head-table guests were in place, then picked his teeth with the corner of his place card. But after Hugh's speech, Wiley was obviously moved. He called him 'Brother Hugh' (to Ethel's delighted amusement) and one of the outstanding novelists on this continent today. Rob't Saunders, Canadian Chairman Hydro-Electric Power Commission of Ontario, on Hugh's other side, had tears in his eyes when Hugh sat down – because for once someone had said something about what Canadians are and what they feel and think – in a way no one else has ever done in the U.S.A.

A reporter said to Hugh, 'That was a swell speech. We listen to so much b-.s. – it's great to hear real stuff for a change. Just wanted to tell you that.'

Then 'they' cornered Hugh in the afternoon. They decided he

was just what they needed in Washington. He was invited to work on *The Heartland* (publication for the ass'n), he was invited to the Canadian Embassy – but he pleaded other engagements, and went for a walk.

At 5:30 he was told that we would both be seated at the head table at the dinner, a reception to be held first at 6:00. Informal. I wore a black faille suit, gold mesh scarf, gold loop earrings, gold bracelets.

Cocktails on two levels – about 1200 present. We were introduced to Robert Taft[,] and I thought less of him in person than in pictures – all politician and fat, plus that grizzly grin he adopted for the Republican Convention (to beat Eisenhower's smile) and never wiped off. Talked awhile with the Hon. Lionel Chevrier, Can. Minister of Transport and speaker of the evening. And again I was told on all sides what a moving speech my husband had made at lunch.

At the head Table, in order, were Syd Pierce, Can. Minister at Washington, soon to be Can. Ambassador to Brazil; Hugh; Sen Homer Ferguson; Hume Wrong, Can. Ambassador at Washington; Dr. N.R. Danielian (who looks like a Syrian rug pedlar though he's a PhD. of Harvard); Mrs. Hume Wrong; Alben Barkley (a darling, let there be no mistake about it); Lewis Castle, ch. of the Ex[.] Com. of the Ass'n; Robert Taft; Sen. Aitken; Gov. G. Mennen Williams of Michigan (heart-throbs, as I once would have apostrophied); Mrs. Hugh MacLennan (with name spelled correctly. Hugh says Americans are always good at getting names, Canadians poor indeed); Sen. Green (who wasn't there, having gone off with Republican Senators to the Burning Tree Golf Club, where Taft joined them); Gerald Lynch of the Ford Motor Co., or head-lobbyist to be exact; Mrs. Syd Pierce; and others I never saw, including Governor Val Peterson of Nebraska. At the tables on the floor were 25 or 30 senators and congressmen, who stood when Barkley asked them to identify themselves.

Louis Bromfield is a director of the Ass'n. and he was a secondary speaker after Hugh, at the luncheon. Unfortunately, his speech was rambling and poor. Gerald Lynch moved over and sat beside me at dinner. He was charming (and very handsome), and he wanted two things badly. First, from me – what tricks had Hugh used to put himself over with such outstanding success in a place like Washington where speeches were used to sell everything from personalities to principalities.

I said it was probably Hugh's Gaelic charm as a man named Lynch should know. He pushed the subject aside with disdain. 'I've taught public speaking at the University of Michigan, and yet I've no idea how he did it. I'd give a lot to find out.' All I could reply was that Hugh never spoke anywhere without a great deal of preparation. And I couldn't add that he was in Washington to sell nothing and gain nothing.

So Lynch gave me up as a female of no further use to him. He leaned toward Gov. Williams across me, and turned on the charm for him. But Soapy Williams (who smelled of all his two families' preparations) was apparently more interested in me than in Gerald Lynch, so finally the Ford lobbyist turned his back on both of us and didn't even bid us good-night when the dinner was over. Gov. Williams met Hugh and wanted to see us more, but we were very tired by then.

Friday – May 1
Ethel and Jim called for us, drove us about the city – Rock Creek Park – out to their house in Arlington. Temp. 85°. Everything in full bloom – salmon tulips, banks of azaleas, pink and white dogwood, lilacs – lovely smells. And the cardinals' spring song. Then back to the Montrealer (by wheelchair for me from car to train), and a quiet trip back in a compartment.

Saturday – May 2
Breakfast at the Ritz. Temp. 41°. Raw, cold, gray, damp – like an ugly girl with her heels dug in, refusing to smile or grow into graciousness.

Spent the day in bed after a hasty unpacking.

NOTES

Dorothy Duncan McLennan's diary is from the McGill Library Rare Books and Special Collections, Montreal, Container 6, file 613, MS 698.

1 The newspaper clipping is dated Saturday, 5 February 1955.
2 The diaries begin on 1 January 1953 and end on 29 March 1957, although the pages between 30 March and 2 April 1957 are missing.
3 See Hugh MacLennan, 'Portrait of an Artist: Dorothy Duncan,' *The Montrealer*, June 1957, 40.
4 See Dorothy Duncan, 'Portrait of the Author,' *Mayfair*, August 1955, 56.
5 Ibid.
6 This was the period in which MacLennan completed his PhD at Princeton.
7 See Duncan, *You Can Live in an Apartment* (New York: Rinehart-Farrar, 1939). Except for the summers, spent in their North Hatley house, the MacLennans lived in an apartment throughout their marriage.
8 Duncan, *Here's to Canada* (New York: Harper, 1941) 28.
9 MacLennan, 'Portrait of an Artist,' 36–8.
10 F. Minden Cole & Co., the MacLennans' insurance provider, was the Montreal division of United States Fidelity and Guaranty Company.
11 As William Weintraub notes, the area of Montreal known as the 'Square Mile' actually covers 'an area somewhat less than a square mile, with University Street on the east, Guy/Côte des Neiges on the west, Dorchester on the south and Pine avenue on the north.' From the mid-nineteenth-century until 1929, it was home to the wealthiest families in Canada. After the stock market crash and the Depression that followed, most of these people left. In the 1950s it was a very pleasant area, but less affluent. Many of the elegant mansions had been demolished to make room for apartment buildings such as the one in

which the MacLennans lived on Mountain Street. McGill University,
the fashionable shops of Sherbrooke Street, and the Ritz Hotel were
in this still desirable neighbourhood. See Weintraub, *City Unique:
Montreal Days and Nights in the 1940s and '50s* (Toronto: McClelland
and Stewart, 1996), 150–1.

12 Duncan, *Here's to Canada*, 123.

13 MacLennan, 'Portrait of an Artist,' 40.

14 Ibid.

15 Ibid.

16 The show is *Stump the Experts*, a quiz show that first went to air in
September 1952; Hugh MacLennan was a panelist along with
Dr D.L. Thomspon and Maxwell Cohen. The moderator was
Steven Brott. Contestants competed for Canadian handicrafts. See
http://www.film.queensu.ca/CBC/

17 This was Camillien Houde, who was mayor of Montreal for most of the
years between 1928 and 1954.

18 The spring show is the same show she refers to in the entry for March
13th: the 70th Annual Spring Show at the Montreal Museum of Fine
Arts (now the Musée des Beaux Arts).

19 This acronym probably stands for the Canadian Institute of International Affairs.

20 Marian Dale Scott was the wife of F.R. Scott, and Peter Scott was their
only child.

21 Chart was a serious boyfriend from her youth. Dorothy was still seeing
him when she met Hugh MacLennan.

22 Steegman was the director of the Montreal Museum of Fine Arts from
1953 to 1959.

Marian Engel
(1933–1985)

AFRA KAVANAGH

In the summer of 1976, Marian Engel used some of the money she received from the Governor General's Award for her novel *Bear*[1] to leave Toronto and stay at a cottage outside Charlottetown, Prince Edward Island. At the time, her marriage was ending, although she had sought counselling in an attempt to repair the relationship and had tried to convince her husband, Howard Engel, to do the same. She thought that the marriage was still salvageable, even though he had embarked on a relationship with a woman whom Engel saw as a younger version of herself. Her angry reaction to being cast as the disposable older wife would receive fictionalized treatment in the penultimate chapter of *The Glassy Sea* and in a short story, 'The Tattooed Woman.'[2]

The diary excerpt printed here was written during that summer in Charlottetown. It opens with Engel inspecting the books on the shelves immediately after her arrival at the cottage. Although she is pleased with the accommodations, she expresses her distaste for housework as she had done earlier in an essay entitled 'Housework Gives Me the Crazies.'[3] Among the people around her that summer, those who appear in the diary include Will and Char(lotte), her twin son and daughter; and John Ormsby, who worked for Coach House Press, a small but soon to be influential Canadian press that was just starting at that time.

Engel writes about the mundane, about her family, and about her art. She speaks of the daily grind – of her fatigue and her need for a change; of her children and their friends; of the cottage and its physical contents – but she also discusses her perceptions of the novel as an art form. As a professional writer, a woman, and a mother, she felt divided. She felt that she must be available to her children either physically or emotionally, and she experienced great guilt when she was not. She was compelled to nurture her own needy self so that she could function as a creative artist, but her attention was claimed largely by domestic duties, especially once she became a single mother.

In writing her diary, Engel used a typewriter, typing single-spaced on sheets of white paper numbered on the top right-hand corner of the manuscript; she sometimes included a date or a month. The typewriter was in poor shape, missing some letters and jamming at others. Despite that, her writing is lucid, her observations noteworthy.

Engel did not intend these notes for publication, although she used some of the reflections and the island site in her next novel, *The Glassy Sea*, which she dedicated to the friends who owned the Charlottetown cottage. In that novel the protagonist, Rita Heber, ponders the pond and the whirlybird, as Engel does in these notes. The 'thereness' of the place and the very being of the bird appeal to the disillusioned Rita, who has been sent away to the island to be kept out of the spotlight as her ex-husband and his younger, more genteel new wife campaign to get him into political office. Rita casts her eyes on this post-lapsarian garden, wishing for a lily's existence, for grace instead of redemption, to be a Mary rather than a Martha. She questions her faith, and debates her role in the world of men and in the order of nuns she spent more than a decade with at Eglantine House, and succeeds in talking herself out of her despair.

Engel's interests, inhibitions, and talents are made explicit in her journal, which was private and self-addressed. That she loved people and parties, that she had a large number of close friends, that she had a temper and often drank too much, and that she wrote clear and expressive prose are all evident in the pages that immortalize that summer of pain and healing. Yet, there is evidence that Engel wrote the journal with an eye on posterity, since much of it reads like the first draft of a story or essay. It is as if the writer no longer has a private life, and certainly no unexamined life. As she lived, she observed herself responding to people and situations, and promptly recorded her perceptions, always finding the best words to express them. Yet, she wrote elsewhere about her dread of and distaste for the public's desire to poke around in the private lives of writers, and cautioned readers against substituting an interest in the life of the author for an interest in her work.[4] Nonetheless, she also admitted to living the previous winter on money she received from selling her papers to McMaster University in Hamilton, Ontario.

Sadly, we do not hear any triumphant notes, any newly gained confidence from the success of her last novel. In these 'Bear summer' notes, there is evident weariness and a recognition of her need for psychic rest beyond that provided by drink or Valium. Yet, the reader can recognize the observant eye that distinguishes the best of Engel's writing. 'It's a life's work,' she wrote in *The Glassy Sea*, 'to keep an eye on the field.'[5] A significant part of her job as a writer was to observe the world around her, and to attempt to represent it in her writing as engaging narratives that reflected important contemporary debates. A product of her time, she considers her personal growth in the wake of her divorce. She wants her independence, but longs for someone (mother, father, husband) to watch over her. She believes in personal liberation, but recognizes and portrays in her protagonists a need to belong to the world. Also, she was greatly influenced by the European literary canon, but sought to represent a Canadian reality in her work.[6]

Engel's writing received positive popular and critical attention during her lifetime. Indeed, she managed to support herself by her writing at a time when only Margaret Atwood, Mordecai Richler, and Margaret Laurence could make the same claim.[7] Her most important contribution, through her involvement with the Writers' Union of Canada, was a compensation package for writers for public lending rights (the topic of the entry for 25 June). She was inducted as an Officer of the Order of Canada in 1983, and was awarded the title Woman of Distinction by the City of Toronto in 1984.

When she died of cancer in 1985, Marian Engel had published, in sixteen years, seven novels, a volume of short stories, two children's books, and a picture book on islands, as well as numerous stories and articles in newspapers and magazines. Her death was followed by the publication of *The Tattooed Woman*, her second volume of short stories. In her lifetime, she had won, along with several other literary awards, Canada's highest award for fiction. There is now, in her honour, a $10,000 prize given annually to a woman writer in mid-career.

Marian Engel, ca. 1980.

DIARY, PRINCE EDWARD ISLAND, JUNE–JULY 1976

Bear Summer
Marian Engel

11 Monday evening

Cool and clear again, wind rippling the estuary. Still intrigued by the idea there might be only two snipe: their calls echo.

Charlotte and Debbie are playing ball on the road. Will is upstairs asleep, no, reading on the can. John O. is asleep. He arrived at 4 with a case of moosehead beer, most of which he has packed in his book traveller's suitcase to take back on the train. He had a great time with the Gools. I like him, he's thoughtful and very together. Must remember him when I feel the young are getting worse.

Cruising the bookcases: treasure. Hesse and Irving Stone, Snow and Powell, Did I come to the country to be distracted and driven by Powell & Well, he'salways there, and at least one falls asleep.

Awesome: a generation, maybe three's, minds formed by Penguins: Snow and Woolf and Orwell, Plomer and Murdoch etc. There's Salinger here, the Nicholson book, Gavin Maxwell, a bunch of thrillers (I thought I was the only one who ever owned 'The Pit Prop Syndicate.' The house is lovely: what I hoped Holstein would be, roomy and shabby enough so one doesn't worry about house-work, and stacked with comfy books and cushions and old post-cards. It manages everything without being cute. It looks as if it artlessly grew. I could use a sieve and a potato peeler but otherwise it's a miracle. Now Hazen's got the stove going. Now Will has a bike and Char a friend, and John O's brought some beer.

Gull on the inlet. The way the water scuds. The bend of the trees. Evening sun whitening gull's body. Hiproofed barns, sod-sided potato barns. Church steeples every direction.

I found a little street tonight. Up past the corner if you branch

right you come about 10 houses in order. Two terra cotta, one
brown, one umber, one white, one bright green, one yella. A blue,
too, I think. Neat, sweet. Carving round the gables. Was there
ever, however poor people are, such a *domestic* island.

Foreground: 104 sand dollars stretched down the railing. Weedy
delphiniums and lilies. Marsh grass, angelica, road, ditch, fence,
iris-marsh. Sky: mackeral.

Men and women: Will's getting all male and taciturn. Where did
he learn it & Thinks a lot, though. Charlotte is confiding, but slier
than he is. He's an awful tease, aget-around. She lacks confidence,
is dumber than Molly, she says. Maybe that's true, but she's also
special. Works out systems.

We're doing experiments. If a wet ball touches the electric wire
what hpens if you catch it.'
His wings whiffle on the downs.
Think I'll go down to the beach. At 5 it was islanded by the incom-
ing tide.
(Last night, trying to read in a room full of whizzing junebugs)
Straight realistic narrative still bores me. I don't think it gives any
meaning to reality. Writing is still selective as the human mind is
selective. Therefore unless one relies on simple genius (a very
uncomforting word that should apply only to mathematicians) one
has to take a chance on infecting one's reality with meaning. Capturing the nostalgia for the kingdom, the love of light that is art.

Does that sound like a sermon on Higher Things?
Look at this/that way: the estuary and the meadows are out there.
Meaningless, complete in themselves. But to each life lived near
them they have a terrific relevance, visual or otherwise. For me
they are a kind of 23rd psalm comfort. For others, they are a place
to fish or to clam or to wander, or just home. They do exist purely
and simply, not only in the mind of God, or else whenever God has
a nervous breakdown they must go away. But just as it is fatal to for-

get that landscape is there, it is also fatal to pretend that anything can exist before a human mind without being interpreted by that consciousness. One of the ways of making fiction out of consciousness is to pretend to have an other consciousness and expel that consciousness's perceptions, which I don't do much. That's doing voices. I'd rather see authors doing their own voices, not pretending to be fishermen and farmers unless they bloody well know what fishermen and farmers think. (not pretending to be bears, either). I suppose that leads to an anthropological view of history which is dangerous and racist but it's also kind of honest. It means finally admitting that most literature is middle class and that most personae are oneself.

Well, does the reader really want the perceptions of a sophisticated city person perceiving a rural pond? Yes, if the words are painted on skillfully enough, and if ideas belong there too: i.e. Walden.

Non-fiction, though.

Fiction & The pond as the world of the snipe? The pond as part of the fishermen's life? 400 pages of pond?

I don't know. Something profound in me says Indians should write about Indians, bears about bears, farmers kids about farmers. One should not try to become anything else. Yet the masquerade has gone on for ages.

But the best masqueraders stuck to their own territory and by dealing very well with it told us something about ours: rose above it. Flaubert, Balzax Dickens, Eliot, Woolf even. You cannot escape your own arrangement with society.

THE POND IS NOT MY SUBJECT.
The pond is my subject as it relates to me (i.e. visually). It could not become any other kind of subject for me unless it was more thoroughly part of my life.

Fiction probably arises out of a need to integrate the elements of one's life in narrative form. Which is why it's so impossible to escape narrative and go into pure linguistic realms. The novel will probably always be about something more than words.

'Purism' is for the very young or the very old. Part of youth's pu[c? d?]eur before lived and messy reality. Older writers and artists refine and simplify and reach a second stage. Or eightieth, life being what it is.

I feel myself becoming less experimental, more classical, recognisin that I'm not Sterne, not Joyce. Still don't want to be Trollope, though. Others see me as turning to fantasy, I think. Don't know if I want to go there, either. What I have to do is work out a number of theories and then give myself enough psychic space (i.e. rest) ((now there's a concatenation)) to let what I have to do occur to me.

Interestingly enough I'm beginning to wake full of energy. A week here has done me a world of good. Hell, I'm gonna get restless. But that's okay too as long as I have thinking mornings, stop popping around my head like loose popcorn esp on booze. Quit being hyper. Let landscape do what Valium doesn't.
I mustn't let that energy take over. I must rest and think. Then decide where I can write the next book. If not Toronto, get the courage to take off for somewhere else. If Toronto, get decent help.

Hell, my mood just changed. I so[?] shot up and got out of the con-templative. Why? sun too hot? Can't sustain. Maybe that's enough writing for now. It's so hot at 9 that even the whirlybirds have gone back to sleep.

A little later
John and Willie have gone to be beach
Hzan stopped by to see how we are

He wanted me to go out with him. In the end we settled for Summerside tonight. I felt all bashful. He's Homer, all right but where's the bear, in Boston?
He sure is a better Homer than that jerk of Saturday night. Colbecks. If I can get up to Colbecks next week that'll be good. Certain sacrifices involved but will they be?

Hat helps.

Steppenwolf reminds of the Outsider.
Everything hangs together. (skip explaining this connection: too hard)
Wonderf there's any Plato around.

Birds do have fun. Else why is that young starling airing his armpits in the breeze?

Find my mind curling around the edges of something. What? Threw out a long letter to Peg and Graeme.[8] Often my letters are to myself. Found some short paper for short letters. Have to get it together (i.e. all papers in one place) to pay my income tax.

Wednesday

Damp and foggy. The view reduced to further foreground. Birds lower, boats blasting the air. John up early to get the 11 am ferry. Nice fellow. Telling me about Turpin's Port Dalhousie poems. Must get.

The fir trees stand out in rows. They must be spruce or hemlock ... classic maritime Christmas card trees, in rows as for windbreaks.

Yesterday I saw a woman doctoring a dying spruce tree with a bucket of stuff. Dipping branches in. Budworm?

John Ormsby has just galumphed off down the road. What a nice young man. Hooked on printing, peddling Coach House[9] books in the Maritimes, 21, together. Likes the kids – always something in a person's favour.

Sitting out on the porch. The fog is clearing but the cloud ceiling is low. Quieting effect. My friend the young starling watches from the wire. Sometimes his cry is quite sweet. I had forgotten starlings were mimics. Will he try being a typewriter?

Re: leaving Toronto. In theory a great idea. If a bldg in Charlottetown were available at a great price I might try. But reading the paper remember that it's Sarnia 30 years ago. The mentality is small. The kids are used to something bigger. School is shorter, probably tougher. Talk to Fran and Ron, Vern and Marlene. Certainly you can't live in To the way you did last year; and maybe you've run through it. But don't
Ctown is a small town, almost in another country (is that its appeal) and don't romanticise it. Winters are bloody awful, too.

You can't live on a farm by yourself with the kids.

Title for Story: Postmen do not pick up histchhikers.

If Toronto were possible again, how? Much, much more silence. Good babysitter. Better rules. You can't do all the things you used to do without domestic help any more. Lunch circuit doesn't work with the kids coming home. You have virtually no evening life except the library board. You go out of your mind with worry because where you want to be and where you're supposed to be never jibe. Therefore: good help.

But it would be so much easier down here! Hardly any phone calls, an easier town to get around and if nothing was going on for you you'd know most of the other people were in the same boat. You wouldn't sit there feeling everything go on for the others and not for you. You had all that superficial social life while it was going on, now you feel left out. Don't be perverse.

Goodness, a goldfinch. Forgotten their dippy flight.

Loneliness of moving, knowing no one. God, that was hard this Christmas.
Could you afford to move? Would it really lower the overhead? Don't worry too much about money: worry about increasing your cool and the quality of your life, I mean improving that. I mean, not worrying so much, stretching out, enjoying. Why do you feel less imprisoned here than there? There's no where to go, here. You'll get bushed.

No telephone, though, and no existential whim-whams.
Got into 2 this week didn't you? No, those were circumstantoial dealt with easily.

Goodness, starlings raiding the sparrows' nest. No wonder he scolds.

8 a.m. Thursday 24 June hot and hazy

Ugh. I drank the wine last night. Baddish head and baddish con-science, but I found out some things about drinking.
My compulsions really are verbal: I started drinking and then wrote letters for hours. It was like the obsessive talking I do at home, esp into the telephone. But more controlled

But booze isn't much good as a tension reliever. It knots me up. It's good for the verbosity but it doesn't do much for the psyche, I notice. Got all very Shelleyan and hectic but that's not my best key. (ah but what a splendid purgative.)

Loneliness: I love it, here. After about 2 hours of company I get very resentful Must orchestrate the children's day so it isn't opressive. They are getting bored with the seashore. Cripes.

One simply has to withdraw once in a while. Toronto was too much last year – all public life and no private and all the bad vibes but not any certainties in the marriage situation. Moving by myself. My God. Some friend helped but I really did it all myself. The television play was a strain. Love Jim but working under a story editor is like working in school. John was right to drop me I think but I need close contact with someone or else absolutely no one but the typewriter.

What a year: buying the house, doing 2 books, moving, getting teeth done, the play, Willie Lawson, Felbert, library board, Arnold, the Marchmount community. Cripes. A whole picaresque novel rolled into one.

The Marshallene idea would be a good one if Marshallene is an ex-nun called Sister Imelda. I could probably do is considering what Hugh[10] wrote about my play: 'if this is true, nobody has learned anything in the past 3,000 years.' I can intuit what he meant but still kind of wonder how it applies to the text. Don't dare get it out but I think it refers to the terrible cellophane wrapping of inno-cence I carry around, which must be more a manner than a reality. Or is it? I have to figure every experience out as if it's the world's first, whereas most people put experience in context.

Too hot.

Later. How gorgeous to be wakened by an idea rather than an alarm clock, even if the idea fades.

All the writers I know swing wildly back and forth between gre-gariousness and solitude. Part of the trade and not to be worried about. One must simply arrange to live so that both aspects are looked after.

Pipedream: a big old frame house near the water in Ctown. Keep it mostly as it is, live in it like an old slipper. Kids up, me down. Shabby as all hell. Put money in insulation.

June 25

The mail worked today. Letters from Mum and Arlene and a telegram from Alma saying we got the vote in Ottawa. My God. That justifies the last 3 years of tearing around, always guilty because I wasn't where the kids were. It justifies the Union's letting me have this house, too. My God, it justifies a lot of things. Mebbe even the half bottle of Scotch last night. I keep wondering if it's good for the kids to see me drinking but the fact is they see what there is to see and judge for themselves. I've never been able to put them away.

How does the ribbon turner work? Mebbe with this thing? Close it up and hoe for the best. Hope. Hope. Yep, it worked.

Off the point.

I have often wondered about the usefulness of PLR (now called Authors' Compensation) but I'm sure it's a form of social justice and I know it's much needed. I can, for instance, now make a good living out of writing, but not out of my best writing, and furthermore making that good living is so tiring that it freaks me write out. Most of us need to live solitary lives most of the time, and the costs are high. The reason that the living is hard to make is beyond a doubt because this is not a book-buying culture. Even I feel slightly guilty at buying new hard-bound books. We get our new hard-bounds at the library and the reserve lists are long for new successful books. The libraries do not buy as heavily in Canadian materials as they claim, but they sure distribute what they have. Now, if faulkner keeps his promise and we get the money we'll have the basis for various kinds of social benefits as well as the annual payment for use. Three or four hundred a year isn't much but it pays one's taxes or one's drink or one's dentist bill: better by far than nothing.

Must stop this and write Alma, tell her to form a collection society instanter.

26 June

Woke earle again but cold and too lazy to write. To my horror Will got up, but he brought me coffee and I went back to sleep.

I always seem to think of good things first in the morning here. I worked out the drinking thing, how one feels freer and warmer and copes better with people but I think they gradually for me at least become smaller and objectified and I grow larger. They are more manageable at one stage but as they are also objects it is easier to insult them or be grossly sentimental with them. Eventually I guess they become Lilliputians and then crawly things. I seem to objectify in ordinary life with great difficulty – I am always afloat in involvement, in my own feeling of inferiority. Booze changes this. Unfortunately it is now changing a good deal more, as my thirst increases and my liver wears out.

Awful lecture on this from Willy Lawson this winter. Gosh, that hurt. I always felt he knew a lot but hadn't lived long enough to be tolerant. I needed him because I was so lost and he was so helpful, but when he laid one of his puritanical numbers on it really hurt. He did as Charlotte said look like Jesus.

It's my diffidence that allows me to allow people in to run my life. Fortunately, it doesn't extend so far it's incurable. I'm pretty certain when I've had enough sleep.
And sleep is such bliss here!
A real gale last night, buckets of rain, thunder, howling wind. We sat in the kitchen and read Sinbad the Sailor. They loved it. Sud-

denly, we were together again, and I was useful, Charlotte read very well when my voice gave out. Rummy, stories ... it reminded me of happy times at Red Bay. We felt so warm and secure in that trailer at night.

But am I just avoiding the outside world? Well, why the hell not, for a while? Need to.

Monday no Sunday June 28

Raining, and cold with it. In fact, a dismal day. Woke early, went back to sleep. When I woke again I made up stories about Imelda. Some of them are funny and sweet and they range over one's Toronto experience all right but would they be anything but drudgery to write? One must give Imelda some other excellent virtue besides innocence: a knowing eye, I guess.

I drank the rest of whisky yesterday; it was good, relaxing. Turned me on, removed care. Then the kids and I read Sinbad in bed and turned in. Also made Will ground ivy tea for his stomach!

Place is a mess today.

They went out last night; I stayed firmly home. Sure enough the funny man came calling. I locked the doors and sent him home. He went. Last chance for a boyfriend in Cape Traverse, Mary Ann! But with the kids around like this?

Dreamt about some official dinner, and visiting the McGibbons and Howard who turned about to be Jas Lorimer. Same core of righteousness there. Think he turned into Ted Whittaker too. Dreams apparently can point out similarities.

About liberation: I'm redefining myself as most women are who have lived with men for long periods and then broken up. The pain is in deciding who you are without reference to that other person, who, having decided whom he wanted you to be forced that image on you. I am further on with the project than I was last year but having decided that I am a) a writer whether I now want to be one or not and 2) heterosexual and lusty doesn't do me much good as there isn't a man around and I'm too set in my ways to go out and look for one in the normal way. Also those who say writers can't live with men may be right. I think I should have my house and my kids but also some efficient method of escape from them as they dominate the scene and much as I love them except in these kinds of holiday times they aren't enough. What I'm enjoying now is enjoying them, however.

Ha. My brain sings with Imelda. How did she meet Liquid Louie? What are the time sequences? She joined the Eglantines when she was 20, an Anglican order in London 8. Coming out of the anglican manse after discussing the matter with Father Cunningham, whose head soared higher and higher as she talked, she met Asher Bowen; ten years later at Holy Trinity, as the K's babysitter, she meets Asher again. He is a lawyer, son of the sheriff of her county. They married, have a son called Charles, whom she calls Chummy. When he is 5 Asher bungs him off to boarding school and runs for legislature. She helps Asher but misses the child and, firmly separated from him, sees the political scene for what it is. Begins, in the gallery of the legislature, a political reporter called Charles, a liaison with, I mean. She has also, briefly and under the influence, had an affair with Asher's manager Talkind. Talkind finds out about Charles; Asher offers her a quiet divorce-separation naming no one if she'll just go away. Compares politics to the war saying she should have waited for him to come home. She's on the loose again. Works for a magazine, finds that other people live quite differently and breaks down quite completely when Asher introduces her to Katie, his new girl, who looks like her 20 years ago, but is of better class. Sent to Windsor for the magazine to interview a writer, she crosses and spends the night with Louie. Then heads up to the ferry house, which had been her uncle's but which Asher owns. There she runs into two hippies, Oliver and Blake, who introduce her to the joys of pot and buggery. Oliver decides to rebuild the house and over her protests does so. If furious when she says she can't pay, nearly burns it down. Asher's secretary Amabel comes up and spends a couple of nights. Katie is pregnant. Asher will pay a good deal for a quick divorce and also wants her to take Chummie, who has had a breakdown at school. She goes back to Toronto and arranges all this ...

No philosophy: book must be all events and surfaces. The wisdom is in the adventures. Imelda grows by her deceptions but never loses her innocence and enthusiasm.

Monday. Crabby, I am. But oh, my goodness, why can't they play outside on a fine day like this? I'm guilty because I've been crabby, but gosh, they wrote letters all morning. Hey mum, how do you spell ... and the T[imes] L[iterary] S[upplement] had just come.

I try to restrict their hours so I can write too. It doesn't work. My job is to be Mrs. Available and it frustrates me. I can't remember Ma as Mrs Available. She was a better manager.

Bitch bitch bit.

I read this stuff over. Like some of it. Some doesn't connect, but the transparent effect I wanted is there.

I've started Imelda. For eight pages it works. Mustn't talk about it any more.

Glorious, the sun, now. And the breeze. Perfect. I put the table in it between the house and the broken down shingled shed. Tee shirts and underpants, badly handwashed, flap on the line. On the oil stove the tea towels are cooking. Haven't boiled laundry since Europe.

TLS review talks of George Sand as dishonest. I wonder. The romantic romanticised but is it her fault? Haven't read enough of her. Perhaps men are right: they see her as maternal but unwilling to be married, a controller. Well, most of us are like that. We want to have kids, sure but we don't want to be men's children all the time. The shrinks are right that the ideal relationship involves parenting, being a child, being an equal. She hadn't had good experiences of being a child. Forgotten who her father was but her big grandmother brought her up. The male parent figures in her life were lgendary heroes. The real males were weak. She set out to rec-reate the pattern. Michel de Bourges wasn't any kid of hers, how-ever. Reviewer is right to talk of the hypocrisy of other romantic solutions in novels but she probably couldn't get away with more than she did. I guess I protect her because she fought a lot of my battles for me. More anyway than Mrs. Browning.

Where shall I find my Nohant and my Musset.

Well, I've had him!

Enough of all this thinking. I've just made myself a bandanna top out of Mum's red silk scarf. Char thinks it indecent and in truth it's not pretty but it puts wind on my skin, better than silk. Will has just peddled off in a winter pullover! I've seen people tie bandanna around themselves better, thogxx though.

Maybe you can't write and look after kids and have a husband too. Maybe Anne's right: that's it. But you can have a fighting try. Because writing isn't living and living alone with kids isn't always living; so one has got to go on trying to find ... people. Even birds come in pairs.

Splendeurs et miseres ... one tries hard to forget they come together.

Later: reading Northrop Frye: fine stuff. Got my head back again and am happy, whether this is good or not.

30 June

How remarkably unterritorial of Libby to lend out her house. It's
full of nice things, too. Herbals and little arrangements of dried
flowers. Rat jelly posters all over: coach house press things. Shelves
and signs and floats. Curtains of old faded country material, just as
they should be.

Not in good shape today. Into the Scotch again last night, dammit.
Guilt. Kids were very nice, I must say.

Why can't I content myself with the view? The wild madder is
green foam in the ditches and when you look down every blade of
grass salutes.

Read a piece in the TLS about a poet called Celan[11] I'd never
heard of. He went from Heidegger to word-coining. Steiner thinks
him better than Rilke. High praise. Sounds like my meat but I
could never do him in German.

The weather is bad and, yes, I'm bored. Want to be active. Waiting
for one of the cars on the road to be for us. Worrying about what
happened to Pat. With the air strike I'll probably never find out.

Charlotte's just left Colonel Sanders to watch over me in the doorway. Such saints we have now.
    Imelda still appears. Wonderf I could get some of the writers'
Union experience in there: Northern Journey, librarians, my own
unwillingness to publish documents. Must write to Gwen and to
Liz and Bob.

2 July

Yesterday was vile, wet and grumpy. Ended up tantrumous. Argh. I
read RIP 7, which covers a lot of Toronto at least, then started a
Hornblower, for my sins. Baked all day. Children bickered. Hazen

dropped by with a slurp of ginjuice. We watched a lot of tv and read a lot of Aladdin Cooked the rest of the meat which had gone off. W. was totally uncooperative. Better day today, surely, as it is warmer.

Where's my lovely headspace gone? Dunno. Don't care. What's headspace anyhow? The acid vocabulary is dangerous. I suppose I mean contemplativeness if there's such a word.

NOTES

The material from Engel's diary is printed with permission from Ms Charlotte Engel, Marian Engel's daughter, and from McMaster University's Mills Memorial Library, Division of Archives and Research Collections. Her papers in the Marian Engel Archive, Ready Division, Mills Memorial Library.

1 *Bear* (Toronto: McClelland and Stewart, 1976).
2 *The Glassy Sea* (Toronto: McClelland and Stewart, 1978); the story is from the collection *The Tattooed Woman* (Toronto: Penguin, 1985).
3 *Chatelaine*, October 1973.
4 Marian Engel Archives, Box 33, File 102, 'Public Psychologising,' 1984.
5 *Glassy Sea*, 17.
6 For a book-length study of Engel's life and work, see Christl Verduyn, *Lifelines: Marian Engel's Writings* (Montreal: McGill-Queen's University Press, 1995). Verduyn edited a volume of Engel's correspondence with Hugh MacLennan (*Dear Marian, Dear Hugh: The MacLennan–Engel Correspondence* [Ottawa: University of Ottawa Press, 1995]). More recently, she prepared an edition of Engel's notebooks (*Marian Engel's Notebooks: 'ah, mon cahier, ecoute ...'* [Waterloo, ON: Wilfrid Laurier University Press, 1999]).
7 Carroll Klein, 'Interview with Marian Engel,' *Room of One's Own 9*, no. 2 (1984): 5–30.
8 This is Margaret Atwood and her partner, novelist Graeme Gibson.

Engel was one of the subjects Gibson interviewed for his book *Eleven Canadian Novelists* (Toronto: Anansi, 1973). Engel was also good friends with Margaret Laurence and Adele Wiseman.

9   Coach House Press was a daring new enterprise, a small press that featured works by new, young Canadian writers. People such as John Ormsby were busy selling those early volumes, promoting them with posters of some of the cover art from the books, such as the colourful pieman from the cover of Michael Ondaatje's poetry collection *Rat Jelly* (1973), referred to later in the excerpt.

10   The novelist Hugh MacLennan supervised Engel's Master's thesis on the Canadian novel and encouraged her efforts to write. They remained friends and corresponded for more than a decade. His letters to her are held in Marian Engel Archives at McMaster University. In his letters, MacLennan frequently mentioned his late wife, Dorothy, whose diary is also featured in this collection. Once he wrote of how sad he felt to think of 'the terrible loss to Dorothy in her own life during all those years' (4 September 1957). Another time, he commended his wife's sharp mind: 'It was Dorothy, an American, who explicitly told me that my basic trouble was not knowing where I belonged, and who explicitly said that this was the trouble with all the Canadians she knew. She saw it from the outside and, as you know, she wrote about it' (10 July 1957).

11   Paul Celan (1920–70) was a Romanian poet who survived the Holocaust and later committed suicide in Paris.

PART SIX:
REFLECTIVE ENDINGS

Mary Eidse Friesen

(1923–1996)

JULIE C. CHYCHOTA

My grandmother, Mary E. Friesen, was born 28 January 1923, a half hour ahead of her identical twin sister, Annie. Mary was the seventh of eleven children born to Abram K. and Anna I. (née Bartel) Eidse, although four of her siblings (including twin boys) died in infancy and early childhood, leaving Mary the third oldest of the surviving seven. Her parents farmed in Rosenhoff, a small Mennonite community (later renamed Riverside) in Manitoba, south of Winnipeg.

On 1 October 1944, at the age of twenty-one, Mary Eidse married Pete S. Friesen (born 3 September 1924), son of C.T. and Mary (née Siemens) Friesen, while her twin sister and close confidante, Annie, married Frank K. Kroeker in a double-wedding ceremony. The twins chose to wear light blue dresses, since at that time the Kleinegemeinde church to which they belonged believed that the colour white imbued its wearers with excessive pride.[1] In the first ten years of marriage, Mary divided her time between tending three children (Diana, b. 12 July 1945; Dennis, b. 5 April 1947; Larry, b. 18 October 1948), milking two cows every evening, cooking, canning and preserving, cleaning, and laundering. These first ten years of married life were physically demanding and financially difficult for Pete and Mary. At some point after the birth of her third child, Mary miscarried a baby boy. Miscarriages, still births,

and infant deaths were common occurrences; like pregnancy, however, miscarriage was rarely discussed, so it was only many years
afterwards that Mary first mentioned this son to her other children.
She recounted that the tiny baby, his features perfectly distinguish-
able, perfectly formed, had been small enough to tuck into a
matchbox, and that Pete had buried it beneath a willow tree. Their
next child was born in 1956 (Lon, b. 4 July). Pregnant for a sixth
time, Mary once again miscarried. She explained that an exceptionally loud clap of thunder during a storm had startled her and
led to her second miscarriage (again a boy). A second daughter
(Gwen, b. 16 October 1962) completed the Friesen family.

Shortly before Christmas 1989, my grandfather was admitted
into the palliative care unit at the St Boniface Hospital in Winnipeg. The following diary entries chronicle his death on 29 January (one day after my grandmother's sixty-seventh birthday) after a
three-year struggle with cancer. Despite the strain of little sleep,
the constant shuttling back and forth to Winnipeg (a forty-five-
minute drive north of Riverside), and all the mixed emotions that
arise from witnessing a loved one's suffering, Mary still managed to
be thankful. Almost every one of her entries for 1990 begins with
the words, 'Thank you, Lord,' or incorporates expressions of thanks
to her children, grandchildren, or neighbours. Rarely does she
dwell upon the intense loneliness she must have felt, choosing,
instead, to remember all the ways in which she kept her mind
occupied on any given day. When she does admit to grieving, she is
given to understatement. For example, she writes 18 February
1990: 'I listened to Pete's Funeral tape. Had my 1st. good cry. Then
was comforted.'

Some recent Mennonite writing – the poems of Di Brandt and
Patrick Friesen, or Heidi Harms's and Katherine Martens's collection of interviews with Mennonite women regarding childbirth, for
instance – has focused on the negative tensions that arise from a
tightly bound religious community. The pages of Mary's journals,
however, contain glimpses of the positive qualities of a close (as
opposed to closed) southern Manitoba community. The personal

manner in which Mary applies the words of the Bible to her own life recall the very reason why her ancestors, three generations before her, emigrated from Russia to Canada: the promise that they could live out their beliefs (pacifism, in particular) without the threat of government opposition or persecution. Mary's words speak powerfully of the rural roots of many Canadian families: hard-working individuals, hopeful in the face of adversity, rallying around family and friends, and exemplifying a faith in a God who is not distant and abstractly paternal, but who cares deeply for the created world, a God involved in every facet of one's life.

In her meticulous handwriting, Mary would, as a rule, draft a rough copy of each day's entry, and then transcribe it into a pocket-sized book. She often remarked that she didn't think anybody would be very interested in her journals: it seems that the need to record, to articulate her experiences for herself, was the prime reason for keeping her diary. Yet there is always an underlying sense that Mary anticipated her reader(s), because it is not uncommon to find a list of visitors she had received that day, followed by a 'Thanks for coming!' (5 April 1990), or 'Thanks to all of you!' (10 April 1990). Over the years, Mary managed to fill with journal entries a total of sixteen small books: many are written in 6-by-4½-inch hard-cover diaries meant to cover one year, while others are contained in yearly appointment books. She may have purchased them at one of the rural grocery stores, or at any one of a number of Winnipeg stores that carried stationery supplies, for these were readily available commercial items. (The books she chose as diaries were manufactured by Rownline in Toronto and by Hutchings and Patrick in Ottawa.) The space allotted dictated the length of Mary's daily entries: in a one-year diary, for instance, each day receives a whole page, while in an appointment-book journal a day is given only half a page. Because Mary usually drafted each entry first on small sheets of note paper, the writing in the journals is of consistent size and quality. In a relatively compact space, Mary inserted a surprising amount of detail. Near the top of the page she habitually entered the day of the week, the temperature for that day, and a sentence or two that either summarized the highlights of that day, or served as a quick-reference guide for those events she anticipated she might return to in the future.

The diary excerpts that follow reveal that Mary found joy in the company of visitors and in the ordinary, daily objects and tasks around her. As I read through the entries, I am reminded of Carol Shields's words in *Swann*: 'Dailiness to be sure has its hard deposits of ennui, but it is also ... redemptive.'[2] When Grandma used to telephone my mother, if I happened to answer, we would play out a familiar dialogue: She would ask me what I had done that day, then I'd reciprocate by asking her what she was doing. Quite frequently she would reply that she had done some gardening or housecleaning, put up some storm windows or screen windows, and then she would inform me, 'nu vell ech noch um bessja on-shrieve,' which translates from the Low German as 'now I want to write a little bit [in my diary].'

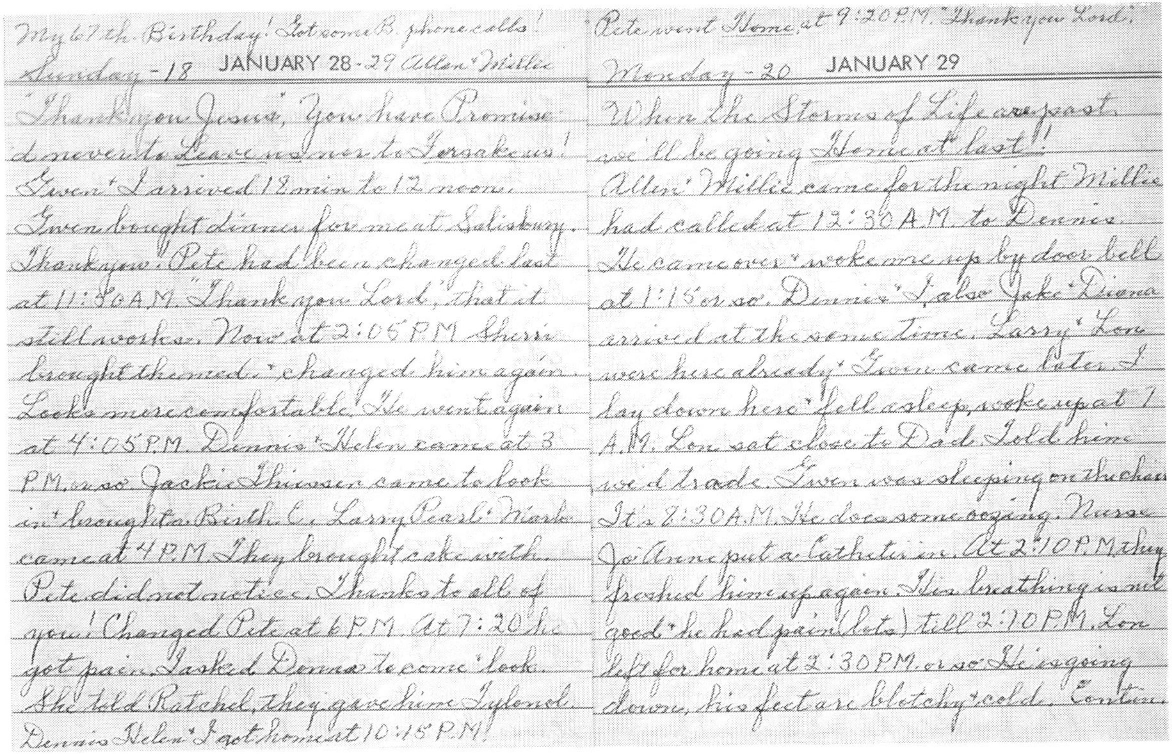

Excerpt from the diary of Mary Friesen, 1990.

DIARY, MANITOBA,
JANUARY–FEBRUARY 1990

My 67th. Birthday! Got some B.[birthday] phone calls!
Sunday −18³ January 28–29 [1990]   Allan & Millie
'Thank you Jesus,' You have Promised never to *Leave us* nor to *Forsake us*! Gwen & I arrived 18 min to 12 noon. Gwen bought dinner for me at Salisbury. Thank you! Pete had been changed last at 11:50 A.M. 'Thank you Lord,' that it still works. Now at 2:05 P.M. Sherri brought the med.[medication] & changed him again. Looks more comfortable. He went again at 4:05 P.M. Dennis & Helen came at 3 P.M. or so. Jackie Thiessen came to look in & brought a Birth.[day] C.[ard] Larry Pearl & Mark came at 4 P.M. They brought cake with. Pete did not notice. Thanks to all of you! Changed Pete at 6 P.M. At 7:20 he got pain. I asked Donna to come & look. She told Ratchel, they gave him Tylonol. Dennis Helen & I got home at 10:15 P.M.

Pete went *Home* at 9:20 P.M. 'Thank You Lord.'
Monday −20 January 29
When the Storms of Life are past, we'll be going *Home at last*! Allen & Millie came for the night. Millie had called at 12:30 A.M. to Dennis. He came over & woke me up by door bell at 1:15 or so. Dennis & I, also Jake & Diana arrived at the same time. Larry & Lon were here already & Gwen came later. I lay down here & fell asleep, woke up at 7 A.M. Lon sat close to Dad. Told him we'd trade. Gwen was sleeping on the chair. It's 8:30 A.M. He does some oozing [dozing?]. Nurse Jo-Anne put a Catheter in. At 2:10 P.M. they freshed him up again. His breathing is not good & he had pain (lots) till 2:10 P.M. Lon left for home at 2:30 P.M. or so. He is going down, his feet are blotchy & cold. Contin. [Insert – 3 × 5″ page of looseleaf:]
Jan. 29th. 1990. Continued. Pete died at 9:20 P.M. 'Thank you Lord,' for taking him Home. Before that Ed Laura & Susan came. The plan was that Susan would come home with Pearl & me at 6 P.M. God's plan was different tho'. We had a real snowstorm this evening. Dennis & Helen came also, hadn't been too bad then, but

later it was very stormy. Helen Wpg. came also. She left about 15
min. before Pete died. Helen Laura & I were in the room when his
breathing changed. Laura quickly [on reverse side of insert: Pete
had to throw up at around 6:10 or so P.M. For the last time!] went
to tell Dennis, Ed, Pearl & Susan to come. They came & saw. Then
somebody told the Nurses. They came & put his teeth in & did
other things. We all stayed in the Lounge for night. Couldn't sleep
tho'. Got home at ¼ to 7 A.M. on Jan. 30th. Tues.
Jan. 29th. The Chaplain Ladie came in to talk to Pete & Pray for
him, & to comfort me. Thank you! Pete passed away Peacefully.

Frank & Marge brought a big pot of soup & brown bread. Thank
you!
Tuesday −25 January 30
'Thank you Lord,' for All Your Special Love & Grace, & for Seeing
Pete thro'! We got home at 7:15 A.M. from Wpg. Slept for about 2
hrs. Got up & felt much better, neck ache was gone. 'Thank you
Lord.' We planned a meeting for 10 A.M. for the Funeral arrangements. Frank & Marge came. Later Cornie & Tina also. In the
afternoon we went to The Morris Funeral Home, to make arrangments & also bring Pete's clothing with. Went to Burke's for coffee.
Came home & made more arrangments. Larry & Lon worked on
the Obituary. Cornie had done some of it. Thank you! Helen looks
after the singing. Pat after the food & servers. Laura brought
Chicken soup & apple pie for supper, was very good! Rick &
Lavina visited here this evening.

'Lord,' You have seen him thro', Thank you!
Wednesday −20 January 31
'Thank you Lord,' that You have kept Pete 'Safely in Your Care,' to
the very End! Helpers & visitors: Bill Schellenberg came to see if
we needed help. Cornie came for the Obituary, it was not ready yet.
Jake & Diana & Larry came over. Diana helped Gwen. Gwen left
this afternoon for Morden. Jake fixed the bathroom door down-

stairs. Larry put new batteries into our Tel. & Lon reprogramed it this evening. Afternoon we went to see Dad at the Funeral Home. We think he looks pretty good compared to what he did in the Hospital after his death. Just had to hurry on. I did a load of laundry & some items by hand. Yesterday the boys carried Pete's bed upstairs. They began working on my new dresser. Seting it up for use.

Frank, Gertie & Kim came at ¼ to 5 P.M. They came over for a short visit. Thank you!

Thursday   −29   February 1

'Thank you Lord,' for All Your Love, Grace, Patience & Care upon us! Lon came over & worked with papers. I washed a few items by hand. Dennis & Helen, Jake & Diana, and Bill & Glenn set the tables at Church for tomorrow. Jake & Diana brought dinner with. Pizza & chicken. Had a good pie from Lori Rempel. Thanks! Jake & Larry put up the light fixchures that we received for Christmas from our family. Dennis & Lon went to the Credit U. for some business. Diana corrected Gwen's papers. Visited & had an early coffee break. I took an early bath & want to get dressed for the viewing of Pete at the Morris Funeral Home. After the viewing most of Pete's family came over for a visit & lunch. Was good. Thank you!

Pete's Funeral day! Wonderful Message!

Friday   −25   February 2 1990.

'Thank you Lord,' for 'Taking Complete Care,' of all of us! Had my devotions, & did the usual. All our family came over. Tina & Sharon brought us lots of soup (chicken) & meat, lots of open faced buns, & tarts for dinner. Was very good. Thank you! Gwen took me with to the Funeral. All people were so good & 'God's Grace,' was best of all. Met our Laotian people before going into the basement.[4] God's Grace was Sufficient for me. Thank you! Met a lot of our friends that came. Everything was well taken care of. Lots & lots of flowers, & lots to eat. I was home at almost 6 P.M.

Tired but 'Thankful,' that Pete's suffering was over *forever!* Our family & Ed & Laura brought the flowers with. The Lord undertook for us, Wonderfully!

NOTES

Mary Eidse Friesen's diary is in the private collection of Julie Chychota and the Friesen family.

1 Back in Russia, some generations before Mary's time, members of the *Kleinegemeinde* (or 'small congregation'), a splinter group of the *Großegemeinde* ('large congregation'), took exception to the more liberal beliefs and practices condoned by the larger Mennonite church body. Like many fundamentalists, *Kleinegemeinder* theoretically eschewed the 'liberal' practices of smoking, social drinking, and dancing; more ludicrous were the prohibitions against such activities as playing hockey, owning two-tone cars, wearing jewellery (excepting watches), and yodelling. Such prohibitions stayed in effect until the early 1950s, at which time the Rosenhoff/Riverside church was rechristened the Rosenort Evangelical Mennonite Church.

2 Carol Shields, *Swann: A Literary Mystery* (1987; Toronto: Stoddart, 1993), 22.

3 The number immediately following the day of the week records the temperature.

4 The Rosenort church sponsored a family from Laos during the early 1980s. Pete and Mary and a few other church couples volunteered to assist the new immigrants obtaining necessary documentation (drivers' licences, citizenship papers, health cards), and other such matters designed to make their transition to Canada easier.

Edna Staebler
(1906–)

JUDITH MILLER

Edna Staebler started writing in her journal when she was sixteen, coming of age in Kitchener, Ontario. Now in her mid-nineties, she can reflect on a long, distinguished writing career from her home west of Waterloo. She and Mally, her cat, live in a small cottage surrounded by helpful and supportive neighbours.

When she talks about her youthful diary-writing, Staebler blushes, recalling its sentimental tone and emphasis on boyfriends. It was not long, though, before her journal transformed itself, proving a valuable aid to a woman who wanted to write; in it, she found her own voice. At the University of Toronto during the 1920s and after graduation in 1929, Staebler knew that she wanted to be a writer, but the voices around her were discouraging. Her mother told her she would never be a writer because she lacked the talent. Her young husband scoffed at her ambitions and thought she should play bridge in the afternoon like the other wives. She wrote anyway – articles for *Maclean's*, *Chatelaine*, *Saturday Night*, and *Reader's Digest*, for example – and in 1950 received the Canadian Women's Press Club Award for Outstanding Literary Journalism.

Throughout her marriage of twenty-eight years and its breakdown, Staebler turned to her journal for consolation, as a place of introspection, to write out the pain and confusion. At other times, diary writing was not as compelling. When she was working on assignments for *Maclean's* or gathering material for and re-working what was to be *Cape Breton Harbour*, Edna wrote only sporadically. 'I didn't need to,' she says. 'I was happy doing the writing I wanted to do.'[1] During those times, diary entries appear when there was something to think through.

Edna began writing her journal in a seven-by-ten-inch science looseleaf notebook with firm covers that she propped against her knees when writing. She still uses the same notebook. In the 1950s, when she became concerned that she could no longer get paper properly cut and punched to fit, Edna asked a friend at Merchant Printing Company in Kitchener what to do. He supplied her with a great pile of paper about two feet high. She thought she would never use it up, but she did. Twice since she has had paper cut to size at the St Jacobs Printery.

The sporadic writing in her journal dwindled as Edna became more and more involved in her writing career. Writing, research, book tours, media interviews, and appearances took up most of her time. Her best-known books are the 'schmecks' cookbooks – *Food that Really Schmecks, More Food That Really Schmecks, Schmecks Appeal* – lively works full of recipes, anecdotes, confession, local lore, and folk wisdom.[2] When she was given an honorary doctorate at Wilfrid Laurier University, John Weir, the university president, introduced her by saying that 'Edna Staebler almost single-handedly raised life in Waterloo County to near mythical status.'

Edna's is a clear example of postmodernist writing, long before it was fashionable. She grounds her work in her local area, but creates a national and international audience. She makes room for voices from the margins. She works with fragments drawn together into a pleasing whole. Her writing has a clear voice. She works in genres that have been marginalized – personal essays, journalism, cookbooks, and, more recently, women's letters, with the publication of her sister's letters from the fifties, *Haven't Any News: Ruby's Letters from the 50s.*[3]

As she worked on the Margaret Laurence Memorial Lecture that she delivered in May 1997 to the Writers' Union of Canada annual conference, Edna Staebler struggled to decide what to include in a talk about her 'writing life,' which then covered most of ninety years. Quite a challenge. One of the things she wondered about was how much of her reading life to include. She has known and read many of the Canadian writers of the last several decades. 'My friends keep publishing and giving me books,' she laughs. 'I have a terrible time keeping up with all the reading.'

Edna also reads all the submissions for the Edna Staebler Award for Creative Non-Fiction, established at Wilfrid Laurier University in 1989. Along with Pierre Berton and perhaps Farley Mowat, Edna is one of the originators of this kind of writing in Canada. She insists on its value and established the prize to encourage young writers who want to work in a genre other than fiction and poetry. She vividly remembers how important the Women's Press Club award was for her. Creative non-fiction combines all those skills, she declares, and research skills in addition. Certainly, the books appearing in the box for the Edna Staebler Award have been steadily improving, so one of Edna's goals is being accomplished.

In her eighty-fifth year, Edna again turned seriously to keeping a journal. The closely written pages now number over 20,000. 'It is much more out-going now,' she says. 'I write about the things that are happening, the people in my life.' She also writes about things that are troubling her, and about feuds with her siblings. 'I still use it as a place to think things through,' she confesses, 'but it is much less self-preoccupied.' Edna writes early in the morning, usually in bed, recording the events of her busy life and her pleasure in the recognition her work has finally achieved.

The excerpt from her diary was written when Edna Staebler received the Order of Canada for her contributions to Canadian literature, in 1995. It is typical of her that she enjoyed the whole process, but did not take it seriously enough to wear her hearing aid to the ceremonies. 'Speeches are hard for me to hear,' she says. She enjoyed the fun but was glad to get back to the quiet of her country home and the loveliness of its surroundings. 'I think this place is the reason I have lived so long,' she suggests. 'I rest deeply here, and I can have the quiet and concentration I need to write: when I first came here, I worried that those hills on the other side of the lake might hem me in, that this might become my whole world: but that hasn't happened.'

It certainly has not. To celebrate Edna Staebler's writing is to celebrate the unorthodox, the adventurousness of moving into writing forms like magazine articles, travel pieces, recipes, anecdotes. It is to acknowledge the validity of the genres traditionally adopted by women, such as letters and recipes. It is to understand that creative writing is found in many not-obvious places – like journals and diaries, drawers and cupboards. It is to be glad that her journal gave Edna Staebler a safe place to talk about her life and her ambitions, continuing to be good company for her – and for any reader lucky enough to see some of it.

Edna Staebler.

DIARY, ONTARIO, MAY 1996[4]

5.25 am Monday May 6/96 –

I've just written a few instructions for Judith[5] who is going to stay with Mally for the 3 days I'll be gone in Ottawa. I should phone & tell her to bring bread & fruit. There's enough other stuff if she can find it.

Yesterday – Marjorie, Jack & her friend Josephine from the Czech Republic came at 2.30 – stayed till 5. They got mice & books. Marjorie worked for 20 years on Fortune magazine as a re-searcher, & on Money Magazine after that. In the 70's, women weren't allowed to be editors or to write articles – until the women from the leading magazines went to Court to lift the discrimination ban! Incredible. It worked. The women won their point.

Josephine wanted catnip seeds to take home with her. Mally was so funny – stole mice, bit them – rolled over & turned somersaults – stole the bag of seeds from J's purse, scattered all the things on the coffee table – candies on the floor – very entertaining.

Josephine would like to be living in Canada, but she does come to Canada for several months to visit friends every year. She's such a pleasant, interesting, interested person.

Gerry, Judith, Sandra, Ralph called. TV & mice at night. Today I must pack my few necessities for Ottawa. I've made lists. Con-cerned about taking my cane. I'll be entirely dependant on hanging on to Barbie[6] or railings – etc – if I don't – but it would be a nui-sance in the planes & buses & when I must carry my flight bag.

6.25 am Friday, May 10/96 raining 10 C –

I feel as if I never will be able to record here all of the past 3 days – wonderful – wonderful, wonderful –

On Monday – here at home – I packed my New Zealand flight bag with just enough clothes for our trip to Ottawa – my long dress, my lilac suit – pyjamas – etc + CBH – & – PP[7] for the Gov Gen (in paperback because hard cover was too heavy). I talked to well-wishers on the phone.

On Tuesday the limousine came at 7.20. Barbie had driven over – & as we passed Playfords, Lois was standing at the edge of their driveway, in her long blue nightgown & dressing gown – to wave us goodbye. She looked so darling – standing there alone in the cold. We spoke of her often in the next 3 days.

Our flight to Ottawa – & a taxi to the Chateau Laurier was fine – but because every room in the hotel was booked & we arrived before check-out time we had to wait, for almost 2 hours for a room. Barbie got a wheel chair for me & wheeled me all around the main floor – ending in the Wilfrid dining room where we had lunch – a delicious seafood chowder for me, with a very friendly waitress.

Our room 167 – was long, narrow, with a very high ceiling & windows facing an inside court – no view of anything – but roof & windows of facing walls. Our walls were a very soft peach colour & we both had double beds.

I lay down to rest – felt tired – Barbie went out to explore – the Sparks St. mall, etc. I read the thinnest paperback book I could find at home to bring with me – The Girl with the Green Eyes, by Edna O'Brien – a good Irish writer. I kept reading throughout our time in the hotel room & was highly entertained by the book I'd had in a carton at home for years without reading.

We went to the Rideau1 dining room for a dinner that was so hotly spiced that we ate little of the ratatouille vegetables – Brochette of lamb was tender but the marinade also was too hot – even the potatoes seemed hot – too bad – Barbie ate little but I finished 4 large chunks of lamb – & we shared an Irish Cream dessert – that was very bland.

As we were leaving the dining room I spoke to an older gentleman at the table next to us. He was wearing an O of C lapel pin – also one that was for the Order of British Columbia he told me. His son John Bell was friendly & introduced his elegantly dressed & coiffed wife. She came from the Ivory Coast, we learned later – & Jack Bell Sr. is a philanthropist in B.C. – a former peat & cranberry farmer who has contributed generously to Vancouver's Art Gallery, Hospital & UBC – etc. – & needy individuals.

Back in our room – we read, went to bed early. I slept until

2.30 – Barbie coughed a lot – I'm concerned about her – she takes medicine & puffers – but the cough doesn't go away. Her lungs hurt & she's worried too – the Dr. said she doesn't have cancer – I said she must go to a specialist & really do something to get better. I lay awake until after 3.30 – dozed off until 6.30 –

Wednesday morning – Barbie walked out for coffee & a bun – brought back 2 Danish – for breakfast I ate crackers – & a couple of slices of Swiss Cheese Barbie had brought. We had lunch in the Rideau1 room while we watched a fashion show of Mondi sports wear being shown by slim young models who walked around the tables.

Back in our room we read, rested until 2.15, then dressed for the Grand Event. My hair is too long & looked wild – like the head of a male lion – I thought – but could simply ignore it –

In the lobby of the hotel we were greeted by a young woman & an aide de camp – a handsome tall young man wearing a scarlet jacket with lots of gold braid – most impressive. We sat in large chairs at the side of the lobby, watched the recipients & their spouses gathering – mostly older men & women – in dress of various vintages – a few very smart. At 3 we were all put into a large bus and driven to huge Rideau Hall – greeted by various members of the house staff – & separated – the recipients going into the Ambassador room – the spouses to be seated on one side of the ball room.

I'd phoned ahead last week & asked if Barbie could stay with me to steady me as I walked – OK. They called our names, lined us up, in rows – then marched us into the ball room where the camera men lined up against the wall & soon the Gov Gen & his wife & a couple of aides & priests in robes came in. O Canada was sung – not very well – 2 prayers were said by the priests – who then sat – & a young woman at a podium introduced Romeo LeBlanc the Gov Gen. His speech was brief – & in both French & English. Then he sat – & the young woman read the citation of each recipient – who then stood & walked down the aisle to the Gov Gen –

with the handsome young aide beside who stepped backward &
waited – until the next recipient was accompanied down the aisle.

The Gov Gen sat beside his wife – dressed in a long apple green
backless gown – both wearing the insignia of the Order around
their necks. When the recipient stood 5 feet in front of the Gov
Gen, he rose – the recipient bowed – & the Gov Gen greeted him
with a welcoming genuine smile & shook his – or her hand, pinned
on the Order – a beautiful medal mounted on a red & white ribbon
bow. The highest honour granted in Canada – it must always be
pinned above all other medals.

The recipient – bowed again to the GG – to his wife – then
moved across the front to a table where he/she signed a book.
There were only 9 women recipients & 36 men – Barbie came up
front with me – & I walked very well – no fear or selfconsciousness.
Throughout the whole investiture the GG was so pleasant &
friendly & genuine – as he greeted each person with his lovely
smile. He never looked bored or supercilious – as we all approached
him & were pinned.

The man sitting beside me – Wm. Tetley – a professor at McGill,
lawyer politician & expert on marine law – etc. talked to me
throughout the ceremony but I couldn't hear what he said because
I'd taken out my hearing aid.

When the investiture was over we were all invited to take a tour
of Rideau Hall with the pleasant young student guides in red jack-
ets. The Grand rooms were spacious, beautifully decorated & furnished – the long drawing room, the queen's room, the small
dining room, the GG's book-lined study – room after room – all
with paintings & portraits of former GG's & royalty.

Then down a long narrow corridor to a dazzling view from a balcony of the Green Houses – all sorts of flowers – colours – breath-
taking – it was so lovely. We walked through to another tropical
room – then back – to see more rooms of Rideau Hall – a long dining room with a table that seated 60 people – & 2 more smaller
drawing rooms. I suppose they all have their uses – certainly they
were impressive.

Then back – thro' a room with all the medals of various orders – & military awards – to the ballroom – where all the chairs had been removed – or placed round the walls – & the GG & his wife stood at one end & received all the recipients & their spouses – smiling, shaking hands very pleasantly as we lined up – but meanwhile we sat – or drank coffee or wine – and had hors d'oeuvres passed to us on big silver trays. The room was so gracious – with its very high ceilings & draped windows.

Barbie went to the washroom. I sat alone only for a second when a spectacular woman – who had received the order of Officer – came up to me & said I know you, Edna Staebler. I have all your books – & she introduced her husband who sat beside me & said he was 'into cooking,' loved reading Schmecks. His wife was Jean E. Pigott, a well known – super lady – wearing a long black skirt & a scarlet jacket, similar to the one on the aide de camp. And she cooks from Schmecks!

All thro' the investiture I felt so incredulous about me – being one of this company of great, useful Canadians, who had done much for their communities, their country. And I was one of them!

After Mrs. Pigott moved off her husband chatted with me until a glamorous young blonde woman, Donna Scott, came up to me & said she knew me too thro' my work. She said she had founded Flare magazine – & is now the Chairman of the Canada Council! She was very friendly, complimentary – & I think – on the Advisory Council that selects the recipients. More than 400 are nominated every year but only 100 or less are chosen. Her husband lingered with me. He is H. R. Farrel – from Cape Breton – & he knew CBH [*Cape Breton Harbour*] & wanted to buy a copy. I said I'd send him one & he was so pleased, wanted to send me a book in return. He kept shaking hands with me – & throughout the evening – whenever he saw me he'd shake hands again.

The whole atmosphere in the ballroom reception seemed friendly & exciting. Many people – recipients & spouses said 'Congratulations' to me – some chatted a bit. We eventually lined up to be greeted by the G.G. & his wife. I gave him my books. He seemed pleased. She was interested. Our pictures were taken to-gether. And we moved on to the old tent room where the buffet dinner was set up on long tables. There were round tables, ele-gantly set. An aide led us to ours – where I was pleased to see Tetley – who called me his 'girl friend.' He talked constantly throughout the meal. I sat between Barbie & a handsome man, Luc Beauregard – 'founding president of Canada's top public relations firms.' I wondered if I could speak to him – but I did – & through-out the meal we chatted like friends. He wondered where he could buy my books – said he'd write me a letter with his address so I could send him one. He was such a charming man.

The food was very fancy & good – the table set with beautiful crystal & silver, with a centrepiece of pale, open roses, iris, & sprays of little yellow orchids. The faded striped tent walls, ceiling, portraits – all so elegant. The whole of Rideau Hall was like that – & the flowers – huge and small arrangements in every room, every-where. I wished Norm could be there to see them. Barbie had me take her picture beside one very large arrangement. She kept tak-ing pictures of me.

We went back to the buffet tables for our desserts – served on plates with the O of C insignia in the centre & a rim of gold maple leaves. I said to the chef, 'They'd be great souvenirs.' He said, 'Expensive!' Back at our table I told my new friend Luc B about them & he said he wanted to know more. He came back with the knowledge that they were designed in the 60's when Lester Pear-son – then Prime Minister – founded the Order of Canada – & they cost $400 each! Now they cost $800. Wow!

Of course we, the taxpayers, pay for all this grandeur – but on seeing it one could not feel anything but pride.

When the dinner was over, we picked up our programmes, leather cases, with our medals & long boxes with a scroll – a large certificate to be framed – telling of our investiture in the Order of Canada.

Many people spoke to me as we were leaving – Congratula-tions – everyone seemed thrilled – I was the only person in the

'Literary Arts' category. Mr. Farrel – & Tetley shook hands with me again & again. We got into the bus & were taken back to the Chateau Laurier – & then to bed – at 9.15. Happy & excited – the most spectacular events in our lives.

Next morning – Thursday – Barbie walked out for coffee. I finished the cheese & crackers – packed my clothes. Barbie & I got our bill on TV – & went down to sit in the lobby where we were being picked up to go to a Media Club of Ottawa luncheon for me at the National Press Club.

We waited & waited – watched many people come & go. Several people spoke to us – 2 were food writers who recognized me – & over half an hour late – we were picked up in a van with 3 very old little ladies who could hardly get out of the van when we got to the N.P. Club.

There was a long table with mostly old ladies down both sides – & Melba Woelfle greeted us, sat us on one end, while she sat at the other & shouted.

I'd called Diane Cress in the morning & she was there beside me – & Gladys Arnold – also 90 whom I'd met perhaps 50 years ago when she was doing a Cdn Club speaking tour & I was our local president. I brought her home with me & we chatted about writing & later we corresponded for several years. She had been so encouraging & helpful to me then – & has since published an autobiography – which she said she'd send me. I had just started working on CBH when we met.

The lunch was good – Mennonite style – & Melba asked me to speak – but people kept talking – until I stood up. She asked me to tell them about Ruby's Letters – but the bookstore had failed to deliver copies – & it was time for us to leave for the airport.

We had a quick flight – a limo ride home thro' rain & fog. In Ottawa we saw many daffodils but few tulips – which are 2 weeks late this year.

Mally hid under the love-seat when we came in – no friendly cat greeting. Norm called. I talked to Judith & Lois – slept in my chair – unpacked my bag – after eating our Ottawa Danish & an apple from the basket of fruit Judith left for me.

NOTES

Edna Stabler's current diary is held in the private collection of Edna Staebler. Older diaries are archived at the University of Guelph.

1 All quotations from Judith Miller's interviews with Edna Staebler appear here with Staebler's permission.
2 *Food That Really Schmecks: Mennonite Country Cooking as Prepared by My Mennonite Friend, Berry Martin, My Mother, and Other Fine Cooks* (Toronto: Ryerson Press, 1968); *More Food That Really Schmecks* (Toronto: McClelland and Stewart, 1979); *Schmecks Appeal: More Mennonite Cooking* (Toronto: McClelland and Stewart, 1987).
3 *Haven't Any News: Ruby's Letters from the 50s* (Waterloo, ON: Wilfrid Laurier University Press, 1995).
4 Staebler's handwriting is not always easy to read, so after Judith Miller transcribed these entries, Edna Staebler checked them for missed or misread words. Judith takes responsibility for any errors not corrected.
5 This Judith is Judith Miller, who prepared the excerpt.
6 Barbie is Staebler's niece Barbara Wurtele.
7 *Cape Breton Harbour* (Toronto: McClelland and Steward, 1972); *Places I've Been, People I've Known: Stories from across Canada* (Toronto: McGraw-Hill Ryerson, 1990).

Select Bibliography

Books

Ahenakew, Freda, and H.C. Wolfart, eds. and trans. *Our Grandmother's Lives as Told in Their Own Words*. Saskatoon: Fifth House, 1992.

Ashley, Kathleen, Leigh Gilmore, and Gerald Peters, eds. *Autobiography and Postmodernism*. Amherst: University of Massachusetts Press, 1994.

Atwood, Margaret. *The Journals of Susanna Moodie*. Toronto: Oxford University Press, 1970.

Barclay, Florence Louisa Charlesworth. *The Rosary*. New York: Putnam, 1909.

Blodgett, Harriet. *'Capacious Hold-All': An Anthology of Englishwomen's Diary Writings*. Charlottesville: University of Virginia Press, 1991.

– *Centuries of Female Days: Englishwomen's Private Diaries*. New Brunswick, NJ: Rutgers University Press, 1988.

Brand, Dionne, with the assistance of Lois De Shield and the Immigrant Women's Placement Centre. *No Burden to Carry: Narratives of Black Working Women in Ontario, 1920s–1950s*. Toronto: Women's Press, 1991.

Bridge, Kathryn. *Henry and Self: The Private Life of Sarah Crease, 1826–1922*. Victoria: Sono Nis, 1996.

Bunkers, Suzanne. *Diaries of Girls and Women: A Midwestern American Sampler*. Madison: University of Wisconsin Press, 2001.

Bunkers, Suzanne L., and Cynthia A. Huff, eds. *Inscribing the Daily: Critical Essays on Women's Diaries*. Amherst: University of Massachusetts Press, 1996.

Buss, Helen. *Canadian Women's Autobiography in English: An Introductory Guide for Researchers and Teachers*. Ottawa: CRIAW, 1991.

– *Mapping Ourselves: Canadian Women's Autobiography in English*. Montreal. McGill-Queen's University Press, 1993.

– *Memoirs from Away: A New Found Land Girlhood*. Waterloo, ON: Wilfrid Laurier University Press, 1999.

Buss, Helen, and Marlene Kadar, eds. *Working in Women's Archives: Researching Women's Private Literature and Archival Documents*. Waterloo, ON: Wilfrid Laurier University Press, 2001.

Carter, Kathryn. *Diaries in English by Women in Canada, 1753–1995: An Annotated Bibliography*. Feminist Voices No. 4. Ottawa: CRIAW, 1997.

Chodorow, Nancy J. *Feminism and Psychoanalytic Theory*. New Haven, CT: Yale University Press, 1989.

Clarke, George Elliott, ed. *Fire on the Water: An Anthology of Black Nova Scotian Writing*. Volume 1. *Early and Modern Writers, 1785–1935*. Lawrencetown, NS: Pottersfield Press, 1991.

Conrad, Margaret. *Recording Angels: The Private Chronicles of Women from the Maritime Provinces of Canada, 1750–1950*. Ottawa: CRIAW, 1982.

Conrad, Margaret, Toni Laidlaw, and Donna Smyth. *No Place Like Home: Diaries and Letters of Nova Scotia Women, 1771–1938*. Halifax: Formac, 1988.

Crozier, Lorna. *A Saving Grace: The Collected Poems of Mrs. Bentley*. Toronto: McClelland and Stewart, 1996.

Culley, Margo. *A Day at a Time: The Diary Literature of American Women from 1764 to the Present*. New York: Feminist Press, New York University Press, 1985.

Drew, Benjamin. *The Narratives of Fugitive Slaves*. Boston: John P. Jewett, 1856; reprint, Toronto: Prospero Books, 2000.

Duncan, Dorothy. *Bluenose: A Portrait of Nova Scotia*. New York: Harper, 1942.

– *Here's to Canada*. New York: Harper, 1941.

– *Partner in Three Worlds*. New York: Harper, 1944.

– *You Can Live in an Apartment.* New York and Toronto: Farrar and Rhinehart, 1939.

Ellis, Miram Green. *Pathfinders.* N.P.: Canadian Woman's Press Club, 1956.

Engel, Marian. *Bear.* Toronto: McClelland and Stewart, 1976.

– *The Glassy Sea.* Toronto: McClelland and Stewart, 1978.

– *The Tattooed Woman.* Markham, ON: Penguin, 1985.

Faderman, Lillian. *Surpassing the Love of Men: Romantic Friendship and Love between Women from the Renaissance to the Present Day.* London: Women's Press, 1981.

Forbes, E.R. *Challenging the Regional Stereotype: Essays on the 20th Century Maritimes.* Fredericton: Acadiensis Press, 1989.

Forbes, E.R., and D.A. Muise, eds. *The Atlantic Provinces in Confederation.* Toronto: University of Toronto Press, 1993.

Fothergill, Robert A. *Private Chronicles: A Study of English Diaries.* London: Oxford University Press, 1974.

Friedan, Betty. *The Feminine Mystique.* New York: W.W. Norton, 1963.

Garvin, John W., ed. *Canadian Poets.* Rev. ed. Toronto: McClelland and Stewart, 1926.

Gerson, Carole. *Canada's Early Women Writers: Texts in English to 1859.* Ottawa: CRIAW, 1994.

Hampsten, Elizabeth. *'Read This Only to Yourself': The Private Writings of Midwestern Women, 1880–1910.* Bloomington: Indiana University Press, 1982.

Harris, Robin S., and Terry Gonçalves Harris, eds. *The Eldon House Diaries: Five Women's Views of the 19th Century.* Toronto: Champlain Society, 1994.

Hassam, Andrew. *No Privacy for Writing: Shipboard Diaries, 1852–1879.* Carlton South: Melbourne University Press, 1995.

– *Sailing to Australia: Shipboard Diaries of Nineteenth-Century British Emigrants.* Manchester: Manchester University Press, 1994.

Herriman, Dorothy Choate. *Mater Silva.* Toronto: McClelland and Stewart, 1929.

Hoffman, Frances, and Ryan Taylor. *Much to Be Done: Private Life in Ontario from Victorian Diaries.* Toronto: Natural Heritage, 1996.

Huff, Cynthia. *British Women's Diaries: A Descriptive Bibliography of Selected Nineteenth-Century Manuscripts*. New York: AMS Press, 1985.

Innis, Mary Quayle. *Mrs. Simcoe's Diary*. Toronto: Macmillan, 1971.

Jackel, Susan. *A Flannel Shirt and Liberty: British Emigrant Gentlewomen in the Canadian West, 1880–1914*. Vancouver: University of British Columbia Press, 1982.

Jameson, Anna Brownell. *Winter Studies and Summer Rambles in Canada*. Toronto: New Canadian Library, 1990.

Jelinek, Estelle, ed. *The Tradition of Women's Autobiography from Antiquity to the Present*. Boston: Twayne, 1986.

– *Women's Autobiography: Essays on Criticism*. Bloomington: Indiana University Press, 1980.

Johnston-Dean, Christina B. *The Crease Family Archives: A Record of Settlement and Service in British Columbia*. Victoria: Provincial Archives of British Columbia, 1981.

Kadar, Marlene, ed. *Essays on Life Writing: From Genre to Critical Practice*. Toronto: University of Toronto Press, 1992.

– , ed. *Reading Life Writing: An Anthology*. Toronto: Oxford University Press, 1993.

Langton, H.H., ed. *A Gentlewoman in Upper Canada: The Journals of Anne Langton*. Toronto: Irwin, 1950.

Lears, J.T. Jackson. *Fables of Abundance: A Cultural History of Advertising in America*. New York: Basic Book, 1994.

– *No Place of Grace: Antimodernism and the Transformation of American Culture, 1880–1920*. New York: Pantheon Books, 1983.

Lévesque, Andrée. *Making and Breaking the Rules: Women in Quebec, 1919–1939*. Trans. Yvonne M. Klein. Toronto: McClelland and Stewart, 1994.

Lowe, Graham. *Women in the Administrative Revolution: The Feminization of Clerical Work*. Toronto: University of Toronto Press, 1987.

McClung, Nellie. *The Second Chance*. Toronto: William Briggs, 1910.

MacEwan, Grant. *... And Mighty Women Too: Stories of Notable Western Canadian Women*. Saskatoon: Western Producer Prairie Books, 1975.

McGann, Jerome J. *The Textual Condition*. Princeton, NJ: Princeton University Press, 1991.

McKay, Ian. *The Quest of the Folk: Antimodernism and Cultural Selection in*

Twentieth-Century Nova Scotia. Montreal: McGill-Queen's University Press, 1994.

MacLeod, Margaret Arnett, ed. *The Letters of Letitia Hargrave*. Toronto: Champlain Society, 1947.

McMullen, Lorraine, ed. *Re(Dis)Covering Our Foremothers: Nineteenth-Century Canadian Women Writers*. Ottawa: University of Ottawa Press, 1990.

Mallon, Thomas. *A Book of One's Own: People and Their Diaries*. St Paul, MN: Hungry Minds, 1995.

Matthews, William. *Canadian Diaries and Autobiographies*. Berkeley: University of California Press, 1950.

Maura, Sister. *The Sisters of Charity, Halifax*. Toronto: Ryerson Press, 1956.

Melnyk, Olenka. *What's Cooking in Women's History: An Introductory Guide to Preserving Archival Records about Women*. Edmonton: Northern Alberta Women's Archives Association, n.d.

Mitchinson, Wendy. *The Nature of Their Bodies: Women and Their Doctors in Victorian Canada*. Toronto: University of Toronto Press, 1991.

Moffat, Mary Jane, and Charlotte Painter. *Revelations: Diaries of Women*. New York: Vintage, 1974.

Moffatt, Peter C. *Time Was: The Story of St Mark's Anglican Church, Port Hope*. Cobourg, ON: Haynes Printing, 1972.

Morton, Suzanne. *Ideal Surroundings: Domestic Life in a Working Class Suburb in the 1920s*. Toronto: University of Toronto Press, 1995.

Neuman, Shirley, and Smaro Kamboureli, eds. *A/Mazing Space: Writing Canadian Women Writing*. Edmonton: Longspoon/NeWest, 1986.

Omori, Annie Shepley, and Kochi Doi. *Diaries of Court Ladies of Old Japan*. New York: AMS, 1970.

Parameswaran, Uma, ed. *Quilting a New Canon: Stitching Women's Words*. Toronto: Sister Vision, 1996.

Pepin, Maureen. *Roads and Other Place Names in Langley, B.C.* Langley, BC: Langley Centennial Museum and National Exhibition Centre, 1998.

Pierson, Ruth Roach. *'They're Still Women After All': The Second World War and Canadian Womanhood*. Toronto: McClelland and Stewart, 1986.

Powell, Barbara, and Myrna Williams. *Piecing the Quilt: Sources for*

Women's History in the Saskatchewan Archives Board. Regina: Canadian Plains Research Center, 1996.

Pratt, Mary Louise. *Imperial Eyes: Travel Writing and Transculturation.* London: Routledge, 1992.

Prentice, Alison, Paula Bourne, Gail Cuthbert Brandt, Beth Light, Wendy Mitchinson, and Naomi Black. *Canadian Women: A History.* 2nd ed. Toronto: Harcourt Brace, 1996.

Prentice, Alison, and Marjorie Theobald, eds. *Women Who Taught: Perspectives on the History of Women and Teaching.* Toronto: University of Toronto Press, 1991.

Ray, Arthur J. *The Canadian Fur Trade in the Industrial Age.* Toronto: University of Toronto Press, 1990.

Reeve, Harold. *The History of Hope Township.* Cobourg, ON: Cobourg-Sentinel-Star, 1967.

Report on the Royal Commission on the Status of Women in Canada. Ottawa: Ministry of Supply and Services, 1970.

Ritchie, Joanne. *Cartographies of Silence: An Annotated Bibliography of Diaries and Reminiscences of New Brunswick Women, 1783–1980.* Feminist Voices No. 3. Ottawa: CRIAW, 1997.

Ross, Sinclair. *As for Me and My House.* Toronto: McClelland and Stewart, 1989.

Routh, Caroline. *In Style: 100 Years of Canadian Women's Fashion.* Toronto: Stoddart, 1993.

Shields, Carol. *Swann.* Toronto: Vintage, 1987.

Sissons, Constance Kerr. *John Kerr.* Toronto: Oxford University Press, 1946.

Smith, Sidonie. *A Poetics of Women's Autobiography: Marginality and the Fictions of Self-Representation.* Bloomington: Indiana University Press, 1987.

Staebler, Edna. *Haven't Any News: Ruby's Letters from the 50s.* Waterloo: Wilfrid Laurier University Press, 1995.

Stoddart, Jack, ed. *T. Eaton Co. Limited Catalogue: 1901.* Toronto: Musson, 1970.

Strong-Boag, Veronica. *The New Day Recalled: Lives of Girls and Women in English Canada, 1919–1939.* Toronto: Copp Clark Pitman, 1988.

Thompson, John H., with Allen Seager. *Canada, 1922–1939: Decades of Discord.* Toronto: McClelland and Stewart, 1985.

Van Kirk, Sylvia. 'Many Tender Ties': Women in Fur-Trade Society in Western Canada, 1670–1870. Winnipeg: Watson and Dwyer, [n.d.].

Verduyn, Cristl, ed. Dear Marian, Dear Hugh: The MacLennan–Engel Correspondence. Ottawa: University of Ottawa Press, 1995.

– Lifelines: Marian Engel's Writings. Montreal: McGill-Queen's University Press, 1995.

– Marian Engel's Notebooks: 'ah, mon cahier, ecoute ...' Waterloo, ON: Wilfrid Laurier University Press, 1999.

Vyvyan, Clara. The Ladies, the Gwich'in and the Rat: Travels on the Athabasca, Mackenzie, Rat, Porcupine, and Yukon Rivers in 1926. Ed. I.S. Maclaren and Lisa N. LaFramboise. Edmonton: University of Alberta Press, 1998.

Weintraub, William. City Unique: Montreal Days and Nights in the 1940s and '50s. Toronto: McClelland and Stewart, 1996.

Whalley, Joyce Irene. Writing Implements and Accessories: From the Roman Stylus to the Typewriter. London: David and Charles, 1975.

Whitely, Marilyn Färdig. The Life and Letters of Annie Leake Tuttle: Working for the Best. Waterloo: Wilfrid Laurier University Press, 1999.

Woods, Shirley E. Ottawa: The Capital of Canada. Toronto: Doubleday, 1980.

Zaslow, Morris. The Northward Expansion of Canada, 1914–1967. Toronto: McClelland and Stewart, 1988.

Articles

Batts, John Stuart. 'Seeking the Canadian Pepys: The Canadian Manuscript Diaries Project.' Archivaria 9 (Winter 1979–80): 125–39.

Buss, Helen. 'The Dear Domestic Circle: Frameworks of the Literary Study of Women's Personal Narratives in Archival Collections.' Studies in Canadian Literature 14, no. 1 (1980): 1–17.

Carter, Kathryn. 'The Cultural Work of Diaries in Mid-Victorian Britain.' Victorian Review 23, no. 2 (1997): 251–67.

– 'An Economy of Words: Emma Chadwick Stretch's Account Book Diary, 1859–60.' Acadiensis 29, no. 1 (1999): 43–6.

Clarke, George Elliott. 'Africana Canadiana: A Primary Bibliography of Literature by African Canadian Authors, 1785–1996/97 in English,

French, and Translation.' *Canadian Ethnic Studies* 28, no. 3 (1996): 107–209.

Conrad, Margaret. '"But Such Is Life": Growing Up in Nova Scotia in the Interwar Years.' *Journal of the Royal Nova Scotia Historical Society* 2 (1999): 1–26.

Cornelia. 'Magic Journey North to Land of Midnight Sun.' *Toronto Telegram*, 28 November 1923, 8.

Cott, Nancy. 'The Modern Woman of the 1920s, American Style.' Pp. 76–91 in *A History of Women in the West*. Volume 5. *Toward a Cultural Identity in the Twentieth Century*. Ed. Françoise Thebaud. Cambridge, MA: Belknap Press, 1994.

Danylewycz, Marta, and Alison Prentice. 'Teachers' Work: Changing Patterns and Perceptions in the Emerging School Systems of Nineteenth- and Early Twentieth-Century Central Canada.' Pp. 136–59 in *Women Who Taught: Perspectives on the History of Women and Teaching*. Ed. Alison Prentice and Marjorie Theobald. Toronto: University of Toronto Press, 1991.

Davies, Gwendolyn. 'Gendered Responses: The Seccombe Diaries.' Pp. 132–40 in *Intimate Relations: Family and Community in Planter Nova Scotia, 1759–1800*. Ed. Margaret Conrad. Fredericton: Acadiensis Press, 1995.

Duncan, Dorothy. 'Portrait of the Author,' *Mayfair*, August 1955, 56.

Ellis, Miriam Green. 'The Backyard of Canada.' *Toronto Sunday World Magazine*, 25 March 1923, 2.

– 'A Business Woman in the Far North.' *Canadian Countryman*, 12 December 1925, 15, 56.

– 'A Business Woman in the Far North – Mrs. Connibear of Fort Smith.' *Vancouver Sunday Province*, 10 April 1927, 3.

– 'The Capital of Esquimo Land.' *Manitoba Free Press*, 11 November 1922, 32.

– 'The Eskimo Presented in a New Light." *Graphic*, 30 September 1922, 484.

– 'Inoffensive Looking Eskimo Shoots His Jailer in Cold Blood, as Policeman Sleeps.' *Calgary Daily Herald*, 4 November 1922, 7.

– 'Natives in Canada's Distant North Are Learning Value of Money –

Able to Drive Shrewd Bargain with Whites.' *Vancouver Daily Province*, 18 November 1922, 27.

– 'Sports in the Far North.' *Onward: A Paper for Young Canadians* 1, no. 22, New Series (28 August 1926): 173–4.

– 'When the Eskimo Celebrates at Aklavik.' *Toronto Sunday World Magazine*, 7 January 1923, 2.

Engel, Marian. 'Housework Gives Me the Crazies.' *Chatelaine*, October 1973.

Gee, Ellen M. Thomas. 'Marriage in Nineteenth-Century Canada.' *Canadian Review of Sociology and Anthropology* 19, no. 3 (1982): 311–25.

Halpenny, Frances. 'Problems and Solutions in the *Dictionary of Canadian Biography*, 1800–1900.' Pp. 37–48 in *Re(Dis)Covering Our Foremothers: Nineteenth-Century Canadian Women Writers*. Ed. Lorraine McMullen. Ottawa: University of Ottawa Press, 1990.

Huff, Cynthia. '"The Profoundly Female, and Feminist Genre": The Diary as Feminist Practice.' *Women's Studies Quarterly* 3–4 (Winter 1989): 6–14.

Jackel, Susan. 'Canadian Women's Autobiography: A Problem of Criticism.' Pp. 97–110 in *Gynocritics: Feminist Approaches to Writing by Canadian and Québécoise Writing*. Ed. Barbara Godard. Toronto: ECW Press, 1987.

Kerr, Rosalind. 'The Flag in Her Flesh: A White Bride's Life in Fort Frances, 1901–1908.' *Tessera* 18 (1995): 20–30.

– 'Reading My Grandmother's Life from Her Letters: Constance Kerr Sissons from Adolescence to Engagement.' Pp. 79–89 in *Working in Women's Archives*. Ed. Helen M. Buss and Marlene Kadar. Waterloo, ON: Wilfrid Laurier University Press, 2001.

Leslie, Genevieve. 'Domestic Service in Canada 1880–1920.' *Women at Work 1850–1930*. Eds Janice Acton, Penny Goldsmith and Bonnie Shepard, 71–126.

McKenna, Katherine M.J. 'The Role of Women in the Establishment of Social Status in Early Upper Canada.' *Ontario History* 83, no. 3 (1990): 179–206.

MacLaren, I.S. 'Touring at High Speed: Fur-Trade Landscapes in the Writings of Frances and George Simpson.' *Musk-Ox* 34 (1986): 78–87.

MacLennan, Hugh. 'Portrait of an Artist: Dorothy Duncan,' *The Montrealer*, June 1957, 40.

Motz, Marilyn Ferris. 'Folk Expressions of Time and Place: 19th-Century Midwestern Rural Diaries.' *Journal of American Folklore* (April–June 1987): 131–47.

Powell, Barbara. 'The Diaries of the Crease Family Women.' *BC Studies* 105–6 (Spring/Summer 1995): 45–58.

– 'Discourse and Decorum: Women's Diaries in Nineteenth-Century Canada.' Pp. 335–46 in *Quilting a New Canon: Stitching Women's Words*. Ed. Uma Parmeswaran. Toronto: Sister Vision, 1996.

– 'Meals and Manners: Women and Language in Upper Canada.' *Textual Studies in Canada* 1, no. 1 (1991): 77–92.

– 'Nineteenth-Century Young Women's Diaries.' *Canadian Children's Literature* 65 (1992): 68–80.

Smith-Rosenberg, Carroll. 'The Female World of Love and Ritual: Relations between Women in Nineteenth-Century America.' *Signs* 1, no. 1 (1975). Reprinted pp. 53–76 in *Disorderly Conduct: Visions of Gender in Victorian America*. New York: Oxford University Press, 1985.

Strong-Boag, Veronica. 'The Girl of the New Day: Canadian Working Women in the 1920s,' *Labour/Le Travailleur* (1979): 131–64.

– 'Raising Clio's Consciousness: Women's History and Literature.' *Archivaria* 6 (Summer 1978): 70–82.

Struan, Bev. 1932. 'It's a Neighborly Land.' *Canadian Magazine* 77 (March): 20, 28.

Thomas, Clara, Carol Shields, and Donna E. Smyth. '"Thinking Back through Our Mothers": Tradition in Canadian Women's Writing.' Pp. 5–21 in *Re(Dis)Covering Our Foremothers: Nineteenth-Century Canadian Women Writers*. Ed. Lorraine McMullen. Ottawa: University of Ottawa Press, 1990.

Van Kirk, Sylvia. 'Frances Ramsay Simpson.' Pp. 811–12 in *Dictionary of Canadian Biography*. Volume 8. *1851–60*. Toronto: University of Toronto Press, 1985.

White, Sister Marie Agnes. 'Early Beginnings: Mount Saint Vincent College, 1925–51,' *Insight* 4, no. 2 (1975): 2–13.

Woolf, Virginia. 'Lives of the Obscure.' Pp. 120–33 in. *Collected Essays*. Volume 4. London: Hogarth Press, 1967.

Contributors

Anita Bonson has a PhD in educational studies (focusing on history and sociology) from the University of British Columbia. She currently works as a writer, researcher, and editor. She became acquainted with the diaries of Susan and Jessie Nagle through research for her doctoral dissertation, which examined the bases of women's identity construction in nineteenth-century British Columbia. Susan became one of the two women whose experiences formed the core of this examination, while Jessie's diary offered complementary insights.

Albert Braz is a SSHRC postdoctoral fellow and assistant professor in the Department of English at Queen's University, where he teaches Canadian literature. He has a publication forthcoming (2003): *The False Traitor: Louis Riel in Canadian Literature*. While researching the response to Riel in nineteenth-century Ontario, at the Trent University Archives, he discovered Dorothy Choate Herriman's diaries.

Kathryn Carter received a PhD from the University of Alberta in 1997; her dissertation was on diaries written by women in Canada. That same year she published *Diaries in English by Women in Canada: An Annotated Bibliography, 1753–1995*. She has taught

Canadian women's literature and history at the University of Alberta, Universität Tübingen (Germany), Duke University, and Laurier Brantford.

Despite her successful transplant to Ottawa-Carleton, **Julie Chychota** treasures her rural roots in southern Manitoba. Julie holds an MA in English from the University of Manitoba. Following Mary Friesen's death in 1996, family members read through their mother's and grandmother's many journals for the first time. The diaries afforded Julie the rare opportunity to see her 'Grandma Friesen' as a multidimensional person.

Janne Cleveland recently completed an MA in women's studies at York University, where she explored the work of the visual artists' collective, Kiss & Tell. She is now pursuing a PhD in cultural mediations at Carleton University, focusing on a feminist literary criticism of the narrative fiction of Jeanette Winterson.

Margaret Conrad has taught history at Acadia University since 1969. A founding member of the editorial board of *Atlantis*, she has a special interest in women's diaries and has co-authored *No Place Like Home: The Diaries and Letters of Nova Scotia Women, 1771–1938* (1988). She held Nancy's Chair in Women's Studies at Mount Saint Vincent University from 1996 to 1998, during which time she and Janne Cleveland collaborated on bringing Mary Dulhanty's diary to public attention through articles and dramatic readings.

Professor of Interdisciplinary Studies at Regent College, Vancouver, **Maxine Hancock** (PhD, English, University of Alberta) is an author, broadcaster, and speaker, seen frequently on Vision Television in such series as *Mandate for the Millenium*, *Harpur vs Hancock*, and *Stories of Our Becoming*. She is the author of seven books, including *Harpur vs. Hancock: Challenging Viewpoints on Faith and Ethical Issues* (1994) and *Child Sexual Abuse: Hope for Healing* (rev.

ed., 1997). Having spent most of her adult life in rural Alberta, where she and her husband farmed, taught school and raised their family, she has a particular interest in the role of geography in shaping women's lives.

Robynne Rogers Healey received a PhD from the University of Alberta, where she completed a dissertation on Quaker women and community in Upper Canada. She has published articles in American and Canadian women's history. While looking for materials related to the history of women in pre-Confederation Canada, she came upon the diary of Sarah Welch Hill at the Provincial Archives of Ontario. Intrigued by the sheer volume of the diaries, which cover a sixty-year period, she made repeated trips to the archives to transcribe extensive excerpts and to learn more about this woman.

Morgan Holmes holds a PhD in English literature from McGill University. He is the author of *Early Modern Metaphysical Literature: Nature, Culture and Strange Desires* (2001). Mina Wylie was Morgan's 'Aunt Mina,' the sister of his great-grandmother, Nell Wylie MacLaren. He received the diary from Mina's son, Robert, who inherited it upon his mother's death.

Afra Kavanagh's main research interest is Marian Engel's fiction, especially the novels *Bear* and *The Glassy Sea*. She is the coordinator of the annual University College of Cape Breton Storytelling Symposium, and has edited two volumes of proceedings of past symposia: *The Power of the Story* (1998) and *Women in Storytelling* (2000). 'Bear Summer' and Engel's other notebooks were a happy find at Mills Memorial Library at McMaster University, offering an intimate and personal glimpse into the life of a beloved writer.

Rosalind Kerr is an assistant professor of dramatic theory at the University of Alberta. She grew up in Whitby, Ontario, where her grandmother, Constance Kerr Sissons, also resided. Despite her austerity and deafness, Sissons was very much a part of Rosalind's life as a child and young woman. Sissons's experiences in Ottawa and Fort Frances operated at the level of family mythology, and it is only recently that the fiction has been measured against the facts.

Lisa LaFramboise, who holds a PhD from the University of Alberta, currently teaches English literature there. She first encountered Miriam Green Ellis's arctic travel diary when writing her doctoral dissertation on travel literature by women in the Canadian North and West. With I.S. MacLaren, Lisa has edited a new edition of C.C. Vyvyan's 1926 arctic travel narrative, entitled *The Ladies, the Gwich'in, and the Rat* (1998). Lisa is currently researching the history and writing of early women mountaineers in the Canadian Rockies.

Nanci Langford, PhD, teaches in the Women's Studies Program at Athabasca University. Her publications include *Politics Pitchforks and Pickle Jars: 75 Years of Organized Farm Women in Alberta* (1997) and numerous historical articles on western Canadian women. Her research focuses on the migration and settlement experience and its impact on women, couples, and families both in past and present contexts. She first read Sophie Puckette's diaries in the Glenbow Archives in 1990 and recognized that they were a unique and rare treasure in the collections of the Canadian prairies.

S. Leigh Matthews has just completed a PhD at the University of Calgary, and her study '"Bound to Improve": Canadian Women's Prairie Memoirs and Intersections of Culture, History and Identity' focuses on how women settlers represent themselves both in alignment with and against dominant cultural narratives. She specializes in nineteenth- and twentieth-century Canadian literature, and theories of life writing, and is researching in the area of eco-criticism. She first read Simpson's 'journal letter' entries during a graduate seminar, and attributes to them her understanding of women's narritive negotiations of cultural texts.

Scholar/poet **Judith Miller** is an associate professor of English at
Renison College, University of Waterloo, where she teaches creative writing, Canadian literature, and women's literature. She is
the author, with composer Carol Ann Weaver, of *Timbrel in Her
Hand, Birthstory,* and *I Have Been a Traveller.* She edited *The Art of
Alice Munro,* and is the author of *Glyph,* a book of sketches, prints,
and word sketches done with artist Nicholas Rees. She has read
and transcribed small sections of Edna Staebler's diary. Early portions are housed at the University of Guelph, but the most recent
20,000 pages are still in Edna's possession.

Barbara Powell is associate professor of women's studies at the
University of Regina, where she is also serving as the associate
dean of Arts. She has made several research trips in the British
Columbia Archives, where she has spent as much time as possible
with the diaries in the Crease family collection. She is especially
drawn to the writings of the Crease family because they take so
many textual forms, including diaries, letterbooks, lists, menus, and
almanacs. The diaries of the year chosen for this excerpt are especially interesting because they record daily life in the Crease family
from the perspectives of both mother and daughter.

Joanne Ritchie is a freelance writer and researcher with degrees in
literature and a keen interest in women's history and women's personal narratives. She discovered a microfilm copy of Amelia
Holder's journals while doing research for an annotated bibliography of New Brunswick women's diaries, *Cartographies of Silence*
(1997), and contacted Amelia's descendants, including her 101-
year-old daughter, who generously shared the journals, letters, and
family stories. Joanne is currently editing Amelia's complete journals and letters for publication. A transplanted Maritimer, she lives
in Ottawa, where she has a day job with the federal government.

Martha Slowe, who lives in Albany, New York, is an independent
scholar with research experience and interests in British and Cana-

dian literature, particularly women's non-canonical texts, and in Quebec genealogy. After receiving her PhD degree from McGill University, she worked in 1993–4 as a research associate on a McGill stage-centred Shakespeare study team. In 1995, she learned of and began to examine the diaries, letters, and manuscripts of Dorothy Duncan MacLennan, which were among recent additions to the Hugh MacLennan Archives at McGill.

A grandmother, musician, and a retired teacher of high school English with bachelor degrees in education, a Master's degree in English, and an ARCT (piano), **Lillian Tuttosi** lives in Saskatchewan. She discovered the diaries of Caroline Porter – which she considers a most distinct voice among many in Saskatchewan archives – while working on her Master's thesis concerning the unpublished writing of Saskatchewan women.

K. Jane Watt, PhD, is a freelance historian, editor, and writing instructor who lives in Fort Langley, British Columbia. She became interested in Phoebe McInnes's diary through her work as research associate at the Langley Centennial Museum and National Exhibition Centre because of the freedom and vitality it expresses and because the loss of McInnes's original manuscript says much about the value traditionally paid to women's artefacts and life texts.

Illustration Credits

Frances Ramsay Simpson: Courtesy of the Hudson's Bay Company
    Archives of Manitoba, HBCA Album 10/82 (N6459)
Sarah Welch Hill diary: Courtesy of the Provincial Archives of Ontario,
    F634, Benson Papers MU113, Box 32
Amelia Holder: Private collection of the Henderson family
Jessie Nagle; Susan Nagle: Courtesy of Don and Phyllis Roberts
Sarah and Susan Crease: British Columbia Archives and Records Services
    (24261 A-8944)
Constance Kerr Sissons: Private collection of Rosalind Kerr
Phoebe McInnes diary: Langley Centennial Museum and National Exhibi-
    tion Centre, Langley, BC
Sophie Puckette: Courtesy of the Glenbow Museum and Archives, NA-
    5166-5
Caroline Brown Porter diary: Saskatchewan Archives Board, R-89
    File 1
Mina Wylie journal: Courtesy of Morgan Holmes
Mina Wylie and her husband Denny: Private collection of Robert Denison
Miriam Green Ellis and unidentified Native woman: Courtesy of Bruce
    Peel Special Collections, University of Alberta
Mary Dulhanty: Courtesy of Mount Saint Vincent University Archives
Dorothy Herriman Diary No. 5: Courtesy of Trent University Archives,
    94-019, Box 1
Jones family portrait: Private collection of Elsie Rogstad Jones

Dorothy Duncan MacLennan: Hugh MacLennan Archives, McGill University, Montreal. (ms 466 C 17)

Marian Engel: Reprinted with permission of the Marian Engel Estate

Mary Friesen diary: Courtesy of Julie Chychota

Edna Staebler: Photograph by Morris Green. University of Waterloo, PG-7-18-37